Coal Dust on Your Feet

Stories of the Susquehanna Valley

Series Editors

Katherine M. Faull
Alfred Siewers
Bucknell University

This book series seeks to develop interdisciplinary and multimedia approaches to the concept of region, place, and ethics in environmental studies. One of the oldest river systems in the world, the Susquehanna stretches from the headwaters of its main stem around Lake Otsego in New York to the Chesapeake Bay, and from the Amish heartland of Lancaster County to wooded trout-fishing highlands of central Pennsylvania. While including a range of disciplines, from sciences and social sciences to literature and philosophy, Stories of the Susquehanna Valley articulates narratives of an eco-region that played a formative if often hidden role in the early American republic, and which today provides potential models for more environmentally sustainable approaches to human community.

Titles in the Series

David Minderhout, ed., *Native Americans in the Susquehanna Valley: Past and Present*

Coal Dust on Your Feet

The Rise, Decline, and Restoration of an Anthracite Mining Town

Janet MacGaffey

Lewisburg
BUCKNELL UNIVERSITY PRESS

Published by Bucknell University Press
Co-published with The Rowman & Littlefield Publishing Group, Inc.
4501 Forbes Boulevard, Suite 200, Lanham, Maryland 20706
www.rowman.com

10 Thornbury Road, Plymouth PL6 7PP, United Kingdom

British Library Cataloguing in Publication Information Available

Library of Congress Cataloging-in-Publication Data
MacGaffey, Janet, 1934–
Coal dust on your feet : the rise, decline, and restoration of an anthracite mining town / Janet MacGaffey.
pages cm
Includes bibliographical references and index.
ISBN 978-1-61148-513-4 (cloth) — ISBN 978-1-61148-514-1 (electronic) 1. Shamokin (Pa.)—History. 2. Shamokin (Pa.)—Economic conditions. 3. Shamokin (Pa.)—Social conditions. 4. Anthracite coal industry—Pennsylvania—History. 5. Immigrants—Pennsylvania—History. 6. Europe, Eastern—Emigration and immigration—History—19th century. 7. Europe, Southern—Emigration and immigration—History—19th century. I. Title.
ISBN 978-1-6114-8687-2 (pbk)

F159.S518.M33 2013
974.8'31—dc23 2013019478

This book is dedicated to the people
of the anthracite coal region of Pennsylvania.

Contents

List of Figures and Tables

All photographs by author except when noted. See figure 1.1 for all place names.

Figures

Tables

Acknowledgments

I first acknowledge my debt to the people of Shamokin/Coal Township. I am deeply grateful for their interest and cooperation in sharing details of their lives and community, for their warmth and hospitality, and their active promotion of my research. I thank all those who have given me so freely of their time. They have made returning to the town feel like going home.

I am particularly grateful to Fritz Reed for the help he has given from his wide knowledge of the community and its history; to Dick Morgan who introduced me to many people and drove me to see many places; to the *pirogy* makers of Transfiguration Church who welcomed me to work with them many times; to Dave and Marianne Kinder for their perceptive comments on town life and for gathering people for me to meet and talk with in their home; to the Chesnay family of Kulpmont for their hospitality, many long discussions, and tours of the area; and to the McCracken family of Mt. Carmel from who told me so much about Coal Region life and with whom I had such good times. Particular thanks are also due to Len Oszko for contributing the results of his interesting research on Polish immigrants, and his accounts of his life and visits to Poland to find his relatives; to local historians Hugh Jones of Mt. Carmel and Dave Donmeyer for sharing their expertise and loaning books and documents; to Pat Segedy, Librarian, who found many library resources for me; to Dr. Edward Twiggar who first started me off on this research by convening for me and my students a group to introduce us to the town. And my thanks are due also to many other inhabitants of the town who greatly helped and talked to me at length, including Ellie Kuhns labor organizer, Walter Neary teacher, Mark Gilger reporter, Mel Farrow whose family goes back to the early history of the town, Reba Hirsch who traced out her extensive family history and detailed the cultural events that she and Irving Liachowitz organized; for guided tours in the area from Adam Klebasko and Joe Chowka; to Jim Kelley Sr. politician, Pastor Sally Dries, Msgr. Fedorovich, Realtor Shirley Persing, the Rev. Richard and Mrs. Wilcock, Anne Wargo of St. Clair, and Lil and Red Miscavage who introduced me to many activities of the Polish Club of Mt. Carmel, and to many others. I am indebted to them all.

My particular thanks for help in writing this book go first to Jean La Fontaine who spent many patient hours reading and commenting on first drafts of chapters and who helped me to see where I needed to go with them. I am grateful to Carl Milofsky for many enjoyable discussions over the years of my research; for Sandra Barnes' ever helpful comments; to Wyatt MacGaffey for our good anthropological conversations; and to Walter Howard for guiding me through the labor history literature of the coalfields. I owe special thanks for help with the graphics: to Ben Marsh for making map 1, to Neil MacGaffey for printing genealogical diagrams and refining map 2, to Shahzeen Nasim for the final design of the diagram of chapter 4, and to George Gerstein for help with constructing map 2 and for subsidizing the cost of photographs. I thank Sam Brawand for her thorough copy editing of the manuscript and her help in putting it all together. But none of these people are responsible for any errors; those are mine.

Introduction

As one drives through northeastern Pennsylvania's anthracite coal region, great black banks of anthracite waste loom over the towns and overlay much of the countryside, but in the towns the golden cupolas of churches gleam in contrast to this blackness. Signs above town doors proclaim the Sons of Italy, the Knights of Lithuania, the Polish Area Cultural Club, the Coal Cracker Detachment of the U.S. Marines and the Black Diamond Navy Club; a board outside a church invites people to buy *pirogies*, made on the premises and sold every Thursday; posters proclaim a *soupie* contest at the fire house, and a block party for a church. A roadside shrine with a statue of the Virgin keeps watch near the remnants of a town where smoke rises from subterranean fires, and on the outskirts of a hamlet there is the replica of a coal tunnel entrance with a statue of a miner holding aloft his lamp with his mule harnessed to a loaded coal wagon.

This study focuses on the small city of Shamokin and the borough of Coal Township that surrounds it; together they constitute one of the principal urban centers of the region. A mountain of culm, or coal waste, looms over the town, through which trucks loaded with this waste spread dust and grime. This scene seems at first depressing, but soon one hears a note of pride as those who live there boast of having the "largest culm bank in the world," an expression of their loyalty and attachment to their coal mining heritage, to their town, and to the Coal Region.[1] "Don't forget that wherever you go, you'll always have coal dust on your feet," was the parting admonition from a woman to her niece as she left for a job in the city. Yet this family had never even been coal miners!

The landscape is integral to the strong sense of place of people from this region, which comes from their coal mining past, ethnic heritage, and militant labor history, and includes the black hills and the slopes and pits that scar the landscape of their countryside. The culm banks are sobering monuments to human endeavor: as in the coal fields of southern West Virginia, "the detritus of history piled high on the local landscape has become central to a sense of place" (K. Stewart 1996, 137).

People from the Region are very aware of the destruction of their landscape by coal mining, of the black hills of coal waste, pools of stagnant water, and stunted trees. But individuals react to it very differently. The black hills are deplored by some for being unsightly and for the dirt and dust they release into the air; for others they are places for bike riding or the enjoyment of the many wild creatures that have come to live there; for teenagers they are getaways where noisy drinking parties are not disturbed; and for those for whom the region is most deeply home no matter how far away from it they are, they are part of the essence of its landscape. What was reputed to be the largest culm bank in the world on the northern edge of Shamokin was truly an awesome looming object of the terrain, a permanent fixture in one's sense of home as a place. And just because of that it had value. Yet as well as arousing pride, it also evoked the oppression of working for the coal companies.

The culture and traditions of people from the Coal Region are so strong and their feeling for the region so deep, although not often understood by outsiders, that many who leave to find work would move back home if there were jobs (Kantz and Saylor 1956, 8). What draws them back? Whence comes this deep rooted loyalty?

The answer emerges from the history of the town. This book is an historical ethnography. It takes a long perspective of more than 150 years to look at changes and their effects, rather than focusing on the networks, internal politics, and relationships of a community at a particular time. It sets the town in the context, local, national, and global, of events and power relations that have determined the course of its history, and looks at the lives of the immigrants who came from different European countries in the nineteenth and early twentieth centuries to work in the coal mines.

Ethnic groups dominated the first one hundred years of town life. Most immigrants were identified in their home countries by region or even just by town or village; strong national ethnic identities arose only after they settled in the Coal Region towns close to those who came from the same country, spoke the same language, and shared the same religion, cultural traditions, and foods. They worked in the coal mines and silk mills of the towns. Religion, ethnicity and class converged in the ethnic neighborhoods they formed. Their churches structured social life, and they married within their own ethnic group. But as the coal industry declined, with the competition from the development of alternative fuels, the miners left to seek work elsewhere. Garment manufacturing moved into the Region from New York in the 1920s, but World War II took many people away again, and after it the G.I. Bill gave veterans who returned the means for social and economic mobility so that they in turn moved to the big towns and cities. Then the garment industry moved on, in the last quarter of the twentieth century, first to the south and then overseas and more people left. The salience of ethnicity greatly declined in town life because of these economic, political and demographic changes. Today Shamokin/Coal Township struggles to recover from economic decline and the loss of over two-thirds of its population from 1930 to 2000. But although many of those who leave abandon their roots, many come back to visit or retire. People's sense of place and their pride in their coal mining and ethnic heritage today inspire their efforts to rebuild sense of community and to revive the town economy.

My definition of an ethnic group accords with its usage and meaning in the town: a group of people defined by common national or religious ancestry and cultural origin, who are so recognized by others, and who organize their common affairs.[2] I use Werner Sollors's definition of ethnicity as belonging, and perceived by others as belonging, to an ethnic group, and see ethnicity as a process not an inventory of cultural features surviving from the past. It emerges in opposition to things nonethnic, as the result of power relations in a given historical time and place. This processual approach requires that we look at both continuity and change over a period of time, and situate local affairs in their wider political, economic, and historical background.[3]

Other writers have pursued the emergence of ethnic difference against the background of power and politics (for example, A. Cohen 1969; Glazer and Moynihan 1963), but this study of a Pennsylvania anthracite mining town provides a different perspective from previous studies of ethnicity in a political framework of which I am aware. To examine the process of ethnicity, it focuses not on one ethnic group, or on one at a time, but looks at all the major ethnic groups of a town in a comparative framework over the long period of a century and a half, and shows how ethnicity is transformed in different periods of time in response to the power relations of the local, national, or global levels. The groups were not themselves homogeneous; some retained hostilities and class distinctions from their homeland that persisted in their new environment.

The English and Scots, the first settlers in the area, were from the beginning dominant in the town's life and economy. These English speakers have not been considered ethnic groups by the townspeople because they speak English, not some other language which is for them a defining feature of an ethnic group. The Germans, fleeing religious, political and economic troubles, arrived earlier than other immigrants and were already assimilated, prosperous, and dominant in local society at the beginning of the coal era in the mid-nineteenth century. The skills for which the Welsh were recruited as experienced miners in the mid-nineteenth century gave them an advantage over the poor peasant farmers from Ireland, and from Eastern and southern Europe who came to work as unskilled miners in the lowest level of the labor hierarchy in the late nineteenth and early twentieth centuries, as the hard coal industry rapidly expanded. Jews, primarily from Russia and Poland, arrived initially as itinerant peddlers in the late nineteenth century. These groups made up a class hierarchy, in which Protestants of primarily German, Welsh, Scottish, or English ancestry ran the town and owned and operated the mines; Jews formed a small merchant class; and poor Catholic farmers first from Ireland and then from Eastern and Southern Europe, worked as unskilled mine laborers.

This study shows how events and power relations of different periods of history transformed the ethnicity characterizing the different groups of the town, from its initial structuring of the lives of the people to its greatly diminished significance today. Ethnicity as it is in the twenty-first century is transformed from what it was in the early years of the town to become primarily a social identity option.

Mining families were semi-subsistent for a good portion of their needs because they had access to land for growing and gathering food, and for raising livestock, and they could glean coal fallen from the train wagons on the railroad tracks or in the culm banks for home heating and cooking. They exchanged or sold the surplus from such activities for goods and services they needed but could not afford to buy. These subsistence activities enabled them to hold out in strikes and hard times, and the networks of personal connections for mutual assistance among kin and neighbors helped the miners to organize strikes and demonstrations. This reciprocal exchange, an "economy of favors," constitutes in the Coal Region what James C. Scott (1985) has termed "the weapons of the weak" as they confront the economic power structure, and which Michel de Certeau has described as the "ingenious ways in which the weak make use of the strong . . . [and] lend a political dimension to everyday practices" (De Certeau 1984, xvii).

In the process of immigration and adaptation to the circumstances of a new country, ethnic traditions in this town were widely recreated, adapted and invented within the limitations of circumstances as Eric Hobsbawm and

Terence Ranger (1983) have described elsewhere. It is, however, apparent that "What is often called cultural 'memory,' 'survival,' or 'tradition' . . . is in truth, always a function of power, negotiation, and strategic re-creation" (Matory 2005, 70). In the Coal Region elements of tradition have been commoditized in the process of their re-creation, adaptation, or invention. Commercial interests benefit from the market for traditional items and markers of ethnic culture and from supplying the materials and food ingredients for the events that celebrate it and raise massive amounts of money to send to the homeland and support its churches and seminaries. This has created ethnic economic niches for the benefit of small businesses so that ethnicity even in its diminished importance in the town today continues to have economic content.

The admonition from which the book derives its title, "Remember, You'll Always Have Coal Dust on Your Feet," reflects the strength of sense of place among Coal Region people. Anthropological studies of native constructions of particular localities and of perceptions and experiences of place show the complex ways in which places anchor peoples' lives in different social environments, in economic and political contexts, and in configurations of class and ethnicity (Feld and Basso, 1996). This sense of place is very evident in the town. It is anchored in the mining past of the people and in the militant heritage of the struggle of the unions against corporate capitalism; in the churches and their festivals; in ethnic traditions; in the tremendous pride of the townsfolk in the successes of the high school sports teams; in town events, parades, and celebrations; and in the surrounding landscape of the culm banks and derelict mines.

The sense of place is so strong that many former residents now living in towns and cities outside the Coal Region remain connected to their home town in the Region and regularly return on visits to family and friends, and to attend the churches and town events. Their desires for the ethnic foods of their childhoods means that very considerable sums of money are raised annually by the production and sale by townsfolk of these foods not only locally but also to these former residents and to their networks of contacts in towns and cities elsewhere. This sense of place draws many people back, not only to visit but also to retire. The town is thus part of a wider community, one of belonging and identity which provides a degree of economic support and boosts the local sense of community. Similar sites of belonging are described by others (Olwig 2002; Kempny 2002; Blu 1996).

People insisted that I could not isolate Shamokin from the nearby towns of Kulpmont and Mt. Carmel; these, like certain other coal towns, are considered to be grouped together. The Coal Region as a whole has a sense of place attached to it for all who live in it, but it is subdivided into these groups of towns.

Historical ethnography poses challenges for methodology and global restructuring transforms many anthropological field sites into transnational spaces, requiring more broadly-based research strategies for anthropological research than in the past. Paul Stoller refers to this as "globalizing method" (1997; 2002). Like Lorand Matory's historical ethnography, my study draws upon a new kind of ethnographic field site with a cultural field that spans space and time. People everywhere are becoming connected and influenced through modern communications and travel and our approaches and techniques must expand to reflect this reality.

My research on the history of the town and region has drawn upon the massive volumes of biographical annals of the early years of the town and county; the city directories; the fine studies already done of different aspects of the history of the area and its peoples; the research and knowledge of local historians; the archives of the local newspaper, and copies of ethnic newspapers subscribed to by residents; and accounts of the past from longtime residents as they gave me details of their family histories. In addition, I have investigated the background conditions and history of the countries from which the ancestors of people came to work in the coal mines.

My gathering of data on the social aspects of life and society has relied on the method of social anthropology emphasizing qualitative rather than quantitative, statistical, research, known as participant observation. This means that researchers immerse themselves in a community and engage in its life and activities as much as possible. It entails gathering data not only from formal interviews but also through participation in what is going on and through observation and casual conversation. Researchers take part in activities and events, attend meetings and other gatherings, formal and informal, in order to get a deeper sense of the realities of life for the people they study and to be known and accepted so that people are willing to talk about themselves and about events taking place. In this way, the researcher learns and records a level of local life denied to those who rely only on questionnaires and structured interviews.

My interest in the Coal Region began the first time I drove through it when I went to teach at Bucknell University in 1988. The black landscapes and golden church cupolas of the towns intrigued me, and I followed up thereafter guiding research projects for my students. Systematic research took place after my retirement, from 2001 until 2008. Although I was not able to live in the Coal Region, I spent a lot of time there, primarily in Shamokin/Coal Township.

I learned about life in the town by participating in what was going on, through observation and through listening to people as they dealt with their lives. I engaged much more in informal conversation than in formal interviews. People seemed quite comfortable if I used a tape recorder, which facilitated the informal nature of the research. My investigation was systematic as I asked consistently about particular details of life in the town, in the past as well as the present, so that generalities could emerge from the data.

I participated as often as I could in life and events in the community, observing life as I took part in it, and I had formal interviews and conversations with people as well as I followed up contacts and introductions, I gathered life stories and family histories from eight to twelve people of each of the major ethnic groups as well as many more from those of mixed ancestry. Our conversations lasted sometimes for hours. I use people's names as much as possible when reporting these conversations because this gives their accounts value as historical documents.

My interviews were open ended and often lasted for hours, but they included systematic information gathering to reveal patterns in the data, and allowed time for people to talk about what they found significant and important. I cross checked information by using different sources and asking the same questions of people of different backgrounds. I weave frequent quotations from these conversations into my text, and I do this not only as they provide data but also as they add insightful comment, seeking to collect oral history that combines "the narrative form with the search for a connection between biography and history, between individual experience and the transformations of society, and the individual's role in the history of society and in public events" (Portelli 1998, 25). Direct quotes sometimes also seem to be a way for more direct communication with the past, giving a somewhat purer image that seems like a direct experience (Frisch 1990, 1).

I participated in the life of the town whenever possible, attending ethnic and other festivals and events, fundraisings and the preparations for them, meetings, church services and other activities. In such a wide ranging study, time constraints prevented anything but participation in a limited way in people's lives. But the increased trust and willingness to help of people in whose activities I was able to participate repeatedly, and the things I learned from just being around that I could not have discovered by asking questions, confirmed for me anew the value of participant observation.

Sally Falk Moore observes that in the study of process, certain kinds of events can be particularly important as forms of diagnostic data (1987, 735). In this town they include: community, ethnic and religious celebrations and festivals; major parades and marches; the merging of the ethnic Catholic churches; high school sports; and events and occasions at which ethnic foods are consumed or produced for fundraising. Descriptions of major community events particularly diagnostic of the political, economic and social situation of the time in which they take place begin each of chapters 3, 6, and 8.

My investigation reached to other Coal Region towns for comparison, for follow up information, and for getting information and attending events of ethnic groups well-represented in Shamokin/Coal Township but for whom important developments historically, and festivities and parades today, occur in other towns of the Region.

The book is divided into three parts. The first concerns the era of the coal industry and the silk mills, from the mid-nineteenth century through the first quarter of the twentieth, the period in which ethnicity dominated life in the town. Chapter 1 is a background chapter. It gives the historical context for which the starting point is the discovery of anthracite and its importance in the industrial revolution, and then outlines the different circumstances of the home countries that gave rise to the waves of immigrant labor that came to supply the labor in the mines and affected the nature of the ethnicity of each group. An account of the organization of mine labor, the dangers and difficulties of the mines, and the living conditions of mining families sets the context for the rise of organized labor and its struggle to improve wages and the conditions of work.

Chapters 2 and 3 compare and contrast the major ethnic groups and their characteristics, culture and traditions during the last half of the nineteenth and the first half of the twentieth century, and give the political and economic circumstances that determined the relative position of the groups in the class structure, as they arrived and worked in the mines. Chapter 2 deals with the Germans, Welsh, and Irish, the earliest to arrive and develop the mines, and the Jews, primarily from Russia or Poland, few in number but significant in town life because of the part they played as a merchant class. Chapter 3 describes the Poles, Lithuanians, and Ukrainians from Eastern Europe and the Southern Italians, who came to fill the demand for unskilled labor as the mines rapidly expanded. These chapters show how ethnicity and religion dominated life in this early period of the town's history and were instrumental in helping people to make their lives in their new country. Foods of the homeland, the material culture, music and dance the immigrants brought with them, and the ethnic beneficial associations and later clubs were the ethnic markers of this period.

Chapter 4 describes the convergence of ethnicity with class and religion during this time, how life was affected by political, economic and social factors, the great divide between Protestants and Catholics, and the division into ethnic neighborhoods. A diagram shows the inner organization of the dominant class through the ties of business, kinship and marriage among prominent and wealthy families. In contrast, miners and their families relied on kin and neighborhood ties in an economy in which little money changed hands, which helped them to last out the protests of strikes and organize demonstrations. In the 1920s and 1930s, ethnic politics dominated the town.

Part Two focuses on national and global influences on the history of the town: the struggle between labor and corporate capitalism; the effects of national and international politics and economics; and the national decline in religion. Chapter 5 shows how labor protested low wages and the dangerous conditions of the mines, and how ethnic loyalties diminished with the coming of the garment factories and the expansion of union activity, giving place to working class solidarity in the strife against the big companies. The Depression brought an expansion of independent mining and the struggle of the miners to eventually achieve the legalization of this activity.

By the late 1930s and early 1940s, the Coal Region had reached the peak of its prosperity, but its industries then declined as global economics and politics and technological change reached down into the area. The population dropped as men and women left to look for work. Chapter 6 describes the town's prosperity as it became a shopping and leisure magnet for towns and cities near and far after the Great Depression. But then it shows how national and global politics and economics brought about a rapid decline of the town's economy and of ethnicity, with the closing of the coal mines, the effects of World War II and the subsequent opportunities for social and economic mobility. The shutdown of the garment factories as the industry moved overseas in the 1970s and 1980s caused another massive loss of population. In 1995, the decision to merge the ethnic Catholic churches for lack of members and of priests definitively undermined ethnicity and religion and their significance in the life of the town.

Part Three describes ethnicity as it is today and shows how people are trying to restore the sense of community of the town as they deal with the consequences of the overwhelming effects of events that took place far away. Chapter 7 shows that despite their decline at the beginning of the twenty first century, ethnic identity and traditions have not been abandoned but they have become much less significant in the process of adapting to new political and economic circumstances. Ethnicity as it is today is transformed from what it was in the early years of the town to exemplify Lorand Matory's view of it in his study *Black Atlantic Religion*, as an identity option, a context of meaning making and a geographical focus. Subscriptions to ethnic newspapers reflect the continuing though greatly diminished ethnicity in the town and connect people to their wider national groups. The chapter shows that traditions have mingled; loyalty and identity are now more focused on the Coal Region and its multiethnic culture than on single ethnic cultural traditions.

Chapter 8 looks at how the town is trying to cope with economic decline and population loss and at the efforts of its people to restore its past sense of community. It examines the intense community pride of the people of the town in their anthracite and ethnic heritage and their strong sense of place. It also shows that the town in the twenty first century cannot be assessed without taking into account the wider community of former residents, who have moved away but who return to visit for life cycle celebrations, to buy ethnic foods, to participate in church and town festivals, attend football matches, and in some cases to retire. This wider community contributes to the town's social and economic life today, and to the efforts of its people to recover from economic decline and population loss. In so doing, it contributes another dimension to the concept of sense of place.

Notes

1. New technology for pulverizing the coal still remaining in the culm for producing power has resulted in this huge bank being re-mined. Its height, size, and outline have considerably changed in the years of this study as the trucks gradually bear it away.

2. Much has been written on the definition and use of the term ethnicity; it has been finely summarized by Marcus Banks (1996) and needs no recapitulation.

3. As proposed by Sollors 1989, xi; Gupta and Ferguson 1992, 1997; Roseberry 1988; Moore 1987, 1981; Wolf 1982.

Abbreviations

AAUW	American Association of University Women
AOH	Ancient Order of Hibernians
CCC	Civilian Conservation Corps
DL&W	Delaware, Lackawanna and Western Coal Company
P&RC&I	Philadelphia and Reading Coal and Iron Company (the coal-owning subsidiary of the Reading Railroad Company)
P&RRCO	Philadelphia and Reading Railroad Company
RRC	Reading Railroad Company
UAM	United Anthracite Miners of Pennsylvania
UMWA or UMW	United Mine Workers of America
UNA	Ukrainian National Association
WBA	Workingmen's Benevolent Association
WPA	Works Progress Administration

PART I

THE COAL ERA

CHAPTER ONE

Historical Background and Conditions of Life in the Mining Era

The contribution of the anthracite mines of northeastern Pennsylvania to the American industrial revolution gives the hard coal region a significant role in the country's history. The book begins with a brief account of how the coal industry developed and how it transformed industrial production. It outlines the reasons why the great waves of European immigrants who supplied the need for labor as the mines expanded left their countries; shows how the differences in the circumstances of the immigrants and the time periods of their arrival determined their social and economic position in the town; and contrasts the nature of the elites of the Middle and Southern coalfields with those of the elites of the Northern field. The chapter concludes with details of the organization of the mines and the conditions of life and work for those who labored in them and in the silk mills that were also a part of the local economy.

The Anthracite Mines

First Settlement, the Discovery of Anthracite, and the Industrial Revolution

Before the 1830s, the United States made little use of steam power and metal machinery. Production took place in small shops, foundries or mills, and used charcoal and wood for fuel; water powered machinery almost exclusively, with the exception of the Pittsburgh area which used steam from its coal, but this steam was much more expensive than it was in Europe at this time.

The lack of good quality inexpensive iron in industrial areas east of the Alleghenies accounts for the small output and lack of metal machinery in the country, and was a consequence of the backward state of the American iron industry. The problem for this industry was the high sulfuric content of Pittsburgh's bituminous or soft coal: its coke produced only low quality iron. In the 1830s and 1840s this situation suddenly changed so that factories were widespread by the 1850s (Chandler 1972, 142–48).

Anthracite was responsible for this sudden change. This new type of coal, almost pure carbon with low sulfur and ash content, burned hotter, longer, and cleaner than bituminous coal. It was hard to ignite, but in the late 1820s and early 1830s after this difficulty was overcome, the eastern part of the country suddenly began to acquire this high quality fuel, so efficient that it was known as Black Diamonds. It was as good for home heating as for industry, and it was cheaper and needed less attention than soft coal, thus keeping labor costs down (Muller 1989, 104).

The problem that then initially delayed the use of anthracite was that it only existed in rugged, mountainous country 30 to 100 miles from any navigable waterways so that transport was a primary constraint on expansion of production. The construction of three major coal canals in the 1820s solved this difficulty and the new coal was widely in use in New York State by the 1830s. Thereafter the New England market, especially the Boston trade, hugely expanded. The canals were soon surpassed by railroads: the Philadelphia and Reading Railroad Company (P&RRCO) operated nearly 2,500 cars more than 105 miles of track by 1842 (Hanney 1985, 14). This high quality coal became available for lower prices than wood, charcoal, or coal from Virginia or Britain. The annual output of the Pennsylvania anthracite fields rose from 21 thousand tons in 1830 to 3.3 million tons in 1847; it is notable that the soft coal fields around Pittsburgh did not see the same expansion (Chandler 1972, 151–58).

The use of anthracite is of historical importance for its profound effects on the output, technology, location and organization of several of America's major industries, particularly glass and paper, and the steam it produced revived the growth of the New England textile industry. The iron industry east of the Alleghenies developed alongside the coal by the 1850s, and it provided manufacturers on the eastern seaboard with iron at lower prices than ever before. This availability of both iron and coal brought about large scale production of iron products for the first time, and the low price of the new fuel kept costs down. The modern rolling mill, and the factory as a continually operating unit with a large working force, became the major units of production in the metal working industry. The adoption of anthracite in converting iron into cast iron in a furnace was quickly followed by its use in making wrought iron.

The opening up of the anthracite fields, because they provided the American manufacturing industry of the northeast with its first extensive supplies of inexpensive iron, had the important consequence of the spread of factories into different industries. With anthracite encouraging large steam-powered factories, by 1845 large wire mills, mills for making rails and other railroad equipment like engines, and all kinds of tools and other products of large metalworking enterprise began to develop (ibid., 159–79).

By the 1860s, the great railroads to transport this fuel were in place. They were the Philadelphia and Reading; Lehigh Valley, Delaware, and Hudson; Delaware, Lackawanna, and Western; and Central of New Jersey, and there were other smaller ones. They reached further than did the canals and broke their monopoly, in so doing creating their own. They opened up a new era for the anthracite industry: Pennsylvania became the nation's leading coal producer as this cheap and efficient transport stimulated production to rise from 11 million tons in 1860, to 28.6 million in 1880, and 57 million in 1900.

The hard coal region consists of the northern, middle and southern anthracite fields, and covers 500 square miles and seven counties. These are Dauphin, Northumberland, Schuylkill, Columbia, Luzerne, Carbon, and Lackawanna counties (see figure 1.1).

They contain 95 percent of the nation's supply of hard coal and, by 1900, were producing over 90 percent of the anthracite in the United States, which made up over three-quarters of world production (Greene 1968, 2). The region includes the large urban areas of Scranton and Wilkes Barre, smaller cities such as Pottsville, towns with populations of a few thousands, small clusters of homes in mining areas known as mine patches, or patch towns, and the villages of the farming valleys in between the mountainous ridges of the coal lands.

The city of Shamokin and the encircling borough of Coal Township is at the western end of the middle coal field. It is situated in a narrow valley and on the slopes of the surrounding mountains. The name of the city is derived from that of an early town at the fork of the Susquehanna River, where Sunbury now stands, which was inhabited by the Delaware Indians before Columbus came to America. It was the oldest and most important of their settlements in the region. On November 5, 1768, Thomas and Richard Penn bought a vast tract of land along the Susquehanna and its branches from the Six Nations. A rush to purchase land by settlers followed, most of them English, German, Scots-Irish and Welsh. The original Northumberland County was created in 1772 for the government of these settlers. The county

Figure 1.1. Map of Pennsylvania's Anthracite Coal Counties. Drawn and used by permission of Ben Marsh

contained one half of the anthracite bearing land in the state, as it was first drawn up; it was later carved up into twenty-six counties. Coal Township derived its name from the fact that when it was formed in 1837, it covered all the coal lands in Northumberland County (Shamokin Greater Centennial Committee 1964, 10). The northern half of the county today is not part of the Coal Region, and is not considered to be so by the people living there.

Stone coal, the first name for what turned out to be anthracite, or hard coal, was discovered in 1790 and used in a blacksmith's forge. In 1824, John C. Boyd bought a tract containing this stone coal, and in 1834 he founded the town of Shamokin and set up iron manufacture in an anthracite foundry. By 1840, the town had 500 inhabitants, in 1864 it became a borough, and by 1875 its population was 8,000. In the 1860s and 1870s coal emerged as king, as the area was dominated by the coal industry. The surrounding Coal Township was incorporated as a first class township in 1901 (ibid., 13–17, 24, 36).

In the last thirty years of the nineteenth century and the first ten years of the twentieth, immigrant workers came to the United States in huge numbers and worked in this industry. Pennsylvania attracted more of them than any other state except for New York, especially in the coal regions. English, German, and Scottish settlers started the anthracite mines. They recruited experienced miners from Wales to set up the mines, and Irish immigrants fleeing from the great potato famine provided the unskilled labor. After 1890 with the great expansion of the industry, Southern and Eastern Europeans came in vast numbers and took over most of the worst jobs as the Irish moved into higher skilled and better-paid ones. The population in the anthracite fields, less than 8,000 in the last decade of the eighteenth century grew to 630,000 in 1904 (P. Roberts 1904, 11).

Very little of the anthracite was near the surface and small-scale mines quickly gave way to large scale operations using expensive and elaborate equipment in slope, shaft and strip mines. Twenty to fifty percent of the coal had to be left as supporting pillars in the slope and shaft mines:[1] most anthracite mines were 400 feet deep, some 2,000 feet. Daily pay seemed good: in 1883 the average miner had the potential to earn about $350 a year. But, in fact, they effectively received only half that sum because overproduction forced these miners into idleness about half of the year. For example, figures cited for 1898 show that the average number of days worked in forty seven Pennsylvania industries was 298, but anthracite miners worked only 148 (Klein and Hoogenboom 1989, 303, 319). Miners thus found it a constant struggle to survive on their wages.

The railroad companies sought to achieve regularity of tonnage by acquiring the coal lands, and they then discriminated against independent operators to protect their own interests in mining and to develop the potential profitability of large-scale mining operations. In 1868, a Pennsylvania law allowed the consolidation and merger of coal companies and the expansion of the railroads' landholdings, and another law in 1869, passed under pressure from railroad interests, permitted the joint ownership of railroad and mining enterprises. The rate-fixing and competition of these heavily capitalized and technologically advanced companies put most of the smaller independent coal operators out of business. Big companies and big capital reigned, backed by money from New York and Philadelphia (D. L. Miller and Sharpless 1985, 79–82). By the 1880s, absentee owners of the Philadelphia & Reading Coal & Iron Company (P&RC&I) gained control of 90 percent of the coal in the Southern field and displaced the local coal capitalists (Kozura 1996, 217). By the early 1900s, New York's J. P. Morgan became the biggest name associated with anthracite.

Why the Immigrants Left Home: Germans, Welsh, Irish, and Jews

"The impetus of a group's migration, the idiosyncrasies of its culture and the nature of its experience in the old world of the Atlantic economy, all worked to determine immigrant destinations" (Golab 1977, 67). In the Coal Region, the immigrants settled into neighborhoods with members of their own groups and formed the ethnic enclaves that were to be the basis of town life. Brief background histories of the immigrants' homelands show how the time and circumstances that determined immigration affected the opportunities available to them in the town, their absorption into its socioeconomic hierarchy, and the differences and relationships between the different groups. Table 1.1 summarizes the reasons for migration and gives the time periods in which the early immigrants arrived.

Germany has one of the highest population densities in Europe. The Germans left their country over the centuries because of religious persecution, land shortage, and the ravages of war and famine. In the seventeenth century, the Thirty Years' War from 1618 to 1648, laid waste the area of the Palatinate in southwestern Germany; further struggles for political domination between Louis XIV and England, Holland and the German Empire beginning in 1674 made conditions even worse. The whole area became politically fragmented, and bad harvests, famine and pestilence hampered its reconstruction.

The Germans were the earliest immigrants to the Coal Region after the English and Scots and settled as farmers. Over the longer period of their settlement, they were assimilated into American culture to a greater degree than other groups by the end of the nineteenth century (with the exception of their separatist religious communities of the Pennsylvania Germans, or Pennsylvania Dutch as they are popularly known). They began to come as immigrants to the Coal Region when, from 1671 to 1677, William Penn visited Germany on behalf of the Quakers to encourage the immigration of religious dissenters.[2]

Readiness to emigrate was widespread towards the end of the seventeenth century and at the beginning of the 18th was increased by a very harsh winter. Large scale immigration began when about 13,000 people from the Palatinate (nearly one fifth of the population) left between 1709 and 1789, and traveled down the Rhine and thence to England. Their goal was America, and most of them were agricultural laborers, servants, and small tenant farmers. Political motives did not enter into consideration among this

Table 1.1. Summary of Early Waves of European Immigrants to the United States

GERMANS	*WELSH*	*IRISH*	*JEWS*
1671–1677 William Penn brings over religious dissenters	**1681–1790** William Penn brings over Quaker gentry seeking freedom of religion. 12,000 Welsh in Pennsylvania		
1709–1789 13,000 from the Palatinate for economic reasons	**1790–1850** Farmers fleeing poor harvests and rising rents		
1815–1850s 1 million fleeing war, land division, and famine	**1830–1890** Immigrants to mines, many recruited from Welsh mines	**1820–1920** 4.7 million Irish came to the U.S.: fleeing partial potato crop failures, population explosion, land subdivision, and the Great Potato Famine. 77,000 fled the famine in 1845 and 106,000 in 1846. More came after the civil war of 1870.	**1850s** Some peddlers and merchants arrived
1880s 1,445,000 religious and political refugees			**1870s–1890s** Mass immigration following the Russian Pale of Settlement pogroms
1920–1950s Immigration increased again			

surge of emigrants; they came for economic reasons (Wiest 1978, 131–33). Many of them financed their passage by signing on as indentured servants. The British sent about 2,800 of them to New York, from there some went to the Schoharie and Mohawk valleys and ultimately to Pennsylvania (Conzen 1980, 407). Of the 30,000 Hessian mercenaries who came to fight for England in the American War of Independence, 5,000 remained after the war in Pennsylvania, boosting the number of Germans (Rippley 1995, 567). Some of their descendents still live in parts of Northumberland County. The first census of 1790 showed a nationwide German population of 8.6 percent, but in Pennsylvania it was more than 33 percent.

There were more major waves of immigration after the end of the Napoleonic Wars in 1815 and the subsequent decline of the German economy: it was overwhelmed by foreign imports; antiquated inheritance laws in the southwestern region involved the continuous division of land holdings so that they became ever smaller; and the rural areas were devastated by a potato famine caused by blight. Thereafter, the failure of the European revolutions of 1848 to bring democracy to Germany resulted in immigration of nearly one million Germans in the 1850s; after some fluctuations it peaked again with 1.4 million in the 1880s (see table 1.1). In the early stages of deep-mining, the coal companies hired skilled European miners, especially Germans and Welsh. The best mining engineers were the Germans (Marsh 1987, 341).

Historically, as a country, Germany had a sense of nationality earlier than the other countries of continental European immigrants in the Coal Region. During the Napoleonic period, the Holy Roman Empire of the German Nation became the German Confederation under a single government with its parliament in Frankfurt. Disagreements arose over the extent of the country until the end of the nineteenth century when Bismarck united the remaining German states into the smaller unit of the German Reich which lasted until its defeat in World War I (Rippley 1995, 565–66). By the second half of the nineteenth century, the increasingly self-conscious and prosperous Germans had a strong economic and political role in the state of Pennsylvania. Their power and influence in Shamokin/Coal Township in this period is shown in chapter 4.

The Welsh came in the mid-nineteenth century. In the Coal Region, they were later immigrants than the Germans, many of them actively recruited from the Welsh coal mines and brought over to set up and supervise the Pennsylvania anthracite mines on the basis of their expertise. Their sense of national identity was established historically in political struggles back in Wales against the domination of the English.

Wales is a small 8,000-square-mile, mountainous country to the west of England in the United Kingdom. Its original Celtic population had arrived in the late Bronze Age and fiercely resisted the later Anglo-Saxon invaders to retain their own distinct culture and language. England and Wales became politically unified under the Tudors when a Welsh nobleman, Henry Tudor, was victorious against Richard III at the Battle of Bosworth Field, and ascended to the English throne. Elizabeth I was the last Tudor monarch and by the end of her reign in 1603, English language, law, and culture was entrenched in Wales and the Welsh people dominated by English rule (Heimlich 1995, 1408–409). Following political union with England, Anglicization of the Welsh gentry in the sixteenth and seventeenth centuries left Welsh Celtic culture to the peasantry or folk (*gwerin*). Since the Welsh urban industrial labor force was drawn from the rural areas during the period of emigration, immigrants to the Pennsylvania mines from the Welsh mines had originally shared a common culture with the rural folk, and came from a background of cooperative community life and self-supporting families (Berthoff 1980, 1012). These features carried over into Coal Region life.

Coal mining in Wales developed during the seventeenth century and was the chief source of energy for the mills of the industrial revolution in Great Britain, which had a fifty year start on American industry. The Welsh then played an important part in the industrial development of anthracite in Pennsylvania. For example, in Wales, George Crane had invented a way to use anthracite in making iron, and Frederick Gessenhainer in Pennsylvania had done the same thing. The two patented the device and formed a company for which David Thomas, a foreman for George Crane, came over to Pennsylvania in 1839 and set up a large hot blast furnace in Allentown; by 1845 there were 28 such furnaces in operation in the eastern part of the state and by 1849 more than 60 (Chandler 1972, 162-63). In the mid-nineteenth century, experienced Welsh miners from the South Wales Coalfield (from whence most of Northumberland County's Welsh immigrants came) were recruited by the mining companies of the anthracite Coal Region to pioneer the development of Pennsylvania's mines (H. A. Jones 1978, 139).

Welsh immigrants came to Pennsylvania in three distinct waves. The first, in the seventeenth century was of Quakers seeking religious freedom from the severe persecution they suffered in Wales. In 1681, a group of Welsh Quaker gentlemen met with William Penn in London and obtained a forty thousand acre tract in Pennsylvania, northwest of Philadelphia, which these Welsh gentry settled, together with a few hundred farmers and servants. Chapter 4 shows three Welsh Quaker families were among the early elite of Shamokin/Coal Township. By 1790, the population of Pennsylvania was about 250,000, of which 12,000 were of Welsh ancestry.

The second wave was largely from the rural areas of Wales. It was a response to the poor harvests of the 1790s and, in the first half of the nineteenth century, the consolidation of estates, and rising rents because of the pressures of a two thirds increase in the rural population. These misfortunes drove out many small farmers and their sons. The chance to escape from the poor Welsh farmland and their oppressive landlords and the possibility of buying a small farm holding in America for the equivalent of a year's rent in Wales, was a great enticement for them. Some came to Pennsylvania, did well and found themselves much better off than in Wales (Berthoff 1980, 1011–12).

After 1830, skills acquired in the Welsh coal mines were the basis for the third wave of Welsh immigrants to the coal region and the founding of Welsh communities there (see summary for each group in table 1.2). At first the Welsh supplied also the unskilled mine labor but as other ethnic groups arrived and worked in the mines, the Welsh soon held most of the skilled supervisory positions.

In Ireland, the struggle against the domination of the English has overshadowed Irish history and resulted in the dire poverty and oppressed circumstances in which many of the Irish lived. The Catholic-Protestant divide dates back to the seventeenth century, with the transfer and ownership of property from the former to the latter. In 1607, the province of Ulster was resettled predominantly by Scottish Presbyterians. In 1603, Catholics owned the great bulk of the land; by 1709, they held only 14 percent (Blessing 1980, 525).

Oliver Cromwell invaded Ireland from England in 1649 and embarked on a career of merciless barbarity as his soldiers besieged and sacked cities, butchering their inhabitants, and devastated the countryside through the 1650s. He died in 1658, but thousands of his soldiers were given land and remained (O'Dea 1923, 158, 181). Loyal Scots and Cromwellians established an English administrative and legislative system that lasted into the twentieth century. The Irish have continuously struggled against this English and Protestant control.

The Anglican Church as the Church of Ireland successfully instituted penal laws directed against Catholics and dissenting Protestants. Catholics were prohibited from sitting in parliament, voting or sitting on juries or in local government. Their schools were outlawed, their children forbidden to marry Protestants, and they were excluded from the legal profession and from bearing arms. Gaelic, the Celtic language, was outlawed (D. L. Miller and Sharpless 1985, 138). Catholics were forbidden to acquire land from a Protestant without changing their religion. In the development of industry, most men of wealth were Protestant and mostly Protestant landlords dominated the rural areas.

The Catholic Irish struck back against this domination with many rebellions and uprisings. In nineteenth century Ireland, bands organized by societies sought revenge for widespread injustices. One such group was said to be named the Molly Maguires after the woman who was their leader. Their violent protests against injustice were to be repeated by some of the Irish immigrants in the Coal Region, to be described in chapter 5.

From 1820 to 1920 about 4.7 million Irish crossed the Atlantic to the United States; only the Germans came in greater numbers. In 1845, the year of the great famine, some 77,000 people left Ireland, and 106,000 left the next year. They were overwhelmingly Catholic, and were largely from the counties with the poorest farmland.[3] There had been partial potato crop failures earlier but the potato blight that caused this famine had much greater consequences.

The destitute, flocked to America in thousands, crowding into the steerage of what were known as "coffin ships" because so many people perished during the crossing (D. L. Miller and Sharpless 1985, 138–39). Typhus and cholera were rampant on these ships and the death rates of those immigrants who did arrive were high, by some estimates they survived less than six years (Morris 1997, 36–37).

The reasons for this large-scale emigration were multiple: religion, politics and economic distress provided the most traumatic ones, but the population explosion was part of it too. In 1767, the Irish population was just over 3.4 million by 1841; it was 8.1 million, with families crowding onto smaller and smaller plots of land (Broehl 1964, 3). Those who made it to the Coal Region thus came from a heritage of struggle against oppression, and most were desperately poor, lacking in any skills for employment, and also in poor health. Many found work as unskilled labor in the anthracite mines.

The Jews in the towns of the Coal Region came primarily from Russia, some from Poland (P. Roberts 1904, 28), but their ethnicity is defined not by nationality but by their religion, culture and language (Yiddish, and Hebrew for religion). The numbers of Jewish immigrants to the United States were not large before 1880; they peaked in 1905–1906.

In Russia, their autonomous and distinctive cultural life had emerged with the hostility of the Tsarist Christian state, which forbade them to own land and restricted their rights of residence, occupations and education in the 1800s. When Russia absorbed Lithuania, Ukraine, Byelorussia, and a large part of Poland, a majority of Europe's Jews came under Russian rule. They were all, with the exception of the economic elite, forced to live in the area of the Pale of Settlement on the extreme western edge of the Russian Empire.[4] Their livelihood was mostly in commerce as dealers in trading agricultural products, and in industry in clothing factories and making shoes, boots and other leather goods (Kuznets 1975, 42–107; Bazelon 1986).

The pogroms and persecution of the Jews in the 1870s and 1890s led to mass immigration to the United States. From the 1850s, a small number of Jewish peddlers and traders arrived in the Coal Region; over time they formed a merchant class. Later a number of Jews were professionals in Shamokin/Coal Township, and in Kulpmont and Mt. Carmel, the two towns nearest to and linked with Shamokin/Coal Township.

Eastern and Southern Europeans

Massive waves of Eastern and Southern European immigrants filled the demand for unskilled labor as the mines expanded. The Eastern Europeans or Slavs as they were generally called, were predominately Poles, Lithuanians and Ukrainians, but they also included some number of Slovaks, Czechs, Hungarians, Russians, and Austrians. The Southern Europeans were Italians from Southern Italy. In 1870, of the 38,161 foreign born persons engaged in mining in the state of Pennsylvania only 3 percent were Eastern Europeans; by 1900, they made up 46.36 percent (P. Roberts 1904, 21). The numbers involved in this migration were huge: it began as a trickle in the 1870s and developed into a mass movement in the 1880s which continued until the outbreak of World War I in 1914. Over four million people came from Eastern Europe to the Americas in this period, nine-tenths of them to North America. Coal mining was one of the five industries in which these immigrants found work as laborers.

The reasons for the immigration of all the Eastern Europeans were markedly similar. Many Slavs immigrated after the Russian abolition of serfdom and the alienation of estates in 1848 in Austria (including the Polish part) and in 1861–1864 in the Russian Empire (including Lithuania) and Congress Poland.[5] Polish and Lithuanian peasants were originally serfs who could be bought and sold, and land ownership included a certain allotment of them. They tilled part of the manor land for their own use, and they were also granted certain rights to take fish, game, wood, kindling and fruit from common land, a practice that as chapter 4 will show, they continued in the Coal Region. In Europe in return, serfs worked the fields of their master, paid taxes, and could be conscripted for military service and public works construction. Their enfranchisement produced cumulative long-term effects on the rural economy of Eastern Europe. A rapid diminution of peasant holdings occurred as a consequence of the division of land holdings, many of which became too small to make a living on. This created a large mass of rural proletarians and many emigrated in search of a livelihood.

A second key factor in immigration for the Slavs was the desire to escape the military conscription for twenty-five years for one son in a family which became universal in 1874 in areas under Russian rule. Many fled from what they considered intolerable oppression by an alien power. This exodus in the last years of the nineteenth and the early twentieth centuries coincided with the demand created by the shift of the American economy to the development of heavy industry and mining, and the massive numbers of Slavic immigrants filled the increasing demand for unskilled labor in the mines (see table 1.2).

Table 1.2. Summary of Later Waves of European Immigrants to the United States

POLES	*LITHUANIANS*	*UKRAINIANS*	*ITALIANS*
1680–1800 A few for personal reasons			
1800–1847 A few political dissidents			
1847–1855 Fled famine and epidemics			
1860–1914 Major wave for economic reasons and to avoid conscription	**1860–1914** 300,000 fled rural poverty, famine, land shortage, falling prices, and Russian military conscription	**1880s–1914** 250,000 from Carpathia and Galicia fled rural poverty, Austro-Hungarian conscription, and land subdivision; 1887 recruitment for strike breakers	**1899–1924** 3.8 million immigrated, 2.1 million returned. Reasons: rebellion, grain prices, and outmoded land tenure and farming
1920s–1930s Political refugees	**1914–1945** Slow because of U.S. restrictions	**1919–1939** After World War I 20,000 immigrated	
1945 and after Exodus after uprisings against Russian control	**1945–1980** 30,000 Nationalists escaping persecution, and displaced persons (mostly professionals and intellectuals)	**1947** after World War II, 85,000 displaced persons came, many of them professionals	
Late 20th century Economic reasons			

In Poland, the Polish speaking Catholic majority had their historical origins in a group of Western Slavs who banded together to form a kingdom, led by a group called the Polanie. The country achieved its Golden Age as a dominant power in Central Europe when the kingdom united with the Grand Duchy of Lithuania in 1386, a union which lasted for nearly two centuries. In the sixteenth and seventeenth centuries, it fell apart as the landed gentry increasingly took over local control, and in the eighteenth century the country suffered partitions by three powerful neighbors: Austria took Galicia in the south in 1772, Prussia the northwestern region in 1793 and Tsarist Russia the northeast in 1795. Thus Poland virtually disappeared as a European country until after World War I. In 1919, its population included Jews, Germans, Byelorussians, Lithuanians and Ukrainians as well as Poles. In 1939, Poland was invaded by the Germans and then by the Russians; they divided Poland between them. Despite this diversity of the population, the vast majority of Poles who arrived in the United States spoke Polish on arrival and was Catholic (Greene 1980, 788–89, 801; S. Jones 1995, 1083–84). Given their history, many spoke several other languages also. "Polish nationalism as we know it, emerged from the long history of invasion, partition, and foreign rule, just as the Polishness of the mass of peasants awaited discovery in a foreign land" (Jacobson 1995, 8).

Polish Americans constitute one of the largest ethnic groups in America: 9.5 million claimed Polish ancestry in their background in the 1990 census (S. Jones 1995, 1087). In addition to the reasons given above, Polish immigration depended on the political or economic circumstances of different historical periods (Greene 1980, 789–91; Jacobson 1995, 35; S. Jones 1995, 1086). From 1800 to 1860, immigrants were largely political dissidents leaving after the partition of their homeland and the harsh Russian retaliation to the rebellion against their rule in 1831 (and to the failed uprising of 1863). From 1860 until 1914 and World War I, economic reasons were primary and a major wave of immigrants, primarily from the rural classes, fled famine because of failed potato crops, and epidemics of typhus and cholera; others fled to avoid military conscription into the Russian army. In the 1920s and 1930s, immigrants were largely refugees leaving for political reasons or ideological differences with the government. In 1945, after the end of World War II, the Russians established Soviet-controlled communist Poland and two major uprising against the Russians led to a great exodus. Later in the twentieth century many left again for economic reasons.

Most Polish immigrants to the Coal Region had been peasant farmers living in rural areas in Poland with the dream of having enough land to make them independent and this craving for money to keep or purchase land motivated them to emigrate. As with other ethnic groups, these Polish migrants generally hoped to earn some money and then return to Poland; two thirds of those who immigrated to the United States from Galicia in the 1890s did so. Those who stayed in America continued their ambition to buy land and put up or buy houses.[6]

Lithuanians are not Slavs but Balts, an Indo-European people originally from the Eurasian steppes. They speak an ancient language related to Sanskrit, completely different from the Germanic and Slavonic languages. At the end of the fourteenth century, Lithuania was part of a vast medieval empire from the Baltic to the Black sea, after the marriage of the Grand Duke of Lithuania to the heiress to the Polish throne united the two countries as a confederation, and the Lithuanian Grand Duchy became the political center of the Baltic peoples. Vytis, the emblem of the knight on a white horse, the state emblem of Lithuania today, dates from this era. Although in this period a Lithuanian literary language did begin to develop among the educated, the Lithuanian nobles and clergy essentially adopted the values and language of the Polish aristocracy, and language was used to reinforce social barriers. The Lithuanian spoken by the villagers became a symbol of their low status, while the aristocracy, Christians, and others of high status were identified by their use of Polish. Each rural parish was almost a folk culture in itself, and spoke its own local dialect. During the eighteenth century, most of the Polish Lithuanian confederation was incorporated into the Russian Empire and the Poles and Russians competed for the right to dominate the country. (Granquist 1995, 881–82; Vardys and Sedaitis 1997, 4–6).

In the 1860s, the Russian abolition of serfdom undermined the political power of the Polish speaking Lithuanian nobility and redistributed much of its landed wealth. In the 1880s, a new social group, a Lithuanian speaking intelligentsia of clergy, teachers, doctors and lawyers, of peasant origins but with a more nationalistic outlook, began to emerge, challenging both Polish cultural domination and Russian political control, publishing a new Lithuanian literature in East Prussia and smuggling their illicit newspapers and tracts into Tsarist Lithuania where they were distributed among the villagers. With the emergence of a new literacy and the first Lithuanian newspaper of 1883, there came a national ethnic identity (Van Reenan 1990, 29–35).

In 1896, a Lithuanian Social Democratic party formed and quickly grew in importance and there were widespread revolutionary outbreaks in the countryside in 1905–1906. In the less repressive years of the early twentieth century, many cultural and economic societies were established and a sense of ethnic national identity intensified. This history explains a strong hostility in the early generations of Lithuanian immigrants in the Coal Region towards the Poles and Russians but it has now faded.[7]

In World War I the Germans invaded and occupied Lithuania, ending Tsarist rule, and toward the end of the war in 1918, Lithuania proclaimed its independence. During World War II, it was subject to Soviet and Nazi occupations, and lost almost a third of its people in the Holocaust,[8] through exile to Siberia, or escape to the West. However in the late 1980s, growing Lithuanian nationalism forced the communists out and independence was declared again in 1991 (Alisauskas 1980, 666; Granquist 1995, 881–82).[9] The Russians tried unsuccessfully to suppress this independence and the last Russian troops left in 1993. In 2004, Lithuania joined NATO and became a member of the European Union.

Lithuanians came to America in two distinct migrations. In the first, from 1860 to 1914, about 300,000 people came to Pennsylvania. They had left because of famine in 1867–1868, the land shortages resulting from continual subdivision of smallholdings, the falling prices of cereals and flax in the worldwide agricultural depression of the 1870s and 1880s, and Tsarist conscription. The return rate of migration was high: one in every five between 1899 and 1914. Migration slowed after World War I with the restrictive U.S. immigration laws of the 1920s. The second migration came after World War II and was much smaller, about 30,000 people, consisting mostly of professionals and intellectuals escaping government persecution or displaced persons *(dipukai)* from the war (Alisauskas 1980, 665–67).

The Ukrainians, like the Poles, are among the largest groups of Eastern Europeans in America: probably about two and a half million people have roots in the contemporary Ukraine. Until after World War I, little distinction was made between them and Slovaks, Russians and Poles in the process of immigration, so their exact numbers have not been known. Officials might arbitrarily assign them to one or the other; all came into the category of Slavs (Luciuk 1995, 109-10). Ukrainians who came to the Coal Region were poor, Lemko-speaking peasant farmers from the Carpathian Mountains, some from the north side of the mountains under Austrian rule (Galicia), some from the south side and Hungarian rule (Transcarpathia).

> The ancient name of the Ukrainians is *Rus* (a Scandinavian word in origin) and they were known as Rusyns (not to be confused with Russians, who are known as Muscovites among Slavic people). When Ukraine was declared independent, they considered themselves Rusyn, but immigration officials put them down as Austrian or Russian. When Russia sold Alaska to the US, a big evangelization was directed at the Russian Orthodox[10] so it was easy to tell the Rusyns they were Russians, but they are not: they speak a dialect of Ukrainian (Lemko) and another Slovak dialect.[11]

Ukrainians are descendants of Slavs who moved into the Balkans in the early seventh century from north of the Black Sea, speaking an Eastern Slavic language. They converted to Christianity in the last half of the 10th century. The greater part of Ukraine and Byelorussia became part of the Grand Duchy of Lithuania, then in the sixth century passed to Poland (Shankovskj 1982, 52–54). In the seventeenth century a Russian Cossack society arose on the plains of the Dnieper River, composed of freemen as opposed to serfs, with democratic rule by elected rulers and military discipline, who organized to fend off the Tartars (Fedunkiw 1995, 1375; Kuropas 1972, 18). They liberated Ukraine from Polish rule and from Turks and other invaders, but its position soon weakened again. Its people were betrayed by the Russians when they entered into an agreement to divide the country between Russia and Poland. Russia annexed much of eastern Ukraine in the late eighteenth century and Russian rather than Ukrainian became the official language.

In 1918, after the Russian Revolution of 1917, Ukraine declared its independence, but it was short-lived and in 1922, Ukraine became a republic of the USSR until the dissolution of the Union in 1991 (Fedunkiw 1995, 1375–376). A catastrophic man-made famine devastated the countryside while the Ukraine was a Russian Republic: Stalin destroyed its agricultural class with a government-created famine to force collectivization in 1932–1933, seizing grain, blockading food shipments into the affected areas, and preventing people from leaving. Over seven million people perished or were deported in the famine (Shankovskj 1982, 43–44, 58; Kuropas 1972, 34).[12] The farming economy of Ukraine, which was one of the largest grain exporters in the world prior to World War I when it was known as the "Breadbasket of Europe," was destroyed.

The Ukrainian American population in the United States began with a large scale immigration of about 250,000 people that started in the 1880s and continued until 1914 (see table 1.2 for comparison with other groups). These early Carpathian immigrants before World War I, like the Poles and the Lithuanians, fled to avoid rural poverty, conscription into the army (in their case the Austro-Hungarian army) and, in Galicia, the extreme subdivision of land (Procko 1973, 218).

From 1887, the coal companies actively recruited large numbers of poor farmers from Transcarpathia, then part of Hungary, to replace strikers in the Pennsylvania coal mines (Dragan 1964, 19).[13] A second period between the World Wars brought 20,000 more immigrants to America and a third period, beginning in 1947, brought 85,000 people who had been displaced by World War II. Those in Shamokin/Coal Township came in the early years.

The Southern Europeans were Italians who came a little later than the Slavs: from 1890–1920 nearly four million of them came to the United States; the peak year of this immigration was 1907 (see table 1.2). Italian migration in general to the United States was overwhelmingly from the South and overwhelmingly of unskilled labor. This migration was nearly 90 percent male in the early years of the twentieth century because so many came intending to return with money to buy land or a house for their family in Italy (Sowell 1996, 143–44). Many were successful in doing this. Italians even more than the Eastern Europeans saw migration as an opportunity to improve life at home: between 1899 and 1924, 3.8 million Italians came to the United States, but some 2.1 million of them returned to the homeland in the same period (Nelli 1980, 547). Migration declined after 1920 because of U.S. restrictions imposed on immigration.

The Italian peninsula was historically made up of small warring states, often under domination by a foreign power, the richest and most powerful of them in the North. They were not unified into one country until 1860. But in some ways, after unification the southern peasants were worse off: the northern dominated government in Rome treated the South as if it were a colonial possession to further the industrial interests of the North. It practiced discriminatory policies in trade, industry and education, and fostered an oppressive agricultural system for the South which already suffered from infertile soils and rapid population growth. The result was a marginal existence for the population of the South. They had few modern farming methods, and were oppressed by the absentee landlords of large estates. In 1900, only Belgium, the Netherlands and England in Europe had higher population densities than Italy, but they were countries which, unlike Italy, were highly industrialized (Nelli 1980, 545–47). In addition, deforestation had made southern Italy an ecological disaster by the twentieth century, and from 1903 to 1908 the Phylloxera pest destroyed vineyards (Grifo and Noto 1990, 2). Early in the twentieth century, the per capita income in Northern Italy was 70 percent higher than in the South and the illiteracy rate in the South double that of the North. The South, being more agricultural than the North was dominated by rural traditions (Sowell 1996, 142).

Unification thus caused worsening economic conditions as well as loss of political autonomy for the South, and resulted in a civil war between the army of the kingdom of Italy and what were called "brigands" in the South. Historians have agreed in interpreting the mass exodus that followed through migration as an expression of rebellion against oppression, an attempt to better their lives that was a conscious rejection by some of the peasantry of their political and economic subordination in the new social order. But an additional factor in the worsening economy was that grain prices on the world market in the 1880s because of expanding American and Ukrainian wheat production, precipitated an agricultural crisis in Italy that was disastrous for small landowners and agricultural laborers alike. Along with starvation wages and high taxes, this also drove out the rural population especially from the hill towns of Calabria and Campania. (Vecoli 1995, 118–20).

Most of the Italians who emigrated in the late nineteenth and early twentieth century settled in New York, New Jersey, Pennsylvania, and southern New England (Nelli 1980, 547). In 1850 there were only 172 Italians in all of Pennsylvania; by 1930, there were 225,979 out of a foreign-born white population of 1,233,051 (Grifo and Noto 1990, 1). From 1899 to 1910, out of 2,284,601 immigrants, 1,911,933 came from the south, and only 372,668 from the north. Among those who returned to their homeland, 56 percent were southerners, 48 percent were northerners. Some stayed a while back in Italy until they needed more money, repeated the process, and eventually settled in the United States. After the turn of the century, the situation stabilized as women and children joined the men.

These differences in the reasons for migration arising from the historical background of the home country and the time of migration contributed to the differences between the ethnic groups as they settled into the coal towns. In the Northern and Southern regions of the anthracite coalfields the elites for whom these immigrants labored were very different.

The Coal Elite: Shamokin/Coal Township in Regional Context

Edward Davies shows that in the north, after 1850, the upper class leaders of Wilkes Barre in the center of the northern anthracite region and the largest community (see figure 1.1) invested time and money in landholdings which gave them control of the coal lands.[14] They established chartered companies which gradually encompassed all mining companies with large capital assets (often exceeding $2 million dollars), facilitating in large measure the control of this class over the cities, towns and villages of the entire northern coalfield. In this process, family ties with Wilkes Barre's upper class drew a large proportion of leadership in the northern region communities into the kinship system and formal society of Wilkes Barre. The city became the headquarters for most of the major companies in the northern coal region and its leadership persisted almost intact in the anthracite industry until the 1920s. Entrepreneurs from cities such as New York and Philadelphia had to lease mining land from them. Their hegemony was challenged after the passage of laws by the Pennsylvania legislature in 1869 which enabled railroads to purchase stock in the coal and iron companies, so that thereafter, the anthracite railroads were competing with the local leadership to control the anthracite industry throughout the region (Davies 1985, 7–9, 19–30).

In contrast, throughout the Southern and Western Middle coalfields, including Northumberland and Schuylkill counties, corporate leaders in Philadelphia in the 1870s had consolidated control of all the mining operations. Their maneuvering affected the nature of the urban upper class in this Southern region. After 1870, it was only loosely organized, not cohesive or persistent and it was unable to build enduring institutions or persist intact into the twentieth century. Its institutions and social characteristics were weak, and its turnover high; few of its leading families persisted into the next century (ibid., 9–11). Thus in the southern anthracite region where Pottsville, the seat of Schuylkill County and a marketing and manufacturing city, was the major community until the late 1800s (see figure 1.1), mobility and achievement not lineage and tradition were the hall mark of the elites. To achieve economic success, leaders of Shamokin or Mt. Carmel had to migrate from their communities in an occupational mobility that was vital to bring them into contact with leaders in Pottsville. But the basis for a regional network that this might have constituted was not realized because the Pottsville elite lacked the social, familial and informal ties to cement such an emerging network; they relied instead on entrepreneurial and economic relations. Such ties were not comparable to Wilkes Barre's with the Wyoming Valley, and Pottsville's leaders were never able to establish a firm hold on either Northumberland County or the southern rim (ibid., 148–58).

The Philadelphia & Reading Railroad Company (P&RRCO) relied on the skills of local coal operators in the southern anthracite region to insure a continuous flow of anthracite coal to the markets. But beginning in 1870, its corporate leaders in Philadelphia had consolidated control of all operations in the area, crippling the network of extra-local ties of the elite of Pottsville. For the future, Philadelphia entrepreneurs and companies ensured that growth in the southern region would come from the anthracite industry as in the past, but entrepreneurs and corporate leaders outside the region would make key decisions and would transfer profits to economic communities and activities outside the coalfields. In consequence, local leaders and families were less likely to maintain their position in the southern half of the region than in the north. The elites in these developing cities had not established economic activities sufficiently productive to generate large enough amounts of capital, and they were hard hit, and many of them bankrupted, by losses in the depression of 1870. After this time the potential for full-scale development and economic hegemony comparable to that of Wilkes Barre's upper class was limited in Pottsville and the southern cities (ibid., 158–74).

Methods of Mining and the Organization of Labor in the Mines

Steam power made possible deep mines below water level, with pumps, air fans and mass-produced iron rails. All these took heavy capital investment and big companies were better able to afford them. Yet the method of the actual mining of the coal changed little over time. It was always done by men using only simple tools—pick, shovel, bar, and drill—working in small teams of two to four men, drilling holes, tamping explosives and firing them from a safe distance, and working at the coal face with only the faint light of their lamps to illuminate a little of the dark around them.[15] Only well into the twentieth century was modern coal cutting machinery used. At the start of the mining era, the miners dug outcroppings on the surface, then quarried or stripped the coal seams. If the outcrops opened on the mountainside, they dug inwards, at a slightly upward pitch for drainage. With the mechanization of the steam age, they excavated holes or "shafts" straight down to the deep coal seams, and then opened horizontal tunnels along the seams. Cage elevators carried the miners and equipment down and the loaded coal cars back to the surface. Today the commonest type of mining is done on the surface by huge shovels or "drags," which can move whole mountains. But for almost a century mining was underground work. Colliery whistles or bells woke the miners who might go to the mines before the sun rose and return after it set, never seeing its light at all. Water was a problem in these mines and the men often worked in very wet conditions.

A marked hierarchy existed in the labor force for the mines and the various ethnic groups worked in different positions in this hierarchy. At the top were the superintendents, below them were foremen who assigned the work, could hire and fire all the men, and visited the miners' working places. Below them were engineers, and the fire bosses who inspected the mines each morning for dangerous conditions. The miners themselves were divided into contract miners, who were the highest paid, were more likely to own houses, and exercised a great deal of independence in the organization of their work, and the laborers who worked for them and loaded the cut coal. The laborers received one third of the wage of the contract miner and worked far longer hours, as much as fifteen hours as opposed to about six for the contract miners. The miners were paid by the colliery operators by the ton or wagon load. They had to purchase their own tools and supplies, such as powder, and they supervised and paid their laborers. In the early years they were mostly Welsh or English, while the laborers were mostly Irish (Wallace 1987, 133). Most men started work in the mines as boys, as young as eight to twelve years old, picking rock, slate and refuse out of the coal in the breakers, the big high buildings in which the newly mined coal was processed: cracked, cleaned and screened. In 1913, there were about 300 coal breakers in the anthracite region. A breaker would hire from 148 to 250 boys (Poliniak 1970, 3, 14). Breakers were cold and dusty and the boys were hit with sticks if their attention wandered. By their mid-teens they were working down in the mines in their foul atmosphere of coal dust and powder smoke, first as door keepers, opening doors across gangways that controlled the flow of air at the approach of coal wagons, then moving up to be drivers and keepers of the mules that lived below ground and pulled the coal cars, and then to the dangerous job of being "spraggers," boys who thrust heavy sticks into the spokes of the wheels of the coal wagons to control their speed on the down-slopes. Full-time work for men in the mines was ten hours a day six days a week; for boys nine hours a day. Sometimes men too old or injured to work underground would return to working in the breakers.[16]

Great resentment was caused by the inequality between the miners and their laborers, in the workload, the length of the working day and the wages received, and it was exacerbated by the ethnic division of the miners which coincided with levels of skill. In the early years in Shamokin/Coal Township, the English and Germans predominated among the mine owners and operators.

The mines were set up by experienced Welsh miners and German engineers and the Welsh subsequently became the superintendents, foremen and bosses; the skilled miners were largely other Welsh miners, English and Scots; and the laborers were predominantly Irish with some Germans. It was the same in Scranton to the north (W. D. Jones 1993, 49–50) and Anthony F. C. Wallace gives the same social stratification for St. Clair to the east. The prolongation of the status of laborer for the Irish was likely in the 1840s and 1850s because the coal owners and the miners distrusted the Irish. "Ethnicity and the status difference between contract miners and mine laborers thus formed a single deepening line of cleavage between Irish and non-Irish workers in St. Clair" (Wallace 1987, 137–38). Wages if continuous throughout the year were sufficient to generate individual income well above subsistence, but the demand for coal for industrial use slacked off in the winter, and at other times employment was not steady but intermittent, because of strikes, mine disasters and floods. In 1870, wages averaged $3.00 a day for contract miners, $2.00 for laborers, and $.80 for breaker boys. In 1900 they were less, $2.25, $1.40 and $.75 respectively (Greene 1968, 52). Often rent for the company house, purchases of food and mining supplies at the company store, together with numerous other possible deductions, meant that there was little or nothing given out on payday. There was no unemployment insurance or death benefits. The employment of women and children was crucial in times of unemployment, under-employment, sickness or injury and for widows; otherwise people relied on the extended family, their neighbors, and the benevolent societies.

Dangers and Difficulties of Mining

Pennsylvania's anthracite mines are reputed to have been some of the most dangerous in the world. From 1876 to 1897, 7,346 men died in these mines (Aurand 1971, 40). They had a high disaster rate because of their geology, which made the shafts very difficult to mine, and the short cuts taken with the technology which could have made them safe to operate. In the soft coal region of western Pennsylvania, the coal beds were level, but the hard coal beds in the eastern part of the state were all steep inclines and folds as they followed the mountains. These difficulties were made worse by the huge amounts of water in the deep mines where they had to pump out ten tons of water for every ton of coal. Laborers and miners were antagonized because wages and safety standards did not keep up with company earnings. The danger of death or disablement in the mines from mine accidents was ever present. In addition to the high accident and disaster rate, mining was very unhealthy work: coal dust clogged the miners' lungs and three out of four of the men who worked in these mines suffered from miners' asthma; many eventually died of it. Thus the miners faced a double exploitation, first from wages that left them struggling to survive, and second, from the very immediate threat to their lives and health of working in the mines.

Anthony Wallace, in his study of coal mining in St. Clair, points out that the system of subcontracting, basically from the mine owners on down, meant that the mines were essentially let out to difference branches of labor, and that this was prejudicial to good ventilation and discipline, leading to a neglect for the safety and welfare of the miner (Wallace 1987, 32). Very little anthracite was near the surface and small-scale mines soon gave way to larger operations which had to use the elaborate and expensive equipment needed for slope and shaft mines. The most frequent accidents resulted from roof falls but miners only wore soft caps not helmets. Fire, flooding and explosions were involved in some of the worst disasters.

The most disastrous fire in the history of anthracite mining occurred at Avondale, near Wilkes Barre, on September 6, 1869. The hoisting machines, the only means of escape in the main shaft (which was also the only means of ventilation), were destroyed by flames. After two days when they finally got to the miners trapped 300 feet underground, all 108 were dead. In another major accident, on December 18, 1885, a miner working near Nanticoke broke into a geological depression or pocket filled with water, quicksand, and culm. Within a few minutes, twenty-six men and boys had lost their lives as the water flooded into the mine (D. L. Miller and Sharpless 1985, 110, 113). In an accident caused by an explosion in 1919 on June 5th, 92 men died in an explosion of powder and dynamite in Wilkes Barre (News Item, May 13, 1980).

People often related details of accidents in which they or family members were involved. The father of one Kulpmont resident (the third town of this study that lies between Shamokin and Mt. Carmel) worked in the Scott Colliery deep mine. Once a cable broke on a cage taking him and other miners down into the mine, all thirty men had broken bones. Another time, he was caught in a blast and blown against a pillar. He didn't have the strength to be a miner after that and worked as a school janitor. He had miner's asthma and could not walk a block without stopping to get his breath. He had eight children.[17] A Lithuanian miner gives details of working in the mines:

> Sometimes, when the top was moving it was scary. You took most of the coal out and only left little pillars, and the weight from the top was so great it sometimes started cracking. You could hear that and it sounded like thunder, then all of a sudden it would break and be like a wind to knock you over. As well as big falls there were gas explosions. It was just like you see in the movies, gas goes right across and you'd jump right down into the ditch in the water because the gas always goes to the top. The heat was there. A couple of times when they had an explosion or blasted coal and there was a spark, it would light the gas, and you could hear it roar. Yeah, it was scary sometimes. You always worked with two guys together, you always had to have a buddy.

He continues to relate a fearful example of a flooding accident in the mines.

> At the time my son graduated from college as a geologist, I worked as a state inspector in the mines and I got him a job. He went there figuring things would open up for him to get a job as a geologist. He worked about a year and they had a heck of a big accident about twelve to thirteen guys killed. What happened, the water broke through and he'd just finished eating and was going back to work. He said, "I heard this rush and turned around and everything was just rolling, I thought I was dead." The water hit him and carried him down into the main hallway and by the time it dropped him, he was stunned and had his leg broken, and the water was up to their noses. He was wedged by a big piece of timber and thought he was going to die. He said a prayer and all of a sudden the timber moved. He could see his buddy's light under the water and he dove down and he took him and crawled six hundred feet with him up about a seventy degree slope to the outside. He dragged that buddy of his up, even with his broken leg. There was an old abandoned mine that no-one knew about, and it was filled with water. When they were driving this gangway, like a tunnel, they came to this point and stopped and had their lunch, and the water started seeping through and nobody realized. Then the pressure got so great that it pushed through and killed six or seven of the men. He said to me, "I'll never go back in the mines." He went back to college and got an industrial engineering degree. Now he is head of management of the Frick Corporation down in Greencastle. The man he rescued was never right again after that time, he was always shaken. He was only in his fifties when he died.[18]

Coal operators blamed careless miners for the high accident rate in the mines, rather than on their own reluctance to install expensive safety measures. The state had facilitated the extension of private enterprise into unexploited regions, financing public works such as canals, turnpikes and harbors. It authorized a geological survey which was carried out in two phases, 1836–1842 and 1851–1854. It was halted after six years because the legislature refused to fund the work needed to complete it. But in 1851 funds were granted to continue. It found there were great difficulties for mining and issued a warning message to mine owners. Its warnings were ignored as the large coal land owners were reluctant to abandon their investments, no matter what the dangers. Safety legislation was not passed until the late 1860s and ventilation safety measures were often ignored. Although the English had invented a good system of mine ventilation which resulted in a far lower accident rate than that in the Pennsylvania anthracite mines, Pennsylvania companies resisted installing it because of its cost. But inadequate ventilation allowed fire damp, a gas, to collect, which resulted in explosions (Miller and Sharpless 1985, 105; Wallace 1987, 201–15, 249). By the end of the century, most mines had at least two shafts, one for hoisting and one for air, but in general extremely unsafe and inefficient mining practices were permitted underground, although the breakers and engines on the surface were relatively advanced.

Miners were not, however, blameless in this respect. For example, they would skimp on timbering to support the roofs in mine tunnels because it cost money that ate into their narrow profits. Also, they allowed debris, or "gob," to accumulate which could cause mine fires. In the end, lost sales followed accidents and deaths, and together with increasing labor costs and repair expenses, eventually resulted in the business failure of operators. The indifference of the courts and the operators to safety issues evoked political response from the miners in St. Clair who called for legislative action to regulate the industry (Wallace 1987, 53, 274–75).

Memories of the callousness of the mine owners last on down the generations; they are engraved in peoples' minds and recalled with great bitterness. They epitomize the resentment of the miners against the total lack of feelings of the big coal and railroad companies for their employees. An intense pride from surviving and coping with such a hard and arduous life, anger at the perceived exploitation and oppression that was part of it, and the strength of community from the common experiences of struggle and achievement, all are part of recollections of the mining past and dominant elements of the mining heritage and the Coal Region identity. They are part of the common interests of the miners that labor leaders called upon in the struggle to improve wages and working conditions, and of the heritage and identity that is today being drawn upon to rebuild a sense of community after economic decline and population loss.

Living Conditions for Miners and Their Families

What was life like for the miner and his family? The bilateral extended family provided security in the Coal Region. It was the source of help for the ill, the injured, the elderly, and widows or orphans. The kin and neighborhood network was the primary resource in times of difficulty. Benevolent associations which paid out for illness and death were otherwise the only source of help. There was no unemployment or life insurance.

The mine settlements or "patches" as they were called, built around the collieries at the mine head (unless they were in or adjacent to a town) in which the miners lived, consisted of from twelve to one hundred houses, built and owned by the coal company and rented to the miners. There would seldom be more than 30 to 40 families in a mining patch, and the patches survived only as long as their collieries (Wallace 1987, 139). Since the companies were importing their laborers, they had to construct housing for them. The company would also run a company store which would charge 10–40 percent more than regular market prices (Klein and Hoogenboom 1989, 319). Rent, food, fuel, clothing, and mining tools and supplies from the company store were deducted from a miner's wage packet, after which there might be little, or even nothing at all, left.

Miners desired large families for the essential economic help children represented: they helped out at home and boys went to work in the coal breakers, girls in the textile factories; they gave their wages to their parents. But these large families could make for very crowded living conditions, as in the following example.

Stanley Parazinski was born in Russian Poland in 1870. His entire family emigrated and came to the United States and settled in Mt. Carmel in 1873. He became a miner, married and had thirteen children. They all lived in a half double. His wife, Anna Chrapowicka, died in childbirth in 1918, after giving birth to all these children and also having three miscarriages. His grandson, Len Oszko continues:

> My grandfather thought that it would help the family if he remarried. So he married a lady who was a widow with six kids. They all moved down to another half double in Mt. Carmel. They'd go to the table in shifts and when they were sleeping, they'd lay across the bed instead of the length of it, maybe four to a bed. A small one would sleep with the parents. This did not work out too well and finally the oldest daughter, Helena, took all the kids [her siblings] back to the homestead in Kulpmont. She raised everybody and they all chipped in to help. Then as the boys grew up my grandfather rejoined them because his wife died after they had a child. They all worked and what money they earned they

handed in to Helena for the household. She did the cooking and all things like that. She never married, though she had chances, because she was taking care of the family.

These details give a vivid picture of how hard it could be for people in the early generations with big families crowded into inadequate housing, and how women gave birth to so many children or gave up life opportunities in order to care for their siblings. "They all paid a heavy price to raise their families and get them educated."[19]

The mining patches usually consisted of a jumble of company-built, small double houses; as late as 1916 few of the anthracite towns had paved streets or garbage collection. As soon as they had any sort of house and plot, the immigrants grew vegetables on it, and expanded food production into adjacent open ground at the edge of the patch by raising livestock. The diet in the early years was primarily cereals, starches, meat and cabbage (Greene 1968, 41–46).

Miners hoped eventually to be able to buy their own houses. The system was that a number of them could buy houses in a mortgage group, but if there was a strike and one person in the group could not make the payments because he was not getting wages, the bank foreclosed on all of them. They had to start over again when they were all earning once more. One former miner told of his mother losing her house three times to the Black Diamond Savings and Loan Association under this system. If there was a strike, no one was earning and no one could make payments. She begged one of her sons to buy it when she died because she had put so much money into it. He did, and now still lives in the house in which he was born. The plot is 30 by 125 feet for two houses since it is a double; each had a plot 15 by 125 feet. "We grew everything," he said, "grapes for wine and jelly, cabbages for sauerkraut, we made sausages from a pig bought from a farmer, and we canned fruit bought in bulk from local farmers. We didn't have much, but we didn't miss nothing."[20]

In the absence of any benefits from the companies, those many women whose husbands were killed or injured in the mines had an appallingly difficult life maintaining their families. They could be evicted from company housing and since they depended for much of their food on what they grew in their gardens, this meant severe deprivation in terms of their livelihood. One Austrian woman for example, had ten children, the youngest two years old when her husband was killed in the mines. The oldest children went to work and turned in their pay packets to their mother. "The family all worked together for the sake of survival." The two youngest sons were eventually

Figure 1.2. View of a Black Landscape

killed in the mines like their father. Anthracite folk had an intense pride in their self-reliance; they never had any welfare and felt shame at the idea of living on handouts. All in this family were devout Catholics. In the past, it was not an option to miss going to church or to be disrespectful to elders. "Discipline was really strong, very different from today."[21]

Typical features of Coal Region family life were the closeness and companionship of family relationships with the constant visiting that maintained them; the hard work; and the big families and crowded living conditions. People lived in the shadow of the huge mountains of coal waste that loomed over the town and blackened great areas of the landscape, in ethnic neighborhoods in which their lives were structured by the churches whose golden cupolas and tall spires towered above them.

Sources of Supplementary Income

Miners could seldom keep their families on just the wages they earned and some were very reluctant to allow their wives to go out to work. Other ways to add cash to an inadequate income were operating a bar or a Mom and Pop neighborhood store[22] in a room of your house, or taking in boarders. All were dominant features of life in the mining towns. Bars and neighborhood groceries served as exchange centers for their ethnic communities: they held immigrants' earnings for them, notarized papers, organized transportation

Figure 1.3. A Golden Cupola

and sent money orders home, interpreted and translated, wrote letters for the illiterate, and afforded generous credit. But the most important function of the bar was as a labor exchange where foremen and employers would look for the labor they needed (Greene 1968, 48–49).

In the whole of the anthracite coal fields in 1901, there were 3,000 licensed bars, with an income averaging $400 a month, and expenses over one year averaging $2,299 (P. Roberts 1904, 237). These taverns were a central community institution. The saloon or tavern keeper was often one of the most powerful members of the immigrant community; most had worked in the mines, and mine workers who frequented a particular tavern were closely linked by class and ethnicity (Broehl 1964, 84; Kenny 1998, 197).

Neighborhood bars in a house meant that the women and children of the family would give their services for free. All bars had to give credit to stay in business. Miners, however, for all their hard-drinking habits do not seem to have had a higher rate of alcoholism than workers in other industries. It does seem, however, that they spent relatively high amounts of money on drinking compared to other workers: one eighth compared to one tenth of their income (P. Roberts 1904, 37). In Shamokin, I was told there were twenty to twenty-four bars on Shamokin Street alone. They would stay open until 2:00 a.m. Miners would stop in for a shot on the way to work, then again on the way home. Women were frequently forbidden to enter the bar area itself. Bars often had an ethnic clientele because they were located in the neighborhoods in which people lived. They also sold food, often good home-cooked meals, for which seafood has long been a favorite: People from the Coal Region are known to love their oysters, hard shell crabs and clams.

One young Polish bartender whose father had a bar and slot machines in half of a double[23] in Kulpmont, started to work in the barroom when he was thirteen years old. His mother fell off a chair and broke her leg and his father was working in the bootleg coal holes,[24] so they had to rely on him to help make ends meet. He remembers that they were mostly Polish in their bar but one Dutch [German] and two Russian brothers who were very good carpenters lived across the street and they'd come in. There was a mixture but in those days Polish would mostly stick with the Polish. Sunday the bars were closed but they were only a block away from the church and after mass at 11 a.m. they would come around the back, and they'd come in and have what they called "the second sermon."[25] There were 45 barrooms for a population of about 4–5,000 in Kulpmont. The bartender detailed some of the troubles he had had: "At night people would come in late and there was always a point where they would have stopped for a drink elsewhere. They'd come in at eleven or twelve o'clock at night and you'd know you were going to have trouble on your hands. They'd start a fight, or argue, or something like that, and it didn't work out that good. A big mug of beer was five cents, a shot in a one ounce glass was ten cents."[26] To compare these prices with earnings, at this time in the early 1920s, the family's boarder working in the Alaska Colliery was making $5.00 a day.

In Mt. Carmel, according to one local historian, "there was a bar literally on every block—they called them cafes and I assure you there was no coffee served in them. . . . These bars, mind you, opened at 6 a.m. Even in the early sixties when it was no longer really a mining community, the tradition hung on."[27] He thought there might be one or two bars in Mt. Carmel right now that open at 6 a.m. A lot of the people going there are retired and they keep going there because they used to. In the mining era, people are fond of saying, there used to be bars and churches on every other street corner.

Taking in boarders was a way of increasing the mining family's income, and being a boarder was the way newcomers got housed. In many families, and particularly among Slavs (Eastern Europeans), women did not go out to work but took in boarders to help cope with lack of cash. The wives of landlords raised their own large families and in addition shouldered the extra work of caring for boarders as well: they cooked for them, made their lunches, and did their laundry.

Boarders were to some degree part of the family, and were often in fact relatives or friends from the home country. They helped out with the chores, and the family was responsible for their funeral if they died. Some immigrants did not live as boarders with a family but were miserably exploited, particularly by English and Irish landlords, and packed into cramped cellars or stables as they tried to accumulate enough money to buy a house or rent land for a one-roomed shanty. As larger numbers of Slavs arrived, the coal companies built them small and poorly constructed houses. Married immigrants saved up to bring their families over by taking in men of their own nationality as boarders. Sometimes as many as twenty or thirty would crowd into the landlord's four room house, sometimes sleeping in shifts, with a lean-to serving as kitchen and living room. Boarders bought their own food and paid for it to be cooked. Rent for a room averaged one dollar a month. In 1890, the average boarder could subsist on ten dollars a month (D. L. Miller and Sharpless 1985, 176–78).

A Ukrainian woman's grandparents had boarders constantly and she remembered that she and the children were always cooking for them. The boarders would be there from two months to a year, until they could get on their feet. She remembered the big black frying pan for pork chops, and the mashed potatoes and pork chops and cabbage, with homemade bread, and then the peaches they had put up in the summer for dessert. Miners' wives worked hard: not only was there all this cooking and the laundry to do, but they had to heat water for the big tub in the basement in which these miners bathed.

Like the bars, the stores were neighborhood institutions. People say there used to be a store on every corner, many of them with an ethnic clientele from the neighborhood. They operated primarily on credit and had a Tick Book in which a family's purchases were entered for payment at the end of the month. The store owners helped mining families to stand up to the hardships of their lives. Many people owed money to them; some debts were paid in kind, some were never called. One man who had a job checking scales in general stores said he often found them inaccurate in these neighborhood stores in favor of the customer, but the owner would just shrug it off saying: "Oh that's all right."

An article in the *News Item* of February 19, 2006 celebrated the oldest neighborhood grocery store in the Shamokin area. Frank and Peggy Rovito are still in business in a Mom and Pop store they have operated for more than fifty years. It is a family business that they bought from Frank's father. There used to be about ten family operated stores on Bunker Hill, their neighborhood, but now they are the only one left in the entire town. Supermarkets, the demise of faithful customers, factories closing and the population decline that followed are the reasons they give for this change. But strikes were also a problem for the neighborhood stores: they always had lots of money out on credit but when there was a strike, no one could pay them back, so they had no cash. During long strikes, a lot of these small stores would go broke. Then later the supermarkets put many more of them out of business. But in the end, it was the recent coming of the convenience stores, open twenty-four hours and all weekend that was the undoing of almost all the remaining neighborhood groceries: they could not stay open all the time. People miss them.

My tour of Kulpmont included a running description of how it used to be before the population decline of the mine and the factory closings. Bars and neighborhood stores featured strongly in the narrative. The town came alive and the sleepy streets seemed suddenly peopled with the vibrant community that had once been there. My guide pointed out that the bakery next to the pizza place used to be a bar; there were five on this block, six on the one before, seven on Chestnut Street. There was only an occasional one on the back streets, but there were grocery stores on every corner. There were also lots of pool rooms. Bars were usually in the front rooms of family homes; stores were also attached to houses in front rooms or the other half of a double. His grandmother had a store. Men might work a store as they got old; sometimes the women ran them. He remembered getting pickled herrings from a Jewish store. "Dell's Hat Shop was one fine establishment. It sold fancy hats from New York and Philadelphia. It was there next door to the fire station."[28]

The Silk Mills

The town depended not only on anthracite mining for a century and a quarter after commercial mining started in the 1820s, but also on the silk mills that located in the area because of the abundant supply of good water and the labor pool of the coal miners' wives and daughters.

The Eagle Silk Mill in Shamokin once rivaled mining as the town's chief employer. The huge mill with its great clock was a landmark feature of the town. In the 1920s, Shamokin was one of the chief silk manufacturing centers in the United States. In 1903, two brothers, Charles Kimber Eagle and John Henry Eagle, sons of a Pottstown farmer, bought out the stockholders of the Shamokin Silk Company, begun in 1899 in Coal Township. They founded the Eagle Silk Company. In 1923, at its height, this company employed about 6,000 men and women in all its branches, and had a payroll of $5–6 million a year. The Shamokin mill, constructed in 1917, which employed as many as 3,300, was the largest of the mills. There was one in Kulpmont (which employed over 500),[29] and in 1925, five area silk mills in Hazleton employed about 3 thousand workers. The Shamokin mill was the largest textile building under one roof in the United States. It produced silk fabrics, weaving, weighting, dye printing and printing them. The company sent two men to China to learn the procedures of silk making. The silk was imported from China to Washington State by sea and then to Shamokin by rail. The cargo was so valuable that armed guards rode on the train (Boback 1994).

Other mills in Shamokin were the Maue Silk Mill, begun in 1931 by two brothers, which had sixty workers and specialized in upholstery and decorative fabrics. In 1964 it still had sixty-five workers (*New Citizen* newspaper, Centennial Issue). There was also a woolen mill.

Workers in the mills often started to work at age twelve to fourteen. The Eagle company required two hours schooling a day until they were fifteen, for which they got paid, at the company operated and sponsored school for these youngsters. The company had its own magazine, The *Eagle Co-Worker*, published bimonthly beginning in 1918. This reported that the school was teaching 500 students a day at that time. Hours were long in the mills, but only men were allowed to work the night shift from 6 p.m. to 7 a.m.; women and children were on the day shift, 7 a.m. to 5.30 p.m. with half an hour for lunch.

In the interviews for the *Shamokin Oral History Project* (American Association of University Women, 1985) on the mill's workers, some commented on what nice people the mill owners were, one said they gave food or money to people in need, another that you could get good meals in the café, a third liked working in the mill with all her friends and found her bosses nice people. A woman who made it up to forelady in her 49 years at the Eagle Mill made $15 per week "which was very good in those days." Workers were paid according to the number of yards of silk they produced. Mill workers were allowed to buy silk cloth cheaply and they would make it up into clothes for themselves and others, so that Shamokin women were renowned for their fine silk clothing. But although the Eagle Mill was considered by some to be a good place to work at the time, others had a different view. One man said that he had been severe getting his daughters to do their homework, he wanted them to get an education and not get a job in the silk mill "working for a New York guy who was getting rich off their labor."[30]

This awareness was realized in 1916 as the labor struggle began in the silk mills. A flyer, excerpts from which are reproduced in the box below, called the townspeople to an organizing meeting for a union.[31]

Do J. H & C. K. Eagle and Co. Inc. Own Shamokin?

Are the citizens of Shamokin going to continue to be owned body and soul by a petty corporation? Do they know what is going on in this Borough of Shamokin? Do they know that girls who have been working in Eagle's Mills for five and six years cannot average $4.00 for a week of 50 or 60 hours. That the men weavers cannot earn more than from $8.00 to $16 per week, the large majority seldom receiving more than $10 per week, for thirteen hours per night. That the day weavers work 50 hours to earn from $3.00 to the large sum of $8.00 per week. Do you know you working men and voters, you fathers, that there are hundreds of boys and girls under the age of 14 and 16 years working in these mills? ... You parents ask yourself "How can your son or daughter live and dress respectably on $4.00 per week under the present high cost of living?" Mr. Boseth, the BOSS, who is so valuable to his employers, and whose salary is so high that he does not know what his position is according to his own admission, says "The employees of the Eagle Mills cannot organize as they do not earn enough money in a week to pay their union dues." Could you have better proof of the necessity of organization? . . . Now you people of Shamokin, you union men and women, knowing that organization is the only weapon with which we can combat this petty tyranny come forward and let us know where you stand. Are you with us or against us? Come to our monster meeting which will be held at the Edgewood Ball Park on Saturday afternoon at 2.30 o'clock (September 2, 1916) and learn more of the facts and conditions of our battle.

Wake Up! People of Shamokin e'er it is Too Late.

Economic and Population Decline

The coal mines and the silk mills which had brought prosperity and expansion for the economy were to lose out to the effects of technological change and innovation. The discovery of alternative fuels and the technological advances to exploit them were major reasons for the decline of the coal industry. The development of synthetic fabrics of various kinds likewise ended the silk industry.

In 1949, after three years of steady production following World War II, the hard coal market collapsed because of the switch to fuel oil, natural gas and electricity for home heating, and because it was losing out to soft coal for industrial use. During World War II, coal still accounted for about half U.S. energy consumption; by 1955 it was less than 29 percent. Without a domestic market, anthracite largely ceased to be a major industry (Freese 2003, 160). The out-migration to find jobs that started after World War II became a flood as unemployment soared with the mines operating only two to three days a week, closing altogether, or consolidating production. Unemployment rose to 17–18 percent in major anthracite districts by 1958 (Dublin 1998, 10). By the 1990s, deep mining had almost ceased and stripping operations performed most of the mining that still existed. When production of anthracite had reached its peak in 1917 during World War I, mining and preparation of coal employed 175 thousand men; by 1992, after its decline, it employed only 1.4 thousand (ibid., 1).

There were other problems beside the reduced demand. The expense of pumping water was another factor in the decline of the mines. While coal was being replaced by oil and natural gas and the mines were in trouble, there was also increasing difficulty pumping water out of the mines as they were made deeper and deeper. At the time the Glen Burn Mine stopped working in the 1960s, they were pumping out four tons of water for every ton of coal.[32] The general opinion was that the prolonged mine strike of 1925–1926 did permanent damage to the industry: during the five months of the strike the population drop began with the departure of many miners and their families, and people turned to using the new fuels of oil and gas. Another problem was that the heating industry failed to modernize heating equipment for using coal.

Over the years the machinery of the silk mills became antiquated, and then silk was displaced in the 1930s, the years of the Great Depression, by rayon, nylon and polyester fabrics. The Eagle Company was bankrupt by 1938. It was reorganized as the Shamokin Dye and Print Works which lasted four years and failed in 1942, but no more silk was made after 1937.

The population of Shamokin-Coal Township eventually declined by between two-thirds and three-quarters as a result of these drastic changes, as shown in the city directories[33] and given in table 1.3.

Table 1.3. Population Decline in Shamokin/Coal Township

1930	40,215
1940	40,210
1950	36,000
1960	33,418
1970	27,204
1980	22,323
1990	19,106
2000	10,000

Source: City Directories from 1930 to 2000 (taken from the U.S. Census).

The devastation of the economy and the huge drop in the town's population profoundly affected the lives of the people who remained.

The next two chapters describe the ethnic groups defined by religion, language, associations and clubs, cultural traditions, foods, and arts and crafts that for more than a century formed a political and economic hierarchy in the town.

Notes

1. This practice was in later years to lead to the dangerous practice of "robbing" these pillars for coal by miners working independently of the big companies.

2. In Shamokin at this time, when the Derr (later to be known as Derk) family came over from Germany, William Penn gave them the whole ridge on the West side of the mountain (Harry Derk, April 9, 2003).

3. According to Donald H. Akenson, at some point in pre-famine migration to the United States, Protestants, both Anglo-Irish and Presbyterian Ulster Scots, significantly outnumbered Catholic migrants. Statistics of the census before 1855 however, he says, are not reliable (Akenson 1992: 105, 109).

4. The Pale of Settlement was the zone established in 1791 by Catherine the Great, Empress of Russia, for the settlement of most Russian Jews on the Russian European border. It lasted until 1915. Jews were expelled from Moscow, St. Petersburg and other cities and forced to settle in the Pale, and later were forced from its rural areas to live in its *shtetls* (small settlements).

5. In 1815, the Congress of Vienna created the semiautonomous kingdom of Poland in the area under Russian control (Greene 1980, 789).

6. In the heavily Polish Coal Town of Nanticoke in 1900, for example, Poles held $500,000 worth of real estate (Golab 1977, 69, 81, 86; Greene 1980, 798).

7. Robert Wislock, August 26, 2003.

8. 190,000 (91 percent) of Lithuanian Jews were murdered in the Holocaust.

9. The famous Hill of Crosses, on which thousands of Latin Rite crosses were placed on a hill near the city of Siauliai, was an anticommunist resistance shrine.

10. There are Russians and Russian Orthodox churches in the Coal Region. There is a Russian Orthodox Church in Mt. Carmel, but not in Shamokin/Coal Township.

11. Monsignor Fedorovich, January 16, 2002.

12. This terrible event and the horrors that went with it, is little known in the West, though a march was held to protest the famine in Detroit in 1933 (Fedunkiw 1995, 1386). In 2003, however, the U.S. House of Representatives adopted Resolution 356, pronouncing the famine a deliberate act of terror and mass murder against the Ukrainian people, and supporting the Government of Ukraine by giving it official recognition (quoted in *The Way*, the Ukrainian biweekly, November 16, 2003).

13. Immigration reports show that from 1899 to 1910, 98.2 percent of the Ruthenians (the early name for Ukrainians from this region) admitted to the United States came from Austria-Hungary (Procko 1979, 219).

14. *Class* is defined by Davies in the Weberian sense as the members of a social group, the upper class being those whose members participate in the same institutions, are frequently related through blood or marriage, often share some commonality of ancestry, are involved in the same social and cultural activities, and nearly always live in common residential areas. *Elite* has a more restrictive sense, of individuals in a community in positions of economic and political power, only loosely organized in a social or familial sense. They lack cohesiveness because of this and often do not persist within or through generations (Davies 1985, 12).

15. Oil lamps were replaced by the brighter white light of the carbide lamp only after the turn of the century; But both had open flames that could ignite gas (Poliniak 1970, 22).

16. For full and vivid accounts of work in the mines, see Aurand 1971 chaps. 4–5; D. L. Miller and Sharpless 1985, chap. 4.

17. Bobby Kaminsky, Kulpmont, December 12, 2004.

18. Ed Narcavage, Mt. Carmel, April 21, 2003, by pernission of his widow, Marie Narcavage.

19. Leonard Oszko, February 28, 2002, by permission.

20. Adam Klebasko, June 22, 2007.

21. Mary Lenig, March 27, 2002.

22. The name for small neighborhood stores run by a man and his wife.

23. Coal Region term for a duplex.

24. The name given to the independent mining operations on company land when the mines were closing and the miners desperate to make a living in the late twenties and the Depression years of the thirties.

25. State law prohibited Sunday sales but Sundays were in fact the saloons' busiest day, doubling the money they took in for any day except pay day (P. Roberts 1904, 236).

26. Len Oszko, February 28, 2002, by permission.

27. Hugh A. Jones, Mt. Carmel, February 21, 2003.

28. Bob Chesnay, Kulpmont, February 25, 2003.

29. There were also silk mills outside the Coal Region in Bethlehem, Phoenixville, Bellefonte, Gettysburg, and Mechanicsburg.

30. Reported from an interview by Bob Hartman, Bucknell student, with a Shamokin resident.

31. A copy of this flier was given to me by Eleanor Kuhns. Accounts of her life and political leadership are given in chaps.7 and 8.

32. Mel Farrow, February 24, 2004.

33. The city directories were put out by different publishers over the years, as follows:

1930: W. H. Boyd and Co. Reading, PA; 1940: R. Polk & Co., New York; 1950: same; 1960: R. L. Polk & Taylor, Boston; 1990: R. L. Polk & Taylor, Maryland.

CHAPTER TWO

Early Immigrants

The Emergence of Ethnic Identity and Social Hierarchy

The immigrants primarily settled in Shamokin/Coal Township near others from the home region of their country. Many came in groups from a particular town or village in the homeland and neighborhoods soon developed in the town and in the "mine patches," as the settlements that grew up around the mine collieries were known. These neighborhoods were centered on the churches the immigrants built which structured their lives. In this process, their original regional, town or village identities were replaced by the national ethnic identities assigned to them as they entered the country. These ethnic identities corresponded to the immigrants' position in the political, economic and religious hierarchy of the town as the structural relations of power and inequality in the years of the coal era determined relations between the distinct ethnic groups that became the basis of town life. Religion, language, cultural traditions and foods, and the associations they formed characterized the different groups. This chapter and the next describe the major ethnic groups of the town during this time.

All immigrants had in common the desire to better their lives and those of their children and descendants by leaving their home countries. Their determination and courage in this endeavor is imprinted on the landscape of the anthracite counties in the dark heaps of coal waste that resulted from their labor in the mines, and in the shining domes and tall spires of the churches and the imposing synagogues that they built in the towns, for which the miners contributed their own labor and such small sums of money as they could scrape together from their meager monetary resources.

At first when they married, some immigrants brought wives over from home, but soon marriage took place in the town within the ethnic group (endogamy) and marriage outside it was disapproved. The groups became exclusive to a considerable degree: children went to their own parochial schools and learned the customs and ways of their heritage, and the different groups were identified by the languages they spoke, by their churches, the different foods they ate, their celebrations and festivities and other traditions, and by the associations and social clubs that they formed. They functioned as interest groups furthering the shared economic and political interests of their members in relation to other groups.[1] The accounts of each group will include a family history to show how a particular family experienced the process of migration, and to document the social mobility of their descendants.

The Germans: Farmers and Men of Influence

Lifestyles and language of the different sub-groups of German-Americans in the Coal Region have varied widely, from the extreme conservatism, use of the Pennsylvania German language, and distinctive lifestyle of separatist rural religious groups, such as the Pennsylvania German Old Order Amish and Old Order Mennonites in some farming valleys, to German-Americans whose lifestyle and language have been since the late 1920s indistinguishable from the other Americans among whom they live. The German farmers who arrived early prospered and became mill, hotel and mine owners; some were mining engineers. They were influential citizens in the town and in the top levels of the power hierarchy from its early years.

The Germans arrived in Jamestown in 1607; in the four centuries that followed they became one of the three largest components of the American population. The Old Order Mennonite and Old Order Amish rural sectarian communities of the Pennsylvania Germans (popularly known as Pennsylvania Dutch) came to Pennsylvania for religious reasons later in the seventeenth century than the earliest German settlers (Nugent 1995, 104). These religious communities were farmers, strongly linguistically and culturally defined: their religion continues to demand that they set themselves apart from other people (Huffines 1985). Today they farm the valleys in between the mining areas, and the mining towns and patches have been important market populations for their produce.

Lutheran and Reformed immigrants came later and settled to the north and west. Large numbers of German immigrants arrived in the Colonial Period: Benjamin Franklin estimated that perhaps one third of Pennsylvania's population at this time was German, the majority of them farmers. Many of them became prosperous. German national identity was thus established earlier than for other non-English speaking groups who immigrated later to the Coal Region, but the need and desire to distance themselves from their heritage during the two World Wars greatly attenuated German identity in the coal towns by the last decades of the twentieth century. Today their observances of cultural traditions are minimal compared to those of other groups.

Many of the influential men of Northumberland County in the twentieth century were descendants of the early German settlers. They appear early among the mine owners. An example is the Northumberland County branch of the famous coal-owning dynasty of the town of Mauch Chunk (now renamed Jim Thorpe), in the eastern Coal Region (see figure 1.1), who are still engaged in coal operations. John Conrad Leisenring, the founding ancestor of this dynasty, emigrated from the German Duchy of Saxony to Baltimore in 1744, and bought a farm of 150 acres on the Lehigh River in the midst of what was later to be part of the anthracite mining fields (Rottenberg, 2003, 7). One of his sons, Peter B. Leisenring, born in 1770, moved to Northumberland County in 1805. He and three generations of his descendants became prosperous farmers and men of influence in the county, owning tanneries, distilleries, grist mills, taverns and hotels, and lumber enterprises. They belonged to the historic Blue Church and were members of the Democratic Party[2] (*Genealogical and Biographical Annals of Northumberland County* 1911, 240–41).

Religion became central to these migrants' identity after the religious revival following the arrival of Lutheran and Reformed missionaries in the late seventeenth century and the rapid expansion of congregations. This religious revival paralleled a similar one among English speaking colonists. It stimulated German identity not only by reinforcing the German language but by laying the foundation of an ethnic parochial school system. Later the Germans were to strive for years to maintain their parochial schools after Pennsylvania had introduced public schools. An expansion of the German press throughout the colonies also contributed to the increase of German consciousness. German literacy was high enough to support thirty-eight German newspapers at various times between 1732 and 1800, which reinforced German ethnic awareness (Huffines 1985, 409). But German immigration on a large scale was virtually brought to a stop with the American Revolution, and for the next fifty years thereafter. During this time acculturation and assimilation proceeded rapidly: Germans Anglicized their names, used English in business and in many urban churches, and increasingly intermarried with English settlers. Only in rural Pennsylvania where the original German religious communities expanded, did ethnic culture strongly persist (Conzen 1980, 409).

A steep decline in German immigration at the end of the nineteenth century, as Germany industrialized on a large scale and internal migration replaced emigration, coincided with the massive Slav and Italian immigration into the Coal Region. But German immigration increased again in the 1920s, after the introduction of a quota system restricted the flow of Eastern and Southern Europeans and for the first half of the twentieth century, first generation Germans and their children were the most numerous immigrant group in American agriculture (ibid., 409–11, 415).

A German Family History

The southern part of Northumberland County and the Lykens valley was originally settled by German farmers, including the Reed ancestors who left the Palatinate in 1709 seeking a good livelihood and freedom of religion. They were primarily Lutheran and Reformed Lutheran. Fritz Reed, former mayor of Shamokin, relates his family history which goes back over thirteen generations.

> They were fleeing religious wars, persecution and an exceptionally hard winter, and were lured by the pamphlets distributed by William Penn's people. Our original name in German was Rieth (in various spellings); the father of the first emigrant was a minor provincial government official. Thousands of people were leaving at this time; this particular group was of 10–15 thousand people and came down the Rhine to Rotterdam, then continued to England. One hundred went in a group to America on a voyage of great hardship on which twenty five of them died. They arrived in 1710 and lived along the Hudson. They had signed on as indentured servants and were effectively white slaves. They did not understand that the land they had been promised was just a little vegetable patch, not like the farms and vineyards they had had back home, and they were unhappy. Some went to Canada; my ancestors went to the Schoharie valley [West of Albany][3] which was Indian Territory at that time. The governor had released them from servitude: he could not afford to feed them because parliament had not paid him. They developed land which they farmed with Indian help and did quite well. But the land was not really theirs and finally the governor sold it out from under them to Dutch settlers out of Albany and New York. One third of the group built rafts and dugouts with Indian help and came down the Susquehanna River to Pennsylvania.

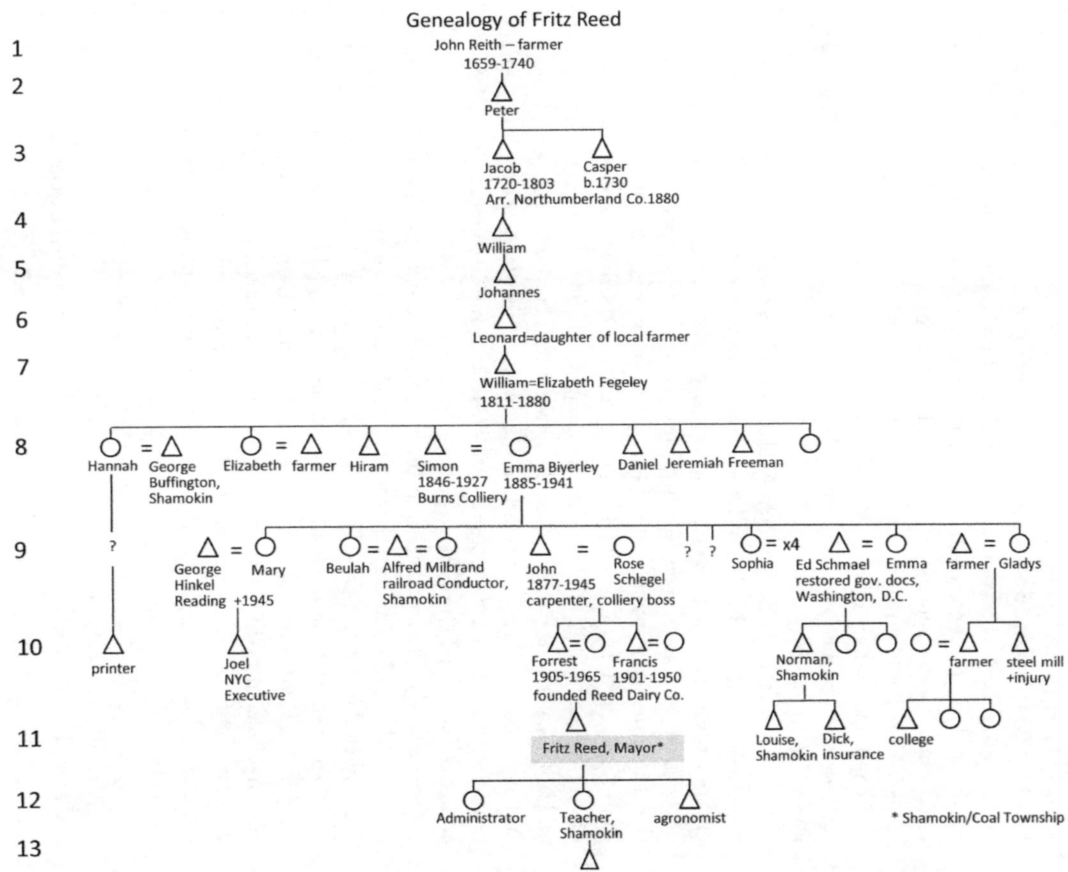

Figure 2.1. Genealogy of Fritz Reed

Generations 1–4: John G. Reith, born in 1659, was the first Reed ancestor to immigrate, but he died of typhus on the Atlantic voyage in 1700. His son, Peter Reed, born 1695, was therefore the first to arrive, and Peter's son, Jacob Reed, 1720–1800, was the first to come to Northumberland County. He speculated in cheap land around 1800 when the county was being formed, which his three sons inherited and became quite prosperous. The family primarily continued to be farmers down through three more generations. In *Generation 8*, Simon, Fritz' great grandfather, worked in the coal industry, but, as is typical for Germans, as a foreman, not as an unskilled laborer.

By *Generation 9*, only one son was a farmer: John, Fritz's grandfather, was a carpenter and colliery boss, and another son a railroad conductor; two daughters moved from rural to urban areas when they married and went to Reading and to Washington.

Generation 10 had one farmer, a steel mill worker, two bankers who founded a successful dairy business, a printer, and a company executive. By this generation, the family had moved from farming to the city and to professional occupations and some members had moved away. This process continued in the next three generations. In 1914 Isaiah Reed, brother of Fritz' grandfather John Reed, started selling milk from his farm. In 1919 the enterprise became a dairy, the Reed's Milk and Ice Cream Company. Its first store opened in 1937 and in 1947 with the construction of a new plant, it became the region's largest and most modern dairy. Fritz's father, the owner of the dairy after his brother's death, was also a director of Shamokin-Coal Township Chamber of Commerce and of the National Dime Bank.

Generation 11: Fritz worked in the business as a route foreman with five milk routes, and ended up managing it when his father died suddenly. It prospered: they covered five counties in Pennsylvania for ice cream, three for milk. They had twenty vehicles on the road. Various problems caused Fritz to sell the dairy early in 1973. He took a state job in Harrisburg, and then became a politician and involved in civic organizations. He was chairman of the City Planning Commission for seven years, mayor of the city in the seventies, and for seven terms the Northumberland County Register of Wills and Recorder of Deeds. He is one of the town's most influential citizens, involved in many of its affairs, a pillar of the Northumberland Historical Association, and much in demand to give talks on local history.

Generation 12: Fritz's three children are all in professional careers.[4]

This history illustrates the features of German immigration of hardships, of long journeys over great distances, of paying passage through indentured servitude, of eventually settling down and becoming prosperous farmers, business and mine owners and influential citizens. Over the generations, this family moved from rural to urban living, to white collar and professional employment, and became powerful and influential figures in the twentieth-century town and its politics.

Language, Food, and Identity

From 1850 to 1970, German was the most widely spoken language after English in the United States, and Pennsylvania second only to California in those reporting German ancestry (Rippley 1995, 570). Up until World War I, in many parts of the Coal Region, the Lutheran Church held regular services in High German. St. John's United Church of Christ (Reformed Church) in Shamokin, for example, had such a service. But the anti-German feeling of the World Wars had very adverse effects. The German press in America had almost disappeared by the outbreak of World War I, and High German in the churches met a similar fate by World War II. By the millennium, among the large numbers of Germans who had completely assimilated into American society, the German language had become virtually extinct.

However, among the Old Order Amish and Old Order Mennonites living in farm communities in Pennsylvania, Pennsylvania German, a German dialect closely related to the dialects of the Rhine Palatinate of southwest Germany, persisted much longer than did the use of High German. Community members still speak Pennsylvania German at home, and with each other, and they use a variety of High German in their church services, though they speak English in their parochial schools and when talking to outsiders. This German is still used in isolated areas of the state, including the Lykens and other farming valleys of the Coal Region.

The Pennsylvania German Sunday service is of recent origin; it is not the continuation of a tradition but deliberately established to celebrate the past. But the language seems to be losing its force and power. Louise Huffines makes it clear that the trends toward English were set before World War I and it just accelerated the process. Although use of Pennsylvania German declined in these communities because of anti-German attitudes during World War I, it enjoyed resurgence in the 1930s, including the performance of new plays, writing of newspaper columns and an increase in radio broadcasts. However, since no effort was made to provide elementary education in the dialect, its prospects are poor; it continues now only in rural, self-sufficient areas, and only among the middle-aged and elderly (Huffines 1985, 243–45).

The strength of German identity and use of the German language has thus varied with these different groups of people of German descent in the Coal Region. In the Amish and Mennonite communities of the farming valleys, there is a strong sectarian identity. Lutheran Germans were never separatists, although their religion divided them from German Catholics who arrived later: the early original German settlers in the Coal Region were Protestants;

the Catholic Germans came in the mid-1800s. There are two big German Catholic churches in Wilkes Barre, and another in Ashland (see figure 1.1).

Strong anti-German feeling developed before World War I: President Wilson's government fostered a vigorous propaganda campaign from the outset and an anti-German attitude was intensified by the newspapers through the ways they were depicted in cartoons and in the headlines referring to them as Huns. As a result, Germans shed identifiable German cultural traits, their social clubs disappeared, their newspapers ceased publication, and their language received no public expression. By World War II there was nothing left that was identifiably German and nothing obvious to bring on them the internment that Japanese Americans suffered in World War II.[5]

Some comments from German Americans show the difficulty of being German during the World Wars in the coal towns with their multiethnic populations, but also how some elements of cultural identity survived even so. People say: "When World War II took place, you were Pennsylvania Dutch, you didn't use the word German." As one Shamokin woman put it, she had always thought of herself as German-American, but as a child she was not proud of being German because she didn't want any association with Hitler and the holocaust. "It was a shame because everyone should be able to be proud of who they are." Her family did not keep German traditions but they did eat German foods for festive meals, such as pork with sauerkraut and mashed potatoes on New Year's Day: for Germans, as for all ethnic groups, foods have been prime markers of identity. Additional Pennsylvania German foods are meat pies and chicken pot pies (potatoes, meat and vegetables in a pie crust), pickled pigs' feet, tripe, and scrapple (a savory mush based on pork liver, meat scraps and cornmeal), Dutch cake (like a coffee cake), and *schnitz un knepp* (apples and buttons: boiled ham, dried apples and dumplings). The custom for east and central Pennsylvania Protestant congregations to hold an annual sauerkraut supper has spread to the Anglo-American Methodists and even to Episcopalians (Yoder 1961a, 56–62).

On the other hand, a man who is a member of a family of German descent that has always lived in Shamokin and has a well-researched family tree, says the family considers themselves to be completely American and assimilated, although he adds: "we do have shoo-fly pie and Dutch cake." Another Shamokin resident of mixed German, Welsh, Irish and English ancestry chooses to consider himself as primarily German, but he says he does not feel any special German identity nor does he observe any special German celebrations. As Fritz Reed puts it: "You see, when World War II took place, you were Pennsylvania Dutch, you didn't use the word German. It isn't a thing that anybody holds to any more, the wartime hostility has faded; it's just a talking thing."

A German Protestant Church

Ethnic churches in the Coal Region are predominantly Catholic, but a few are Protestant. An example is Salem United Church of Christ in Coal Township, in the West End of town. In 1904, members of St. John's Reformed Church in the Borough of Shamokin who were living out in the West End of town, built a chapel and in 1912 formed a congregation. At this time the neighborhoods in this area had more of a mixture of people than those of the East End. Originally the area was primarily German and Protestant but quite quickly there were Poles and other Catholics too. All of Salem's families lived near the church, so it was in that sense a neighborhood church and the congregation was primarily Pennsylvania German in origin. The church rolls and list of charter members show names that are mostly German, with some English, from 1912 to the 1940s. Men among the older members of the congregation today worked in the mines in the past and women in the textile factories; the church is more a working class church and more ethnic German than its parent church, St. John's in Shamokin, in which the more influential and wealthy of the area's families are dominant.[6]

The Welsh: Mine Supervisors, Bosses and Company Owners

The Welsh immigrants who were miners came in far greater numbers than those who came from rural areas; all left overwhelmingly for economic reasons in search of a better life (W. D. Jones 1993, xviii). They were attracted by the comparatively high wages of the developing coal industry of Pennsylvania. In the 1840s and 1850s, they were about $36 a month, double those in Wales (Berthoff 1980, 1012). They also wanted to escape crowded living and poor working conditions. At first the Welsh filled rank and file positions as well as supervisory ones in the mines, but as other immigrants arrived, they came to dominate the power structure by the superior place they filled in the political and economic hierarchy. They were mine owners, state mine inspectors, mine superintendents, supervisors and bosses, and as contract miners, superior in class position to the Irish and then to the Slavs, later arriving groups who worked as unskilled mine labor.

Welsh foremen recruited expert miners directly from the mines of south Wales (H. A. Jones 1978, 138, 143). The town of Minersville (see figure 1.1) was populated initially by Welsh coal miners who were recruited to settle there. The whole town was built up by two coal companies, hence the name. It was the same with Mt. Carmel.[7] The miners' great ambition was to give their sons a school education and a better position in life than being a miner. This was fulfilled since succeeding generations of Welsh Americans mostly went into white collar jobs, business or the professions (Berthoff 1980, 1014).

The U.S. Census shows that in 1850 there were just under thirty thousand Welsh foreign born in the United States; by 1890 there were over one hundred thousand. The figures are uncertain and were probably higher still, though the number is still small compared to Welsh immigration elsewhere. They were remarkably concentrated: in 1900, nearly 38 percent of the 93.5 thousand of first generation Welsh in the United States were in Pennsylvania. They were to be found particularly in the Scranton and Wilkes Barre areas of northeastern Pennsylvania (W. D. Jones 1993: xvii, xx; see figure 1.1). For immigrants in America, marriage with Welsh girls, even if this meant returning to Wales to find one, was general. Out of seventy-five Welshmen married in the Scranton area in 1886, forty-eight of them married women born in Wales and another twelve of the wives had Welsh parents (Berthoff 1980, 1014).

Scranton, in the north of the Coal Region, was described as the greatest Welsh Center in America. William D. Jones' (1993) detailed documentation of the Scranton community gives us a close up view of the Welsh in the nineteenth century Coal Region, and provides a picture of the role the Welsh played also in other towns which lacked such numbers of them and therefore such a clear historical record. The community of the Hyde Park section of the city was overwhelmingly Welsh speaking. It was also a major center of the Welsh American press, with a number of Welsh newspapers and periodicals. Nonconformist denominations of Welsh Baptist, Congregationalist, and Calvinistic Methodists had seven splendid churches in this section of the city, each with auxiliary organizations attached of schools, bible classes, and women's societies, all with a full calendar of social activities. Between 1864 and 1875, they held services in Welsh (W. D. Jones 1993, 88–90).

Culture and Tradition: "The Welsh Have Their Singing"

Welsh-Americans expressed their Welshness in cultural activity; their idea of Wales was an active force which led to the holding of cultural events as well as the organizing of institutions and societies (ibid., xxi). The Scranton Welsh community organized singing festivals called *eisteddfodau*. These originated in the meetings of the bards in early Welsh history. The first records of them are from 1176, of meetings for poetic competitions among the bards at which prizes were awarded for stanzas sung with the harp (*penillion*); by the Middle Ages, the bards were licensing reputable performers in this singing.

In the seventeenth century in Wales, however, Anglican religious evangelism followed by Methodism drove out ancient Welsh culture, music, dancing and the bardic poetic tradition, transforming ancient rituals and devising a new way of life that cut Welsh people off from their past. Thus we later find in Wales a deliberate revival, and even invention, of tradition derived from the common people whose lives had been so drastically changed but who were the last practitioners of Welsh lore, music and learning, and the Welsh language. The first attempt to retrieve this culture was around 1700 with the revival of the *eisteddfodau*. In the 1780s, this revived tradition was linked to the Welsh Societies that had begun to appear in both Wales and London. These societies proceeded to organize *eisteddfodau* in which musical rather than poetic competition gradually came to dominate the proceedings. By 1815, they were held under the auspices of Cambrian clubs in Wales, and popularized the idea that the Welsh bards were the heirs of the ancient druids and their rites, rituals and mythology. During the nineteenth century about five hundred ceremonial *eisteddfodau* were held in Wales. The national one created a great interest in genuine as well as mythical Welsh history, and was aimed at reviving a national culture for Wales (Morgan 1983, 53–57, 59–61).

Before this very ancient musical tradition was brought over from Wales to America, it had therefore undergone both change and reinvention; once in its new country the process continued. Over fifty recognized Welsh bards lived in Scranton. Joseph Parry, born in Merthyr Tydfil and raised in Danville (see fig. 1.1), developed and nurtured the local literary and musical talent with choirs, fundraisers and festivals. In 1875, a national *eisteddfod* was held in Hyde Park under the auspices of the Philosophical society.

There were also secular societies, prominent among them the Welsh Philosophical Society which aided upward mobility with its educational programs (W. D. Jones 1993, 88–95). It had members who became mine superintendents, mine inspectors, legislators, and judges (Bertoff 1980, 1016). Other Welsh communities in the Coal Region in Ashland, St. Clair, Minersville, Pottstown, and Shamokin, were not as large as Scranton's, but held singing festivals and celebrated St. David's Day as their primary manifestations of Welsh identity.

The Welsh were Protestants (Congregationalists, Methodists or Baptists), and their churches constituted the preeminent Welsh institution. A Welsh Baptist church was first organized in Mt. Carmel in 1872, and lasted until 1888. The Welsh Congregational Church of 1870 is still in existence. In Shamokin a Welsh Baptist Church existed from 1865–1870, and the Mt. Zion Congregational United Church of Christ (UCC) is still a strong institution and is referred to as the honorary spiritual center of the Welsh in Northumberland County (H. A. Jones 1978, 146).

From the churches in Wales came the annual assemblies of the *gymanfa bregethu*, preaching assembly, and the *gymanfa ganu*, singing assembly. The former was a series of sermons that might go on for several days. The latter was developed in 1860 to improve hymn singing in small village chapels and churches, through the practice of having the congregation stay on after the Sunday service for an hour of hymn singing (Bertoff 1980, 1014, 1017). For months a few hymns and anthems would be rehearsed, then in a common meeting place, congregations would perform them with a conductor. Hymns were composed or adapted especially for this event, which was devoted to four-part singing of hymns and anthems. The *gymanfa ganu* in modified form came over to the United States in the 1920s, and is now the annual event for Welsh communities, in Shamokin/Coal Township and throughout the country (Heimlich 1995, 1413).[8]

Hymn singing has always been a unifying cultural feature for Welsh Americans: not only were hymns sung in church, at *gymanfa*, and by families around the parlor piano, but Welsh miners also used to sing them in eight part harmony as they walked over the hills to the mines (H. A. Jones 1978, 146). These examples show the vigor and strength of Welsh musical culture.

The Welsh in the Mines

The Welsh held a near monopoly of positions of power and responsibility in the mines throughout the whole anthracite coal region. Until the last decade of the nineteenth century, the Welsh were the second largest immigrant group in Scranton, and the Hyde Park section was Scranton's Welsh town, though never exclusively. The Welsh churches, Welsh Sunday school, Welsh *eisteddfodau*, Welsh societies, Welsh street names, Welsh businesses, and many Welsh doctors, lawyers and bankers made it seem another Wales. The Welsh were pillars of the Republican Party and occupied some of the key positions in the most powerful coal and railroad company, the Delaware, Lackawanna, & Western (DL&W), which dominated the industrial life of Scranton in the second half of the nineteenth century.

Their high position in the industry's hierarchy was the result of their expertise and of the discrimination in favor of their countrymen that they exercised in giving out jobs. The majority of Welsh males in Scranton, however, were mineworkers: in 1870, 45 percent of Welsh household heads were contract mineworkers, and, since mining was a family tradition among the Scranton Welsh, in the early years, sons followed their fathers (W. D. Jones 1993, 29). To maintain their predominant position in the hierarchy of the mines, they brought in their own countrymen when jobs needed to be filled. A Welsh foreman or mine superintendent could obtain workers for the jobs he had vacant simply by writing to his home newspaper in Wales (Magda 1986).

The mine superintendent had the daily responsibility for running the mine. Below him were the inside and outside foremen in charge of surface and underground operations. An inside foreman was in charge of about two hundred men, depending on the size of the mine, among them he had a number of assistants known as fire bosses. The tendency towards favoritism at all levels of the industry as the Welsh discriminated against other nationalities in favor of their own was much resented among the miners of other nationalities who accused the coal companies of colluding with Welsh foremen and miners to keep them out of good jobs (for a detailed account see W. D. Jones 1993, 1–39).

One woman of East European ancestry in St. Clair details the way the Welsh had dominated that town up until World War II:

> One of the things that caused dissatisfaction in the mining community was that the Irish, who were farmers, came over and got in the mines, and then this kid who would be fifteen years old, would come along from Wales, because his brother called, and he'd move right in as a contract miner because he knew what to do. So that caused a lot of friction with the older mine workers. The Welsh were very tight knit you know, when they were here. They were mostly the mine owners and mine bosses and favored their own people when it came to giving out jobs. They separated themselves from the rest of the people and did not interact with them and were very unhappy if their children married out. It was like that all over the coal region. They were definitely resented, in fact hated. But all that changed with the next generation, my children don't feel that way at all.

A Shamokin Welshman commented on how much resentment there had been against the Welsh and how they experienced it as a feared hostility: "My mother kept the blinds down tight until she died, but that's all gone now." However, some still say they feel it: "There is prejudice against the Welsh—it is less OK to talk about being Welsh than about being Ukrainian or Polish, Italian or Irish," was the view of one Welsh woman. She added, "I don't think we brag about it as get accused of it." Some reject their heritage entirely. A Welshman to whom I was referred, declined an interview, saying firmly that he was not interested in being Welsh and would not be a good person to talk to: "My family never spoke the language, they are just Americans of Welsh ancestry. They never practiced or were involved in it." A Catholic priest discussing ethnicity in Shamokin emphasized this reluctance of the Welsh to be recognized compared to other ethnicities: "I don't know anybody in this town who has told me that he or she is of Welsh heritage. I know the names, Thomas', Davis', but they don't seem to talk of it, they are Americans. They stay with the leek, and their singing."

This resentment of the Welsh domination of the coal industry, however, conflicted with the common bond felt between all mineworkers. In fact, for all of them, the ever present danger of the mines was a unifying force that counteracted any barriers. As Hugh Jones points out in the context of the animosity against the Welsh, they were also among the founders of the unionization efforts of the miners (H. A. Jones, *News Item*, May 13, 1980). In many ways, the fortunes of the whole Welsh community fluctuated with that of the mining industry. All Welsh mining families lived, like others, under the constant threat of death or injury in mining accidents, of irregular wages and intermittent working days. In the Avondale mine disaster of September 1869, nearly all of the 108 victims were Welsh (W. D. Jones 1993, 33–44).

The coming of Eastern European and Italian immigrants to the coal industry of the region lessened the appeal of mining to the Welsh. These new immigrants were willing to accept lower wages than the Welsh, English, Scots, Irish and Germans demanded. Mining became a less and less skilled occupation with the improvements in blasting techniques, and also the richer seams of coal were getting worked out. Welsh mining skills were becoming irrelevant. By 1910 a visitor recorded that managers and superintendents were Welsh, foremen and bosses were Irish, and contract miners were Polish and Lithuanian. Thus in the early twentieth century, the Welsh were retreating from the mines and other groups moving up to take their place (ibid., 83–84). One miner who came from Aberdare, Wales, wrote home that "labor is so plentiful that the operators can do just what they please. Pennsylvania is swarming with foreigners—Poles, Hungarians, Slavish, Swedes, and Italians, etc.—who are fast driving the English, Welsh and Scotch miners out of competition" (Conway 1961, 205).

A Welsh Family History

This history of a Welsh family from Ashland and Shamokin includes many of these features of being Welsh in the Coal Region.[9] A group of families with the names of Price, Bridal, Roberts, and Morgan, all came over together from Aberdare, S. Wales, in 1887 or 1889, in the third wave of immigration, twenty-three of them in all. They all settled in Ashland in the same street, living close to those from home. The group included four generations of Richard Morgan's family: his own, his parents, his paternal grandparents, and his paternal great grandparents. They came over for economic reasons hoping to make better money than they could in Wales. His grandfather spoke Welsh

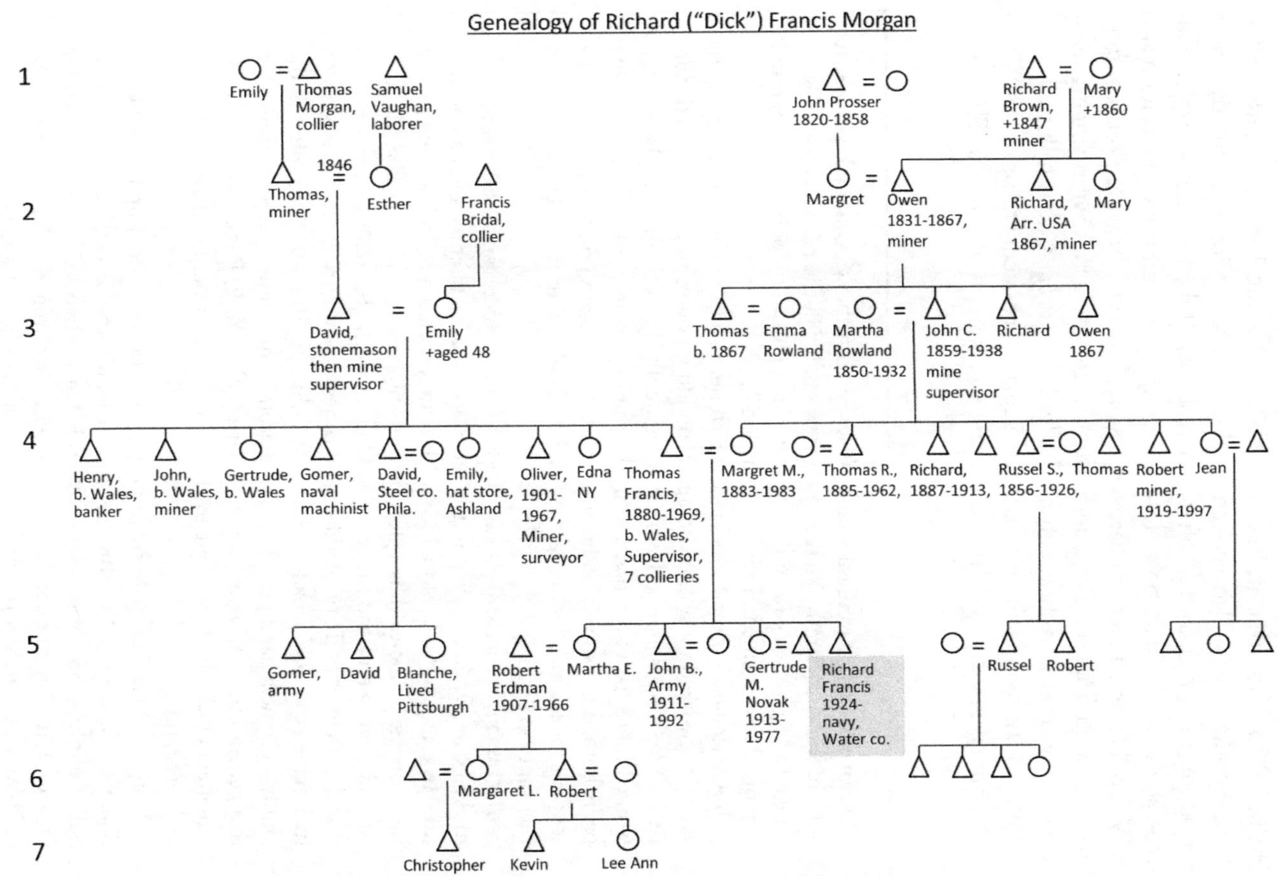

Figure 2.2. Genealogy of Richard Francis Morgan

in Ashland when he first came from Wales, but discontinued it in time and spoke English. All of Richard's father's people that he knew spoke English. His father told him that in English school in the late 1880s and early 1890s, teachers punished Welsh spoken in the classroom. But at about the same period, his mother said that often when she was taken to the homes of relatives, she was told to sit on a stool and be quiet and all the conversation was in Welsh. He remembers all through his life, however, hearing Welsh phrases mixed in with English. The family went to the *gymanfa* (hymn singing festival) every year and to the traditional Welsh tea *(te bach)* that followed.

Lives in this family show the typical supervisory occupations of the Welsh in the mines, and the deaths and injuries so common for miners. The family

Generations 1 and 2 were miners in Wales in both the Morgan and the Brown sides of Richard's family. Richard Brown was killed in the mines. His son Owen emigrated to Minersville and went into the mines to support his mother and siblings. He was killed in the mines in 1867.

In *Generation 3*, David Morgan was a stonemason. He came in the group to America, worked for a mine company building houses in Ashland, and married a Welsh woman, also from a mining family. John C. Brown, Owen's son, worked in a supervisory position in the mines, first as a fire boss. After being badly burned in a mine fire, he became an inside supervisor, and then superintendent for seven collieries of the Reading Coal and Iron Co. He retired from the mines in 1926.

Generation 4: Richard's father, Thomas Francis Morgan, 1880–1969, born in Aberdare, Wales, worked in the naval yards as a carpenter then a contractor. He came to Ashland in 1889 with his mother, aunts and cousins to join his father and uncles. His wife was from Shamokin and he was a Methodist and a trustee of the Lincoln St. United Methodist Church for forty-two years. Only one of Thomas Francis' brothers was a miner, and he was killed in a mine explosion outside Ashland, his oldest brother, the wealthiest of the family, became a bank president and a prominent Mason. Despite dispersal in this generation to Washington, New Jersey, New York, Pittsburgh, the family remained close; those resident in the Coal Region would gather every Labor Day weekend.

Margaret May Brown lived to be one hundred years old and is buried in Shamokin cemetery. On this side of the family too, this generation moved out of mining and dispersed after World War II. Two sons were salesman for tobacco and insurance companies; another retired from the Air force and lived in Hawaii. A daughter married and lived in Plainfield, Indiana.

is advanced by World War II, one finding a permanent career in the service, another funding for college education. Down the generations they moved from work in the mines to professional careers.

The Decline of Welsh Identity

In the last twenty years of the nineteenth century, big changes took place in the cultural life of the Welsh community: the Americanization of Welsh culture, the waning of the language, and Welsh assimilation into mainstream society. By 1909 in the churches, those most powerful bastions of the Welsh language, services were half in English. Growing numbers of people could not, or would not, speak Welsh. In the twentieth century, churches were faced with declining attendance and a nationwide drift away from religion. Cultural organizations with their proceedings in Welsh declined and disbanded, new ones formed using English. Welsh cultural activities increasingly focused on a few specific events and dates, in contrast to their frequency in earlier years. Successful Welsh days were held in Scranton from 1907 until well into the twentieth century and were large and prestigious events: twenty-three thousand people were present at the first one. But the bards became redundant, and Welsh literary culture declined. Welsh language and culture came to be replaced by a generalized American culture (W. D. Jones 1993, 122–41).

A complaint of the lack of preservation of other Welsh traditions besides music in the Coal Region which appeared in the Opinion column of the Welsh monthly *Ninnau*, deplores the decline of Welsh identity in the Region and shows a wider range of markers of it existing in other areas of the country.

This local decline of Welsh culture reflects the early arrival of Welsh immigrants to the Coal Region compared to the Eastern and Southern European immigrants, and their social mobility and assimilation owing to their privileged position in the mine labor hierarchy. The mining expertise of the Welsh

> In the past number of years, there have not even been any Welsh events sponsored by our local organizations, outside of the annual St. David's Day celebration. Welsh societies in other parts of the country have Welsh language classes, teach folk dancing (yes, dancing), and have many programs throughout the year, not just March 1. In a part of the United States that once boasted the largest concentrations of Welsh-Americans in the country, there are now very few activities that promote our culture (Megan Landmesser, a fourth-generation Welsh American of Wyoming Valley in the Coal Region, *Ninnau* March 2004, vol. 28, 5:2).

gained in their home country was the basis for their high position in the power structure of the mines and in the town. The waning of their ethnic cultural events is a part of the process by which class interests overrode ethnic interests and identity in the town as the coal era progressed.

The Welsh and the Germans in their high position in the structural relations of power in the town contrast with the Irish who were fleeing famine and desperate poverty and arrived to be situated in the lowest position in the power hierarchy. The historical circumstances of these groups and the time periods in which they arrived in the Coal Region thus account for the differences between them.

The Irish: Fleeing Starvation and Poverty, and Fighting Prejudice

The Irish like the Welsh had an identity forged back in the homeland in opposition to their English oppressors. The political divide in the homelands of the Welsh and the Irish was in both cases associated with language: the Welsh and the Irish spoke Gaelic languages and the English who conquered and dominated them historically imposed the English language on them in the process. The bitter repercussions of the Irish struggle against English domination came to the Coal Region with Irish immigrants and appeared in their violent protests against the oppressive conditions of the mining life and the discrimination they faced. The Irish were the lowest in the power hierarchy, and their culture and identity were submerged in the Coal Region in the aftermath of these violent protests, but they subsequently moved up in the political and economic power structure and reasserted their cultural heritage, particularly through the Celtic revival that swept America in the last half of the twentieth century.

Irish Farmers

The way of life of the nineteenth century Irish farms from which the immigrants came was well-adapted to the reciprocal assistance of the family based economy that developed in the Pennsylvania anthracite towns, as will be shown in chapter 4. Small farmers in Ireland had gardens of potatoes, cabbages, some oats, turnips and maybe some rye. The rest of the land consisted of hay meadows which were grazed in winter, and pasture land grazed in summer and winter. Sheep were taken up in the mountains. Production of cattle for the export of live animals and some dairy production for the sale of butter were the chief occupations, with the raising of ducks, geese, chickens and pigs for consumption. The basic diet was potatoes with cabbage and bacon or salt pork, bread baked on a griddle, and tea. A far greater number of persons supported themselves on small holdings (one to fifteen acres) than on large ones (fifteen to thirty acres). The family of the owner worked the small farms, agricultural laborers the large farms.

Parental dominance continued throughout the father's lifetime, and the sons' earnings were largely contributed to the household expenses (Arensberg and Kimball 1968, 7–36, 62–70). On most small farms in Ireland, reciprocal help in cooperative labor on the farms was the norm; meals were given to the helpers, not money. Women did the milking, helped with fieldwork and took care of the house and children; their work was considered to be as important as that of the men.

The Great Famine obliterated by death or emigration nearly three million of Ireland's poorest inhabitants, drastically altering the social structure. Those who survived were middling sized commercial farmers. The ties which had bound young Irishmen to their communities and associations were severed; wakes and harvest festivals that had united rural communities across class lines were abandoned; Gaelic poets and ballad singers were vanishing. Landless laborers, who were mistreated and despised, developed a deep resentment against parents and communities which offered them little except celibacy and servitude. The Catholic Church helped to erode the cultural cement which held the community together, as religious strictures reinforced and sanctified middle-class Victorian lifestyles and parish priests gained effective control of education. The Protestant clergy were heavily puritanical (Miller 1985, 404–23). There were outbreaks of violent struggles between commercial and subsistence farmers as the latter formed a variety of secret agrarian societies to resist evictions, protest low wages, unemployment and the commercialization of agriculture (Miller 1990, 100).

In America, those left behind and in desperate need were not forgotten. Kinship networks from strong family bonds of affection and obligation were channels for remittances and passage money for brothers and sisters, nephews and nieces, sent home by immigrants. In the last half of the nineteenth century remittances alone amounted to over $8 million in some years (Blessing 1980, 530). Irish Americans scraped together not only money but also clothes and consumer goods to send home. Ten percent of immigrants returned and were agents of broad cultural change which encouraged further immigration (Miller 1985, 425–26). Many farms in Ireland were partially supported by Christmas gifts from sons and daughters abroad. Immigration from a local region tended to perpetuate itself as sons and daughters of each generation went out to join the members of the last (Arensberg and Kimball 1968, 143–44).

A small but significant number of affluent Irish Catholics emigrated and paid their own passage, generally faring much better than their poorer countrymen (Blessing 1980, 527). Some remained very aware down the generations of the social difference between the two groups: "We were not shanty Irish," remarked one Irish woman from Shamokin when recounting their family history. The more affluent upper middle class who came over after the famine were conscious of and maintained the class position they had back home after they had settled in the Coal Region.

But the Irish culture and language was not lost despite this history of oppression. Most migrants entering the United States were under thirty-five years old and unmarried. The literacy rate was high among them: at mid-nineteenth century about 57 percent, and by 1910, 97 percent, could read and write English. After 1831, government financed schools in Ireland had provided English instruction (Blessing 1980, 529). But before that time, Irish Hedge Schools, with some of the teaching in the Irish language and taught out in the open under the hedgerows with as many as a hundred pupils, had been set up since the suppression of Catholic education in Cromwell's time and continued after the closing of Catholic schools in 1745 under the penal code of William III.

These schools were a channel of surreptitious education till the early nineteenth century, passing on the love of literature and learning. Many of the school masters taught in the Irish Gaelic language and were instrumental in the preservation of legends, songs and poems and in perpetuating the Irish language and culture (Dowling 1935). The poorest gave instruction only in reading, writing and arithmetic, others in addition some mathematics, Latin and Greek: "The national literary tradition had become, in the 18th century, the heritage of the tiller of the soil" (ibid., 11). Perhaps one can see the high literacy rate of the nineteenth century Irish immigrants as the legacy of these schools with the enthusiasm for learning inculcated by them in the parental generation, and perhaps some of the immigrants themselves, who must have been of school age before the Hedge Schools disappeared, had attended them. These schools gradually died out after the introduction of the state system of education in 1831 (ibid., 153).

A quarter to one-third of Irish immigrants consisted of Irish Gaelic speakers and another quarter were children of speakers of this language. Gaelic was still a living language in 1891 and all were familiar with the concepts and traditions it expressed. Thus from 1856 to 1921 the majority of Catholics arriving as immigrants were from regions of great poverty but ones where peasant folkways and remnants of an attenuated Gaelic culture still existed (K. A. Miller 1985, 350–51). They brought these cultural elements with them to America. Catholic churches were built and parishes formed wherever the Irish settled. They were ethnically exclusive, building churches separately from the German Catholics (Kenny 1998, 161).[10] Minersville Irish were predominantly from Kilkenny; Ashland's from Mayo and Galway. Immigrants to the Coal Region before the famine came primarily from Kilkenny and Laoighis in the South, then the famine emigration, outnumbering them three to one, came from Galway, Mayo, Sligo and Donegal in the West.

Associations

Some associations that were formed back in Ireland in the struggle to better the conditions of life, carried over into the Coal Region with the immigrants. Some, such as the Whiteboys, were vigilante groups operating in Ireland 1775–1840. They fought to secure better conditions for tenants and to abolish the tithes exacted by the church from poor farmers (O'Dea 1923, 13, 438).

In America, the Mollie Maguires, of the same name as one of these groups back in Ireland was said to have been brought over by the immigrants. The Society of St. Patrick, which paraded on St. Patrick's Day in every city in which it had members, was established in 1831 to afford relief to Irish immigrants in America. In 1838 the Hibernian Benevolent Society was founded in Pottsville. The Ancient Order of Hibernians (AOH) was first founded in New York in 1836 and spread through the Coal Region after the massive immigration following 1845. It became the only ethnic organization besides the church and the tavern available to the Irish. Its initial intention was to provide protection to Irish Catholics in times of hostility, but it quickly grew to be a fraternal society with branches across the United States, Britain and Ireland, and was the Catholic equivalent of Protestant groups like the Masons, the Odd Fellows and others from which the Irish were excluded (Wallace 1981, 323). It had initiation rites, handshakes, signals, passwords and toasts; gave out aid to dues-paying members in times of need; and was a clearing house for advice and favors.

The AOH had always been a peaceful fraternal organization, but its requirement of a secret oath from members and its reputed association with the violence of the Mollie Maguires in the 1860s and 1870s aroused the condemnation of the Catholic Church (Kenny 1998, 162). Although there was never proof of a connection between the AOH and the Mollie Maguires, in the early 1900s the AOH was suspended.

From the late 1860s, however, the situation of the Irish in the mines began to gradually improve. Many more Irish became contract miners as the Germans moved out of mining into other occupations and the Irish took their place. By 1870, the Irish were beginning to get better educated, to own

Figure 2.3. Badges for the Ancient Order of Hibernians and the Maine Fire Company

houses, and to be more prosperous. Wallace cites the census for St. Clair in 1880, which showed that by then there were more Irish born contract miners than either English or Welsh, while the Germans had virtually withdrawn from mining (Wallace 1987, 375). In Shamokin/Coal Township from the 1880s to 1914 and World War I, the Irish came up from being laborers to being foremen.[11] After the turn of the century, they were replaced at the lower end of the hierarchy by later comers—Poles, Ukrainians, Lithuanians and Italians. In their move up the socioeconomic ladder, the Irish had the advantage of speaking English, unlike the Eastern and Southern Europeans. The use of Gaelic quickly disappeared among them however.

The church and politics have been the paths for upward socioeconomic mobility for sons of Irish immigrant parents, and seem to have provided a way for Irishmen to get recognition and respect. Irish women moved into trade, manufacturing and especially teaching. Until 1880 endogamy was likely, yet they were among the least segregated immigrant groups in America and often

An Irish Family History

Tom Coakley's family descended from two Irish couples who emigrated after the famine, coming to the same place as relatives had come to before them, with the men going into the mines. Both sets of his great-grandparents came over from County Cork in the mid-1800s after the famine. On his father's side they had some relatives already in the Coal Region, so they migrated to the same area. His great grandfather settled in St. Clair and was a miner. When the coal ran out in St. Clair, he moved to Shenandoah. For a while, he belonged to the Mollie Maguires, until his wife told him to get out because there was going to be trouble, and the priest at the church told them they were going to be excommunicated if they were involved in any of the violence. His mother's maternal grandfather was a superintendent in the mines in Pottsville and died of the smoke when fighting a mine fire.

Tom's maternal grandfather worked in the mines and then got a job as a salesman with the National Biscuit Company and traveled a lot. His mother had one brother, a doctor who died in France in World War I, and four sisters, who were all teachers. His paternal grandparents both died when his father was a young child. His father had ten or twelve siblings, all went into the mines when they were seven or eight years old, except for two brothers who died in infancy in the great flu epidemic. Another brother died in the mines in St. Clair. Because of his parents' death, Tom's father was raised by a wealthy family. He went to Lehigh University, became an engineer and worked for Allied Chemical, and he and his family moved around, living in Cleveland, Buffalo, and Philadelphia. When the last member of this family that had raised him died, he felt obligated to go back to Mt. Carmel and run their lumber business.

After working in the lumber yard, Tom enlisted in the Air Force in World War II and went to navigation school. After the war, he went to night school on the G.I. Bill in construction and returned to the family lumber yard in Mt. Carmel. He has a brother, who was in the grocery business, and two sisters both of whom were teachers and moved to the South. His son is a priest and his daughter a teacher in Mt. Carmel. His granddaughter teaches in Baltimore.

acted as cultural brokers for groups struggling to learn English, extending credit and advice to recent arrivals (Blessing 1980, 532–33).

In addition to his family history, Tom Coakley recounted the customs of the old days, in particular how Irish weddings went on for three days with dancing and songs and music. They would bring in a couple of fiddlers and some Irish girls who could do an Irish jig and were good singers of Irish songs and ballads. Sometimes the men would wear kilts and the girls would be in green with white blouses. Locust Gap was famous for its three-day-long Irish wakes to which relatives would come from a distance. The fiddlers played slow dirges, and women would keen. The neighbors brought food, hams, cakes; they never went to a restaurant as they do today. They would have the body there, the men would gather in the kitchen and the women would sit with the corpse. Some of the older people spoke Gaelic among themselves then. The language has not been passed on, but the music continues.[12]

Memorial Day was a big event for the Irish. People would all gather in the cemetery and spend the day there and have a picnic.[13] It was like a family reunion: all the neighbors came as well as people from places like Philadelphia. "I remember when I was sixteen or so, I'd take my aunt up in the morning with all this food and stuff and set it up and we'd be there the whole day. But today, the Irish have a good time in the bars on St. Patrick's Day and put out a lot of green, and that's about the extent of it."[14] Chapter 7 reports elaborate celebrations elsewhere in the Region, however, for this day.

The Jewish Community

Most of the small Jewish population who first settled in the coal region became retail merchants; later there were business and factory owners and professionals. Although the Jews do not all come from one country, they fit the definition of ethnicity since they perceive themselves and are perceived by others as belonging to an ethnic group, one that is a religious and a cultural but not a national community.

A few Jews came to the Coal Region as early as the mid-nineteenth century, but the only opportunities they found at first to make a living were as peddlers. They later came to dominate the retail trade of the three towns, some of them setting up family businesses which were carried on by their children. By the late nineteenth century, they were concentrated in clothing, dry goods, liquor, and later in private banking (P. Roberts 1904, 29). Their linguistic abilities from their background of European migration were an advantage in these multilingual towns. Over time, they formed a small merchant class, a mainstay of the town's life. These Jewish merchants, unlike most of the other European immigrants, were not from a rural background of poor farmers. They were from an urban background and highly literate, so it was easy for them to enter the small scale retail trade (Kuznets 1975, 112–16).

In Shamokin/Coal Township, when these merchants had accumulated some money, they were joined by relatives and compatriots; by 1887, they had formed a religious congregation and they built a synagogue in 1923. Many of the succeeding generations entered the professions or the arts. The community was later to include some of the owners of the New York garment factories that came to the coal towns in the mid-twentieth century. At its peak in the 1930s and 1940s, it consisted of ninety families.

Kulpmont's six Jewish merchants from Russia and Hungary had stores for groceries, clothing, dresses, furniture, and work clothes; one was a Variety 5&10. But in the late twentieth century, the shopping malls that featured in the demise of small retailers made it impossible to sustain the Jewish retail businesses in the Coal Region (Bazelon 1986). "They were fine people and a great prop of the town's economy. When they went, the town went down" commented one resident.

A Mainstay of the Town Economy and Cultural Life

Liachowitz Jewelers is an example of one of the longtime Jewish family-owned stores in Shamokin. The business started in 1888 and lasted until 2005, when it was one of the few remaining stores from the town's great shopping era days. In 1888, Aaron Liachowitz, a watchmaker, was on his way from New York to Chicago, where he was proposing to open a jewelry store. The train got caught in the blizzard of '88 and only got as far as Shamokin. He liked the look of the place and decided to stay there. He set up a jewelry store, prospered, and his brother, who was trained in clock and watch repair, came from Passaic, New Jersey, to join him. Eventually, in 1941, Aaron's nephew Maurice took over the store, and in time, passed it to his son, Irvin. The business thrived for many years but, like the others, was eventually put out of business by the shopping malls.

Irvin Liachowitz said that it was the relationship of trust they had with customers that enabled them to remain for so long. He considered that they had managed to stay in business because of the service they provided and the trust their customers had in them. "They come back again and again, even if they have moved away. We have some customers that have been coming for two and three generations. If they want diamonds reset, for example, they feel they can trust us to do it."[16] Such trust, based on the personal relationships of a small community, was a strong element in establishing and keeping the customers of small business and stores. It was likewise evident in the Mom and Pop neighborhood groceries and the long lists of credit in their tick books. In the case of Liachowitz Jewelers, the trusting relationship lasted even down the generations of original customers who had moved away.

Over time, the Jewish community also contributed greatly to the cultural life of the town. Shamokin's past has included periods of extraordinary musical activity. Appreciation of, and participation in, good musical performance has been a marked feature of this town with its many choirs, bands,[16] and concert series. An early example of the last was the Great Artists Course, which lasted from 1920 to 1925, and was devoted exclusively to classical music, and included such legendary stars as Amelita Galli-Curci, Rosa Ponselle, Tito Schipa, Fritz Kreisler, Jacques Thibaud, Pablo Casals and Vladimir de Pachman. The concerts were managed for these five seasons by Conrad Graeber.[17] Later, the Central Community Concerts, three or four a year, from 1979 to 2002, were organized by jeweler Irvin Liachowitz and Reba Hirsch, who had a career in public relations and advertising in Philadephia and Harrisburg, before returning to her hometown (her family history is given below) to be a mainstay of the cultural life of the town. The series brought many world class artists and attractions to the town in an annual series of close to one hundred events in total, including symphony, swing-era favorites, big band, opera singers, orchestras and solo instrumentalists, folk music and dances of different cultures, and choral groups, reflecting the broad cultural interests of the people of the town.

A Jewish Family History

Events very distant from Shamokin brought Reba Hirsch's father to the town as an immigrant in 1905 from Riga, Latvia. He and other Jews fled that city because of the lack of any future there for Jews and to avoid the twenty-five-year conscription into the army of the Russian Czar (the Republic of Latvia before 1918 was a province of the Russian Empire). In 1904–1905, in the Russo-Japanese war, the Czar's army of conscripts, ill-trained and low in morale, was fighting a losing battle in the Far East. Although obligated by treaty, Russia had refused to withdraw its troops from Manchuria after the Boxer Rebellion. Japan launched an attack on the Russian Far Eastern Fleet and defeated the Russian army and navy, capturing the fortified naval base of Port Arthur and the port of Vladivostok. Jews in Riga were so desperate to avoid conscription at this time that some of them even inflicted serious injuries on themselves. Reba's father emigrated.

The history of the Hirsch (or Arsch) family goes back to 1790. They originated in Kreuzburgh, Latvia, as boot makers and repairers, and in the course of eight generations moved to Riga, to flourishing businesses in Shamokin, and to professional careers in major cities in America.

The first three generations of the family lived in the small town of Kreuzburg in what was then East Prussia; some of their descendants may still live there. This town, northeast of Danzig and Elbing, and southeast of Konisgsburg, was just over the border of what was then Latvian Russia. Sometime in the second half of the nineteenth century, some of the third generation of the family moved from Kreutzburg to Riga, migrating from a small town to the city as did many other Eastern European Jews of the time. Riga was outside the Pale of Settlement; Kreuzburg was within it. In the early eighteenth century there were only about 200 Jews in Riga because of the restrictions on their living there. They included skilled craftsmen, producing furs, boots, shoes and furniture, and intellectuals, who led in finance, medicine and law. By 1824, there were 513 Jews in the city. In the early years, success in trade had aroused animosity against both Jewish and British traders, but in 1842 the city council expressed fears that the restrictions imposed on Jews were adversely affecting the commerce of the city with Poland, and they were given the right to trade, but not to own property in the city.

In 1850, the city synagogue in Riga was built. In 1858, those Jews who had had a permanent abode in Riga were granted the right to own their property, though they were not allowed to be citizens. By 1897, there were more than twenty thousand Jews in the city (8 percent of the population). In 1848, a member of the Hirsch family and her husband immigrated first to Riga and then overseas to Cleveland, Ohio, a pattern that was typical of Eastern European Jewish families at the time. Eventually twenty two of the extended family lived in Shamokin.

Members of the fourth generation of the Arsch family continued to leave Kreutzburg for Riga early in the twentieth century to improve their prospects and escape the dangers of the persecution suffered by Jews. Some who left later in the century fleeing the horrors of the era of the Nazis and of the Stalinist regime were widely scattered, reflecting the terrible dangers from which some of them escaped. They fled in desperation to wherever opportunity offered sometimes going to kin they had never seen before. Their descendants live in Israel, England, South Africa and the Netherlands, as well as in other countries. Not all of them escaped. Some of the previous generation of the family in and around Riga perished in the troubles there, and one cousin is known to have died in Siberia. Many parents and children never saw each other again after the younger generation left.

Reba, of the sixth generation, daughter of David and Eva, studied journalism and fashion in Philadelphia and had a career in advertising, public relations and newspaper writing. She returned to live in Shamokin; her long involvement in community affairs is described above.

The seventh generation includes a distinguished Professor of pediatrics and genetics at Harvard University Medical School. He received the Mead Johnson pediatric research award in 1978, and was deeply involved in cytogenetic research to eradicate children's diseases through genetic engineering. He published almost 200 articles during his short life. His sister, with a B.A. from Wellesley, M.A. from Columbia, and a PhD from Northwestern, is a freelance art historian.[18]

Photographic mementos and letters are part of a people's heritage, and are carefully preserved. Many from Shamokin/Coal Township make visits to Europe to seek out their relatives and visit the place in which their ancestors lived. Reba, who has not herself been to Latvia, recalled a member of the fourth generation of the Hirsch family who took his wife and daughter back to Kreuzburg where they had all lived. She comments: "The roots of the past, of the European culture, have a very strong pull. He had a movie camera, and when he returned, there was the old house, the gate, the well, and the aged relatives, all on film. I found myself deeply drawn to it, it was part of me. The old house was not at all palatial, but it was still there."

Ethnicity and Language

The association between language and ethnicity shows a range of difference among the ethnic groups described in this chapter. These differences are related to the political and economic situation of these groups. In its early history, Germany was a nation that was a political patchwork unified by use of German (Chapman 1992, 132); the Welsh and Irish each historically spoke languages of the Celtic language group which in each case came to be the language of a group marginal in relation to their English speaking conquerors; Yiddish, a Germanic language written in Hebrew characters, the vernacular language of the Ashkenazi Jews of Eastern and Central European countries and their descendants, was the language of an often persecuted religious minority, providing a unifying feature for these Jews, with their backgrounds in different European countries. For these groups in the Coal Region, for the most part, pressure was exerted on children of immigrants to learn English and abandon their own languages in order to advance and improve their conditions of life by assimilation into American society.

The Germans settled in the area long before coal was discovered. This chapter has shown how the assimilation of these later German arrivals into American life, and the decline of the use of their language happened earlier than for other groups in the nineteenth century. Subsequently, the two world wars against Germany in the twentieth century caused Germans in America to actively reject their ethnicity and heritage and with the exception of sectarian rural communities, to abandon their language to avoid the hostility of their neighbors. This further weakened their ethnic identity, and their thorough assimilation and economic prosperity brought them a dominant social and economic position in town life. In the twentieth century, use of the German language and German identity and traditions virtually disappeared in these towns.

The Celts emerged sometime in the first millennium BC in Central and Southern Europe. They were the barbarians from the north who brought about the collapse of Roman order in Western Europe. Later they were confined to the northwest of Scotland, Ireland, Wales and Brittany, countries in which relatively small numbers of people still speak Celtic languages. Wales and Ireland contributed immigrants to the Coal Region; Brittany did not, and there were few if any from the Scottish Highlands. Malcolm Chapman argues that the continuity of the Celts is not derived from anything intrinsic to them as a people but rather from a particular kind of cultural interaction between a powerful central culture with written records, and a much less powerful culture which left few if any such records, and that the continuity of this kind of cultural interaction has provided the continuity of the Celts (ibid., 1–3).

Modern Celtic languages are divided into p-Celtic (Welsh and Breton), and q-Celtic (Scottish and Irish). Irish Gaelic is regarded as the indigenous language of the Irish, spoken for most of the first millennium as a rural language. After 1922, it was the official language of independent Ireland and taught in its schools (ibid., 8).[19] In Wales, the speaking of Welsh declined after public schools prohibited the teaching of Welsh in the late nineteenth century, but with the revival of a strong Welsh national consciousness in the twentieth century, the Welsh Language Act of 1993 put Welsh on an equal basis with English in public life. About 20 percent of the population speaks Welsh today.

According to Chapman's thesis, in early history the Celts existed in opposition to the classical world and when that disappeared, they reemerged in opposition to the Germanic world.

> The continuity between the Celts of the Iron Age, the Celts of early mediaeval Europe, and the Celts of the modern day, is not a simple continuity of genetic lineage of culture, of race, of language. It is rather a continuity of symbolic opposition between a central defining power and its own fringes; this continuity can be, and has been sustained, regardless of overwhelming changes in the cultural content involved. (ibid., 69)

He observes that this runs counter to the more usual assumption of continuity of linguistic, cultural and racial forms. For the Celts, cultural processes are involved not in the continuity of culture but in the form of being like or unlike other people in a center-periphery relationship. Thus ancient traditions that seem on the point of dying out, in practice do not do so; their content is redefined in every generation (ibid., 96).

For the Celtic Irish in the Coal Region, their language was initially a part of their ethnic definition in the peripheral relationship they had to the dominant class of the English, Scots, Welsh and Germans. This relationship was to lead to the outbreaks of violence of the Mollie Maguires in the 1860s and 1870s and to their defeat. As a result, Irish culture and language was stifled until well into the twentieth century; its later revival in music, song and dance, detailed in chapter 7, was to be different. For the Celtic Welsh, on the other hand, manifestations of Welsh culture and the use of the Welsh language in Shamokin/Coal Township faded early in the twentieth century. In the Coal Region, the Welsh have not been defined as on the periphery: they rapidly moved up to be influential in the social and economic hierarchy of the coal towns in the nineteenth century. As they did so, use of the Welsh language almost died out, as did the remnants of the ancient Celtic Welsh culture. In Shamokin/Coal Township, vestiges only remain in their musical heritage: singing some Welsh is still part of the St. David's Day hymn singing festival. Their musical tradition, however, includes at least some Welsh today and gives them a sense of Welsh identity.

It is likely that Yiddish arose in Central Europe in the eleventh to the thirteenth centuries from Middle High German dialects. By the twentieth century there were 10–11 million Yiddish speakers worldwide, but as a result of the Holocaust, cultural assimilation in the United States and the USSR, and the shift to Hebrew in Israel, at the end of the century there were probably fewer than 2 million speakers left, and it was not the primary language of most of them (Jacobs, 2005). In the United States, most Yiddish speakers did not pass the language on to their children who spoke English. In Shamokin-Coal Township, there were Jewish shopkeepers who spoke Yiddish in the nineteenth century.

Conclusion: Comparison of Groups

To compare the groups, the first four so far described had an established national ethnic identity before they arrived, in contrast to those who were to arrive subsequently. German settlers in America were not a monolithic ethnic group (Conzen 1985, 133). In the Coal Region, the earliest had settled in the area long before coal was discovered. They were primarily Protestant but were also divided by different varieties of this religious adherence. The earliest ones formed the distinctive sectarian rural farming communities with their own language of the Pennsylvania Germans. Many of the later Lutheran German farmers became prosperous and influential in their local communities. They owned mills and hotels, participated in the development of the coal industry and became mine owners. This extended participation in the life and economy of the town led to assimilation, which was completed after two world wars that caused them to avoid all expression of their ethnicity because of the conflict with Germany. The disappearance of the German language was related to their move into the politically powerful level of society.

The same was true with the Welsh and the Welsh language. The Welsh sense of national identity was established back in Wales. Early Welsh immigrants many of them poor farmers, came for religious and economic reasons; the later massive flow of Welsh immigrants was essentially recruited from the Welsh coalfields and brought over to set up and supervise the Pennsylvania anthracite mines. Welsh ethnicity faded and use of the Welsh language declined as they moved up the social and economic ladder in the Coal Region. Their Celtic culture waned and their Welshness ultimately came to be expressed only in their love of music, their singing skills, and their singing festivals.[20]

The Irish arrived like the Welsh with a sense of identity formed in contrast to the dominance and oppression of the English. Both had in common that they spoke their Gaelic languages in opposition to the English language of the dominant class. For the Irish, religion intensified the contrast: they were Catholic; the dominant English, the Anglo-Norman Irish and the Scots-Irish Presbyterians of Northern Ireland were Protestant. But the Irish were quite different from the Welsh and Germans in Shamokin/Coal Township: most of them were fleeing famine and desperate poverty in the mid-nineteenth century when they entered the local town hierarchy as unskilled mine labor; they confronted pejorative stereotypes from the beginning from those above them in the social hierarchy. Their identity was Irish-Catholic, historically oppressed as such by the dominant English-speaking Protestants of Northern Ireland. The Irish manifested a clear connection between their oppressed past in Ireland and their bitterness and violent resistance to the discrimination and prejudice they faced from Protestants in the Coal Region. However, they subsequently gradually rose in the mine hierarchy as the Germans and Welsh moved into occupations of higher economic and social status, making room for the Irish, who were able to better their circumstances. In this process, speaking English gave them an advantage over the Eastern and Southern European immigrants who followed them. With the revival of Celtic culture in America since the 1960s, they have strengthened and expressed their own heritage and solidarity but have not revived the Gaelic language.

The Jewish community is very small in number but Jews have been disproportionately significant in the three towns through their economic success and cultural influence. They contrast with the other three ethnic groups of this chapter in that they did not originate in one country, but were fleeing from a long history of persecution in the different countries of Europe that terminated in the holocaust of Nazi Germany. In the twentieth century, despite being relatively few in the three towns, they dominated in commerce and the garment industry, which brought more Jews to the town in the mid-nineteenth century. They were characterized in comparison to the other groups by their religion and the strength of their religious community.

Ethnicity among these four groups covers a wide range of variation determined by the considerable differences in the historical, political and economic circumstances of their homelands, and by the position in the socioeconomic hierarchy of the town into which each group moved. The range of differences is narrower between the four groups that are described in the next chapter.

Notes

1. It has been long recognized by social anthropologists that political organization in a society does not only consist of formal political institutions, but includes also institutions that are not formally political, like marriage, friendship, and security for old age (A. Cohen 1969, 193).

2. The Blue Church (St. Peter's) out in Ralpho Township countryside is a tiny United Church of Christ church and cemetery, built in 1863. It has many graves of historical interest.

3. In 1723, according to John M. Carter 1936.

4. Fritz Reed, details from many informal interviews and conversations from 2001 to 2006.

5. Walter Neary, February 1, 2007.

6. Pastor Sally Dries, Salem Church.

7. H. A. Jones, February 21, 2003.

8. Minersville has a *gymanfa ganu* in the spring.

9. Family in this case, as in most of the family histories, refers to the bilateral extended family.

10. Irish churches were built in the Coal Region in Pottsville, 1828; Tamaqua, 1836; Minersville, 1846; Port Carbon, 1847; Ashland, 1857; Heckschersville, 1858; St. Clair, 1864; New Philadelphia, 1867; Shenandoah, 1872; Mahanoy City, 1873; Gilberton, 1874; Girardville, 1876; and West Mahanoy, 1880 (Kenny 1998, 161).

11. Walter Neary, December 22, 2004.

12. Tom Coakley, March 22, 2003.

13. Garden cemeteries were popular in the nineteenth century. Even smaller cities, towns and villages set aside land and laid it out for the double purpose of burying ground and pleasure ground (Linden-Ward 1989, 322).

14. Tom Coakley, March 22, 2003

15. Irvin Liachowitz, May 1, 2002.

16. These were: Our Band, the Shamokin Band, and the Ruthenian, Springfield, Hibernian, Italian, Fairview, Silk Mill, Municipal, American Legion, Uniontown and the UMW Bands (Marlok 1976, 4).

17. Reba Hirsch's article on Conrad Graeber for The Achievers series of the *News Item*, June 25, 2006. The Graebers were one of Shamokin's influential families in the nineteenth century.

18. Reba Hirsch interviews; Jono David 2000.

19. Scottish Gaelic was spoken in the southwest of Scotland by Irish immigrants from northeast Ireland in the fifth and sixth centuries A.D. as the Romans retreated. In the middle of the eleventh century, it was the language of much of mainland Scotland. But it was displaced by Anglo-Saxon and Norman invaders by the twelfth century, and Scottish Gaelic thereafter became the language of the Scottish Highlands and Islands and remote Western peninsulas only. In West Brittany, Breton is unlikely to survive (Chapman 1992, 8–12).

20. In keeping with the social and economic position they have gained, there does not appear to be much interest among Welsh Americans in the Coal Region in the recently gained political independence in 1999 of Wales, with the formation of a Welsh National Assembly and the extension of its powers in 2006 to amend laws of the United Kingdom's Parliament, and the revived use of Welsh and of Celtic culture in Wales today. This revival, following Chapman's thesis, can be seen as a function of that country's peripheral relationship to England. *Ninnau*, the Welsh American newspaper, however, reports more interest in cultural activities besides singing among the Welsh in States other than Pennsylvania, as does the letter quoted from it earlier in this chapter, but a comparison with the socioeconomic position of the Welsh in these communities is beyond the scope of this study.

CHAPTER THREE

Eastern and Southern European Immigration

Ethnicity at Its Peak

Matthew Jacobson observes that parades and other civic spectacles were critical as forms of communication in the nineteenth century: "Parades communicated above all ideas about social power" as they demonstrated to employers, unions and local politicians the impressive numbers of the group and their solidarity (Jacobson 1995, 79). The significance of ethnic groups in the town by the end of the nineteenth century is dramatically represented by a huge Ukrainian parade and its following events during the convention of the Ukrainian National Association (UNA) in Shamokin June 1904, as reported in the Ukrainian newspaper *Svoboda.* It marked the UNAs tenth Jubilee Anniversary. This parade by its extent and splendor communicates in terms of sheer imposing display the importance, numbers and cultural impact of the Ukrainians in the town. Civic pride in, and the acceptance of, Ukrainians in the town's population were represented by iconic representations of America in the veterans, firemen, and Native Americans, at the beginning and at the end of the parade.

> Everybody who witnessed this parade could not help but be proud of being Ukrainian . . . the Ukrainian brotherhoods . . . joined the American societies in what was a truly magnificent march. The city police led the parade, followed by the firemen's police. Then came the Spanish War Veterans with rifles on their shoulders. They were led by their officer who rode a horse, followed by the flag-bearer and an orchestra. . . . Then marched five units of firemen, all in red shirts, carrying flowers. . . . Between units, horses pulled the fire engines, also adorned with flowers. They were followed by a group

> of Indians, representing the first inhabitants of America. Each of them carried an open umbrella. They were led by Chief White Eagle. Riding a white pony, he was clad in white clothes with wings attached to his shoulders and a feather cap on his head. And then came the Ukrainians. First, the Sts. Cyril and Methodius Brotherhood which founded the UNA. It was led by Mr. Talpash, mounted on a beautiful horse, looking like a Kozak [Cossack]. . . . He was followed by the bearers of the new UNA banner and two American flags. The Taras Shevchenko Brotherhood[1] marched second, led by Mr. Kolodiy, on a horse, followed by a flag-bearer. Then the Saints Peter and Paul Brotherhood with church banners and an orchestra, then the St. Demetrius and St. Michael Brotherhoods. All these brotherhoods were from Shamokin. They were followed by three brotherhoods from Mt. Carmel, with banners and an orchestra. Then came the delegates, being driven in carriages. Closing out the parade were the Civil War veterans carrying sticks, and their sons with rifles. Altogether over 6,000 people marched in the parade, accompanied by five orchestras. The weather was beautiful and for the first time the Ukrainian people showed their strength and unity to the world. (*Svoboda*, June 9, 1904. Quoted in Dragan 1964, 46–47)

After the parade, all the brotherhoods attended the Holy Liturgy in the Ukrainian church, a requisite feature of all major occasions serving to mark the importance of the church. A blessing of the new Ukrainian National Association banner followed. The convention ended with a concert held in the local theatre, attended by everyone not just Ukrainians. A choir with seventy singers performed, soloists and a children's chorus sang patriotic Ukrainian songs, there were recitations and a piano solo, and all attended a party at the end (ibid.).

This impressive celebration of Ukrainian ethnicity stands out as a seminal event because it signifies the ethnic heritage, established strength and power, and acceptance into the town, of one of the major groups during the time when ethnicity was at its peak. Its reporting illustrates the way an ethnic newspaper could function to foster both the sense of pride and unity of an ethnic group and its place in a city, and the acceptance of its place as a nationwide ethnic group in American society.

This event introduces the account in this chapter of the ethnic groups in the town from Eastern and Southern Europe and reflects the ways in which ethnicity structured people's lives in the early period of the town's history. In their home countries most of these immigrants had not had a sense of national ethnic identity. National identity was an idea that appeared in the eighteenth century and spread; previous to that time, there was not always the understanding that "all the people within a state were of a single identity or shared anything in common besides allegiance to the monarch. They spoke different languages, had different cultures and were often rigidly separated" (Banks 1996, 125). When these immigrants first came over to the Coal Region, most identified themselves in terms of a region, or even a town or a village, for their notion of who they were, and where they had come from; it was often immigration officials who allocated to them the national category that seemed to fit their names. A strong sense of national ethnic identity emerged later in the neighborhoods of the town established by immigrants who were of the same nationality. But in the comparison of the town's major ethnic groups, it is noteworthy that there is some variation in the sense, or lack of it, of national identity among these Eastern and Southern immigrants when they first arrived.

The Slavs were better off in the coalfields than they had been at home, with a more plentiful food supply and higher wages (P. Roberts 1904, 345). Slavic aspirations were focused to begin with on establishing themselves in working class America. Their achievements were modest for the first generation and their children showed little advance beyond their parents; the labor of children was seen as necessary for family survival until after World War I. In the early generations of immigrants, parents saw education as a means for cultivating morality and preserving ethnic culture and language through the parochial schools of their churches not as a means to social mobility (Bodnar 1979, 336–38, 341–47; Greene 1980, 797).

The Poles

Immigration and the History of a Polish Family—Written with Len Oszko, Coal Township

Immigrants relied on personal networks to help them in the process of migration. When a Polish immigrant to America found steady work in a locality in which there was no Polish settlement, he would try to attract friends and relatives to join him from other Polish-American communities or from back home in Poland. Usually a small group of Polish working men would coalesce. In time they would have a Polish boarding house, often run by the wife of one of them (Znaniecki and Znaniecki 1984, 242).

In the scattered small villages of rural Poland, the church of one village in a group within a ten to fifteen mile radius would serve all of them. This group was like a parish, and the people attending this church of a group of villages were your *rodaki*. The meaning of this term depends on context; it can also mean fellow countryman or woman when speaking of Poles generally, but those belonging to the same Parish are close *rodaki* to each other. According to Caroline Golab, these agglomerates of villages entailed close-knit networks of roles and expectations and represented an "urban" tradition, which was different from that of the isolated farms common in parts of America and in much of Northern and Western Europe. There were minor cultural variations between these village groups which made them distinct: some linguistic in vocabulary and pronunciation; some in foods and eating habits; in dance, costumes and music; and in religious observances of specific devotions to the Virgin Mary and the Saints (Golab 1977, 68, 155).

Len Oszko researched the origins of the Poles living in Kulpmont (the town between Shamokin and Mt. Carmel), where he was raised, and in Coal Township, where he now lives. It showed that Poles in the churches and neighborhoods in these two towns had originated from four clusters of villages, each belonging to a single church back in Poland. He discovered that these immigrants consisted of groups of close *rodaki* who had found or followed each other in the process of immigration and had settled down in the same church and neighborhood in the Coal Region.

> *Group 1*, including Len's paternal grandfather and a group of Poles who went to the Mother of Consolation church in Mt. Carmel, came from the cities of Suwalki and Sejny, and a group of villages located in Suwalki Gubernia in the Mazurian Lakes region, northeast of Warsaw and close to Poland's northeastern border of Lithuania and Russia. The people there are 75 percent Polish, 25 percent Lithuanian, only a few of them Jews.
>
> *Group 2*, of Poles who lived in the Springfield and Ranshaw area of Eastern Coal Township, (see fig. 4.1) came from northeast of Warsaw around Lomza. A lot of the Poles who came to Springfield were sponsored by one man. In the early 1900s, he made a successful business out of sponsoring immigrants, taking care of the paperwork for immigration and naturalization and providing them with board and lodging in his hotel and bar.
>
> *Group 3*, including Len's father, came from the village of Mrokow, part of a cluster attending the church at Korytnica, 50–55 miles southeast of Warsaw, including the village of Elzbietow, the birthplace of Len's great grandfather. These villages were in Garwolin county and Mazovia province.
>
> *Group 4* came from Galicia (which used to be Austria-Hungary but is now Southern Poland) from villages around Rzeszow. A minority of groups 1 and 4, and a majority of group 3 lived in Kulpmont, belonged to the Jan Sobieski club, and made up 85–90 percent of the congregation of the Polish St. Casimir's church.[2]

This data shows that these immigrants used the social network of kin and *rodaki* among those who had gone ahead, to help them in a strange country in finding a job, a place to live, and in coping with language problems.

Len's family history now follows to show the details of this family's migration, the help of kin and *rodaki*, and how the family's circumstances improved down the generations as they moved into skilled employment and professional life. It starts with the two earliest generations back in Poland for which they have records. Over the generations, since Polish inheritance laws divided the land equally between all the sons and daughters, the fields had been divided and divided again into narrow strips of land. As a result the family barely existed on subsistence production from their tiny plots and from the sale of the very small surplus they produced. These people were not only emigrating from Russian-Poland to escape this land shortage and its desperate rural poverty but also to avoid conscription into the Czar's army, since one son from every family was drafted (see genealogy and box below).

The relationships of *rodaki* and the networks they formed were for this family a means for gathering people together to help each other in settling into the strange land to which they had immigrated. In the last two generations, the descendants of those poor Polish farmers have become well-to-do and cosmopolitan, some taking American names which made social mobility easier.

It was worth the family's combined moneys to send Jan to America. Polish immigrants in the United States have from the beginning sent remittances back to their families in Poland and demonstrated a strong drive to save money in order to do this. In Pennsylvania's anthracite district in 1884, the ordinary Polish mineworker was said to be saving close to $135 a year. Around 1910 it was estimated that about $40 million had been sent back from America to Poland: Austria-Hungary, Russian-Poland, and Galicia in southern Poland alone were supposedly receiving $4 to $5 million a year (Greene 1980, 797). These remittances made a substantial contribution to impoverished families back home and even played a significant economic role in the poor provinces in which they lived. The importance of kin and ethnic networks has faded, but over the years, Len's family has continued to send money and clothing to their relatives in Poland.

Associations and Clubs

Immigrants established mutual benefit associations soon after they arrived in the town and established ethnic neighborhoods. At first in the Polish community's evolution, spontaneous collections were made for those in distress but this soon became regularized into dues paying associations (Znaniecki and Znaniecki 1984, 245–46). The first purpose of such associations was for assistance in emergencies, illness and death especially. A family's insurance policy, with its monthly payment to the beneficial association, paid out $500 as a death benefit to cover funeral expenses and a tombstone.

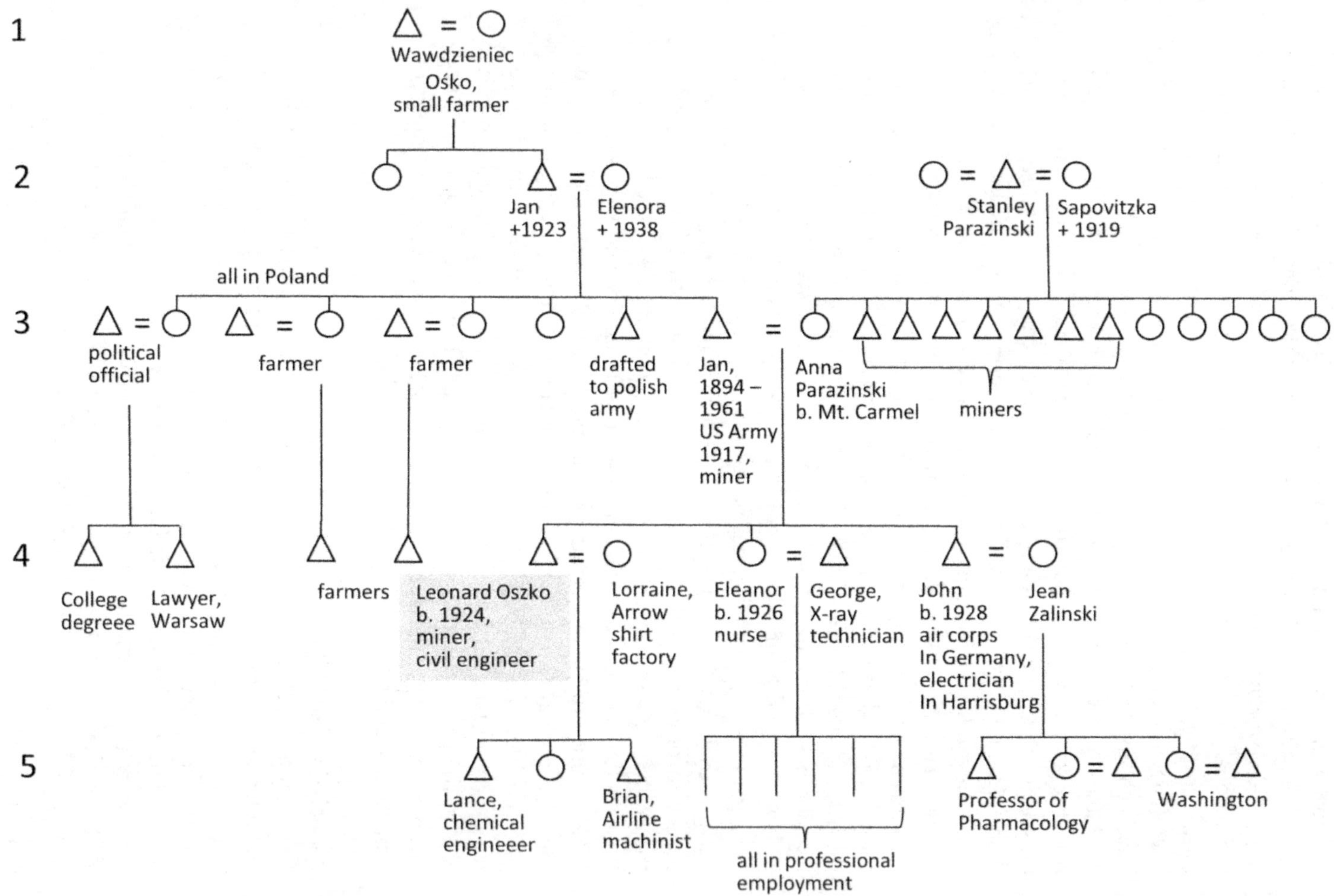

Figure 3.1. Genealogy of Leonard Oszko

Generations 1 and 2 lived in the small village of Mrokow. Len's paternal great grandfather, Wawdzieniec Osko (Laurence Oszko) was a small farmer who married a widow with land and two daughters, and they had two children of their own.

Generation 3: In 1914, the family pooled their money to help Len's father, Jan, aged 20, to immigrate to the United States. He had learned a little English in night school. First, he went to a cousin in Minnesota, then to Kulpmont, to a family of one of his *rodaki*, where he lived as a boarder from 1914 to 1917, and worked in the mines. Of his six other siblings, one brother got drafted into the Red Army, one sister married a political official and their children are educated and professionally employed, the others remained very poor farmers. Jan enlisted in the U.S. army in 1917, worked in the medical corps, and learned English. Afterwards, he returned to Kulpmont and worked as a miner. He opened a grocery store in his house in 1920. In 1932, he was elected to be a school director for one term, and was thereafter in politics a little. The mines were going into decline by this time. By 1935 with the Depression, they turned the store into a bar and also took in boarders, three of whom were their *rodaki*. Jan worked in the independent mines. He died, aged sixty-seven, in 1961.

Generation 4. Len was born in 1924. He graduated from high school. In 1940–1941 the mines were being shut down and the younger people, like his aunts and uncles went to Bridgeport, Connecticut to look for work. They settled there, boarding with two Polish families. Len got machine shop training in a Federal program and, at the age of eighteen, went to New York to work in a defense plant. From 1943, he was in the Marine Corps and fought in the Pacific. He returned to Kulpmont in 1946. Len then worked as an independent miner in Centralia. He had learned surveying in the Marines and through a program of continuing education and on the job practical experience, he was able to learn all the basics for his subsequent successful career Civil Engineering. His wife, Lorraine, of Slovak nationality, typically for a miner's daughter worked in factories, including the Arrow shirt factory, for thirty two years. Len's sister, Eleanor, graduated from high school in 1943 and trained as a nurse during World War II. She married the son of a Kulpmont Polish immigrant who became a sales representative for Bristol Meyers. Len's brother, John, finished high school, and was in the Air Corps in Germany after World War II. An electrician by trade, he worked in construction in the Harrisburg area. He married a Lithuanian American. They have lived in Kulpmont in the family homestead since the death of his mother in 1971.

Generation 5. The grandchildren of Jan Oszko, are college educated and hold professional careers or skilled employment, including a professor of pharmacology at the University of Kansas, a construction inspector in the Corps of Engineers, an instrument technician for United Airlines in San Francisco, a mine reclamation supervisor for the Pennsylvania Department of Mines, and a sales representative for a realty company. One grand-daughter was in the Peace Corps, and another a dental technician.

In later years, ethnic social clubs formed: some ensured economic security, others worked for nationalist goals as well, or worked to build a parish or to cultivate music and arts. In Shamokin there were two Polish ethnic clubs, the Polish Cadets and the St. Francis Society; in Mt. Carmel there was the Sons of Poland; in Kulpmont the Jan Sobieski.[3] Len's father was the secretary in the early years of the club when Len was a boy; all the *rodaki* belonged. This club in Kulpmont owned two plots in St. Casimir's cemetery at Marion Heights for burials of any single members of the club. Club members volunteered to dig graves.

Len remembers many ethnic clubs: on 10th Street in Kulpmont, there was the Hungarian club; on Pine Street, a block up, there was the Russian club; on Spring Street, between 9th and 10th the Lithuanian club; and the Italian club was down on Poplar Street. They were basically to socialize, drink and play cards. Len comments that "For the new immigrants, there were only the days in the dark, cold and dusty mine, no streets paved with gold. That's why they would all get together in the club."

Voluntary associations among Polish professionals began to appear just before 1900. In the 1920s, after Polish independence was achieved, the politically inspired fraternal societies replaced their nationalist goal with sending aid to their homeland, though these societies still continued to have an insurance function.

After prohibition ended, bars were licensed by the state and drinks were cheaper than in the local bars. Bars and especially clubs had slot machines or some other gaming device. These were illegal, but if there was a raid in the offing, someone would call you up to warn you to put the slot machine away. During the mid-thirties, both clubs and bars got their money from the slot machines. The Jan Sobieski had a hall for dancing. The music and dancing were mostly Polish, but other groups would mix in their dances too. The clubs became less and less exclusive over time as young men of all ethnic groups mingled on the High School football team, and the young people were serving together in World War II. According to Len: "We were all young and everybody was really socializing and dancing looking for girlfriends and boyfriends and getting married." This increasing intermarriage was a factor in the gradual decline of ethnicity in the life of the town.

Traditional Foods and Celebrations

In the Coal Region, Poles had a series of traditional celebrations based on the religious calendar and the life cycle. Such traditions, the special foods that went with them, the use of the vernacular language, and membership in their ethnic Catholic churches were strong markers of ethnicity for Poles, as they were for all the Eastern and Southern Europeans.

For *Wygilia*, the traditional Polish Christmas Eve supper common to all the Slavic groups, families gathered in their homes to participate in a meatless meal of an uneven number of courses. It included fish such as herring and carp, beets or mushrooms, cooked wheat, *pirogies*, noodles, sauerkraut, dried fruit compote, and Christmas cakes. The children would watch to see when the first star came out, before the meal could begin. They started with the Christmas wafer (it still comes in a decorated envelope from the Polish church every year). The entire family lined up and the father dipped the wafer in the wine, gave them each a piece, and wished them all a Merry Christmas. On Christmas morning it was the custom to visit relatives and sing carols, the same on St. Stephen's Day. The main dish for this day was *bigos*, (Hunter's Stew), as it was for New Year's Eve parties, with cold meats, stuffed carp, torte and cakes (Chrypinski 1977, 8, 15).

In March, Bitter Lamentations, *Goszkedzaly*, a service of the chanting of the Passion story by the priest took place in the church. In April, at the ceremony of *Swieconka*, the priest blessed the baskets of food for Easter breakfast on the morning before Easter Day. The baskets would be filled with sweet bread with raisins, colored and decorated eggs, ham, kielbasa sausage, cakes, and usually a butter mold of a Paschal lamb, some cheese, horseradish, salt, vinegar and oil. On Easter morning the head of the house began the meal by sharing the blessed egg, the symbol of life. Bread and salt are the essential elements of Polish hospitality.

In June *Wiankia na Wode*, a very ancient ritual, took place when wreaths with candles on them were floated down a stream by young girls. The one whose wreath got to the end first was supposed to marry first. Weddings were elaborate staged events, celebrated with traditional dances and a great consumption of vodka and festive foods, such as roast pork, sausages, beet soup, cabbage rolls and poppy seed cakes. Baptism celebrations lasted over several days, and feasts with music and dancing followed funerals (S. Jones 1995, 1090–91). These traditional Polish events all stressed and reinforced family and community ties.

The Lithuanians

Lithuanians differed from the Poles in that during the nineteenth century, the struggle for independence from Russia and Poland gave Lithuanians a sense of nationhood and an involvement in the politics of their home country. More than the Poles, they thus always had a sense of national identity in America. With their background of the long struggle for independence and an end to cultural domination from Poland and Russia, many Lithuanian-Americans remained involved and interested in the continuing efforts to achieve Lithuania's independence, an interest which sustained their ethnic identity and traditions in America. In the three towns covered in this study, Poles seem to have depended more on outstanding individuals to foster this interest.

Immigration and Settlement

Like the Poles, Lithuanians immigrated to escape desperate rural poverty, land shortage, conscription into the czar's army, and famine. Like other groups, these immigrants drew upon the patterns of mutual assistance of family and of the village community as they immigrated: those who were established in America helped their relatives and friends to join them, sending back money for tickets and providing temporary board and lodging. Such networks also helped them to move about in America.

Before 1890, the largest number of Lithuanians in America had moved to the coal towns of Shenandoah, Hazleton, Pittston, Mahanoy City, Mt. Carmel, Plymouth, Freeland and Scranton, where they worked, to begin with, as unskilled labor in the mines. A strong Lithuanian ethnic presence and identity soon developed in the Coal Region (Alisauskas 1980, 668). In 1864, the first Lithuanian language newspaper published in America, the *Lietuwiszka Gazieta*, was established in Shamokin (Budreckis 1976, 7), and Lithuanian books were published, starting in the early twentieth century. There was a publisher in Shenandoah and another in Mahanoy City, which also put out a Lithuanian newspaper that was sent to all the other coal towns.[4]

Schuylkill County was the major center of Lithuanian activity in America during the first wave of Lithuanian immigration, and Shenandoah, "*Shenandorius*" as it was known to Lithuanians, was its capital city (see figure 1.1). The church of St. George in the town, founded in 1871, was one of the first Lithuanian Catholic churches in America.

In the 1870s, Shenandoah only had about sixty Lithuanian residents, but by the late 1890s they made up nearly 25 percent of the population of 16,000. They soon moved up from their low position as unskilled miners: by the end of the nineteenth century they owned over 200 businesses in the town, and a Lithuanian lawyer was elected mayor in 1895. Five other Lithuanians held this office thereafter. By the late 1800s, Lithuanians also made up 25 percent of the population of Mahanoy City where the first Lithuanian school had been set up (Chernoski 2004, 14–15). In Coal Township, after being closely associated with the Poles and attending St. Stanislaus (the Polish Catholic Church), Lithuanians founded St. Michael's church in 1888, which achieved full parish status in 1910.[5] Today in the anthracite region, the towns of Minersville, St. Clair, Frackville and Shenandoah are "the heart and strength of the cultural movement of the Lithuanian people."[6]

Lithuanian Catholicism had been Polish in language and orientation for hundreds of years and at first this domination by the Polish church extended to the immigrant communities in the United States. But the growth of Lithuanian nationalism and ethnic identity brought about great changes in the Lithuanian American religious community. Under the leadership of a priest, Aleksandras Burba, Lithuanian Americans began to establish their own parishes, more than 100 being formed by 1920. This revolt against the Polish Church created tensions in immigrant communities but also increased the sense of ethnic consciousness. In 1914, Lithuanians founded their National Catholic church in Scranton, breaking away from the American Roman Catholic hierarchy. This national church founded religious orders and established a large parochial school system (Granquist 1995, 887-88).

A Miner's Life and Family History

The following family history is of a Lithuanian miner, Ed Narcavage of Mt. Carmel as he told it to me. His grandfather was rewarded with land for fighting for the Russians in war, but his father emigrated to flee conscription, in which he was helped by kin who had gone before him. The closeness of family and the camaraderie among miners stand out in this account. Again, the second generation of the family shows progress to increasingly skilled jobs in the mines and the third, college education and mobility into white collar and professional employment.

> My grandfather was a lieutenant in the Russian army. They gave him a piece of ground when he'd served his time because he'd fought in one of the wars over there (the Prussian War maybe). So he had a farm and he had eleven sons. My father and mother came over [to the United States] from Lithuania in 1903, my mother from Vilnius and my father from a little town, Gubundia, on the border of Russia. The Russian Tsar was taking young men and putting them into the army. My father had an uncle that worked in St. Louis and he gave part of the fare for my father to come over. My father worked first in St. Louis, but then another uncle who worked in Mt. Carmel said there was a lot of work in the mines, so he moved to Mt. Carmel—and it was terrible. At that time you got the lousiest job in the mine. The bosses were Welsh and they gave the lousiest jobs to the immigrants. 'We really worked,' my father said. He worked fifty-five years in the mines, retired at seventy and died aged ninety three in 1969.
>
> We spoke only Lithuanian [at home] in our family. My mother could speak seven languages (Lithuanian, Polish, Czech, Russian, Yiddish, a little German, and then English to get her citizenship papers). Her father in Vilnius was caretaker of the big basilica and the priests would teach her their languages. I had

> four brothers and a sister. Three of us went to the mines; one learned to be a machinist in the service with the Seabees. He got a job in Philadelphia. My other brother had a little restaurant in Chester, Pennsylvania, and made quite a bit of money. We all went to High School, except my sister who was married young to a fellow that took care of apartments in New York and she lives there. I had a scholarship to Fordham but my Dad got sick and I went into the mines. I had five children, two sons and three daughters, and ten grandchildren. All my children except for one went to college.
>
> I enjoyed mining, I never had any problems with it. We were healthy that was one thing and it was a challenge. We were shifting maybe 40 ton of rock every day. It was nothing to us to pick up a piece of timber of 300–400 lbs. The Department of Mines used to have tests which I took, and I wound up being a mining foreman. I went to the Mining School at Penn State in the evenings. Then I worked for the Glen Burn. Everybody depended on each other. It carried on even when you got out of the mines, families would get together and have a little cookout or something. My buddy would bring his family over and we would have a cookout, or go over to one of the parks and have a cookout there. We always had happiness.[7]

Ed was one of those who found mining a satisfying occupation. He brings out the miners' tremendous physical strength and their pride in it. The strength and closeness of mining families is clear, as is the bond between people of mining communities inside and outside the mine. Over time, such bonds forged in the mines contributed to the breakdown of ethnic boundaries.

Associations and Fundraising

Soon after they arrived in the early 1880s, Lithuanians like the other groups set up beneficial societies for insurance against personal crises, and they began to raise funds to sustain their churches and send aid to Lithuania. In the Coal Region, the first purely Lithuanian society was St. George's in Shenandoah. Others followed and from 1886 to 1972 they paid out $10,000 in death benefits and sick benefits covering 100,000 Lithuanian Americans, and raised $250,000 for charitable and cultural endeavors. Lithuanians in Shamokin/Coal Township and Mt. Carmel formed social clubs. Members had Christmas parties, Easter egg hunts for children, and an annual memorial mass for those who had died. The Clubs continued to be active into the 1960s, but by the turn of the century, they functioned as social clubs for anyone who wished to join, not only Lithuanians.[8]

The Knights of Lithuania is a national organization of men and women of Lithuanian ancestry, first established in 1913. Members had to be of Lithuanian descent, or married to a member, and practicing Catholics. It aimed to assist in the assimilation of immigrants and emphasized the preservation of their culture, language and religion. The organization offered no welfare benefits, but appealed to ethnic exclusiveness to a greater extent than with other groups: in the first half of the century preservation of the culture was a constant concern and debate and friendship outside the group was discouraged because it could lead to intermarriage (a resolution against marrying out was even passed at the Knights' convention as late as 1944). But gradually, especially among the youth, ethnic awareness dropped to a low level; by 1963, 50 percent of marriages were with non-Lithuanians and in the 50s and 60s the Knights became a social organization for all ages (Wolkovich-Valkavicius 1988, 21–23).

Traditional Foods and Festivals

Ed Narcavage continued his earlier account with descriptions of his childhood and family life. It shows the hard work of children as well as how much they relished their mother's Lithuanian cooking and the good foods they gathered or grew. The importance of food as part of people's sense of identity, of tradition, of family life, comes out very clearly in this and other family stories. These foods, remembered as an important component of the different ethnic traditions of the past, are now part of the multiethnic food tradition of the region today.

> These kids today don't know what life is, we enjoyed every bit of it, the good and the bad. We worked so hard. When we were kids, we'd get up every morning at 5 o'clock and go up on the mountain and pick berries; every day, five days a week. My mother would jar all these berries for the winter. We had blue berries and black berries, and whatever kind of berries, we had them. We had jams and my mother made wine out of the blackberries and elderberries. My mother used to make like a cottage cheese. We'd get milk from the farmer, put it in the crock, and then take the water off for about two weeks, and that would come out like a big yoghourt. We would have it with baked potatoes. That was a Friday meal too, and oh, that was delicious. My wife makes some stuff like that, and we still make chow-chow (peppers, cucumbers, lima beans, corn, celery, cauliflower, little onions, all cut up and soaked overnight, cooked next day with mustard powder, and cold packed into jars).

Ed emphasizes that their family still set great emphasis on keeping up the old traditions even in the third generation here in the United States. "We do keep the traditions and we have a good time." He describes *Kucios*, the Christmas Eve dinner, the Lithuanian version of the major traditional feast for all Slavs in the ethnic neighborhoods.

> Traditionally in Lithuania the table would be covered with a hand-loomed linen cloth with fresh hay beneath it, a reminder that the Christ Child was

> born in a manger. A crucifix and a plate of the blessed Christmas wafers would be in the center. The head of the family begins the meal with a prayer and breaks and shares the wafers with each member of the family. For *Kucios* we had twelve types of dishes, with fish but no meat. And we'd have the poppy seed roll, and poppy seed ground with milk, and a rye flour dumpling with this milk over it; farmers' cheese and butter; a big pot of oyster stew which everybody liked, and pickled eggs. We always had three breads, white, rye and raisin. We used to pick mushrooms and dry them and my mother would make a soup too. She'd make red beet soup (like *borscht*, cold in summer hot in the winter, just potatoes and beets). My kids still do it and make the foods. I send them the wafers from here; they don't get them in North Carolina.

The presentation of the Christmas tree, traditionally decorated with the finely woven straw ornaments that are a distinctive Lithuanian craft in the Coal Region, and with fruit, nuts and cookies (see figure 3.2[9]), took place

Figure 3.2. Decorating the Christmas Tree of the Knights of Lithuania in 1975. Used by permission of Anne Klizas Wargo

after dinner. Finally the entire family attended the first mass of Christmas at midnight.

The biggest festival for Lithuanians in the Coal Region, marking and celebrating the strength of their ethnicity, was Lithuanian Day, held on August 15th, the Day of the Assumption of the Blessed Virgin Mary. It started in the Coal Region in 1914 after two Lithuanian priests of the region "set aside a day for friends and relatives from Lithuania to gather and observe the ancient and honored customs of the land of their heritage" (*Pottsville Republican*, Wednesday, August 2, 1978). This festival was held at Lakewood Park, a ten-acre amusement park at Barnesville, and was a major ethnic event. Thousands of Lithuanians flocked to it, coming from all over the Coal Region and from cities as far away as Baltimore and Philadelphia, by train and bus. Ed Narcavage describes it:

> August 15, Lithuanian Day, was the biggest thing in this whole Coal Region: everything closed down. Everybody went, not just Lithuanians. All the collieries shut down, all the stores closed, and everybody went up to Lakeside (the ballroom at Lakewood) by Tamaqua. There'd be 50 thousand people there.[10] They used to run excursion trains. My Dad would go up there the night before to get a table. Everybody had a big table and had beer and pork chops, bread, steaks, half a pig to roast, water melons and all kinds of fruits. Everybody that was there that was anybody, knew everybody. The people that came from the old country used to get together and reminisce about things over there. They'd come from New Jersey, Connecticut, New York anywhere—even from Chicago. People with accordions would sing Lithuanian songs. They had dancing: they brought in Lithuanian dancers in costume from Connecticut. It was really, really ethnic.

Anne Wargo of St. Clair, recalls flags all over the park and travelling musicians playing Lithuanian music and going from table to table. Foods, costumes, music and dance, and connections to the homeland are the central markers of ethnicity for Lithuanians in this cultural celebration. It continues today on a much smaller scale at the Schuylkill Mall in Frackville as described in chapter 7. It is the oldest continuing ethnic festival in Pennsylvania.

The Lithuanians, among the Slavic groups of the town, are the most involved with their home country, and came out of an independence movement back home that gave them a greater sense of national identity before migration than either of the other two groups. They also have been more consciously concerned with trying to preserve their Lithuanian identity and exclusiveness, especially notable in their efforts to sustain endogamy for longer than the other groups.

The Ukrainians

Ukrainians are Catholics. The "Uniate" (or Greek) Ukrainian Catholic Church resulted from union with the Catholics in Rome by a segment of the Ukrainian Orthodox church, first in Galicia in 1596, then in 1646 in Carpathian Ukraine also. Virtually all the early Ukrainian immigrants to

Generation 1. George Pollyniak's paternal grandfather (also named George) lived in Austria but was of Ukrainian descent. His wife was married six times. George's maternal grandfather was a coalminer in the United States. His brother, also a coalminer, was killed in the mines. George's wife, Mary Steffanik's paternal grandfather was a farmer in the Carpathian Mountains of Austria (see figure 3.3).

Generation 2. George's father, George Sr. was Greek Catholic. He had a brother, Nikita, who came to Shamokin and became a miner. George Sr. wanted to escape conscription into the Austrian army and Nikita wrote him to come and take a job in the mines too. So George Sr. and five other men walked from Austria to Hamburg. They missed the ship by a week and had to wait two months for it to return; they finally arrived in the United States in 1898. The group dispersed, most of them to Canada joining Ukrainians already there. George Sr. went to Shamokin where he worked in the mines for forty five years until he was seventy years old. He married Mary Mastuk who was Greek Catholic. His brother Nikita married Mary's sister Pearl (Pazia). Nikita was injured in the mines and sick thereafter. There were three other siblings but they stayed back in the Carpathathians. George Jr.'s wife Mary's father was Charles Steffanick, who came to work in the mines in Mt. Carmel to escape conscription into the Austrian army (see figure 3.4, photo of him and his wife Anna Remish on their wedding day in 1920.) Mary's three sisters moved away. One of her brothers worked in bridge construction in Baltimore; another was a store clerk in Shamokin.

Generation 3. George's father, George Sr., and Mary's daughter Anna lived in Mt. Carmel. She owned the Shamokin Baking Company and married a Polish salesman. Their daughter Susan married a Jew in New York City. Their daughter Helen married an Irish supermarket clerk in New York City, and worked in a textile factory. Their two sons were Theodore and George Jr. Theodore worked in Harrisburg for an architecture firm and married a Slovak girl.; George Jr. lived in Shamokin, worked in Shroyer's dress factory, and married Mary Steffanik. She worked in the Eagle Silk Mill (see figure 3.5, photo of George Jr. and Mary on their wedding day in 1942).[11]

Generation 4. George and Mary's son Dennis went to the Philadelphia College of Pharmacy and moved to work in Marietta, Georgia.

Generation 5: Dennis' son is a businessman and lives in Georgia. His daughter graduated with highest honors from Georgia Technical College, had a one year scholarship in Oxford, has a management position with General Electric.

Figure 3.3. Photographs from three generations of George Pollyniak's genealogy: (1) Anna Ladna and her two children. Used by permission of George Pollyniak

Figure 3.4. (2) Wedding of Charles Steffanik and Anna Remish. Used by permission of George Pollyniak

Figure 3.5. (3) Wedding of George Pollyniak and Mary Steffanik. Used by permission of George Pollyniak

the Coal Region were of this Eastern Byzantine-Rite Catholic Church.[12] They have been known variously as Rusyn (Ruthenian in English) or Russian nationals, and their regional groups as Russniak, Carpatho-Russian or Lemkian. Most of the Ruthenian-American community, however, now calls itself Ukrainian, but most only thought of themselves as Ukrainian after they arrived in the United States.

Immigration and a Family History

As with other Slav migrants, the first Ukrainians who came encouraged and helped others, providing them with temporary homes. Often men came first and brought their families after they found jobs and could support them. Ukrainians in Shamokin say that whole villages left, meaning some people came from every family in a village. But finding relatives in the Ukraine has been made very difficult by the events of the twentieth century.[13]

These immigrants worked in the anthracite mines of Northeastern Pennsylvania, the steel mills of Pittsburgh, and the factories of New York and New Jersey, and moved up in time into trade, small businesses, and the professions (Magocsi 1980, 999). Ukrainians were among the first of the Slavic workers to come to the mines and they did not speak English. There was tension between them and the English, Irish, and Welsh miners because some Ukrainians had been recruited to immigrate and be strike breakers, and they were pejoratively referred to as "Hunkies," (a word reflecting their origin in the Hungarian part of the Austrian Empire).

The extended family history that follows illustrates the effects of historical circumstances on a family who chose to flee to improve their existence and the lives of their descendants.

The ancestors of George and Mary Pollyniak were poor farmers from the Carpathian Mountains in the Austrian Province of Galicia. The men did all the farm work and took the animals up to pasture in the high mountains. It was bitterly cold in winter, and herders could die of cold or be killed by wolves. In consequence, it was not unusual for women to be widowed and married several times, as was George's paternal grandmother. These early immigrants were almost all from poor rural backgrounds and left to come to work in the mines of the Coal Region to escape the hardship of their lives and to avoid military conscription.

The five generations of this family genealogy show the improvement in life chances of these poverty-stricken farmers who left the Ukraine to work in the anthracite mines, and how over the generations their descendants moved up into professional careers and married into other ethnic groups. While their parents were still alive, they kept the old traditions and the family all came together for Christmas Eve dinner. Like other families in the town, they stayed close and those who moved away returned to visit until after the death of their parents.

Church and Community

At first, Ukrainians attended the Latin Rite churches of the Poles, Slovaks or Hungarians (Procko 1973, 220). After the arrival of their own priests and organization of their own churches (Shenandoah had the first parish, Shamokin the second), the priests initiated Ukrainian organizations, and they founded *Svoboda* (Liberty), a Ukrainian language newspaper, in 1893. It was these priests who fostered a national ethnic awareness and unity that, over time, overrode the divisions between some of the priests themselves and within Ukrainian American communities (Procko 1979, 53).

The Transfiguration of Our Lord, Ukrainian Greek Catholic Church in Coal Township belongs to the Byzantine Rite Catholic Church. It is in the South Anthracite Deanery of the Ukrainian Archeparchy (Archdiocese) of Philadelphia, and did not have to merge like other ethnic Catholic churches in town which belong to the diocese of Harrisburg. It was therefore able to keep its parochial school, and the church and its school have played an important role in sustaining Ukrainian ethnic identity and culture, tradition and sense of community. "In this area, they are still very, very much aware of their ancient roots. We are surviving strongly with a strong identity and sense of community."[14]

In the Ukraine, church based institutions, festivals and traditions were the center of community life. In America, they were modified as part of the process of adapting to American society, reflecting a different class structure in which the clergy had a less dominant class position. In Ukraine, they had a higher status and church members were peasantry of inferior status. The church in the United States became dependent on the support of parishioners for investment in church property such as land and buildings, and the church committees that arose to manage them resulted in parishioners gaining control of parish policies in a way that had not existed in Ukraine. The income of the clergy was dependent on parishioners in America, and, until 1924, pastors could be fired by them. The American Latin Rite church pressured the Ukrainian Byzantine Rite church to have celibate clergy. They carried their case to Rome, were finally successful and after 1929, Ukrainian priests in the United States were forced by Rome to accept celibacy, whereas in the home country, the village priest had been a family man, giving him more status than one who was unmarried. Finally, there was competition for membership because of the conversion activities of American Protestant churches, which did not happen back home (Isajiw 1979, 82–84). Thus the institution of the church itself, as well as its traditions, had to be modified and adapted in the process of settling into the new society.

Religious and Other Associations

Associations and societies appear to have been stronger and more influential for Ukrainians than for the Poles and Lithuanians because circumstances did not force the closure of the Ukrainian church in Coal Township. For Ukrainian immigrants arriving before World War II, religious brotherhoods and fraternal associations were the primary vehicle for Ukrainian education, cultural and social life. Fraternal societies are the oldest Ukrainian organizations in the United States, and were the most influential force in the life of Ukrainian communities after the church. Brotherhoods, sodalities and clubs preserved Ukrainian traditions and brought together people of different degrees of assimilation into American life. Their newspapers and almanacs also helped to maintain contact and cohesiveness within the community, with their news of their activities as well as of the homeland (Magocsi 1980, 1002; 1995, 254).

In Shamokin, the Sts. Cyril and Methodius Brotherhood was founded in 1897, together with other small Brotherhoods in Shamokin and Mt. Carmel. They were united into the Society of Ukrainian Brotherhoods, with its own building, meeting hall and about two hundred members. Initially it was an insurance company for paying funeral expenses, gradually taking on other kinds of insurance and preserving culture and tradition through education. It published *Svoboda*, the Ukrainian language newspaper.[15] For women there was the St. Anne's Society and the Society of the Blessed Virgin Mary which helped the pastors in their work, cared for children, helped members with benefits for caring for the sick, and paid nominal death benefits. These associations all donated stained glass windows in the church, memorializing their importance in early times.[16]

But the Ukrainians were affected like the other groups by the population loss as the coal and garment industries declined or moved. The Ukrainian Club formerly had a membership of 1,400–1,500. After World War II numbers began to decline because so many people moved away in search of work. They sold the building and by 2002, membership was only forty-five,[17] a great contrast with the strength of the Ukrainian community reflected in the parade in 1904 which begins the chapter. The Ukrainians follow the pattern found in all ethnic groups: the vigor and elaboration of ethnic culture and organization in the early years of the town's history declined by the mid-nineteenth century in response to changing economic and political circumstances and opportunities for social mobility.

The Arts: Crafts, Music and Dance

Like the Poles and Lithuanians, Ukrainians brought with them the arts and crafts tradition of their farming homeland. They consisted of ceramics, embroidery, wood carving and decorated eggs (see figures 3.6 and 3.7). Today these items are imported from Ukraine, sold in specialty stores and at booths on national days, and displayed in many homes. Some people do continue to practice the art of decorating eggs and instruction classes are offered at the church.

The Ukrainian strong music and dance tradition was a feature of town life in the past; there used to be dance groups and choirs in every parish in the Coal Region. By 1894, Transfiguration Church had a choir, which gave concerts. A group of thirty or so would visit all the parishioners' homes to sing carols at Christmas. They stayed out until 3:00 a.m. or 4:00 a.m. and in wealthy homes were treated to lavish spreads of food. In the early 1930s, this choir had seventy-nine members and there was also a junior choir. They sang unaccompanied and in Ukrainian. The choir was asked to sing in other local churches, including Protestant ones, especially Christmas carols. It was disbanded in the 1960s when the director had to leave for lack of funds. A Ukrainian band of fifty instruments also used to give regular concerts.

Figure 3.6. Ukrainian Ceramics and Embroidery

Figure 3.7. Ukrainian Decorated Eggs (*pysanky*)

Ukrainian dancing was a major tradition. "If you got together in a group with a few drinks, somebody would be dancing; 90 percent of the men could do it. On Saturday nights they would pull the rugs in the house back and dance."[18] Dances were performed at weddings or birthday celebrations, and into the thirties dancers would still come to dance at the church's annual block party. In the *Jubilee Souvenir Book of 1939* the Transfiguration parish dance group had twenty eight dancers; in 1935, thirty-five children had summer instruction in dance and performed in local theaters and high schools; and in 1938, a dance group of Ukrainian high school graduates in the town performed at graduation, and came first in an ethnic festival at Susquehanna University. This went on until after World War II but then declined after so many young people went away and did not return. Today a dance group comes from Hazleton to perform at the annual Ukrainian picnic in the village of Primrose near Minersville, but there is no longer a dance group or choir in Shamokin/Coal Township nor in other coal towns nearby; choirs do exist where there are still resident directors, as in the town of Nanticoke, near Wilkes Barre (see figure 1.1).

Like the other groups, Ukrainians had their ethnic festival, Ukrainian Day, held annually in Lakewood Park in Barnesville (see figure 1.1). It was a huge event at which there would be over 1,000 people on the dance floor, with famous bands like Guy Lombardo and the Blue Baron.

The Italians

Immigrants from Two Southern Italian Towns

Ninety percent of the Italians in Shamokin/Coal Township, Mt. Carmel and Kulpmont came from the same two small towns: Ischa and San Sostene in Calabria in the extreme south of Italy. The massive Italian immigration to the United States and the high rate of return of migrants meant that those wanting to immigrate had extensive knowledge of the new country and of the places in which the immigrants had settled (Sowell 1996, 145). Contacts made on the job helped Italians from particular regions and even villages in Italy to concentrate in the same towns or city neighborhoods in the United States, as the immigrants helped family members find employment (Grifo and Noto 1990, 7). The *padrone* system also increased the numbers from these two Calabrian towns as the *padrone* got jobs for immigrants from their home towns.

In the 1890s, *padroni* operated as private labor agents without licenses or offices. They provided a number of skilled as well as unskilled jobs for immigrants, including masons, carpenters, stone cutters and machinists as well as mine workers. The *padrone* knew employers, spoke English and was familiar with American labor practices, which made him very useful to newcomers and employers alike. He was instrumental in bringing people over from Italy and would get orders from employers for specific numbers of workers. These immigrants paid him a commission secretly and in advance. In Shamokin's "Little Italy" in the Fifth Ward, "Jimmy" Christiana, a highly respected leader, was the *padrone*. He found hundreds of jobs for these Southern Italians and brought them over to Shamokin, providing labor for the mines, for the laying of water mains from Brush Valley into Shamokin, and for the road and building construction business (Marlok 1976, 65).

A *padrone* would also supply services for new immigrants, such as advancing them money, writing letters, taking responsibility for housing and transporting them, and handling relations with employers.[19] Sometimes this tight control resulted in abuse of the immigrants as *padroni* protected their investment and exercised a prison-like control over the workers. The system was in decline after 1900 and dying out by 1920 (Nelli 1964, 153–58, 164, 167; Sowell 1996, 165).

In Shamokin/Coal Township, Kulpmont and Mt. Carmel, almost all Italians came from these two small Calabrian towns, the majority of them from Ischa. They came over in groups, beginning in the 1870s.[20] They are still identifiable through their names which can be found in disproportionate numbers in the local phonebook: Gidaro (18), Pupo (16), Procopio (16), Mirarchi (15), Anolia (9), Coroniti (8), Lacroce (7).

These Southerners were likely to have worked as sharecroppers or farm laborers in Italy rather than as self-supporting farmers; many had lived a marginal existence owning a small piece of land and providing labor for the estates of large landowners. They came with a living pattern of extreme thrift and of pooling family effort and money (Sowell 1996, 147; Vecoli 1995, 119). As one town Italian put it: "People SAVED and did not spend money. My mother wore the same winter coat for seventeen years and saved her money for her kids." These Italian peasant farmers also tended to view the clergy as oppressors; in Italy, they had fought against the church's feudal tax obligations and in America were less likely to contribute to the churches than Germans or Poles (Morris 1997, 129).

This background is reflected in the emphasis by Italians on the strength of family, with festive meals and winemaking as the most important elements of Italian ethnicity in the towns, and in the perception by some of the threat of education to family solidarity and traditional ways and their consequent reluctance to contribute to parochial schools. In parts of southern Italy education had been actively resisted and schools were even burned because children were needed to work to supplement meager family incomes. The lower classes of Italian society suspected that schooling would be of little help for them and instead would undermine the family solidarity on which they relied for survival. The rate of illiteracy was higher in the South than in the North. Typically in the early years of immigration to America, Italians would not pay for schooling when they ran their own parishes, and had to be subsidized by their dioceses (ibid.). This refusal to invest in education contrasts with the emphasis on it in other ethnic groups in the towns: Italians were to move up socioeconomically through blue-collar skills, rather than by becoming educated and entering the professions.

The first generation of Italian immigrants in the Coal Region went into the mines, as did their eldest sons. But thereafter Italians primarily went into different businesses. Typically in the earlier times, they were shoemakers, in road and building construction, brick making, restaurants and other businesses.

Stigmatized in the early years by powerful stereotypes referring to their illiteracy, poverty, clannishness, and ill health, Italians suffered discrimination in jobs and housing (Pozetta 1995, 767). Hostility against them contributed to the coalescing of "Little Italy" neighborhoods in the towns. In Shamokin, they were concentrated in the Fifth Ward where the Italian/Irish church was St. Edwards. In Mt. Carmel they lived in Atlas, a section on the edge of town, and the Italian church was St. Peter's. It was founded by immigrants from the Tyrol.[21] Kulpmont was mainly founded by Italians and Hungarians; by about 1910 each group had its own section in the town.

Some Italians became low level civil servants but, for a long time in the United States, not many were doctors, lawyers, intellectuals or in politics. Fiorello LaGuardia, Mayor of New York three times 1934–1945, was the first major Italian political figure (Sowell 1996, 143, 146, 165).

Associations

In Southern Italy, rural villagers depended on the family to provide aid in times of need, clubs were few and for social functions only. The voluntary mutual associations that arose to help new immigrants in their new home in America are part of the movement away from the family based social system of Southern Italy. As with other ethnic associations, these nation-wide Italian associations provided insurance and welfare services in the Coal Region communities. They organized aid for newcomers and assistance in times of sickness, unemployment, accident, and death. The Sons of Italy was the largest and most influential association. It was started in New York in 1905 and by 1921 had 125,000 members in 887 lodges all over the country (Gans 1962, 552–53). Members contributed fifty cents to one dollar a month and got six dollars a week during illness and their families $200 at their death. Over the years, it broadened from insurance and protection to social activities like playing cards and *bocce* if the society was affluent enough to rent a clubhouse (Grifo and Noto 1990, 18). There is a local lodge in Shamokin. Such clubs along with Italian newspapers, churches, theaters, and bands helped initially to create an emerging Italian-American culture in Italian neighborhoods, (Pozetta 1995, 767). Today, in Shamokin, it is a social club and is no longer exclusively for Italians.

Family, Festive Foods and Winemaking

"Festive meals with special holiday foods and traditions, and activities such as making wine, cheese and sausage, are integral to the Italian way of life" (Rauche 1988, 208), and are an important part of ethnic identity for them (Waters 1990, 118). Details of foods and festive meals, family get-togethers, investment in the home country, a family business and winemaking from several families follow.

The relish of Italians for their traditional foods and their association with family is vividly conveyed by the accounts of family events by two sisters from Ischa.

> We'd have Christmas Eve dinner at 7.30. We have all kinds of different fishes and wine. It could be pike (sometimes in a jelly), mackerel, cod, flounder, sea bass, shark, and it was all cooked expertly, with side orders of spaghetti. My Dad

used to have a big pot of snails. It was a feast. For desserts, we'd have *cippoli*: fried dough with jelly or raisins. My mother would always make *capusata*, (it was a special gift for special family or friends, like a prayer for you. It was a pastry of a special dough with eggs around it). On Christmas and Easter Day we'd have lamb or baby goat or chicken (but no gravy), veal cutlets (turkey only came in because veal was expensive). Good Friday was a fasting day. We'd have fish and pancakes . . . my mother would make them of potato and garlic and onions with parsley. And we'd have spaghetti with olive oil, onions and anchovies.

The mother of the family made Italian Wedding Soup for Christmas time. "It takes a long time too. I make the dough, then the next day I make the meat balls, and the next I boil the chicken separately, and there you are. Other foods are *gnocchi* ("Little Pillows"), very light, you roll and cut them, you use flour and eggs and some people put potatoes in. Boil them until they come to the top and have them with a butter or tomato sauce. In the old days everyone had a coal stove and cooked the sauce all day, you basically had a pot simmering on the back of it. Also we had *pastazoli* (spaghetti with beans), spaghetti and meat balls (ALWAYS, always), and a big pot of vegetables: potatoes, peppers, onions, garlic, everything except corn. . . . I can remember in 1941 when I got married . . . the church was jam-packed, not just with those invited, everybody. Just the family came back for the big meal, they received invitations. . . . We bought the cake, but we made the meatballs and the Italian *biscotti*, and wedding soup and a salad. That's family."

Italian families celebrated together with festive meals at Christmas, Easter, Confirmation, First Communion, marriage, and the birth of a baby (you would have a dinner for the godparents who are very important for Catholics and Orthodox Christians). "Christmas was family, not gifts. . . . We would go from one aunt's house to another's on Christmas Day, telling stories and eating: wedding soup, spaghetti and meatballs, ham baked in wine, hot Italian sausage, cow's heart and tongue, and blood pudding."[22] Dancing and singing Italian songs were part of festival occasions: the Tarantella, a dance of Neapolitan origin, was danced at weddings and birthdays; Italian carols were part of Christmas. But this music has declined with the decline in the use of the Italian language.

The Silvanos are from San Sostene. The head of this family was first Aristes, then Freddy (Alfred). Aristes's wife was Rose Marie Schiavone, from Ischa. This is a big family.

When Rose Marie died, her funeral was the largest ever recorded in Mt. Carmel. Freddy had four brothers and five sisters in Mt. Carmel. They got together all the time in their home in Atlas, Mt. Carmel, even if they lived out of town, and they used to have huge picnics to which family members came from all over. In the old days they would even sell things at these picnics. They stay in touch with relatives in Italy now by phone, which is easier than letters. Freddy's daughter Marianne says: "I can remember having dinner at my aunt Rose's and they would have a table put together all the way from the kitchen to the front door and everybody would sit down." They are in touch with frequent phone calls and e-mails, at weddings and funerals, and formerly at family reunions. These reunions used to be coordinated by Aristes, who was the head of the family to whom everyone went for advice. After he died, Freddy kept the family together. He was the first American-born child and the only one who did not work in the mines. Now Marianne and her sister Suzanne are in charge of holding the family together and are planning a family reunion again after a long time.

Sam Feudale is an example of an immigrant who invested heavily in the Home Country. He came from Ischa in the early twentieth century to make money for his farm back in Italy. In the past his family included two who were clergy and another who was a mayor of Ischa in 1870. Sam went into the mines, but did not like it and used the money he made to open an olive oil business and to buy more land for the farm. He was one of the many immigrants who invested in farming in their homeland and periodically returned to it, earning more money than was possible by staying in Italy. He had made seven trips back to Italy by 1929. He has a house in Atlas, the Italian neighborhood on the outskirts of Mt. Carmel. His mother's family came over first, and he helped the rest of them come. In this family the parents pushed their children to get educated. Sam's son Tony, went to Philadelphia but did not like it and came back to Atlas and worked in a construction business. Many Italians of Tony's generation worked for the owner of this business, and many others were in the craft of stone masonry. Those without craft training worked as laborers.

Many young Italians dropped out of school because their future was in the Coal Region in their parents' business, especially restaurants. Mary and Rose Procopio, said their father with his store was the most successful man in Atlas. Back in Italy in San Sostene, Calabria, he had been a shepherd boy taking his father's sheep up into the mountains. He left when he was sixteen years old in about 1905, along with everybody else. First he worked in the steel mills around Pittsburgh. But, said Mary, "one day he nearly fell over a banister into the molten steel, so that was the end of that and he came to Mt. Carmel." He joined his brother in Kulpmont and worked in the mines. A family member gave an account of the family store.

> He was almost killed in the mines too, so he said again, this is not for me, and left them and went into business. He had a grocery store and meat market. Somebody would have a cow that had a calf and he'd get it and slaughter it and they'd sell all its parts and then the skin. Little by little, he progressed to having a big store, Procopio's it was called. It was a general store that sold everything: clothes, supplies, dry goods, a meat market and grocery. He came

from Italy about 1905 and by 1920 he had this big store. He did it pretty much on his own. All he had was our Abby and our Bel to help. It was a busy, busy store. I was a clerk in that store at eleven years old. He built more buildings in the 1930s and 1940s and he was always in debt. He knew how to borrow here and there. He had ten children.

The Procopios were an example in Mt. Carmel matching Glazer and Moynihan's observation in New York City that despite the peasant background, lack of commercial experience and educational limitations, the first generation of Italian immigrants showed a strong proclivity for business enterprise (Glazer and Moynihan 1963, 206).

An Italian winemaker and wine connoisseur in Shamokin used to have his own vineyard and showed me a fine collection of wines in his basement. He is a member of a typical large family, who stay in touch with the family remaining in Italy.

My mother's father came from Ischa and he brought all his daughters and a son here to Kulpmont. They are all buried up in Kulpmont cemetery. My Dad and a couple of his brothers came from Rome [he does not know what they did]. Two stayed but one went back. I've been to Sicily and twelve times to Rome. I have lots of cousins there. My Dad worked in Trevorton in the mines and got married to my mother there. I've been making wine since 1952, and I'm known as a winemaker. Last year in Kulpmont, we had a *soupie* (a hard, flat, Italian sausage) contest, a pasta contest, and a wine contest. At the end they put it all out to be eaten free. We had twenty two bottles of wine to be judged.

Many Italians in the towns had a big vat for stomping grapes. The juice would run out and fill as many as twenty two barrels. The grapes used to come from California and they would get a whole truckload of them for $100 and put them down in their cellars. All Italians liked to make wine, were they wealthy or poor, as recounted by one from a poor family:

Italian neighbors would get together to make wine. All the men in the neighborhood would put their money together to make the wine. When Pop died, I used to make wine with Mom. These are continuing traditions, people still make wine. My father and mother would have a little glass with every meal even though they were poor and we lived on beans, *pasta vazou* (beans, spaghetti and tomato sauce) twice a week, and my Mom's homemade bread. We made our own pizza. My Mom would make wedding soup for special occasions. But nobody is poor now like we were.

As they grew older, children of Italian immigrants were brought to look on their old neighborhoods and institutions with disdain and it was left to the generation coming of age in the 1960s to revive interest in ethnic origins and traditions (Nelli 1980, 545, 554).[23] Very few of the second, third, or fourth generation of Italians still have the language (Grifo and Noto 1990, 18). It is a pattern that is repeated in Shamokin/Coal Township, but nevertheless there is a strong sense of identity among Italians in the town focused on family and foods.

To make some broad comparisons of these Catholic ethnic groups, those from Eastern Europe have in common an historical background of shifting national boundaries from a long history of conflicts in their home countries and between nations in Eastern Europe, resulting in varying degrees of economic deprivation, political oppression and national loyalty. People migrated in the hope of improving the conditions of their lives and those of their descendants. The continuing independent existence of the Ukrainian church in Shamokin/Coal Township has strengthened and maintained the traditions of the Ukrainian community based upon it, and made it the most identifiable ethnic community in the town today. They have retained a strong sense of the regional identity of their home country while taking up a national identity and referring to themselves as Ukrainians. The history of the Lithuanian people and their struggle to establish their independence from neighboring powers in the last century has involved Lithuanians within and outside the country in its political affairs to a greater degree than either the Ukrainians or the Poles, giving them an earlier and stronger sense of national identity. This appears to be a factor in their greater insistence on cultural exclusiveness in the past than is found in the other groups. Both the Lithuanians and the Poles have been able to participate more directly in getting aid to their home countries and their relatives there than have the Ukrainians; the reason seemingly the destruction of the Ukraine by Stalin.

As shown above, the three Eastern European groups whose borders have continually shifted in the course of history, share many cultural similarities. All groups utilized family ties in the migration process, but the Poles could also draw on the more extensive *rodaki* ties of membership of a group of villages. The Southern Europeans were not recently colonized by other countries as were the Eastern Europeans, but were exploited in somewhat similar fashion by the northern part of the country. The Italians, in the three towns of Shamokin/Coal Township, Mt. Carmel and Kulpmont, are distinguished particularly in that almost all came from just two small towns. The Poles relied on *rodaki* ties to help in the process of migration which similarly resulted in a concentration in these towns of people from four village groups in Poland. And the Welsh family in chapter 2 came over together in a group from the town of Aberdare in South Wales. The frequent rate of return and investment in their farms in Italy seems to make Italian migration more of a search for opportunity than that of the Poles, Lithuanians and Ukrainians, for all of whom escaping economic hardship and political oppression were the dominant motives.

The language spoken by each group and all the religious and family celebrations, festivals and parades, the traditional special foods, the clubs and associations, and the music, arts and crafts all manifested the strong ethnicity of different groups in this period of the town's history.

The Depression of 1929 reduced the immigrant flow, and in 1934 Congress introduced the quota system to restrict immigration, which diminished it further. In 1945, at the end of World War II, Eastern European immigration was to resume with a wave of displaced persons and war refugees (Morawska 1995, 97–101). "When coal was king," as people would say, during the rise of the coal industry and during its peak years, ethnic and religious identity located individuals in the social and economic hierarchy of Shamokin/Coal Township, as it did also in Kulpmont and Mt. Carmel. The importance of religion in the towns in manifesting and sustaining ethnicity, and the intersection of ethnicity and religion with class in the power structure of the towns during this time is the subject of the next chapter.

Notes

1. Taras Shevchenko (1814–1861) was Ukraine's most famous poet who was exiled to Siberia by the Tsarist regime.
2. Data for all four groups was researched by Leonard Oszko.
3. It was named after a Polish hero at the time of the Ottoman Empire, who rescued Vienna from the Turks.
4. Ann Wargo, St. Clair, February 22, 2006.
5. Lithuanian national parishes besides Shenandoah in the Diocese of Allentown were founded in Mahanoy City in 1880, Minersville and New Philadelphia in 1895, Maizeville and Girardville in 1907, Tamaqua in 1911, St. Clair in 1912, Coaldale in 1914, Easton in 1916, and Frackville in 1917 (*Catholic Standard and Times*, August 11, 1983).
6. Robert Wislock June 26, 2003.
7. Ed Narcavage, Mt. Carmel, April 21, 2003, quoted by permission of his widow, Marie Narcavage.
8. Robert Wislock, June 26, 2003.
9. Printed with the permission of Anne Wargo, St. Clair.
10. Estimates given by other people ranged from 30,000–150,000.
11. With thanks to George Pollyniak for permission to publish these three photos, figures 3.5, 3.6, and 3.7.

12. These Eastern Byzantine Slavonic Rite Catholics are part of the Roman Catholic Church and recognize the Pope as head of the church. The rite of the Mass differs slightly from that of the Western Latin Rite and uses Old Slavonic and Ukrainian in the liturgy. In the 9th century, Sts. Cyril and Methodius, founders of Slavonic literary culture, were missionaries to the Slavs in Moravia. Harassed by the German bishops, they were however welcomed by the Popes in Rome who approved the Slavonic liturgy and supported their missionary activities.

13. Going over to the Ukraine to visit, some Coal Region Ukrainians were able to find the same names in the villages of origin that were found in particular communities over here. But not others: one woman whose parents immigrated to the US, tried unsuccessfully to find records of the ship on which they arrived, and then her brother, who was in the service, went to Ukraine and found the location of their hometown, but there was nothing there, it no longer existed.

14. Monsignor Fedorovich, January 16, 2002. Some years after my research finished, I learned that the school had had to close.

15. The *Souvenir Booklet of the 75th Anniversary of the Transfiguration of Our Lord*, put out by the Ukrainian Catholic Church, Shamokin, 1884–1959, gives details of these and other associations.

16. Msgr. Fedorovich, November 10, 2005.

17. George Pollyniak, February 13, 2002.

18. George Pollyniak, October 23, 2003.

19. In 1897, *padroni* controlled an estimated two thirds of Italian labor in New York, at a time when they made up about three quarters of building labor in the city (Glazer and Moynihan 1963, 190).

20. 60–70 percent, Hugh A. Jones, local historian, Mt. Carmel, said that two families came first, and then the others rapidly followed, March 16, 2003.

21. The Tyrol on the extreme northern border of Italy was ceded to Austria by Italy after World War I. The Tyrolesi looked down on the Calabresi from southern Italy and at first there were no Calabrisi in the church. However, it was later taken over by these Southern Italians as their numbers greatly increased (Hugh A. Jones, March 16, 2003).

22. Shirley Persing, February 30, 2003.

23. In the West End of Boston at the beginning of this decade, Herbert Gans found that acculturation had almost eroded Italian cultural patterns among the second generation, and was likely to erase the remainder among the third (Gans 1962, 34).

CHAPTER FOUR

Religion, Class, and Ethnicity

The last two chapters described the development of ethnic enclaves and the strong ethnicity that dominated life in the town in the late eighteenth and early nineteenth century, the era which people speak of as the time when coal was king because the industry so dominated the town. This chapter looks at the ways ethnicity converged with religion and class in this period of the town's history. During this time the most intense division seems to have been religious rather than ethnic, and to have existed most bitterly between Catholics and Protestants. It did not fade until the 1950s and early 1960s, and was linked to a class structure in which Protestants of primarily German, Welsh, Scottish or English ancestry ran the town and owned and operated the mines; Jews primarily from Russia and Poland dominated in the small merchant class; and Catholic immigrants, first from Ireland and later from Eastern and Southern European countries, made up the laboring class that worked in the mines.[1]

These local religious and class differences were the basis for the relations of power and inequality that affected the process of ethnicity in these early years. In this period, religion, ethnicity and class mapped the town's neighborhoods and even its cemeteries. Connections forged by relations of kinship, marriage, business partnerships and employment between the prominent families of the dominant class consolidated this class and formed its internal structure.[2] The use of nicknames, long widespread in Shamokin/Coal Township, featuring ethnic, religious, or class stereotypes both in the past and today, contributed to notions of otherness that reinforced relations of power and inequality between the people of the town.

An internal structure existed also for the working class of the town, different in nature from that of the dominant class. It consisted of an economic system in the mining communities that functioned through an exchange of favors based on relations of mutual help and the exchange of goods and services. An account of this "economy of favors" and its connections to the early ethnic associations and to the politics of the town completes the chapter.

Religion: The Great Divide

As neighborhood communities grew, they organized religious congregations. In the nineteenth century, the Catholic Church in the United States established specific ethnic parishes to fill the needs of non-English speaking newcomers and to help them to adjust to their new country and be able to use their own languages in church outside of the Latin of the mass. In Coal Township, primarily inhabited by the different groups who formed the laboring class of mine workers, the Irish, Poles, Lithuanians, Ukrainians, and Italians, once their groups were large enough, founded, built, and attended their own churches in the neighborhoods they had formed. These churches were seen and referred to in the town as the ethnic churches, even though over time the reality of membership was not so strictly defined. Essentially, they were churches set up for the particular immigrant communities living near them. "Most of our Protestant churches were not ethnics. It was basically the Catholic ones that were."[3] Language was the distinguishing feature of an ethnic church for the people of the town. The Lutheran churches initially using German were consequently considered ethnic despite not being Catholic, as were the Welsh churches which used to have services in Welsh in the early years, and still use it at the annual hymn singing festival.

The churches organized the life of neighborhood communities and were an important feature in the consolidation of ethnic groups. The golden cupolas of the Ukrainian Catholic and Russian Orthodox Christian churches that shine over the majority of coal region towns surmount churches built with the small contributions and the labor of the miners themselves; they are an extraordinary witness to the importance of religion in these early mining communities. A Ukrainian scholar of Ukrainian immigrant communities emphasizes the carry-over of the importance of religion from the rural homeland villages back in Europe to the Coal Region towns; the point he is making applies to other Eastern Europeans as well as to Ukrainians.

> In the European homeland, religion was an integral part of existence, especially at the village level, where church-related functions were embedded in many commonplace activities and daily occupations. . . . It was inevitable that Ukrainian immigrants would try to recreate this religion-oriented environ-

ment in their new homeland. Characteristically, the church was one of the first buildings constructed and it became the focal point in immigrant communities (Magocsi 1979, 9).

The Churches and Synagogues

Members of the seven ethnic Catholic churches built in the less affluent neighborhoods of Coal Township were not included in the nineteenth and early twentieth century elite. All these churches had parochial schools. They are listed in the sesquicentennial booklet of 1939. Details are given in the box below.

Although accurate comparison is difficult and religion everywhere in the nation seems stronger in its observance in the nineteenth and early twentieth centuries than today, it is the case that churches do appear to be unusually numerous in Shamokin/Coal Township. This is not unusual in Coal Region towns and reflects the importance of religion and the variety of different ethnic groups in many of the towns. Mt. Carmel for example has six churches on one block (see figure 4.1).

In the early years, in Mt. Carmel, there were two Polish churches in the town founded for congregations of different class backgrounds: St. Joseph's, thought of as being for upper class Poles from West Prussia and with some German influence, and Our Mother of Consolation, originally of "the real peasantry," founded by immigrants from Russian Poland and parts of Austria and Hungary that were poor areas. There were some opportunities for mobility

Ethnic Catholic Churches

St. Edward's Roman Catholic Church, the oldest church in town, combined Italian and Irish with some German Catholics.[4] It was established as a parish in 1874, with a church built in 1881. *St. Stanislaus Kostka*, the Polish Catholic Church in the East End of town, established in 1874, is the oldest Polish parish in Pennsylvania, and built its church by 1881. *St. Stephen's*, the Polish Catholic Church in the West End of town, was organized 1897 with a church a year later. *The Ukrainian Catholic Church of the Transfiguration* was organized in 1884, with a church first built in 1888 and then built again after a fire in 1904. *St. Mary's*, the Slovak Church, was organized in 1892 and a church built a year later. *St. Michael's*, the Lithuanian Church, founded 1894, built its church in 1924. *St. Joseph's* Catholic Church, founded in 1913 for German Catholics, Irish, and Italians in the West End of Coal Township, was a Parish Church, based on an area rather than an ethnic church based on ethnicity, and was founded to accommodate all Catholics in that end of town who were not Polish. The Poles attended *St. Stephen's* listed above.[5]

Figure 4.1. Street with six churches on it in Mt. Carmel

in the town, of which the Irish and German Catholics were able to take advantage. They founded Our Lady of Mt. Carmel Church, now referred to as the Irish Church but early on it was as much German as Irish.[6] Holy Cross was the Lithuanian Church in Mt. Carmel (it included Kulpmont Lithuanians too), and St. Paul's the Italian Church. In St. Clair, to the East (see figure 1.1), there are five churches in one block: Russian Orthodox, Episcopal, Ukrainian, and two Roman Catholic. Two blocks further down there is a Byzantine church, a Lutheran and a United Presbyterian one.[7]

Unlike the Catholic churches, Protestant churches were not directly founded as ethnic parishes, but some were dominated by particular ethnic groups who brought with them the particular form of Protestantism of their region in their home countries. Wealthy and powerful Protestants built the churches of the denominations with which they were associated, in the affluent neighborhoods in which they lived, which were primarily in Shamokin, but it should be noted, that there were a few later Protestant churches, especially the Evangelical ones, whose members were not drawn from among the affluent.

Shamokin's 1939 Diamond Jubilee booklet put out by the city, also listed the Protestant churches of the town. Those in the early period were all founded by Welsh, German, English, and Scots. The Welsh were Congregationalist, Methodist or Baptist; the Germans, Lutheran or Reformed Lutheran; the English, Scots, and some Germans, Episcopalian and Presbyterian. The language to be used in the services in the early churches of the

Germans and Welsh rather than English, was a disputed issue and they could be considered as ethnic churches.

Protestants were thus found at all levels of society, though the well-to-do were unevenly distributed among the different Protestant churches and some of them had a much higher membership of them. St. John's United Church of Christ was and still is the largest Protestant church in the area; it has always been very influential because of its size, money, and prestige. At its peak, in the 1920s and early 1930s, it had over 2,000 members. At that time it was called the Reformed Lutheran Church, which in Pennsylvania was primarily German.[8] As one Protestant recalled: "If you wanted to belong to the elite in Shamokin you belonged to St. John's United Church of Christ, if not you were more or less nothing. All the other United Church of Christ (UCC) churches came from it. They had all the attorneys and doctors, all the millionaires. It did not include the coal barons [of the big coal and railroad companies] because they did not live locally." The wealthy people of St. John's had made their money before the Depression, especially with family wealth from the coal mines. There were three or four families of the sort of wealth who, as one pastor put it, "if the furnace went out and you made a phone call, [they] would write you a check for $40,000 without blinking an eye." Not only did they control the purse strings but also the politics. It created a cold church of members who looked down their noses at blue collar folk. Social recognition was based on where you lived, who you knew, who you married, or who you could pick up as a patron. Blue collar folk would not go there because they did not feel welcome.

But despite its preponderance of affluent members, the Protestant-Catholic ethnic division was by no means so entrenched in this church. The reason

Protestant Churches, Some Using Welsh or German

The Welsh Congregational Church organized in 1865 and built a church in 1865; *Lincoln St. Methodist* organized in 1838, and built in 1859, with services in Welsh; and the *Welsh Baptist Church*, a congregation in 1865, built a church in 1890. The Germans of *St. Johns Reformed Lutheran* (now *United Church of Christ*) organized in 1855, and built a church in 1967, and a mission in the West End of Coal Township, *Salem Church*, in 1912; *Trinity Evangelical Lutheran* organized in 1854, built a church in 1867 and held services in German every other week; and *Trinity United Evangelical Lutheran* was built in 1869.

The English, the Scots and some Germans went to *Trinity Episcopal*, organized in 1865, with a church built in 1866 and rebuilt in 1890, and to *First Presbyterian* organized in 1845. (Sesquicentennial Booklet 1939)

gives an interesting glimpse of the process of social change and how the actions and attitudes of individuals bring it about. St. John's had a very ecumenical, much revered priest, Rev. Schneder (1891–1931). Catholic/Protestant couples whom the Catholic Church would not marry would come to him and he would marry them and they would usually end up coming to St. John's. A parish administrator gave details.

> He had a deep friendship with the Catholic priest at St. Edward's, and I think they opened a lot of doors for people who thought Catholic and Protestant couldn't be friends. He looked at things very differently and wasn't narrow-minded by any means, and he welcomed everyone and all. . . . We worshipped a little differently. We weren't taught that we couldn't be friends or couldn't hang around together. . . . The first time I experienced it was when I was working at Knoebel's and there was a girl working there, who said I was the first Protestant friend she ever had, because she was taught Protestants were going to hell.[9]

Being a haven for intermarriage between Catholic and Protestant and between different ethnic groups made a difference in the ethnic makeup of St. John's membership. According to the interim pastor:

> If you look at the roster today, most German Reformed churches have a listing of people with very German names. St. John's doesn't. We probably have more Welsh, Russian and Polish names than we do German, and we have an amazing amount of people with Italian names. That is simply because our theology said you were a Christian first and Reformed second. If you considered yourself to be a Christian the doors were opened at St. John's for you. One of the things that contributed to St. John's in those days was that if you weren't wanted somewhere else, you could come here.

The intense disapproval of religious and ethnic intermarriage has gradually faded. Today, it is finally gone and people say you can marry whom you please. But the rich people have also gone with the change in the local economy and the congregation must find others to take their place.

The more educated and professional people have tended to be in the more mainline Protestant denominational churches, the blue collar people to be more non-mainline denominational, like the Evangelical churches and especially the outlying rural churches. According to a Protestant pastor, broadly speaking, members of the Christian Missionary Alliance, Calvary Bible Church, and Assembly of God were originally less affluent. They have tended to be the younger churches with younger rather than well-established families. Other older Protestant churches are the Independent Baptist Church on Lincoln St. in the Academy Hill area, Trinity Evangelical, and St. John's United Methodist. The latter has a lot of people in the educational field, some in social work, some in prison work, but basically not doctors, lawyers, and high end professionals. They have some of the elite, but not so many as did St. John's, which had not only wealthy members but politicians like the men of the Lark family in the twentieth century, who took them into the county arena. The First Methodist, the Lutheran and Episcopal churches also have more elite members. Evangelical United Brethren merged with the Methodist Churches in the 1950s and became the United Methodist Church, but it was not traumatic because the change was only in name.

There were no Protestant churches on the East End, but the West End of Coal Township was much more diverse. It was newer and had two Catholic and two Protestant churches that are relatively young. The East End had all the ethnic Catholic churches (listed above); Brady (or Ranshaw as it is now called) to the east had United Methodist and Catholic; Tharptown, near the hospital, in the northwest section of the town, had United Methodist and was Protestant. There was more intermarriage and mingling in the West End than in the East.[10]

There were two synagogues: one in Shamokin and one in Mt. Carmel. B'nai Israel Congregation was organized in Shamokin in 1887, by Charter 1903, and its synagogue built in 1923 on Sunbury Street. Anti-Semitism existed in these towns, but was said by some to be minor compared to the extreme prejudice that existed against Catholics among Protestants. The Jewish community was dominant among the city merchants, although it was always small; it also included professional people and the factory owners of the garment trade when it moved down to the town in the late 1920s. At its peak in the 1930s and 1940s, it consisted of 90 families, but the community became depleted when retail stores were put out of business by the malls and the young left for jobs elsewhere. Older people retired to Florida or died, and by 2002 the community was down to five families, plus a few single people, and was lucky to have a *minyan* of ten men, a ritually legal congregation; the synagogue closed a couple of years later.

Maintaining the Divide

Two accounts of childhood show how the Catholic-Protestant religious divide was internalized in childhood. The first is of a Catholic deacon born and raised in Shamokin of Irish-Slovak ancestry, who attended twelve years of Catholic parochial school:

> I lived within an Irish Catholic ghetto. I went to school there, I went to church there across the street, and I was an altar boy. We had a Boy Scouts group and a youth group. But my whole social life until I graduated from high school was more or less confined to our own Catholic environment. We never talked about the Protestants in our community; it wasn't in our radar space. When I was going to school, I thought all Catholics were Democrats and all Protestants Republicans. I just thought that's the way it was. I thought all Irish were Catholic; the

> good sisters in school never told me about the six counties of Northern Ireland. When I came of voting age, I automatically became a Democrat.

But, he says, he never developed an appreciation of ethnic foods or traditions, nor, it seemed, of the ethnic identity that went with them; his religion provided the parameters of his existence.

The second account, by a Protestant, speaks of the same sort of religious segregation:

> I was a Protestant kid who grew up in Mt. Carmel and strangely had all Protestant friends, at least in Elementary School. The reason was that your parents organized it that way. You didn't realize that but that is how it happened, that those were the people who you hung around with. All of my friends, exclusively, when I was in Elementary School, were Protestant: the families in the same religion pretty much stuck together. . . . If you were from a Protestant family, you probably bought all your clothes from a Protestant clothier and had your hair cut by a Protestant barber. And at the end of life you were buried by a Protestant funeral director; you tried to cover all bases within your religion.

For the Jewish community, the synagogue was the center of activity. Here adults and children formed their friendships at numerous celebratory events and meetings for holidays and organizational purposes. Hebrew lessons were given for boys preparing for Bar Mitzvahs, and, in later years, for girls preparing for Bat Mitzvahs, and children of all ages got their religious schooling. Wednesdays and Sundays were days when relatives visited from Philadelphia and New York.

High school was a different matter. The mixing up of children of different ethnic backgrounds took place at this level when Coal Township and Shamokin School Districts were merged in 1965. There is a Catholic High School, Our Lady of Lourdes, as well as the public High School. But all children were raised with a strong taboo on marriage outside one's religion and ethnic group. One Protestant remembers his grandmother telling him: "Don't go out with any of those Catholic girls." A Protestant who wanted to date a Jewish girl as late as the 1950s met with strong objections from his parents, her parents, teachers, and friends: "You just don't DO that," he was told by his parents. Another youth from a prominent Catholic family did nevertheless date a Jewish girl for a long time, but the relationship was really discouraged by his parents and it finally ended.

Intermarriage did happen, as our case histories show, but it was very strongly disapproved in the early years. The sort of conflict this could produce for a child from a mixed marriage is encapsulated in a description of what it was like for a small boy with a German/Welsh mother and an Irish Catholic father who went to private school.

> Every Wednesday you went to whatever church you went to for religious instruction. Now, I go there, and the nuns are there and my first big problem is my name. My name is Frank, not Francis, I was named after the one and only Frank [his maternal grandfather], whom my mother idolized. I was not named after St. Francis of Assisi. And when I got there they called me Francis, and I said my name is not Francis, it is Frank. Now all of a sudden I am talking back to the nun and I have to go to the back of the room. I was only 3rd or 4th grade. Then there was the theory that there were two buses on the highway to Heaven and the Catholics were in this bus, and it's OK for all the Catholics thinking, yeah I'm on this bus, and I'm thinking, where's my Mom? Where's my Granma, where are they? You mean to tell me that Dennis' Mom is going to get up there and my Mom isn't? No way. I mean I had issues.

Intermarriage has now greatly reduced the great Catholic-Protestant divide. The barriers to religious intermarriage lasted until the 1960s but were really gone by the latter half of the 1970s. Their disappearance was accelerated because grade schools were consolidated during this time so that children of different ethnicities and religions were all mixed up instead of going to their separate ethnic parochial schools. In Shamokin, the Ukrainian school remained the only ethnic parochial church school. The others were closed at various times and in 1985 were consolidated into one, Queen of Peace, for all Catholic children from the churches of the Harrisburg diocese.

Transfiguration Ukrainian Catholic Church is in the diocese of Pittsburgh.[11] The first Ukrainian parochial school in the United States, it was established in Shamokin in 1894. Until about 1980, it used to teach the Ukrainian language, history and culture, but after that lacked a qualified teacher. The school had about 130 children, kindergarten to eighth grade, but about two thirds of them were not members of the parish. In 2002, fees were $900 a year for parishioners and $1,000 for non-parishioners. It had an excellent reputation with young and committed teachers and small classes; its graduates, often valedictorians[12] at the high school, doing very well at getting college scholarships.

Neighborhood Communities

A Religious, Class, and Ethnic Map

The religious, class and ethnic divisions of Shamokin/Coal Township used to be mapped out in its neighborhoods: "Formerly (I'm going back fifty or sixty years), if you gave me someone's name in Shamokin or Coal Township, I could tell you where they lived"[13] (see figure 4.2).

As people settled in the town and the surrounding coal patches, the social divisions among them came to be reflected in the neighborhoods in which

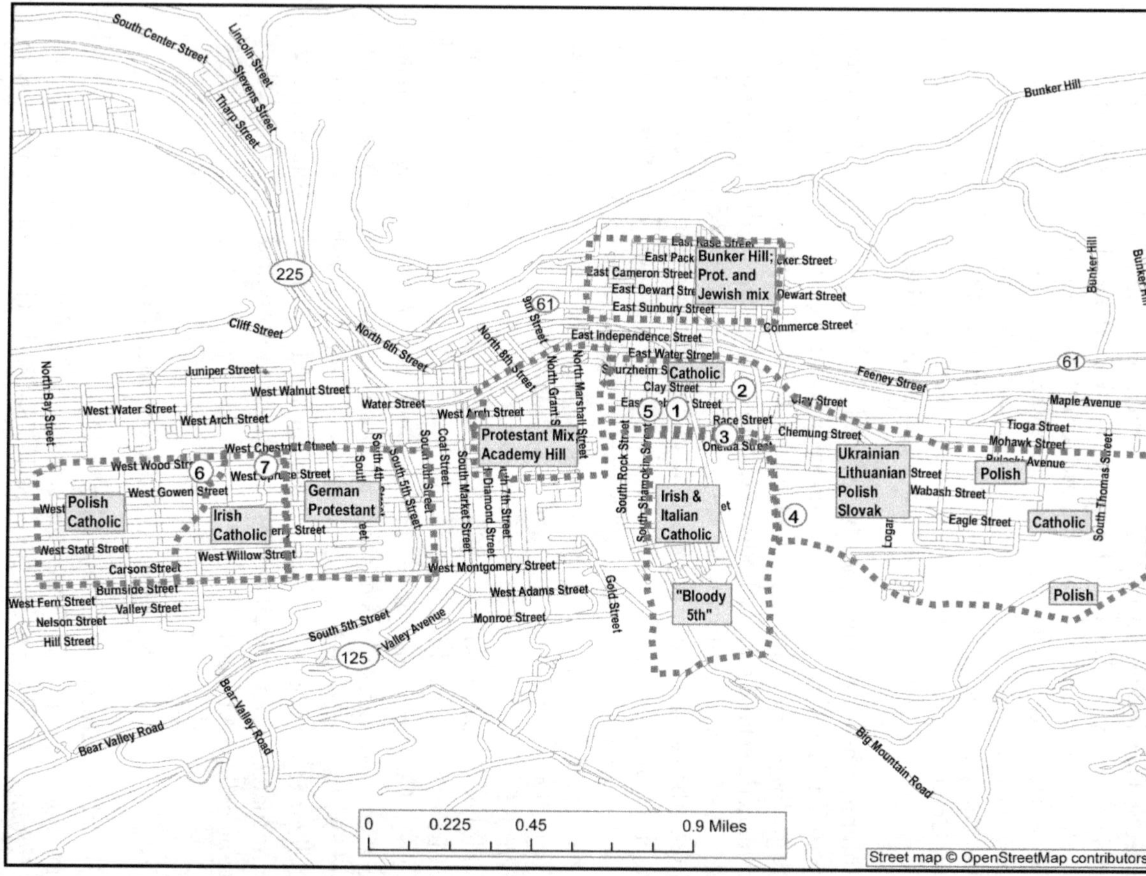

Figure 4.2. Map of Ethnic Groups and Neighborhoods of the Town up to the 1960s. Drawn by Janet MacGaffey, Neil MacGaffey, and George Gerstein

Key to Figure 4.2—Location of Churches and Synagogue

Catholic Churches

(1) *Transfiguration—Ukrainian*, Clay and Franklin Sts.
(2) *Saint Mary's—Slovak*, Clay and Vine Sts.
(3) *Saint Stanislaus—Polish*, Race and Vine Sts.
(4) *Saint Michael's—Lithuanian*, Hemlock and Cherry Sts.
(5) *Saint Edwards—Irish & Italian*, Shamokin and Webster Sts.

WEST END:
(6) *Saint Steven's—Polish*, Chestnut and Oak Sts.
(7) *Saint Joseph's—Irish*, Chestnut and 1st Sts.

Protestant Churches

Holy Trinity Episcopal, 150 E. Lincoln St., Academy Hill
Grace Lutheran, 7th and Chestnut Sts., Academy Hill
Trinity Evangelical Lutheran, 65 East Sunbury St., Bunker Hill
First Presbyterian Church, Liberty and Sunbury Sts., Bunker Hill
Mt. Zion Congregational, Welsh. Grant and Church Sts., Academy Hill
St. John's United Church of Christ, 117 N. 8th St. Academy Hill
First United Methodist, 102 East Sunbury St., Bunker Hill
Lincoln St. Methodist. 112 East Lincoln St., Academy Hill
St. John's United Methodist, 1201 West Arch St., Academy Hill

Jewish Synagogue

B'Nai Israel Congregation, 7 East Sunbury St., Bunker Hill

they lived. Those higher in the social and economic hierarchy, coal owners and operators, mine supervisors and foremen, professional people such as lawyers, bankers and doctors, built fine houses up on some of the hills, creating the affluent neighborhoods of Shamokin. The immigrants who came to work the mines settled in the mine patches, around the collieries, and in less affluent areas of Shamokin downhill from the railroad, and of Coal Township, close to those who came from the same region, town or village of their homeland. They often started off as boarders, in time rented housing from the mine company, and some finally managed to buy their own house. In this way they built up ethnic neighborhoods and formed the clientele of the neighborhood taverns and grocery stores.

In these neighborhoods, people spoke the same language, got help obtaining housing and jobs, and built up networks of mutual help and assistance based on the trust of shared culture, values, and family and neighborhood ties. Such networks, as will be shown below, were instrumental in helping the coal miners and their families to survive the difficulties of adjusting to their new existence and to the hardships of the mining life, and also in their successful contesting of the oppression of the coal and railroad companies.

These neighborhoods were clear enough in people's minds that some were still able so many years later, to delineate their boundaries by specific streets on the city map. As one Lithuanian resident described it:

> Business people and the moneyed class, owners of companies and people high up in commerce, lived on Bunker Hill (on Packer, Cameron and Dewart Streets), there were English, Scots, some Welsh, German and Jewish (the latter especially on Dewart and Sunbury Sts.) and on Academy Hill (bounded by Marshall and Arch Streets, with Welsh concentrated around the Welsh church), which was also an elite area (see figure 4. 2). If you lived in these two sections you had to marry within the neighborhood. You could also marry into the elites of Sunbury, Pottsville, or Philadelphia. It was like a caste. The business district of downtown is in the center bounded by Sunbury St. (Route 61) on its northern side. Some of the mine owners and other people of wealth and influence (including the McConnells, McWilliams, Robertsons and Graebers) had their big houses on this street, [others had them on Bunker Hill]. The railroad, [marking a division in the town] ran parallel a block or two below Sunbury St. The Farrow and Lark families lived up on Dewart, [see the next section on politics and class] as did the Jewish factory owner Morris Fishman. In the Coal Region, the Welsh, German and English were part of the establishment. They were the moneyed class, the owners or administrator of the companies. It was the companies versus the workers in a definite antagonistic relationship. It was a distinct social relationship, if you were an owner or a company boss, you didn't shop in the same store, you didn't eat in the same place, you didn't socialize, you didn't do any of that stuff together, you did it separately, and you lived in separate areas of this little town, which wasn't so little then.[14]

You did not, if you were an immigrant, go up on Academy or Bunker Hill. As the map shows, there were no Catholic churches up in these two neighborhoods; they were in the 5th Ward and the West and East ends of the town. There were four Protestant churches on Bunker Hill, four on Academy Hill, and the synagogue was on Sunbury Street on Bunker Hill.

The Italians said that Italians had never had the opportunity to be counted among the wealthy local families. They named a few who had made good money in the 1940s and 1950s, but in independent mining, in making whisky, or in running a tavern. The "greenies" (immigrants who worked in the mines) lived downhill from Bunker Hill and Academy Hill. "Don't cross the tracks" was the idea. "When there were strong ethnic backgrounds, the people stuck together and formed an alliance that was strictly 'if you do something wrong to one of us you are going to hear from all of us.' It was a sort of unwritten law. If you did not fit in, you were an outcast in some places."

East of Academy Hill was the 5th Ward in which lived Italian and Irish immigrants. Marion Heights, near Kulpmont, was also an Italian area. In the east end of town were Springfield and Marshalltown, Pulaski Avenue to Ranshaw at the edge. This was the Polish area: its hills were known as The Polish Poconos. They included as well as Poles some neighborhoods of Lithuanian, Ukrainian and Slovak immigrants.[15] East of Bunker Hill was a mixture. To the west of Academy Hill, it was German and Austrian, and to the west of that Irish, and then Polish (see figure 4.2). The newer homes of Edgewood Park were at the Western end of the city. The patches surrounding the town around the collieries were predominantly of different ethnic groups. Excelsior and the Big Mountain Colliery end of Shamokin was predominantly Ukrainian; Centralia was Irish; Bear Valley English and Pennsylvania German; Coal Run was Polish. The Welsh miners lived up around Germantown and Locust Dale for the Potts Colliery just before Ashland[16] (see figure 1.1).

The endogamy (marriage within the group) that sustained these neighborhoods was in some areas enforced by the proprietary attitudes of the youths of a neighborhood towards its girls. In Coal Township, the Irish-Italian "Bloody Fifth" Ward was so named up to Race St. from its reputation for violence over these and other matters. It was said that gangs with brass knuckles would hold you up and turn you back. One Lithuanian recalled walking ten blocks off the Polish Poconos into the Bloody Fifth to date his future wife, hoping he wouldn't get into a fight; another was actually beaten up by Polish guys for bringing a Polish girl back to her house in a Polish neighborhood after a date. A Ukrainian recalls his father walking to work along the rail tracks and having his lunch pail taken by the Polish and Irish living along the tracks. This ethnic rivalry and hostility lasted until the early twenties. It was easier for the Ukrainians after they got their church: "People mingled as a group instead of as single persons. It was tough until then."[17] This comment underscores the role of the churches in structuring communities.

In Kulpmont also ethnic neighborhoods were clearly demarcated by streets: "There was hostility between ethnic factions. Children had to keep to their home neighborhood: they could get beaten up if they strayed over boundaries . . . parents wanted their children to play together so that they would not marry out."[18] In Mt. Carmel ethnic blocks existed but are said not to have formed such well-defined neighborhoods as in Shamokin/Coal Township.

Cemeteries

"They remained divided even in death:"[19] Ethnic and religious divisions of the past and other social distinctions are as clearly marked in cemeteries as they were in neighborhoods. Shamokin Protestant cemetery has a big section of English, Welsh and German graves. They include tombs of eminent citizens from the past such as Charles Helfenstein and David Llewellyn, big coal owners, and the Shroyer family, owners of a garment factory. There are specific areas for other social distinctions: war graves form circles around a large tree at the side of the cemetery, with parts of the circles for each war, starting with the Civil War; there is another area on a different side for the poor who could not afford plots. St. Edward's cemetery, the oldest ethnic Catholic cemetery, is Irish, Italian, and has a large section of Polish names only. Transfiguration Ukrainian Catholic Church cemetery has a fence around it, gates to enter it by, and has all Ukrainian names on the graves, with three-barred Ukrainian crosses on most of them (see figure 4.3). The Jewish cemetery is fenced, with a graceful cast iron arch over the gate saying B'nai Israel, and tombstones engraved in Hebrew (see figure 4.4).

Cemeteries seem to be anchors of identity in the Coal Region. When parents die and the family home (referred to as "the homestead") is sold, families who have moved away no longer return so much for ethnic festivals

Figure 4.3. The Ukrainian Cemetery in Shamokin

Figure 4.4. The Jewish Cemetery in Shamokin

and family celebrations, but they do return to visit family graves in the cemetery. Yvonne Milspaw reports similar ethnic segregation in the cemetery of the mill town of Steelton, Pennsylvania, (east of Harrisburg) commenting: "For the residents of Steelton, separation was a way of life and of death." Both Steelton and Shamokin/Coal Township have the park-like atmosphere of nineteenth century rural cemeteries, with shade trees, paths and careful upkeep, and the same centrality of the German and English section with "the ethnics" at the back and edges. "And thus the landscape of an early twentieth cemetery emerges with ethnic, racial and religious separation as its major premise" (Milspaw 1980, 38.)

In Minersville, one climbs up the steep grassy slope of a cemetery in the town, where the forsythia blooms in spring and there is a view across to the blue, gold-starred onion dome of the Ukrainian church on the main street. Here are row upon row of Irish graves from the second half of the nineteenth century. The inscriptions are blurred with age but the names can be made out and frequently also the parish and county of origin in Ireland: O'Connor, Shannon, Murphy, Reilly, Flanagan, O'Neill, Brennan, Kennedy, O'Brien, Donohoe, and many first names are Patrick or Bridget. Many of the men died in their twenties, doubtless many of them in mine accidents. Newer graves contrast with other ethnic names at the bottom of the slope. On the other side of town is a big disused cemetery. Here there are many Welsh names, with dates on the graves from the same early period: Williams, Davies, Morgan, Lewis, Edmunds, Evans, sometimes specifying South Wales where miners were recruited, or sometimes a southern county of Wales like Glamorgan or Monmouthshire.

In Locust Gap near Shamokin, St. Joseph's cemetery is mainly Irish Catholic. Though the church now belongs to a Protestant congregation, many of the names are Irish, but of people born in the late nineteenth century who died in the mid-twentieth, later than in the Minersville cemetery. These cemeteries reflect the early predominance of Irish mine laborers in Minersville in the early years of the mines, and the later dominance of the Irish in Locust Gap (McCafferty 1929).

Newer cemeteries are not divided ethnically, reflecting the decreased significance of ethnicity in town life by the late twentieth century. The new Catholic All Saints' Cemetery for Mt. Carmel, Kulpmont and Shamokin at Bear Gap is on the road to Elysburg. Protestant ones are the new Odd fellows' cemetery for Shamokin on the road to Trevorton, similar to All Saints but commercial, with many flags scattered through it to indicate veterans' graves, and one passes a new Protestant cemetery for Northumberland County on the way to Sunbury. Funeral directors however still operate for the great majority of their funerals, though not exclusively, within religious and ethnic divisions: "That is still very clearly defined" according to a Protestant pastor, who says that nine out of ten of funerals of members of his church are with Farrow's. The Farrow's Funeral Home, family owned since 1876, serves Protestants; James Kelley Jr.'s, Irish Catholics; C. J. Lucas, family owned since 1891 and with branches in Kulpmont and Mt. Carmel, other Catholics; and Stephen A. Chowka takes Catholics from Transfiguration Church and the Orthodox Church (from the church in Mt. Carmel).

These ethnic differences have been both reinforced and resisted by various constructions of otherness.

Constructions of Others: Stereotypes and Nicknames

Stereotypes can play a significant role in everyday life. The use of stereotyping, either of the national self or some despised "other," acts as a basis for both contesting and reproducing power relations at the local level (Herzfeld 1997, 158–60). This function fits the prevalent and frequent use of nicknames in the Coal Region, which often take the form of ethnic stereotypes. *Guinea*, *dago*, *wop* are all ways to refer to Italians; *cucumber* and *toad/jugie* refer to Lithuanians because in northern Europe they used to grow cucumbers and often lived in marshy country with lots of toads and frogs; "*honky/hunkies*" refers to Poles, Russians, and Ukrainians; and "*yonko*" means someone of any

Eastern European descent. Depending on the context, these nicknames both reinforce the power structure and resist it: when used among themselves by members of an ethnic group, they express unity and strength in opposition and resistance to outsiders;[20] when used by anyone else, they are considered insults and are a way of putting people down and reinforcing the ethnic hierarchy. Similarly, "coal cracker" a term for the people of the Coal Region as a whole, when used by the people of the region among themselves expresses their unity against the rest of society, but when used by an outsider, it is insulting.

An excerpt from the transcript of a discussion among a group gathered to discuss the town with me[21] shows that nicknames for particular nationalities can be perfectly acceptable, or offensive and insulting, depending on the situation.

> *Frank*, a Pole: "When you are asked what [nationality] you are . . . you may very well use a slang word. If you would call someone a *wop* somewhere else, then that would be very bad.
>
> *Dave*, a Lithuanian: "Between Lithuanians, if you would say you're a toad, that's OK between me and you, but if he (Frank) calls me a toad that is really insulting. That's a bad name for Lithuanians. A guy I knew in Kulpmont made the comment once: "every guinea in Kulpmont will be mad at me." We can call each other "Guineas," "wops," "dagos," "toads," "honkies," and "Coal Crackers" [and it is not insulting]. But if you (an outsider) would call someone a Coal Cracker, you would have Lithuanian, Polish, Italian, arm-in-arm walking together fighting you. Once you get that whole brew and call them Coal Crackers, you've got the bigger umbrella. Coal Cracker to us signifies hard-working, trustworthy, loyal. If I say Frank's a Coal Cracker and need him to be there at 8 a.m. one morning, he'll be there." But used by outsiders Coal Cracker can have a very derogatory connotation. "Things did not calm down in terms of religious and ethnic rivalries until the late 1950s and early 1960s."

Rivalry in the form of interethnic hostility was shown in violent reactions to interethnic dating and to strike breaking. Ethnic nicknames were used to express resentments between ethnic groups in the struggle of organized labor to improve working conditions, described in the next chapter. In the early years, union organizers were hostile to Italians because they were strike breakers. Some strikes were defeated in Pennsylvania in the 1870s and early 1880s when employers recruited Slavic, Hungarian and Italian workers to work in the mines in order to defeat the striking miners of different ethnic origin. This angered the strikers who maligned and stereotyped Slavs in general as Honkies, and Italians as Wops. The following example shows how Italian children in the public schools, who were Catholic, suffered the prejudices of Protestant teachers and were also tormented by their school mates whose fathers were on strike or sympathizing with the strikers. Further details of the life account of an Italian Catholic from a poor Italian family begun in chapter 3 show how it felt to experience this ethnic hostility. The story shows how the shame of being labeled by these ethnic stereotyping nicknames contributed to the loss of their language among Italians, in a desire to distance themselves from their heritage and even to actively feel ashamed of it.

> When we were growing up my mother spoke Italian, and so did my father and my aunt. But my mother went to school when she was working in the factory: they had a school for young girls (employees) and she learned English. I had to talk to my grandmother and my family in Italian. But I was ashamed of it because when I went out, if I was with my mother and talked Italian, the kids would make fun of me and call me a "wop." In the playground, they'd call Italians "spaghetti benders." Today I can understand Italian but I can't speak it. I was ashamed I was Italian. I was ashamed to go shopping with my grandmother because she couldn't speak English. I'd speak to my grandmother in English and she'd get mad at me. I had to get away from that.

She married and went to live with her husband out west for some years before eventually returning to Shamokin/Coal Township.

This painful example of the hostile use of ethnic nicknames between members of different ethnic groups had the consequence in this case that an Italian heritage was felt to be shameful. But connotations of ethnic nicknames were also situational. Marianne, an Italian, grew up thinking of herself as a Guinea, to her as an Italian this was a perfectly neutral term. (Italians were so called because they used to raise Guinea chickens.) Only after a family moved into the neighborhood and used it as an insult to describe an Italian small boy, did she learn that it could be derogatory.[22]

This data exemplifies the Comaroffs' comment that "the Janus-faced nature of ethnic consciousness—the fact that it involves both the assertion of a collective self and the negation of collective other/s—is a cultural expression of the structuring of inequality; it emerges as groupings come to signify and symbolize their experience of a world of asymmetrical 'we-them' relations" (Comaroff and Comaroff 1992, 56).

Prominent Families in the Coal Era

Ethnicity, religion, and class are shown to have converged in the town in the coal era. Some documentation is available for the early years of the most prominent families, of their religion and ethnicity, the sources of their wealth, the positions they held in the town and its economy, and the ways they were connected by ties of marriage, kinship, business partnership or employment. Such connections formed the internal structure of this class, giving it an inner organization that helped to maintain its boundaries.[23] The businesses owned by its members were the foundation of the town's economy and the source of the wealth and power that were the basis of their dominant position. The significance of connections formed by business partnerships and between employer and employee in Shamokin/Coal Township, is expressed in a comment by a lawyer who is also a local historian: "If you were in business, you generally took care of the people that did business with you. . . . You first took care of your own ethnic group and your own religion. But then you also took care of people who did business with you."[24]

Women did not hold overt power in the economic and political system at this time. Their power came from being members of powerful families, from the connections their marriages forged between these families, and from the part they played in social life and philanthropic enterprise, all of which were sources of considerable influence.[25] Ann Duffy emphasizes that: "the exercise of power is not restricted to nor does it entirely rely upon economic, political, and/or military decision making." It encompasses "the broader range of activities in which bias is mobilized, in which agendas are set, in which respectability is lent or withdrawn, and so on," and she includes the social capital women accumulated through ties of friendship and social networks (Duffy 1986, 36–38). In the Coal Region in this period, women of the dominant class were denied public political power but wielded these forms of indirect power. In their control of social life and in their civic and philanthropic activities, they could be instrumental in setting up advantageous connections for men and for women to make good marriages and to meet those who were powerful and economically important, and likewise in excluding those whom they did not favor.

As noted in the introduction, the English and Scots are not thought of as ethnic groups as are the other nationalities of the town. Both are Protestant and they speak English (the defining feature of an ethnic group for people of the town is speaking a language other than English). Dominant groups rarely define themselves as ethnic (Royce 1982, 3) and these have dominated in the national class structure since the early colonial settlement. 'British' has not been an overarching category for English, Scots, Welsh and Irish.[26] The Welsh and Irish, as chapter 2 shows, were very distinct components of the population in the early period of its history. The Protestant English and Scots belonged to Episcopal and Presbyterian Churches and the Welsh to other

Protestant denominations. The Irish immigrants to the Coal Region were primarily Catholic; they did not come from the Protestant north of Ireland. Exceptions to the Protestant dominance in religion among the prominent citizens of the time are John Mullen, an Irishman and a Catholic, whose parents were earlier immigrants who arrived in the United States in 1831 and were not fleeing famine as were those who came later in the 1840s and 1850s, and the Graebers, who were a German Catholic family among the dominant families of the town. Otherwise, Catholics were not part of this nineteenth and early twentieth century Protestant elite.

Prominent men and families in the nineteenth century appear in the diagram of figure 4.5. The data collected here, although by no means comprehensive, includes a majority of the most prominent individuals of the town's dominant class at this time.[27] It confirms that they are primarily Protestants and of German, Welsh, Scottish, or English Quaker descent. Coal, timber, and railroad companies were the greatest sources of their wealth.[28]

Figure 4.5 shows the web of connections between these individuals in their ties of business partnership or employment, marriage and kinship. Only the names of the women of these families who connected to other families by ties of marriage appear in the diagram. Such dates as are available are included: they are primarily for the nineteenth century. Broken black lines indicate business relations of employment or partnership—the former sometimes leading to the latter, == signs indicate marriage, and solid black lines indicate kin ties, between siblings or between parents and children.

Ethnicity, Religion, and Sources of Wealth of Prominent Families of the Nineteenth Century

This section gives details of the individuals shown in figure 4.5 and of the connections between them.

Kimberley Cleaver. English Quaker, mining, railroad and road engineer, and surveyor, worked for *John C. Boyd*, the founder of the town, laying it out with Quaker William H. Marshall, a developer of anthracite as a fuel. Cleaver was chief engineer for the Philadelphia-Sunbury and Shamokin to Pottsville railroads, mapped the Middle Coalfields, and surveyed Shamokin and then Trevorton. He later worked with *Judge William Helfenstein*. All of his nine children, save one daughter, died in childhood.

The German Lutheran brothers *William* and *Reuben Fagely*, came to Shamokin in 1838, started with small stores, became railroad contractors, leased coal mines, and accumulated great wealth. They worked with and formed a coal company with Kimberley Cleaver. They were pioneer businessmen in coal, commerce and real estate and were the principal employers of the

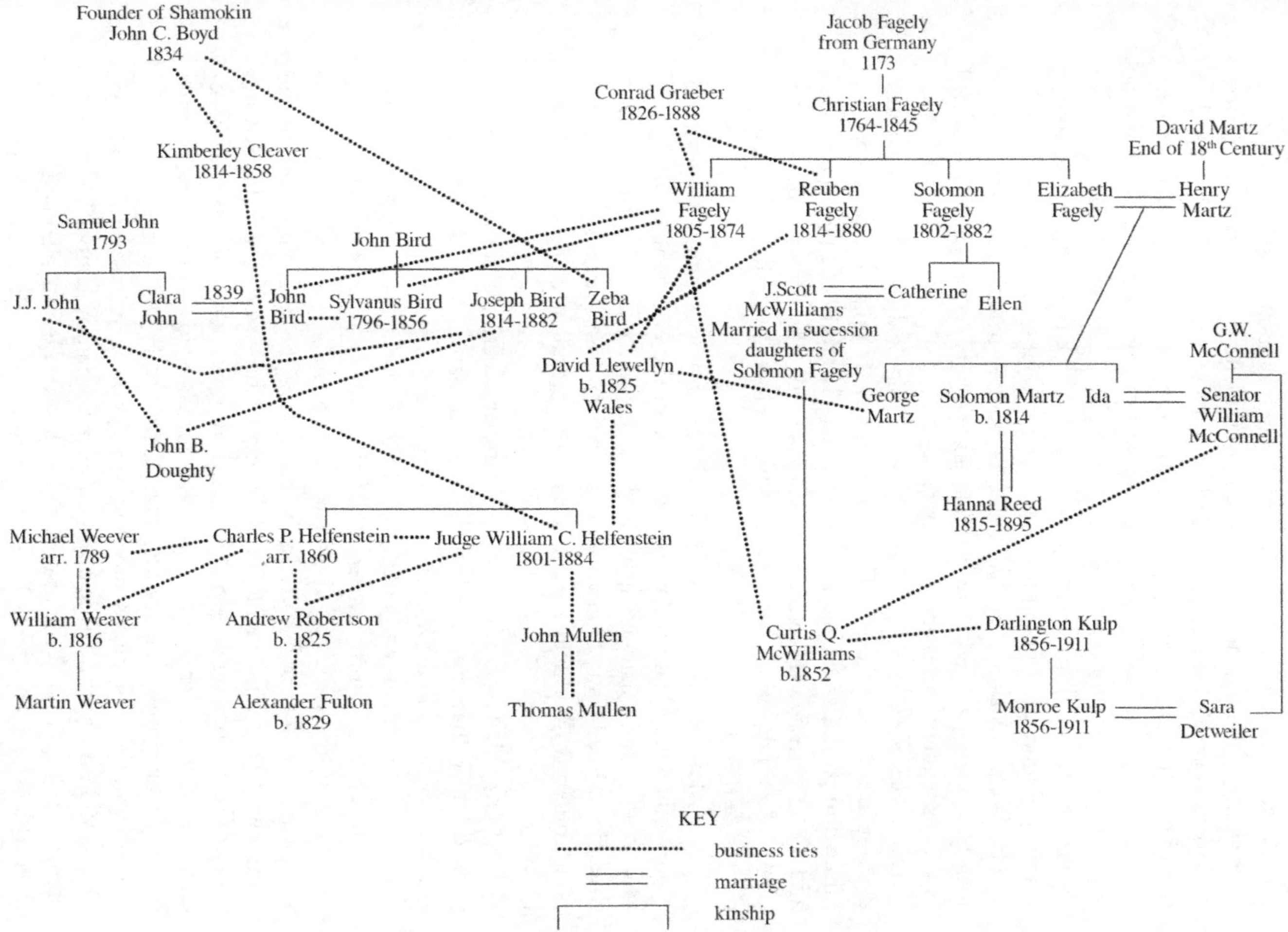

Figure 4.5. Diagram of Connections between Prominent Families in the Eighteenth Century. Redrawn by Shahzeen Nasim

town. Their influence is borne out by their many business connections with other prominent men in the community. Their economic prominence seems to have given them almost autocratic power. Neither of them ever married.

The English Bird family: *James Bird*, from New Jersey, an English Quaker, was one of the early farming pioneers. His sons were among the prominent men of the town: *Ziba*, one of the founders of the town, was the building superintendent for John Boyd in 1838, and also in charge of the family coal mining operations; *Sylvanus* and *John* worked for the Fagely brothers building many of Shamokin's houses; *Joseph* was a successful coal operator.

The Welsh Quaker *J. J. John* made his money in coal and worked with *John B. Doughty*, a Welsh Presbyterian and colliery owner, who also owned mills, department stores and real estate.

David Llewellyn, Welsh, Protestant, and a big coal owner was a wealthy pioneer of the Coal Region. Born in Wales, he immigrated, developed the mines and partnered a coal firm with the Fagely brothers. He was a banker, and along with W. Helfenstein, director of the school board, the Electric Light Co. and the Water Co. His descendants lost the family money through poor investments.

David Martz immigrated to Berks County from Germany and came to Northumberland County to farm at the end of the eighteenth century. The Martz family had a dairy company and David's son *Solomon* married *Hannah Reed* of the Reed Dairy family. *George O. Martz* was a partner in Big Mountain Colliery with David Llewellyn and the president of Bear Gap Water Company.

Curtis Q. McWilliams, a Scot and member of Trinity Lutheran Church, worked for William and Reuben Fagely, and married first *Catherine Fagely* and then, when she died, *Ellen Fagely*, both daughters of Solomon Fagely. Curtis Q. McWilliams was a partner in 1878 of *Darlington R. Kulp*, a German and a member of Trinity Lutheran Church, who was one of the largest timber dealers in the state, and also a partner to Senator *William C. McConnell*, a Scot and member of Trinity Lutheran, one of the wealthiest men in the county with both an ice and a brick business who also founded the Roaring Creek Water Company in 1884. It is still in operation today. Senator McConnell, who was for one year in President Garfield's cabinet, married *Ida Martz*, the daughter of Henry Martz and Elizabeth Fagely Martz.

Darlington Kulp's son, *Monroe Kulp*, was prominent in several local businesses, and on his father's death, took over the family lumber business (by then extending from Williamsport to Lewiston). He was a congressman in 1895–1899. He laid out the Edgewood amusement park in Coal Township and sponsored the real estate development that grew into the town of Kulpmont and was named after him.

Andrew Robertson, a Scot, was a member of Trinity Lutheran Church. He owned coal companies and was one of the coal barons, owned a mill, and was a director of utility companies.[29]

Alexander Fulton, a Scot and a Presbyterian, was a prominent coal operator, a banker and president of the Shamokin Water Company.

The *Helfenstein* brothers, German, Episcopalian, and Presbyterian, came to the town in 1850. *Judge Helfenstein* organized and invested in mines and a railroad and worked with Kimberley Cleaver. He brought in capitalists from New York, Philadelphia and Lancaster. *Charles Helfenstein* invested in lumber and real estate and was president of the Shamokin Gas Light Co. J. J. John and Andrew Robertson were also among its officers.

The *Weaver family* were German farmers for three generations. William moved to Shamokin in 1845, owned hotels, became a banker, and invested in real estate with Charles Helfenstein.

John Mullen (son of Irish immigrants of 1831) and his son *Thomas* were Catholics and partners in the Shamokin Iron Works. Their products included mining machinery. John Mullen worked with Judge Helfenstein in directing utility companies, and was president of the 1st National Bank.

The *Graeber family*, German Catholics, were wealthy in coal, banking, and the Water Company.

As these details show, employment could lead not only to partnership, but sometimes to marriage with the founder's or partner's daughter or sister. Kin ties are also significant in business relationships: they may transfer business control, expertise and useful connections from one generation to the next. Likewise, marriage ties forged connections between the prominent families of the town. This web of connections constituted the inner organization of this class: personal ties gave an advantage to those who had them over those who did not, which sustained the class boundary.

The prominent families of the nineteenth century did not continue as dynasties; as chapter 6 will show, different families ran the town by the mid-twentieth century, most notably the Lark family. This reinforces Edward J. Davies's (1985) findings that while influential families persisted over the generations in the northern coalfields they did not do so in the southern fields (see the regional context of the coal elite in chapter 1).

The working class, to which we now turn, did not live in the affluent areas of the town. People in this class also operated through networks of personal connections, but their networks were different from those that formed the inner organization of the dominant class. They lived by means of an economy in which very little money changed hands. The exchange of goods and services did not depend on money but on a system of delayed reciprocal exchange based on personal ties. The networks of personal connections developed in this economy played a significant part in the struggle of organized labor to resist and challenge the power of corporate capitalism, the subject of chapter 5.

Differences in the inner organization of the classes of this coal town are similar to the findings of John Corbin's study of Andalusia, where classes differed in the nature and extent of the personal networks of their members and these differences contributed to social inequality. He found that the social networks of the dominant class were better instruments for getting things done than were those of the subordinated class which were isolated from the system of personal influence or only had access to it through attachment to a particular member of the higher class (Corbin 1979, 108–9). The same was the case in Shamokin/Coal Township.

The Economy of Favors: A Means of Survival and Resistance for Mining Families

The miners and their families lived in an economy that was in many ways one of near self-sufficiency. It was outside the cash economy because they had access to land and to other means of supplying their needs, and they exchanged the surplus from what they obtained in a highly developed system of reciprocal exchange.[30] The networks through which this economy functioned were based on ties of kinship, friendship, neighborhood, ethnicity, and religion. An informant of John Bodnar's raised in the Depression commented that there was no such thing as welfare or public assistance but you had the help of other people: "You sort of worked in a cooperative thing" (Bodnar 1982, 70). I call this system the "economy of favors," following others who describe similar systems elsewhere.[31]

Many mine families had house plots big enough to have gardens that produced most of the family's food, those that did not leased plots further away, and all were able to graze livestock on the grass and scrub of the hills behind the town, to hunt over these hills and fish the streams, and to gather berries and nuts. The area was rugged and rough, not rich farmland as it is in West Pennsylvania. The land was owned by the coal companies, who had subsoil rights to the coal underneath. People walked all over it and pastured their animals for a small fee. Their hunting, fishing and gathering in season supplemented the food supply. Additionally, they were able to obtain fuel for cooking and to heat their houses in the winter by gleaning coal that fell off the coal train wagons along the railroad tracks or could be picked from among the rock and slate of the culm banks.

As one former miner put it: "Everyone had a garden: you had to grow vegetables in order to survive." Women and their children, helped by their men when they were not working, grew vegetables and fruit in their gardens and canned and preserved the surplus in various ways. "Producing vegetables and other food in World War II was a war effort" but, as Fritz Reed emphasized, "it had always been a strategy." Miners who lived in company housing did not own the land, but they had what was called their in-lot, the plot attached to their house, and their out-lot, land which they could lease from the coal company on the outskirts of town, where they grew much of their food.

The peasant farming way of life from which the first generation of most immigrants came, meant that people brought with them not only the desire for the foods they were used to eating but also the knowledge of how to grow them. Even if they only had a little space they would contrive to grow some favored food they had always eaten in the home country. People who did not grow their food or who only had little patches, supplemented what they produced by buying from the local German farmers, who took advantage of this market population living adjacent to their farming valleys between the coal hills.[32]

Two Italian sisters who lived in a half double in Atlas on the edge of Mt. Carmel had a garden about twelve feet by sixty-four feet, the standard size of house plots there, once the area of the house and the outhouse were subtracted, which provided a quite considerable area for cultivation. A German family in Tharptown had a lot 50 by 150 feet, of which the house took up 50 feet and they planted close to 100 x 50 feet: "We had a big garden." Yards were long and narrow "and you'd plant that with everything." People grew vegetables of all kinds: cabbage (of major importance), potatoes, tomatoes, radishes, celery, lettuce, horseradish, red beets, cucumbers, pole and string beans, peppers, corn, onions, rutabagas, kohlrabi, herbs, and carrots. They put up the surplus in jars, stored them in the root cellars found in all the old houses, or salted, dried or pickled them. They dried their own beans. Lots of people had grapevines and made wine, jam and jelly, and dried the grapes for raisins. Some grew fruit trees, peach, apple, cherry and pear trees, water melons and cantaloupes, and hops for root and birch beer. They made homemade wine from grapes, elderberries, tea berries and dandelion flowers. The surplus from what they produced, gathered, gleaned, or hunted, was used in the exchanges of the economy of favors.

The Slavs in particular survived in large measure outside the monetary economy in this way, as is indicated by the fact that the average per capita expenditures for Slavs in a store in Schuylkill County in the 1890s was \$2.86 per month, while English speakers averaged \$5.48 (Roberts 1904, 106). The Irish were accustomed to such reciprocal cooperation back in Ireland where the *meithal* was a group that cooperated in seasonal farm work. Members gave each other assistance in turn and were rewarded each time by food and drink (K. Miller 1985, 55). Such practices were widespread in other European countries also.

Families did not only grow food in their gardens, many of them also raised livestock on quite an extensive scale: one Ukrainian family always had about 100 chickens and two roosters; a Lithuanian family raised 200 to 300 poultry in a field alongside the house, in which they built pens for them, and they would sell the eggs, another family raised as many as 500. Chickens, geese, and sometimes ducks were the commonest livestock, but some people kept cows for milk and for making butter and cheese, and pigs, goats (as many as six to twelve, which they would milk). Goats were favorites since they would eat anything. Some people had a stable for them at the end of their house plot, In addition to their gardens, people had access to land for pasture for larger stock. They could graze animals up on the hill at the edges of town where there was grass and scrub. There was hardly any forest because it had already been timbered. The cattle had cow bells and in the summer they would come back by themselves. But some people remembered their cows being sent along the trails up to the rough grass on the mountain in a herd and how they had to go up to fetch them in. The farmers would come in from the countryside with a horse and wagon full of hay and you could buy that if you were not able to take the cows up the mountain to pasture.[33] One Coal Region resident in Lyndora in the Depression years recalled that pasturing cattle cost three dollars a year (Bodnar 1982, 70).

Men hunted deer, turkey, rabbits and squirrels (for pot pie), and fished, providing food in season. Children were essential for the upkeep of the family in the help they provided: in the gardens and in going up in the mountains to gather berries, mushrooms, and nuts. They would sell or barter for goods or services, the buckets of coal they gleaned or of the huckleberries (blueberries) they gathered that grew in abundance on the mountains; collect old rags and sell them to the rag merchant who came around to the door; and collect and sell old newspapers. They gave all they earned to their mothers until they were twenty-one, sometimes being given back a quarter to go to the movies or buy candy.

In the system of reciprocal exchange, payment for many goods and services could be made in kind instead of with money. For example, fences would be built for a pitcher of beer or people could barter the surplus food they produced for a bucket of coal or some other thing they needed. One Shamokin funeral director (of a family business that has lasted over three generations) told how his grandfather would take payment for funerals in homemade pies or chickens or eggs. People could not afford funeral expenses.

"In those days, funerals generally cost around $100–150, and if you figure that the average weekly wage then was around $10, that worked out to be fifteen weeks' work."[34] Doctors too were often paid in chickens or eggs or bags of coal. In the northern region, a Nanticoke woman's mother was a midwife paid in chickens and ducks (Bodnar 1982, 22). At the Mom and Pop grocery stores in the towns, goods were bought on tick (credit) and entered in the Tick Book, but many people never paid off their bills. Some paid in kind or by working for the store owner.[35] "Attorneys provided services—and here is the connection to politics;"[36] their services might be given in exchange for votes. During strikes "the hardships of wide-spread unemployment, over a prolonged period, were alleviated to a great extent by the continuing co-operation of local business people. Countless merchants were generous in extending credit to the jobless for necessary food and clothing" (Centennial Committee 1964, 58).

People commented that "the mine women were hardy like their men." Many of the coal patches only had water from pumps shared by as many as twenty-five families. It had to be carried home for bathing and for washing clothes. Women baked twenty or more loaves of bread a week in a brick oven in their yards, depending on the size of their family and number of boarders. Bread was the staple for every miner's lunch (Bartoletti 1996, 71–72). As well as caring for their household, many women also worked in the factories. Many were widowed or were the sole support of their families because of the high rate of death, accident, and sickness in the mines; the coal companies paid them no death benefits and they heroically and successfully managed to raise large families on their own by earning money taking in laundry, working as cleaning women or scrubbing floors. But they also survived because of assistance from their children, and help from kin, neighbors, and friends, with food, childcare, and even house room.

The next chapter will show that this economic system in the coal towns' neighborhoods and patches was an important element in the struggle of the miners and their families to resist the power of the dominant class, the state, and the big coal and railroad companies, because it helped them to survive in long strikes, and through its networks of connections and communications to rapidly mobilize demonstrations. The help for strikers from their degree of self-sufficiency through the economy of favors was commented on at the time of the strikes. Peter Roberts noted in 1904, that in the strike of 1902, hundreds of mining families could not have carried on the strike if they had not been able to cultivate the small farms and large gardens that were attached to company owned houses or available for leasing (P. Roberts 1904, 107). John Mitchell himself, the president of the United Mine Workers said after the 1900 strike that "the economical living of the Slav's boarding houses with their little vegetable gardens and livestock did much to sustain the non-English-speaking mineworker during the contest."[37] A prominent Knight of Lithuania said of the Slavs: "These men can stand out two weeks to the one week of English-speaking miners. If we stand alone for three months, they are good for six. They can live on almost nothing" (Greene 1968, 109).

Michel De Certeau (1984) emphasizes the political dimensions of everyday practices in people's lives. We have shown here how the economy of favors of mining families brought support to relatives or neighbors with food, shelter or child care in times of crisis, given with the expectation of likewise receiving such help in return. These arrangements helped the miners to cope with strikes and with frequent periods out of work for longer than if they had had no other resources to live on than their wages. As chapter 5 will show the networks of personal relations through which the economy of favors operated also facilitated the mobilization of peaceful demonstrations so rapidly and on such a large scale that the miners were able to achieve political ends. It enabled the miners and their families not only to survive but also to protest the hardships of the mining life.

This system involved an exchange of favors in an expectation of delayed reciprocity. It was not a calculated exchange of objects of equivalent value as in a monetary economy (as explained by Marcel Mauss in his study of the gift). The personal ties of kin and neighbors that bonded the members of the ethnic and other neighborhood communities in Shamokin/Coal Township were sustained and even created by this reciprocal exchange of tangible and non-tangible necessities for living. Anthropologists have defined the reciprocity of this kind of exchange as a series of transactions which need not maintain an exact equivalence but which are directed towards securing it (MacCormack 1976, 90, 94). The norm of reciprocity morally obliges people to return benefits or favors to the giver, so that the recipient is in debt until repayment is made. These outstanding obligations are means of maintaining social relationships: they constitute mechanisms which "induce people to remain socially indebted to each other and which inhibit their complete repayment" (Gouldner 1960, 175). Continuation of any relationship depends on exchange, but not necessarily an immediate or identical exchange. Material services can be repaid with nonmaterial returns, such as social approval and esteem, and nonmaterial reciprocation can help exchange relationships to persist and develop (B. Roberts 1973, 171).

The economy of favors was connected to politics. Ethnic politics dominated the town in the 1920s and until the late 1930s in the Coal Region, after which the New Deal and the increased federal role in social welfare made city bosses the middlemen for federal policies and the significance of local and ethnic politics faded.

Ethnic Politics

One view of associational ties is that they are instrumental in the development of ethnic politics. Second generation immigrants had few direct memories of village life in their home countries. Instead, membership in beneficial organizations and ethnic clubs reinforced their sense of identity with others of the same ethnic group outside their family. These organizations were prime vehicles for the organization of mutual interests and the exchange of goods and services; from there it was easy to see politics as a device for trading favors for votes. The urban political machine incorporated this organization and exchange into a system of ethnically based politics by providing social welfare, political privileges and alternative means for social mobility (Litt 1970, 42–44). Those seeking political office used ethnic solidarity to mobilize a political following. When other options were lacking or when it seemed to give a strategic advantage over other possible political networks, they relied on networks of dependency and alliances structured along ethnic or religious lines (Wimmer 2002, 45). Some remnants of this strategy remain in the Coal Region, as seen in chapters 3 and 7.

In the United States in this form of politics, the ethnic group sought protection and self-advancement for the group and especially for individuals within it. In the first appearance of ethnic politics, the Democratic and Republican parties, which are relatively open to pressure groups at the state and local government levels, organized immigrant groups into voting blocs to give a strategic advantage over other possible political networks (Kellas 1991, 98–103).

Ward bosses in ethnic wards in Shamokin/Coal Township used to control blocks of ethnic votes, in a system in which individuals were paid by the number of people they could deliver to the polls. Sometimes people were paid fifty cents to vote, or given a favor, or they could be threatened and told not to come out to vote at all. There was a connection between getting loans, and having debts forgiven at savings and loan associations, and voting for bankers trying for political office. Italians, Poles and Russians all formed Building and Loan Associations in the town, and one law firm serviced the religious divide by having Protestant, Catholic, and Jewish attorneys. Such connections especially mattered when it was time to get out the votes.[38]

Jobs in the school system and local government in particular needed political contacts, but it used to be the case that the promise for most jobs came in exchange for your vote, you would be likely to be asked whom you were going to vote for, and pressured to contribute to the politician favored by your boss. This situation gradually changed but continued to a limited degree until the 1980s.[39]

Ethnic politics flourished in America until after the 1930s, when ethnic influences diminished in the political system because there was a power shift from the local to the national level (Litt 1970, 48). Decline in the use of the national languages of different groups also contributed to the decline of ethnic politics. In the Coal Region, these languages continued to be spoken at home by the parent generation only into the 1930s and 1940s.

Ethnic ties were, however, and it is said to some extent still are, part of how politics functions at different levels. A lot of people when they deal with the Coal Region know that politics will come into play. As one banker put it: "traditionally—if you were set up politically, you could do alright—that is, if you had the connections and they were to good old boys that kind of ran things around here. There were loyalties to those people, they employed you or could get you work, and I still think you see a little bit of that."[40]

Ethnic political influence was still evident in 2005, when local politicians promoted the Girardville St. Patrick Day's parade and their support from the voters, by marching in it and pausing at intervals as they walked along to shake hands and greet people. It was the same at other ethnic festivals. Religion could reinforce politics and ethnicity too: a Lithuanian of St. Clair, said that "On Lithuanian Day, in the old days, there would be maybe fifteen, maybe more, priests that always sat on the stage, and they always had local politicians who I guess helped them a little."[41] This marked the close connection between religion, politics, and ethnicity.

People gradually moved up through the different levels of political office. "minor political office was considered a sort of testing ground. Looking back you could see that people on the school board or the council or in county office were being trained to be politicians. They moved up and some of them stayed in politics and got some sort of small state job or county job connected with politics but not in political office. Then they'd go on to political office."[42] Mostly they were in commerce or worked in a bank, rather than in the mines.

A comment on the operation of structural relations of power and inequality and the significance of ethnicity sums up the way that the political system operated within the boundaries of the Coal Region: "It was all a question of who was in power and who wanted to stay in power. . . . The ethnic, economic, political, and cultural and religious components were . . . all closely interwoven and formed a delicate, balanced system which was not in existence outside the region because any changes in the particular configuration of ethnic groups found in the hard coal region disrupted the connections through which the system functioned."[43]

Conclusion: Part One

Ethnicity is a process and the power relations of a specific time and place determine the strength and nature of the manifestations of this process. The three parts of this book will show how the relative significance of ethnicity, religion and class has shifted over time in Shamokin/Coal Township. Part One has focused on the early years of the last half of the nineteenth century and the first quarter of the twentieth century, the era when coal was king. During this time, ethnicity was a dominant feature of life in the town and converged with religion and class: the salience of ethnicity varied between groups, and reflected their history, the circumstances of their immigration, and the position in which they were placed in the socioeconomic hierarchy of the town. Its strong significance appeared in the ethnic neighborhoods, use of national languages, endogamous marriage, churches, associations, foods and cultural traditions which rooted people's lives in this era. Chapters 2 and 3 laid out the details of how ethnicity dominated life for each of the principal ethnic groups in these early years of the town's history. Chapter 4 has showed how the religious divide was felt even more strongly than the ethnic one, and how both coincided with class divisions. Power relations in the early years of the town's history were those at the local level as the coal industry developed, but as the coal mines were bought up by the big coal companies, the wealthy and powerful coal barons lived in the big East Coast cities and power relations shifted from the local to the national level.

Part Two presents this shift in power relations and the economic changes at national and global levels that brought the town to the peak of its economic prosperity and then to its decline and loss of population. It shows how the salience of ethnicity in the lives of people in the town greatly diminished as a consequence of these shifts and changes far outside local control. Chapter 5 focuses on the gradual change from ethnic to working class solidarity that took place with the rise of organized labor, the prolonged struggle between labor and capital, and the domination of class over ethnicity and religion.

Notes

1. Conversations with people in Mt. Carmel and Kulpmont, the other two towns to which Shamokin/Coal Township are closely linked, indicated the same dominance of Protestants of the same ethnic groups in these towns, and that retail

business was dominated in them likewise by Jews till the latter part of the twentieth century.

2. I link Marxist and Weberian approaches to class, envisaging a single system for both economic and social hierarchies. This usage corresponds to the constructions of the hierarchy of this town by the people themselves.

3. David Donmoyer, January 19, 2002.

4. Germans were primarily Protestant, but there were some working class German Catholics who came later.

5. These two churches have now been merged into Our Lady of Hope.

6. Hugh A. Jones, Mt. Carmel, February 25, 2004.

7. In St. Clair, ethnic neighborhoods were built near to the ethnic churches, but there was no Italian area since there were only four Italian families in the early years; they were shoemakers. There were no English or Scots in this town either (Ann Wargo, St. Clair, November 29, 2004).

8. In 1934 Reformed and Evangelical Churches joined, and in 1957 with Congregational and other churches, they combined into the United Church of Christ.

9. Cheryl Thomas, Secretary, St. Johns, September 17, 2003.

10. Pastor Sally Dries, Salem Church, May 4, 2004.

11. There is no Russian Orthodox Christian Church in Shamokin/Coal Township, but there is one in Mt. Carmel.

12. The top student of the graduating class.

13. Fritz Reed, January 23, 2002.

14. Dave Kinder, May 10, 2006, by permission.

15. There were twenty-one Ukrainian families living in the neighborhood of the Ukrainian church, which was moved and rebuilt after a fire in 1904, on North Shamokin St., see figure 4.1 (George Pollyniak February 2, 2010).

16. Sources for this whole section: Fritz Reed, January 23, 2002; Dave Kinder, March 3, 2002; Dave and Judy Shade, September 10, 2003; Ralph and Mollie Victoriano, January 23, 2003; Harry Dietz, January 30, 2003; Sally Dries, May 4, 2004; Shirley Persing, February 30, 2003; Mel Farrow, February 24, 2004; Gerald Breslin, Walter Neary, Adam Klebasko.

17. George Polyniak, July 13, 2007.

18. Bobby Kaminsky, December 12, 2004.

19. Richard Morgan, on a tour he gave me of cemeteries on April 30, 2004.

20. June Nash in her study of Bolivian tin miners, quotes a worker speaking of the solidarity he feels with his working companions in the mines, and notes that Marx speaks of shared experience as basic to class consciousness. In the Bolivian tin mines each worker had a nickname that captured his characteristic qualities (Nash 1979, 12).

21. Convened by Marianne Kinder at the Kinder home, December 15, 2003.

22. Marianne Kinder, April 14, 2004.

23. Such inner organization is documented elsewhere. Anthony Leeds found in a study of Brazil that informal groups and personal connections constitute the inner

organization of classes and sustain boundaries between the classes and the masses (Leeds 1965, 292, 295). Abner Cohen documented the networks the Creole elite of Sierra Leone developed that connected the members of the elite and coordinated action informally through mutual trust and co-operation (A. Cohen 1981, 222).

24. Hugh A. Jones, February 25, 2004.

25. Edith Wharton's novels illustrate admirably the nature of the power and influence wielded in these ways by women in American urban society of this period.

26. In Britain today, the Welsh, Scots and Irish have their own parliaments and the majority of the people in each case have a fierce sense of their national distinctiveness as opposed to the English.

27. Sources for the data of this section are as follows: I asked four of the town's prominent citizens both Protestant and Catholic, variously knowledgeable in local history, genealogies of town families, and politics, to tell me whom they considered to have been dominant in the town, past and present; I consulted Herbert C. Bell's *History of Northumberland County* (1891); *Genealogical and Biographical Annals of Northumberland County* printed by J. Floyd and Co. (1911); Harold Shomper's 1967 article on *Kimberley Cleaver*; the Centennial and Sesquicentennial Book and Pamphlet of the Town of 1964 and 1939 (Great Shamokin Centennial Committee), with their lists of people on the committees for these events; the city directories for the twentieth century; and the Achievers' Series of the *News Item* newspaper, 2006.

28. Most of these men were active in their churches, but did not otherwise use their wealth much to build up the town (Dave Donmoyer, December 3, 2008).

29. The *Farrow* family, Anglo-Norman-Irish Presbyterians, owned a livery stable, furniture business, and a funeral business started in 1876 and continued to the present day. It was helped in its initial capitalization through the marriage of *Walter*, one of the first Farrow brothers, with Andrew Robertson's daughter.

30. Local people described this as "helping each other out."

31. In the former countries of the Union of Soviet Socialist Republics (USSR), the economy of favors ("*blat*") means the use of personal networks and contacts to obtain scarce goods and services and find a way around restrictive procedures and the oppression and failure of the state run economy (Ledeneva 1998). In Chile, society and economy function through networks of connections in which direct or indirect favors are exchanged in a system of reciprocity among the urban middle class: obligations are stored in a sort of savings account in which future services will be rendered to various persons as the need arises (Lomnitz 1971, 94). In my research on the Democratic Republic of Congo, I have included the economy of favors in the second (unofficial and unrecorded) economy (MacGaffey, 1991, 2005). Goran Hyden (1980) earlier used the term "Economy of Affection" to refer to a broadly similar phenomenon in Tanzania.

32. These farmers sold potatoes and cabbage in quantity and also corn, apples, peaches, vegetables, meat, and fodder for animals in the Coal Region towns. Ruth Schrader remembers at least three who came around regularly: one selling butter, milk, eggs and other dairy products; one garden produce; and one meat and sausage.

33. In 1850, St. Clair householders owned 46 cows (Wallace 1981, 129).

34. Mel Farrow, February 24, 2004.

35. This system of nonmonetary exchange operated in the rural areas also: Dutch farmers could barter dried apples (*schnitz*) which were, like sauerkraut, a staple of the Dutch household (a family could dry one hundred bushels in the fall) for goods they needed at the country store or even for the pastor's wedding fee when they married (Yoder 1961b, 45, 51).

36. Dave Kinder, March 3, 2002.

37. S. J. Kent to Mitchell, October 8, 1900, in John Mitchell Papers, Catholic University Archives, Washington, DC. Quoted in Greene 1968, 174.

38. Sources, Dan Strausser, October 20, 2003; Jim Kelley Sr., May 6, 2004; Dave and Marianne Kinder, March 13, 2002.

39. George Pollyniak, April 1, 2008.

40. Chuck Yoder, April 8, 2003.

41. Anne Wargo, St. Clair, February 2, 2006.

42. Mel Farrow, February 24, 2004.

43. Dave Kinder, March 13, 2002, by permission.

PART II

INDUSTRIAL STRIFE, NATIONAL AND GLOBAL POLITICS, AND THE DECLINE OF ETHNICITY AND RELIGION

CHAPTER FIVE

The Militant Heritage of Labor and a New Industry for the Town

The resistance to the power of the coal and railroad companies by the anthracite miners, the subject of this chapter, has been the basis for Pennsylvania's reputation as a strong union state and for its importance in labor history. Labor historian Walter T. Howard observes that few areas in the United States can boast of a record of such labor militancy as the Pennsylvania anthracite region (2001, 97). The memories of this struggle, handed down in families, are part of the mining heritage of the townspeople, and form a strong component of their sense of place, a concept not only of a physical environment but also the circumstances of life lived in it. The fierce struggle of the independent miners against the power of corporate capitalism during and after the Great Depression, culminating in the legalization of independent mining, is a high point of this militant heritage.

The changes in the relative strengths of ethnicity and class that came about in the first half of the twentieth century were contingent on this rise of the unions, on historical events at the national and international level and on technological change. World War I, from 1914 to 1918, benefited the hard coal industry as it increased the demand for anthracite, but in the 1920s the industry declined with the strikes of the workforce threatening the coal supply and the competition offered by gas and oil as alternative fuels. The town economy was revived by the New York garment industry and the job opportunities offered by its factories in the Coal Region in that decade. This was the beginning in the garment industry of the process of the globalization of capital in its search for cheaper labor. In the 1930s, the town was overtaken by the Great Depression, the closing of many of the mines and a drop in population as many miners left in search of work.

These events and their consequences reflect a shift of power relations and economic changes from the local to the national and global levels that was to profoundly affect the town. These changes are presented chronologically in this chapter as far as possible, but sometimes overlap; if so, they are presented in separate sections that are parallel in time.

The Early Years of Organized Labor

In the last half of the nineteenth century, coal miners rapidly proved adept at organizing small local assemblies to struggle against the problems of their trade, and then going on strike to protest them (Muller 1989, 107). But early in this period, the most violent manifestation of protest came in the activities of a group of Irishmen known as the Mollie Maguires. This protest is relevant here for the long term effect it had on Irish ethnicity and identity in the Coal Region.

The Molly Maguires, the Reading Railroad Company, and the Early Unions

The following account of the variation in what it has meant to be Irish and how that has changed over time, bears out the approach taken here that ethnicity is a process contingent on the power relations of the day.

Many people mentioned the Mollie Maguires when they talked about the past. Their activities seemed to typify the old days of ethnic division and rivalry and the harsh oppression by the mining companies. The violent assaults, assassinations and robberies perpetrated by this Irish vigilante society were seen by the authorities and many of the townspeople as the operations of criminals and thugs, but they can equally well be interpreted as one of the initial forms of labor protest by the Irish against the job discrimination, ill-treatment, dangerous working conditions, and low earnings suffered by unskilled Irish mine labor. A short account of the Mollie Maguires is important for understanding the low esteem in which the Irish were held for a long time after the violent episodes of this protest, from which they suffered for many years and emerged only relatively recently.

In the 1860s and 1870s, national attention focused on the anthracite fields of Pennsylvania for two violent outbreaks of assaults, beatings, arson, industrial sabotage and the killings of men, most of them mine officials and the majority of them Welsh (H. A. Jones 1978, 146).[1] All were believed to have been carried out by the Molly Maguires, said to be an Irish secret society, a vigilante organization brought over by immigrants from Ireland to which members were bound by taking an oath. This society got its name from the woman who was the leader of the original society back in Ireland. Pinkerton agency detectives were sent in to track down the Mollies, which resulted in a series of showcase trials and convictions and the hanging of twenty Mollies alleged to have been guilty of the murders. Thereafter, the idea of inherently evil Irishmen brought to justice by heroic James McParlan, a Pinkerton detective, dominated newspapers and local history. But this interpretation was denounced as a myth in the 1930s by historians who emphasized the need to place the violence of the Mollies in the context of the conflict between capital and labor, arguing that the Mollies were the equivalent of a secret type of labor union with a different strategy, ideology and ethnicity from the unions organized by other mineworkers (Kenny 1998).[2]

Molly Maguire violence came in two distinct waves. The first, 1862–1868, was to some extent a violent continuation of labor's earlier organizing efforts and reflected the earlier intersection of draft resistance with labor organizing under the conditions of the Civil War. By the end of the war, the term Molly Maguires had everywhere become an explanation for labor activism, violence, and disorder (ibid., 102). The second wave of Molly Maguire violence was 1874–1875 and included eight assassinations. It occurred in opposition to the Workingmen's Benevolent Association (WBA) labor union in northern Schuylkill County. But both the union and the Mollies can be seen as trying to improve the conditions of life in the Coal Region. Kenny quotes a letter from a Molly Maguire to the *Shenandoah Herald*, October 2, 1875, stating that the aims of the Molly Maguires were for just wages and fair working conditions: "I have told ye the Mind of the children of Mistress Molly Maguire, all we want is a fare Days wages for a fare days work, and that's what we cant get now By a Long shot" (ibid., 201). But both the union and the Molly Maguires were to be defeated in this early period by Frank Gowen, the president of the Philadelphia & Reading Railroad Company (P&RRCO).

The trials of the Molly Maguires in 1876–1878 appear to have been a travesty of justice. It seems clear that three of those hanged should not have been convicted as charged.

> But to argue that the Molly Maguires were the entirely innocent victims of a diabolical plot against the Irish or against the labor movement is to replace one form of conspiracy theory with another. . . . There was a very real pattern of violence in the anthracite region in the 1860s and 1870s, and much of it was committed by Irishmen. The task of historians is to try and explain why. (ibid., 214)

The Molly Maguires were active in the lower region of Pennsylvania's hard coal fields, in a triangle that reached from Shamokin at the west end to

Mauch Chunk (Jim Thorpe) at the east end, and which included Mt. Carmel, Ashland, Shenandoah, Mahanoy City, Tamaqua, Lansford, and Hazleton to the north (see figure 1.1). The history of the Mollies was explored in detail for Schuylkill and Carbon Counties but not for Northumberland County, until in 2001, Katherine Jaeger made an investigation of their activities in the county. She wrote an unpublished paper, showing that there was equally uncontrolled violence by the Mollies in Northumberland County as there was elsewhere. There were two Divisions of the Ancient Order of Hibernians (AOH) in the county: one in Locust Gap including Mt. Carmel and the mine patches;[3] one in Shamokin, including Coal Township and its patches. But it is notable that the Mollies met in particular taverns in each town; their activities were never planned at AOH meetings. Jaeger details ten violent incidents reported to have been committed by known Mollies (verified by court records or newspapers) from 1866–1874. Those on her list of 60 Mollies in Northumberland County come from Locust Gap and Shamokin, except for two, one from Mt. Carmel and one from Ashland (Jaeger 2001).

The Mollies were struggling in their own way for justice against patterns of discrimination in the mines (Kenny 1998, 57). Their acts of violence against the mine supervisors and their gang warfare against the skilled miners must be seen in the context of the ethnic and religious discrimination that kept the best jobs for the English and Welsh, most of whom were Protestant, and the worst for the mostly Roman Catholic Irish. The elite of the workforce were the skilled miners, both contract and waged. The mostly English and Welsh contract miners controlled the production process and the length of the working day. They were paid by the amount they produced and they employed their own laborers at about one third of their income. These nineteenth century miners thus had considerable independence, while their laborers had to struggle filling six to seven coal cars a day. The apprentice system moved Welsh, English, and other miners up into skilled jobs, but the Irish were seldom considered eligible for apprenticeship (ibid., 61; Wallace 1987, 134–35); seemingly a clear convergence of ethnicity and class.

The divisive effects of ethnicity were partial, however, because there were many varieties of Irish immigrants in the anthracite region and relatively few of them joined the Molly Maguires. Most Irish mine workers joined the trade union movement that started in the 1840s and produced the Workingmen's Benevolent Association (WBA), the last of a series of local unions; it lasted seven years, from 1868 to 1875 and was led by John Siney. He advocated arbitration, and opposed strikes (except as a last resort), and also violence. The Association directed its protests against poor wages, long hours and lack of safety, minimal vacations and preferential assignments of work (Hanney

1985, 15). Siney's most important accomplishment was not any particular achievement of the WBA but the idea of the large industrial union and the development of a higher consciousness of class and of pan-ethnic solidarity among the miners (Wallace 1987, 395–96, 403).

Divisions among the Irish dated from their background in different regions of Ireland. Some Irish immigrants who had worked as miners in England or as skilled miners in the coal mines of Kilkenny and who were experienced in unionism, were founders of the WBA, whereas the most unskilled of the Irish immigrants were from the north-central and northwestern regions of Ireland from a desolate and unproductive part of the country such as Donegal, which was oppressively ruled by large, often absentee, landowners or their agents. The tenants, many of them destitute or dispossessed in the clearance of land for pasture for livestock rather than wheat growing resorted to violent protest and retributive justice for the wrongs done to them.[4] In Pennsylvania, some historians have thought that this culture of violent protest brought from Ireland to some mining communities was an element in the tension between Welsh and Irish in the ethnic divide between miners and laborers. It was played out in street gang warfare and violence, a precondition for Molly Maguire activity (Broehl 1964, 5, 11–20; Kenny 1998, 31–38, 61–65). But some Coal Region Irish dissent from this view and point out that Kilkenny men were as much involved in violent resistance as any others.[5] Kenny resolves the argument:

> To make sense of the Molly Maguires in Pennsylvania, two forms of labor organization and protest need to be kept analytically and ideologically distinct: the trade union movement and the pattern of violence that developed alongside it. In terms of personnel there was undoubtedly a degree of overlap, but the trade union and the Molly Maguires represented fundamentally different answers to the same question: How to improve conditions of life and labor in the anthracite region? (Kenny 1998, 66)

This struggle of the Molly Maguires must be seen in the context of the rise of the Reading Railroad Company (RRC) under Frederick Gowen, its president, and his efforts to bring the Schuylkill anthracite industry under the control of the company, and to displace the small independent mine owners. Unlike the upper anthracite region of Wilkes Barre, Scranton and the Northern Coalfield, the lower region was still a bastion of small scale coal operators in 1870. By defeating these small operators, the trade union and the Mollies, Gowen eventually secured control of the hard coal industry for the RRC. His strategy was to drive the independent operators out of business and to get control of the marketing of coal in Philadelphia because he believed that an efficiently managed regional monopoly was in the best interest of stockholders and the general public. In opposition, the WBA held that the heart of their strategy should be to control the production, as well as the distribution of the coal mined and sent to market, by limiting the amount of coal produced to keep prices high; to achieve this, they linked wages to the price of coal to benefit both mine workers and the mine operators.

Gowen insisted to the contrary, that corporate control of the industry would guarantee stable wages and prices and that the best way to make profits was to market as much coal as possible.

Gowen's unprincipled strategy to achieve this end, was, first, to drive out the independent operators by manipulating freight rates, by purchasing thousands of acres of coal lands,[6] and by the marketing, production and transport of coal by the RRC; and, second, to slander the union by repeatedly identifying it with the Molly Maguires, insisting there was no difference between the two, despite the fact that infiltration of the WBA by another Pinkerton operative found no evidence of any union involvement in violence. It seems to have been an effective manipulation of public opinion by Gowen in a time of general terror created by the violence of the Mollies (Kenny 1998, 131–33, 156–58). In 1871, he raised freight rates so that with the stranglehold of the RRC on transport it was no longer profitable for the independent operators to mine coal. He manipulated the committee appointed to investigate this situation.

By the summer of 1871, the real power in the lower anthracite region lay with the Reading. Its coal-owning subsidiary, the Philadelphia & Reading Coal & Iron Company (P&RC&I), had purchased 65,605 acres of coal land; by 1874 they owned 100,000 acres (Kenny 1998, 131–48). The final confrontation between the Reading and the WBA was the Long Strike of January to June 1875, which was marked by violence and disorder. Labor was on the defensive everywhere and the defeat of this strike was their most spectacular failure during the economic depression of the time. By 1877, wages had been forced down to 54 percent below the 1869 level (ibid., 180). The collapse of the union and the upsurge of Welsh/Irish ethnic tension was the precondition for the second wave of Molly Maguire violence. Thereafter, all striking mineworkers and the Mollies were lumped into a single conspiratorial category and condemned in people's minds as violent. And the Ancient Order of Hibernians (AOH) was simply considered to be one and the same as the Mollies. Both were denounced in 1875 by Archbishop Wood of Philadelphia (ibid., 212).

In Kevin Kenny's view, the dimension of the internal divisions of the Irish in discussion of the Molly Maguires has been ignored. The Catholic Church was a powerful condemnatory voice within the Irish community in both Ireland and America, and a specifically Catholic version of Irishness emerged in the anthracite region in the 1870s, in a power struggle between rival, sometimes overlapping, groups and institutions: politicians, saloon keepers, labor activists, the slowly emerging middle class and the Catholic Church. The Church hierarchy itself did not adopt a unified stance: while some priests condemned the Mollies, others supported them. A considerable number of men convicted of Molly Maguire crimes, including all the alleged leaders, kept taverns or hotels. As noted in chapter 1, the tavern keeper was one of the most powerful members of the community and as such would have been a natural leader among the Irish (ibid., 195–96).

The later process of ethnic definition among the Irish involved the eradication of the less acceptable versions of Irishness, especially the wild alternatives embodied by the Mollies. They included the speaking of Gaelic, various forms of local customs and folk beliefs and the unorthodox practice of boisterous wakes, with women leading the keening (a distinctively Gaelic practice), singing, music, and drinking, as described in chapter 2 by Tom Coakley for Locust Gap, a mining patch near Shamokin, which was famous for its wakes. Such wakes were discontinued in the late 1800s. "Now" says Tom Coakley, "instead of spending three nights at a wake, you spend one in a funeral parlor." This version of Irishness practiced a different version of Catholicism than that propagated by the Catholic hierarchy of Rome, Dublin, and Philadelphia. The meaning of Irish Catholicism was thus in question throughout the nineteenth century (Kenny 1998, 157-59). The significance of religion and its convergence with class and ethnicity in the town is evident here.

The prevailing view of the time condemning the Mollies lasted down the years, but has not gone unchallenged. One powerful example of this was in 1978, when Governor Milton Shapp paid tribute to the martyred Molly Maguires with a group of members of the Pennsylvania Labor History Society, and in 1979 signed a posthumous pardon for Jack Kehoe, a leader of the Mollies. That such sympathies underlie some versions of what it is to be Irish today, were evident in the gathering following the 2006 St. Patrick's Day parade and celebration in the coal town of Girardville at the tavern that formerly belonged to Jack Kehoe, described in chapter 7. This parade is an event which attracts large crowds of Irish from all over the Coal Region today.

Kenny's conclusion is that the Molly Maguires were a group of Irish immigrants who assassinated their enemies but whose existence was put to all sorts of ideological uses far beyond their limited use of Irish collective violence. Some of the Mollies wanted to settle personal grievances but most engaged in battle to defend what was fair and just in social relations. Unlike the trade unions, they did not see their struggle as part of a wider class conflict. The WBA denounced the violence and condemned the Mollies as a misguided deviation from the goals of the labor movement. Despite this the Mollies were identified as one and the same as the union by those in power, which resulted in the destruction of both. Any vestiges of an Irish tradition of retributive justice perished with the Mollies, but trade unionism was soon to reemerge (ibid., 286).

The Shift from Ethnic to Working Class Solidarity

The Slavs and Italians were initially brought in as strike breakers so that ethnic hostilities and interests, and differences of language and culture appeared as divisive elements in the efforts of labor to organize. The common experience of all mine workers, however, skilled and unskilled, was the inadequate wages paid by the big coal and railroad companies and the hardships, dangers and threat to their life and health of working conditions in the mines. As the labor movement grew, these common interests and experiences of the workers overrode divisive ethnic interests as miners from all ethnic groups joined to support the union's call for strikes in the coal fields. The common interest of mineworkers as a powerful element uniting ethnic groups in the labor struggle was to be a factor in the decline of ethnicity. It is one of the contingent economic and political factors determining this process in the Coal Region.

Mine operators by means of force and playing off ethnic interests to divide workers attempted to foster the lack of solidarity among miners in the hard coal fields, and coal strikes until the end of the century had an ethnic character (Sterba 1996, 10). The first truly national labor body had appeared in 1869, when the shoemakers banded together in Philadelphia and formed the Knights of Labor. In the early years, the Knights' members in the anthracite fields were predominantly Irish, and tension arose between them and the English, Welsh and German miners, then later with the Slavs also (Greene 1968, 7, 87). An example of these tensions came from a Polish resident of Shamokin: "My Grandmam came over [from Poland] and opened a little grocery store. She came from a place where there was a lot of lakes and fishing. They lived in Mt. Carmel at the time, and she'd send my grandfather to Ashland to get fish and he'd have to go with a horse and buggy. And almost nine out of ten times, the Molly Maguires would get him. They never took his horse and wagon but they always took the money he had and the fish. They didn't like the Polish."[7]

The establishment of a union in 1903 was a tremendous achievement because the anthracite industry had become an industrial empire under the financier J. Pierpont Morgan from its beginning in the early 1820s to its maturity in 1900. His monopoly had stabilized the industry, and the mighty trust that he created had previously appeared able to withstand any attack. Morgan's grand edifice and the stability that he and other men of capital had brought to the industry, however, were not able to stand up to the introduction of a new proletariat into their workforce, the Eastern European Americans. In 1880, 84 percent of the foreign born of the hard coal region were from English speaking groups; by 1900, they were less than 52 percent. Meanwhile the Slavs grew from 2 percent to over 40 percent of the foreign born in the same period (Greene 1968, 35). By 1910, 50 percent of the anthracite coal workforce was Eastern European, with Poles exceeding all other nationalities in numbers. Between 1900 and 1920, 12,032 men were killed in the anthracite mines; 3,177 of them were Poles (Miller and Sharpless 1985, 186).

The inability of the miners to establish any permanent labor organization was initially blamed on this influx of Slavs who were considered to be unreachable because language barriers made organization difficult. In fact, according to Victor Greene, there was very determined Slavic support for the union cause, and it was the dualism and jealousy between the two unions, the Knights of Labor and the Amalgamated Association of Miners and Mine Laborers, and their incomplete organization that sapped union strength into the 1890s. Although contemporary writers blamed the Slavs for breaking the miners' solidarity, contest for members between the two unions was more to blame, and the general disapproval of the Catholic Church towards unions did not help. Thus union-Slav relations in the years until 1887 shifted back and forth (Greene 1968, 79–87).

In September 1887, Slav support for union action became evident: the call to strike for a rise in pay brought out 9,000 men on the first day and 30,000 by the thirteenth day, half of them from the Lehigh field and the others from around Shamokin and Shenandoah. By the middle of January, the number of operating mines was reduced to only a few in the entire field and half of the work force was idle. Dissension among the unions arose, however, and ended the strike in early February (ibid., 88–90). The anthracite union was temporarily crushed again.

The infamous Lattimer Massacre took place in Hazelton in 1897 in the Lehigh coal field, during a protest initiated by Slavs and subsequently joined by the Italians. They demonstrated at McAdoo, and then marched to confront the police at Hazleton. The sheriff and fifty deputies fired on the unarmed marchers killing or injuring twenty-six Poles, twenty Slovaks, and five Lithuanians. This was one of several outbreaks in the Lehigh Field in which Polish, Slovak, Lithuanian and Ukrainian mine workers had demonstrated separately. But from 1889 on, with the momentum of this Slav enthusiasm, the United Mine Workers (UMW) organized the entire industry, and the Slavs were a strongly united force in strikes.

Slavic communities were so tightly knit and in such close communication with each other that workers walked off their jobs on the basis of grass roots consensus rather than of organization, exhibiting great militancy and willingness to strike. This was what brought about the Lattimer demonstration and thereafter broadened the dispute. Striking Slav miners, with the active strong support of Slav women, violently attacked any dissenting mineworkers in an almost leaderless movement. On the whole, they won their point. They were joined by the Italians and stimulated the English speaking mineworkers to action as well (Greene 1968, 125–50; Miller and Sharpless 1985, chap. 7; Sterba 1996, 11). In these militant actions, the networks of relationships of the economy of favors of the miners' communities described in chapter 4, functioned as "grass-roots consensus," and their communication networks helped to organize the labor struggle.

In 1900, the mine owners refused to negotiate the mineworkers' list of grievances and John Mitchell called for a general strike on September 19th, the first industry-wide strike. Eighty thousand men responded. Initially they were mainly from the north: only half of the mineworkers went out in the two lower regions at first, but the rest soon joined the strike. By October, 97 percent of the workforce was out. They were granted a 10 percent increase and the men went back to work at the end of the month. The prestige of the union grew with this successful outcome and membership increased (Greene 1968, 160–62).

The dominant ethnic components of the population of various towns differed, and so did their participation in the strike and the course it took. Shamokin and the Mt. Carmel area were heavily Polish; Ashland was predominantly non-Slavic, primarily Irish, German and Welsh, and none were members of the UMW. At Mahanoy City the Lithuanians could not agree to strike. Shenandoah had a population of 20,000, two thirds of it Slavic and the union was strong, chiefly with Poles and Lithuanians. They beat up those who worked and forced colliery closures. The Coal and Iron Police and mine guards fought back and by the end two miners were dead and a dozen injured. The governor sent in the National Guard. But immigrant militancy won: in a few days the only working mine in Shenandoah closed down, and later the Mahanoy City workers who had hesitated went out on strike. In Lehigh and

Hazelton violence subsequently broke out with women taking a strong role (ibid., 165–70).

Greene argues that at issue were the material achievements of the immigrants. In the Hazelton area, their material wealth, despite the work suspension, enabled immigrants to send in total about $50,000 per month to the home country. Their powerful drive for wealth, however, did not mean their subservience to the conditions imposed by the mine owners or the worker abandoning his dignity—it was the collective organization of the immigrant community that compelled conformity in this crisis and more than any other force gave the union victory (ibid., 173–74). Parades, messengers, newspapers and, especially, word-of-mouth spread and directed opinion through these communities. Community networks of kinship, friendship, and neighborhood ties again seem to have united and rallied the Slavs and others to the strike. This shows the operation of the inner organization of the working class. Later, there was even a name for word-of-mouth dissemination of unity: it was named from the way by which the news from Radio Free Europe in World War II in Lithuania was spread around by those who had hidden radios, called "women-told-women." A Lithuanian in Shamokin commented: "There was a lot of that in the Coal Region."[8] Any dissent and opposition to the general will was quickly known and action taken to exert pressure on individuals to ensure unity in the crisis.

The 1902 contest in the Coal Region "was to show even more clearly than prior strikes the particular ethnic reaction of a firmly resolute Slavic community" (Greene 1968, 177–78). The problem for the miners of lack of work began about 1890. In a normal year, a mineworker had worked somewhat more than 200 days on average, but in 1890 and for every second year to the turn of the century, the number of days worked annually declined as follows: 198, 190, 174, 152, 166 (Greene 1968, 119).

The coal operators had asserted they would only deal with their employees directly, not as members of a foreign labor organization; they refused to meet with Mitchell and the mediating body, the National Civic Federation (NCF). In March 1902, the UMWA presented their final demands of a 20 percent wage increase, and an eight-hour day, an equitable docking procedure, and a collective bargaining agreement to be agreed upon by the union. Under pressure from Mitchell and the NCF, the union agreed to delay this ultimatum for a further month. Despite further concessions the company presidents held to their position. The strike began May 12 and continued all summer, until there was public hysteria at the approaching winter and the prospect of no fuel. Under pressure from President Theodore Roosevelt and the Secretary of War, J. P. Morgan was finally persuaded to pressure his anthracite colleagues to accept arbitration. This intervention by the President forced corporate employers to deal with the UMW and began a new era of labor management relations (Dublin 1998, 8). Agreement was reached and the miners returned to work on October 23, after a strike of 165 days closing down the entire industry and involving about 100,000 men. Since 1900, the union had followed the successful policy of granting the Slavs high office in their organization to attract immigrant membership. The reaction of leaving the region and seeking work elsewhere, however, was more pronounced during this strike than in the previous two, with the departure of about one-third of the 147,000 work force.

Once again, the Slavic immigrants' ability to live just above subsistence and to maintain themselves so long without visible income within their economy of favors dumbfounded Anglo-Saxons. Roberts comments: "In the strike of 1902, hundreds of mine employees' families could not have carried on so brave a fight if it were not for the small farms and large gardens they cultivate, which are leased to them or are attached to the company houses" (P. Roberts 1904, 107). It was at this time that the sale of coal gleaned from culm banks and of huckleberries picked in the woods for miles around in the late summer was critically important. Huckleberries (similar to blueberries in appearance and taste) were of surprising value: the *Mount Carmel Daily News* sent out as many as 1,500 quarts a day by one shipper. It was estimated that a large family could make $5 a day on berry picking.

Some of their support came also from fellow countrymen in other regions. Also important was the aid paid to strikers by the fraternal organizations. On the national level, the National Slovak Society pledged its $50,000 surplus for 5,000 members in the strike district in case of hardship. Local branches expelled members who refused to strike, or fined them. Considerable violence broke out against strike breakers and police in this strike also, and again women played a significant role. Eventually, the strikers and the union got more or less what they wanted (for detailed accounts, see Greene 1968, 179–98; Miller and Sharpless 1985; and chapters 6, 7, and 8).

These strikes at the turn of the century definitely had ethnic support. They demonstrate the cohesion of the Slavic community, locally and nationally, and the strength of the Slavs' identification with other members of their particular ethnic group. These immigrants showed extraordinary militancy and powers of resistance. Greene concludes that were it not for these powers of the Slavic immigrants, the UMWA would certainly have lost the 1900 strike. The achievement of the 1902 strike was to make the union secure in the Coal Region. This brief and necessarily selective account of the early years of the labor movement in the Region has shown how after the initial attempts by the coal companies to bring over Slavs and Italians as strike breakers, the working class interests that the movement represented gradually overrode ethnic divisions and made the strikes successful.

World War I and the Era of the Garment Trade

World War I brought economic prosperity for the coal industry because the mineworkers benefited from increased demand caused by shortages of coal and of labor. In 1917, production reached its peak of 100 million tons and almost as much again in 1918. Miners worked a record number of days in both of these years, 285 and 293 respectively. Their material conditions of life improved during and after the war because of these expanding opportunities for work and increasing wages. Thus from 1916 to 1921 the anthracite miners averaged 273 days a year, almost full-time work, and wages were roughly comparable overall to most other industrial occupations, a marked change from the underemployment of the last decade of the nineteenth century (see chapter 1), although they were still inadequate and very uncertain for miners' helpers and laborers. Ethnic organizations and churches flourished.

The improvements in the coal industry made in this period came from increased work opportunities and the wage rates obtained during and after the war, especially in 1922 and 1925. The strikes of the 1920s show the growth of class solidarity among the anthracite mineworkers, as the openness of the UMWA to immigrant groups in its membership diminished the divisive effect of ethnicity. The union's commitment to industrial unionism and its use of democratic procedures set it apart from other unions, but the strikes of this period intensified not only the anthracite mine workers class solidarity but also the class struggle because of the determined response of the coal operators to recapture the real wage gains of the workers (Blatz 1994, 228–31, 258).

The New York garment industry started to move down into the Coal Region in the 1920s seeking to escape from the gains of organized labor in the highly unionized factories of New York. The availability of the cheap labor of miners' wives and daughters, with few employment alternatives and little union experience (Sterba 1996, 34), and the reputation of the strong work ethic of the area drew them to the Coal Region. The existing local factories expanded as new ones moved in, which they did in great numbers to Shamokin/Coal Township and to the north around Wilkes Barre and Scranton; all primarily worked under contract to New York factories. This new industry provided jobs for women in the area, so that by 1925, 31 percent of women in mine families and 57 percent of adult daughters were already employed in silk mills, garment factories, and commercial establishments (Kozura 1996, 205). This change in the economy for a time compensated for the decline of the coal industry faced with the militant demands of labor and the development of alternative fuels.

Working in the Garment Factories

The coming of the garment factories had major economic impact on the town. The larger factories in Shamokin included Shroyer's Dress Factory; the Taubel knitting mill, a manufacturer of women's hosiery which had factories in Mt. Carmel and Tamaqua also; the Lark Dress Company and Hosiery Mills; the Anthracite Shirt Factory; Morris Fishman's uniform factory (uniforms were made for the army and navy in World War II by the garment factories); and later the Arrow Shirt Company. There were many smaller ones. Their labor force was primarily women, but men went into them too as mechanics and foremen.

The Shroyer factory was the largest of the early ones and a good example of a local family firm. It was started in the 1920s and run by the four sons of John Shroyer, the German founder. He eventually went into politics and became Pennsylvania's Secretary of Highways. In the twenties the factory mostly made gingham house dresses, but the business grew and hugely expanded. The market was seasonal. It was a family business, with a few outside stockholders; the oldest of the four sons was president, the second brother was the production manager, the third was the floor manager and handled all the credit side, and the youngest brother dealt with finishing the product. There were three daughters in the family; one of them made a marriage uniting her family and the Larks.

Together with a couple of other plants they owned, the factory turned to working on contract for outside manufacturers in the New York City garment industry and became one of the largest plants in the state. In the depression, they went into bankruptcy because their two major suppliers could not agree on pricing policies that would enable them to stay in business. However, a new group formed and the company was rebuilt to operate successfully in the post-World War II period.[9] In 1964, their output was 20,000 dresses a week and the payroll was over $1 million a year.

Employees had high praise for the factory. According to a former foreman, by the time John Shroyer, the founder, left in 1977, he had salesmen all over the United States and Cuba, and he planned to expand to South America, too. People used to come from all over the country to buy their dresses: one woman came from Chicago every year and took back as many as a dozen dresses each time. They were beautiful clothes. But John Shroyer, had a heart attack and died, and from then on it went downhill. Every year they had a big Christmas party, and the foremen would be taken out at least once a year to a dinner out of town. They gave them beautiful gifts, worth a lot of money. There was never had any union troubles, though they had a union. They liked the owners so much that the founder was made treasurer of the union in New York City. Over a thirty-year period, the union at the factory demanded the company give a 3–4 percent wage increase every three years; in that thirty years wages went up 40 percent.[10]

The Lark Hosiery Mills (owned by members of the Lark family) also was given favorable mention as a good place to work. By the late 1930s, the fine clothes the garment factories produced attracted crowds of shoppers who came by train from other towns and cities.

The Cluett-Peabody Company/Arrow Shirt Manufacturers, another of the biggest garment factories, had a big manufacturing plant and also a warehouse in Shamokin/Coal Township which was the distribution center for the Eastern States. This factory started operation later than the others in 1945, with 100 workers and made army supplies. It expanded vastly with the switch to making Arrow shirts, and subsequently casual wear as well. In 1964, they employed 1,100 workers and their estimated payroll was $2.5 million (Centennial Issue of the *Shamokin Citizen*). Some former garment factory workers gave favorable accounts of their bosses and conditions of work, as quoted above. Many of the women I talked to had worked in these factories. They spoke of them favorably saying it was hard work but fun. "They were good to us and we had our breaks and lunch hours, everyone knew each other." But others dissented: "No, we were slaves." I also heard how women factory workers had their own ways of keeping some modicum of control of their working conditions, as in the following excerpt from a transcript of an interview with a woman who had worked in a clothing factory, a spontaneously given example of James Scott's "weapons of the weak:"

> WORKER: The bosses we had were nice. Now and then you'd get a bad one. We were a gang of women and could soon put them in their place because we could slack up on our work you know, make believe it was hard and things, they'd come down to it you know.
>
> MACGAFFEY: You could make them give in?
>
> WORKER: To a certain extent. We'd slow down. Or we'd make believe we were having a hard time with our machine. Then a mechanic would have to come and fix it. Well he couldn't fix eight machines at one time and there was eight of us in the gang. We had our ways.

MACGAFFEY: Anything else you'd do?

WORKER: We'd go to the bathroom and smoke. You know, everybody smoked. You'd go smoke, and they couldn't come in the bathroom after you, you know. So there were ways of getting things done. Yes, if you stuck together, there were ways of getting things done. But if you don't...

MACGAFFEY: So in that factory you did get on well with your coworkers?

WORKER: Yeah! There was one or two you know—we always called them "Brown Noses"—they'd yield to the boss for everything.[11]

But the deadening monotony and pressure to keep going was another reality of working in a factory. It is made vivid by the following account given me by Eleanor Kuhns, a union organizer whose story is given in chapter 6. She spoke of a woman stricken by Alzheimer's disease, who had worked for Arrow attaching collars and cuffs to shirts, for which the rate of pay was about a penny and a half a collar: "Imagine how hard you would have to work," was Ellie's comment. Her son had her in his home for a while until she was put in a nursing home. Whenever you would see her, she was always still sewing. She would do it with the hem of her skirt, she would crease it, then she would take it and sew it. She was sewing the whole time. She didn't know who you were, but somewhere in her mind, she knew she was a cuff attacher and she was still attaching cuffs to the sleeve of the shirt.[12]

There were problems for the workers in the garment factories that contrasted to the favorable reaction to the Shroyer factory given above, and labor found the need to organize in the garment factories as well as in the mines. The militancy of the labor struggle in the region continued in the era of the garment industry, and women again played a strong role.

The General Strike in Textiles

On September 1, 1934, the United Textile Workers of America called an industry wide general strike of cotton, silk, wool, rayon and textile workers in the whole country, demanding union recognition, industry-wide collective bargaining, a reduced workload with no change in pay, and the enforcement of federal labor guidelines. By September 15, 400,000 workers were on a strike that lasted for three weeks. While the strike did not obtain good results on a national basis, in the Coal Region it was able to do so.

For example, the Duplan Silk Corporation employees in Hazleton managed to establish an autonomous union local and their strike was successful: they got the cooperation of local craft and industrial unions. At the beginning of the century, as noted earlier, for previous strikes by the miners, women had played a forceful but indirect role; they played a direct role in this textile strike. They had been suffering severe verbal abuse by foremen for any mistakes they made in operating the complex looms and they worked long exhausting hours standing up at these machines. The Hazleton silk mill union made up a flying squadron, mainly of women pickets, who intercepted workers entering factory gates in McAdoo and other places, and shut down operations.

These young women differed from their immigrant mothers not only in the American education they received and their roles as family wage earners, but also because they were consumers in a popular culture: the 1920s and 1930s saw the creation of a leisure culture of movie houses, dance halls, department stores, and popular music on the radio. The increased independence of these women combined with the excitement of traveling in cars and buses, singing songs and picketing to generate tremendous energy in their protest as shown in their flying squadron raids. They had supported their miner families in strikes for higher wages; they received support when they went on strike in their turn and the UMWA District 7 publicly declared for them (Sterba 1996, 24–27).

A spectacular event diagnostic of the textile era took place with the strike of 1934. On Labor Day in the labor parade in Hazleton (see figure 1.1), members of the city's craft and industrial unions joined the 3,000 striking silk workers, with 14,000 miners from 34 locals of the UMWA following them in a three and a half mile procession (Sterba 1996, 27, 30–33). This huge parade marked the significant progress and unity of organized labor. In this strike, city newspapers did not identify workers by ethnicity as in previous UMWA strikes and clergy from the immigrant churches played no role:

> In stark contrast to the conflicts of the anthracite miners at the turn of the century, the labor parade symbolized the essentially non-ethnic character of working-class protest in Hazleton in the 1930s. (ibid., 32) . . . The protest and march articulated an awareness of class interests powerful enough to unite people of numerous ethnic backgrounds and such disparate groups of workers as anthracite miners, skilled tradesmen, and female machine operatives. (ibid., 35)

In the 1930s the unions achieved a strong presence in Shamokin-Coal Township. The city directory for 1936–1937 lists the following labor organizations: the Amalgamated Clothing Workers of America; the Brotherhood of Railroad and Trainmen; the Brotherhood of Railroad Firemen; Carpenters and Joiners; the Electrical Union; the National Association of Letter Carriers; Painters, Decorators and Paper Hangers of America; the Labor Union; the International Ladies Garment Workers Union; the Plumbers and Steam-Fitters

Union; the Shirt Workers Union; the UMWA ; the United National Association of Postal Clerks; and the United Textile Workers.

Later in the century with the decline in the area's economy, the town's labor organizations diminished from 1970 through 1992, until there were only three left (Polk's City Directories). By the early twenty-first century, the only remaining one, however, the International Brotherhood of Electrical Workers (IBEW) still had a strong chapter, Local 607, in the town. A postscript was given by a Shamokin banker in 2003: "You think of this as a depressed area, yet we have our own little local here which is a very strong chapter of the electrical union. I think some of it is fathers and sons who have done this for years, gone into this field, and they earn a pretty good living."[13] This comment indicates the contribution of the union struggle to the town's sense of its heritage.

But alongside the success of organized labor, the decline of the coal industry in the twenties with the development of alternative fuels decreasing the demand for coal, the many strikes that beset the industry, and the closing of mines from the onset of the Great Depression at the end of the decade, brought about the start of a population exodus as miners left town in droves in search of work. The overriding of ethnic interests by class interests combined with economic, political and demographic changes to begin a decline in the strength of ethnicity in the life of the town.

The Last Years of the Coal Era

The mines had reached their peak in 1917–1918, with production of nearly 100 million tons, but dissatisfaction with the union began to appear soon thereafter as declining anthracite production and underemployment gradually worsened in the late 1920s with the onset of the Great Depression. By this time, the mines were only working one to two days a week (Michrina 1993, 145). The decade had seen fierce labor struggles in the coal strikes of 1923. Also, alternative fuels made inroads into the home heating market at this time.

The Depression, Union Strife, and Independent Mining

The Great Depression after the crash of the stock market in 1929, did not result in a single bank failure among Shamokin/Coal Township's five banks, but it closed mines, factories, and businesses, and caused bankruptcies, unemployment and wage cuts in the town and throughout the Region. Between 1926 and 1933, many coal operators cut production by one-third, displacing nearly 65,000 workers from the labor force of the mines. By 1932 in Schuylkill county alone, with a population of 235,000 and an 82,000 labor force, 39,000 displaced workers, including 16,000 miners were jobless (Kozura 1996, 205–6). In Shamokin, the number of collieries had dropped from fourteen to two. The southern region was especially hard hit: the rate of joblessness was 50 percent and union leadership failed to wrest any concession on work-sharing of the available jobs.

Business closings and unemployment were widespread in the town from 1933–1935. The Salvation Army, the Miners Relief Committee Projects and President Roosevelt's New Deal after 1933, including the Citizen Conservation Corps in which young men on relief rolls were recruited for work camps, provided some relief. The appropriations for public improvements of the Works Progress Administration projects provided jobs and community kitchens which fed five hundred families daily (Toscano 2000, 30–59).

During this period of the Depression, from 1928 to 1931, a small but determined communist movement flourished in the anthracite region and organized the militant National Miners Union (NMU), the Red Miners Union, to challenge the coal operators and the dominance of the UMWA, and to mobilize working class militants. The NMU drew its support and membership primarily from eastern and southern European immigrants, having some 500 members in twenty locals at its peak, and undoubtedly many sympathizers among the miners. In 1930, foreign born miners made up 57,517 of the total of 82,053 anthracite miners (*The Daily Worker*, quoted by Howard 2001, 97). The aims of the NMU were not rebellious but focused on the more immediate needs of higher wages, shorter hours, better working conditions and union recognition, nevertheless anticommunist forces strongly opposed it. For radical miners, on the other hand, it was an important alternative to the UMWA whose interests were perceived to have diverged by this time from those of the miners. In the mid-1920s, communist miners and union dissenters joined in opposing John L. Lewis' leadership of the UMWA, and membership in the communist party peaked during the bitter strike of 1925–1926. This strike lasted 170 days.

But the NMU met with stiff resistance as they tried to make themselves into a viable trade union, and their attempts to take over leadership of strikes failed. Anticommunist feeling was running high in the region and in the nation in 1930 and ultimately doomed this union; it no longer functioned after 1931 (ibid.).

Job equalization became the central objective of the miners as a response to the decline of the mines. They demanded the even distribution among the different collieries of a company for mining and processing the coal, rather than its restriction to the collieries in which coal was closer to the surface which made it easier and cheaper to mine, so that the available work should be widely distributed to benefit all miners. In 1933, 15 thousand men went on strike in the Lehigh Valley over this job sharing. The coal operators argued against this demand on the grounds that it would further weaken the competitive position of anthracite relative to the new fuels of oil and gas. While John L. Lewis and the UMWA were more concerned with higher wages and shorter hours, the rank and file considered the union view to be self-serving and not helping to stabilize employment. Dissatisfaction with the UMWA spread, as it was felt that the company and the union leaders went hand in hand: if you did not support the union leaders you did not have a job. This separation of interests between union and rank and file had begun in 1930, when union dues began to be taken from wages by the company before the workers got their checks, so there was no longer any direct dealing with the union for the men (Bodnar 1984, 79–83).

As the mines began to decline and close, the union loyalists turned to the UMWA to protect their jobs; the dissidents formed the United Anthracite Miners of Pennsylvania (UAMP) in 1933 to fight for equalization and attack Lewis' integrity and leadership (Sperry 1973, 301). Their struggle took the form of a series of violent strikes that ended with one hundred dead and many injured. In the Lehigh Navigation in the south, a work-sharing arrangement was finally achieved in a series of illegal strikes; in other areas more than half the collieries permanently closed and their workers resorted to mining the coal themselves.

Miners and particularly their wives and children had always scavenged coal from the culm banks and used it for fuel or to barter or sell, and the coal companies had tolerated it. In the hard to endure six-month strike of the fall and winter of 1925–1926, however, the banks were picked clean and some strikers began to open makeshift mines on company property and dig from any exposed veins. They cracked and screened the coal and sold it to businesses in the towns. This was the start of illegal, or "bootleg," mining. The companies would not, in general, tolerate strikers opening their own mines on company lands, though a few did permit the miners to continue their digging. Within a few years, over 600 of these mines could be seen on the hillsides of the anthracite fields. The costs to their owners were little more than the wages they paid the miners who worked for them, so they could sell coal at prices lower than those of the mine companies (Greater Shamokin Centennial Committee 1964, 67).

From 1936, recovery set in for Shamokin/Coal Township. In 1935 a new shirt factory had opened, there was some improvement in the mines, and with the community projects of the New Deal and the reemergence of community activities, the town began to lift out of the Depression (Sperry

1973, 117). By 1939, the year of the town's Diamond Jubilee, its prosperity was again in evidence, and the coal miners were mining the coal on company lands as "bootleggers" or independent miners as they soon insisted they should be called.

The Triumph of the Independent Miners

The militant heritage of the mining past of the town culminated in an extraordinary resistance by the independent miners to state and corporate power. Thousands of unemployed miners illegally occupied coal company property, engaged in independent mining operations in defiance of the corporate powers arrayed against them, and eventually gained their legal right to these mines. By 1941, independent miners produced 10 percent of anthracite production at this time of the decline of the coal industry and in their total production rivaled the output of the largest legitimate company. The story of this struggle and its successful ending, and some accounts by the miners themselves of operating these mines, conclude the chapter.

Most of the independent mines were dug by a group of five to eight men; some were family enterprises. Two accounts by former independent miners from Shamokin/Coal Township describe how this mining was done and the physical strength, ingenuity and persistence of the men driven to do it to support their families.

The most complete account is from John Kwasnoski. He described how, during the Depression, people started mining on their own account. Later, they started building breakers where they sized the coal and trucks would come in and buy it and take it to the city. A group of them had a mine that he worked in most of the time. He had the best job and was mostly the engineer. He did not work in the mine, but used to go down to get coal ready for the next day. Their mine was 165 feet deep, straight down: "about 15 feet from the top there was no ladder, you had to get on the cross-pieces in order to get a footing. Going down, when you came to the ladder, you were alright and you could keep going down. Today, I'd never go down that hole, not for $5,000: you'd make a misstep and down you'd go." His brother who worked there too always scattered coal dirt around for a better foothold. He always did that, every morning in the wintertime because it would be all ice. The newspapers used to write up the victims when they were killed in those coal holes.

They had a regular crew of five or six men and used to hire what they called slaves (work was scarce and people were willing to take what they could get). Kwasnoski was the treasurer and kept track of all the expenses for the week and then when the week was up he produced a rundown of the division of the money between the five men and the slaves—the slaves got fifty cents a load, the miners eight dollars a truckload. They had five or six regulars and two slaves. The regulars were lucky to make five dollars a day and they worked six days a week. They made twenty-five to thirty dollars a week if the operation was good and they struck coal. This was not more than in the mines, where it was $5.35 a day, $4.62 a day outside, but they did not pay any taxes. It was a ten hour day, six days a week. This was in the early 1930s. The job ended when the seam ended.

Coal was only taken away between the two holes they dug. They dug with hand tools, then they would tap it with dynamite and blow it. They could get away alright, there were different exits. They shored up the mine with pit props, it was not big enough for coal pillars. They cut the props themselves in the woods and had to know the right kind of tree. They had to get wedges and make four pieces out of one tree. In the early stages, they set up a scaffold and windlass to crank up the bucket. Later, they hooked up a car to drive it and haul it to the top. The police were not active by that time; they would have blown down the scaffold. The miners would raise the back wheel and have a drum on it with a steel cable to the coal tip and then right down to the bottom of the hole and then they would put it into low gear. At the top, they had a top man who used to dump the bucket. They sold the coal to a colliery that came round and picked it up. They had to crack the coal with a hammer to make it stove coal size, then run it over screens to size it for sale in the cities and put it in a twenty ton bin from which a big truck was filled. One mine they dug took a year straight down through 165 feet of rock, and there was no coal. It took them a year to sink that mine, and then the water flooded it. So there was no money. They quit then and all went their own ways.[14]

Dan Strausser, a former mayor of the town, worked in a bootleg coal hole by Stirling Colliery after he finished High School until he was in the army. When he came out there were no jobs and he went back to bootleg mining. It was in the 1930s after the collieries closed and there was no industry. Five to six men formed a group, one of them being a skilled miner to direct them. The coal would be taken to the cities by truck and sold twenty tons at a time. The bootlegger miners found their mining sites in old mine workings in the mountains. It could be frustrating. They might try new areas, work for two months, and then discover there was no coal there.[15]

Michael Kozura faults anthracite scholarship for emphasizing the analysis of community at the expense of class, and for neglecting collective action in favor of union organization. He argues that the emphasis on family, community, and union cannot explain the cohesiveness and resourcefulness of the working class of the coal towns, and does not account for the complex motives of the jobless miners' action. The independent miners' movement "waged a struggle that transcended the bounds of kinship, community, and union . . . the far reaching aims and radically oppositional practices of the bootleggers' movement require a conceptual approach that is more sensitive to the transformative potential inherent in collective action" (Kozura 1996, 202). John Bodnar, on the other hand, considers that the workers were not inherently radical but that their behavior and perceptions were motivated by the family and community obligations of the family economy (Bodnar 1983, 14–15). Despite their fierce militancy, miners are considered to have aspired to nothing more radical than their desire for secure employment and better wages and working conditions. Pragmatism and radicalism are considered to be antithetical mental states, as if the concern for the realities of economic survival were incompatible with commitment to social transformation. I do not find the obligations to family, church and community and the networks of ties and communication they entail to be necessarily a conservative force; they can also, as suggested in the last chapter, be organizational forces that in various ways and in different times and places have been harnessed for militant and transformative ends. Kozura's account of the independent miners' struggle and its successful outcome, on which I primarily rely for the following summary of these events, with its many quotations from the miners themselves, convincingly supports this point of view.

The miners were able to harness the personal networks developed in the survival strategy of the economy of favors in their struggle against the state and the big companies. These networks contrast with those of the business, kinship and marriage connections of the wealthy and powerful members of the dominant class of the town presented in the last chapter. The connections between the elite of the town had helped maintain their dominant position, but the networks of the miners and their families helped them to survive, hold out for longer, and organize strikes, their weapon in the struggle against the power of corporate capitalism.

Miners' accounts of independent mining make vividly clear the dangers and difficulties of the independent mines that proliferated at this time. If the Coal and Iron Police found a bootleg mine, they would dynamite it, so it was necessary to work fast to get out the coal before the mine was found. Men sometimes worked day and night, and safety precautions were neglected (Wolfgang n.d.). Lacking any enforcement of safety measures, these mines could be extremely dangerous, and the conditions of mining hard to endure, as the following examples show.

George Pollyniak worked in an independent mine for one year before the accident that made him stop. His cousin Steve worked in the bootleg mines and had persuaded George to join his group. George tells of climbing down a fifty-foot ladder, then sliding down ten feet to the workface with only a wooden barrier between him and a 400-foot-deep shaft with water in its depths. They were working in a breast at the top of a shaft in a mine that had been closed robbing a coal pillar (the coal left as a thick pillar to hold up the roof). They would dynamite at the end of the day, and then in the morning when the dust and smoke had cleared, they would get out the coal. One day, Steve was working fifteen feet from him and George's carbide lamp went out, indicating a flow of methane gas. A great rush of coal followed, burying him up to his hips so that he could not move. Steve managed to get his lamp lit and dug him out after about fifteen minutes. He had just escaped falling down into the deep shaft which was where the rush of coal went. George's father would not let him work in the mines again after that extremely narrow escape.

Others were not so lucky. Dave Donmoyer recounts that "Grandfather Donmoyer was killed in his late thirties robbing pillars. But thank God he didn't have any children, so his wife wasn't left to do that. People were paid extra for robbing pillars, it was very dangerous but they were desperate for money to live on." Joe Tumollo gives details of working in these mines as a boy: "at sixteen I went to work in a coal hole. That was around 1939. We used to get paid by the load, a dollar a load for a big truck. I worked inside. My mother used to make me a waterproof cover she sewed on my back because I used to get wet, the roof was so low. I worked about five or six loads a day." That was a lot of money at that time.

Adam Klebasko remembered the desperation of the miners in that period. In the Depression there were many independent mine holes and the mine police would come and blow them up. But the miners would reopen them and keep going. He and his brothers were desperate to support their families. Once in a vein they were entitled to follow it, but depending on the quality of the vein the company might claim it. Sometimes the Coal and Iron Police would wait until they were mined right down to the coal and then come and blow the mine shut. Or the miners might work a 450-foot tunnel through the rock and then find all the coal had been taken out when they got to it. There was no reimbursement for all that work, no reward. It was a hard life. Adam's recollections of mining and the treatment of miners were very bitter and contrasted with those of Ed Narcavage (in chapter 3).

There is tragic nobility about men willing to work so hard in such dangerous conditions for such long hours. The result was often that their lungs were full of coal dust and many died at an age that would have been before their time in easier and safer occupations.

Independent miners were able at first to use the coal they produced to survive through exchange in the barter economy. Soon, however, they were building their own breakers to crack and size it and setting up interstate trucking operations to get it to market. The rise of the trucking business was related to the bootleg mining, since the miners could not sell coal to the breakers on whose land they were illegally operating. Men took up trucking to market this coal, peddling it from door to door locally for home heating and eventually driving to the big cities (*News-Item*, May 13, 1980). The miners' defiance was essentially successful: 20,000 miners and truckers defied the coal companies and the state government and overwhelmed the coal and iron police. In Schuylkill and Northumberland Counties, where independent mining predominated, it provided one in four jobs (Kozura 1996, 199–200).

Hundreds of independent mines were dug as the men determined to get the coal: whether this was stealing or not, they were set on making a living regardless; the miners were desperate, bitter, and above all angry. Kozura describes a deeply felt anger among them directed against the companies and explicitly expressed in quotes from interviews with the miners themselves. They reveal a class anger fueled by a history of struggle: accounts of the hanging of the Molly Maguires, the Lattimer Massacre, and the pitched battles of women and children against the Pennsylvania militia; all are retailed down the generations in the mining communities. The Molly Maguires and the Massacre in particular were often brought up by men and women alike in the course of my interviews and in conversation. They are an important component of a live oral tradition. "The culture of the coal towns was thus enriched by a legacy of class struggle" (ibid., 207).

This was the militant heritage of the Coal Region; it is as important today as a part of the people's identity as is their ethnic one. The motivation of their militancy was a pragmatic need for survival, for miners to take care of their families. Some of the women even worked alongside their men in these independent mines. More importantly, women encouraged pro-bootleg sentiment and provided a supportive environment, as the efforts of individual independent mining families coalesced into a region-wide economic force (ibid., 209–10). The independent miners' union thus mobilized the ties of the web of interdependency of the economy of favors. They also utilized the connections through which this economy worked to provide a network of customers for their coal.

The independent coal trade rapidly expanded and soon coal was being hauled directly from the coal holes to cities like New York, Baltimore, Philadelphia and Harrisburg. By the early 1930s, more than 2,000 bootleg truckers were hauling coal to Maryland, New Jersey, New York, and New England.

Unless the police could catch them in the act of taking coal off company property, they could not be prosecuted. The coal towns began to revive. Mining outgrew family labor and groups of men formed to work the mines, working in solidarity within the group, between groups, and with legitimate miners. The miners held their ground against any attempts of the companies to shut them down. Two miners quoted by Kozura, described it as "a rebellion of the people against the coal companies" and "a fight for what people rightfully believed was theirs" (Kozura 1996, 214). They would get together with other groups of independent miners, fight off the company police and chase them off the mountain. They finally formed organizations called bootleg unions to engage in self-defense, arbitrate disputes, set prices, and defend arrested members in the courthouse.

In 1934, the companies launched an offensive against these miners, in Schuylkill County and then in Northumberland County with detachments of coal and iron police, backed by state police. They were met with organized, nonviolent opposition, which eventually resulted in victory for the independents. The miners did not do so well in the north where this form of mining was more successfully repressed. But in the southern field by 1935, the coal companies had lost control of the situation and the independent miners operated with impunity (ibid., 211–19).

The truckers were more vulnerable, however, and bills were proposed in the state legislature in 1935 to keep them off the highways. The independents established a committee to unite the region's truckers and miners in one association. Sixty delegates representing 10,000 truckers and miners assembled in Shamokin for the first region-wide convention of independent unions on April 7, 1935. This convention demanded a public hearing on the proposed legislation and called for a march on Harrisburg. Ten thousand miners and truckers went and marched through the streets to the Capitol Building in a huge demonstration. It was clear that independent mining could not be legislated away, and although an association of all truckers and miners did not materialize, their capacity for organized and united action was demonstrated and sustained. Until 1939, these miners flourished: they gained the tacit support of the new governor of the state and the state police were instructed to remain neutral in conflicts between them and the companies unless there was violence.

After 1939, with a pro-business Republican governor, the situation was less favorable. The governor failed to defeat them by legislative action but brought together representatives of the coal operators and the UMWA, though not the independent miners, in a committee designed to regulate the anthracite industry, the Anthracite Emergency Committee; this opened another legislative assault on the miners. At this time, technological change brought strip mining on a large scale to the Coal Region, with the use of enormous mechanical shovels. These were blockaded by the independent miners. On February 10, 1941, thousands of them converged on Minersville to defy the Anthracite Mining Committee and they again organized a huge demonstration in Harrisburg on April 16, which was successful in achieving an amendment of the legislation that satisfied the truckers. The miners continued their blockade of the stripping for the next six months. This protest ended in a violent confrontation that had to be put down by the state police, who remained thereafter to prevent any further attempt to disrupt these operations (ibid., 219–24).

After 1941, the miners refused to consider themselves as "bootleggers;" they were all independent miners. Shamokin had its own independent miners' union, as did other coal towns; these unions helped mobilize the demonstrations in Harrisburg. They achieved enough support in Shamokin/Coal Township that local businesses at various times sided with them: in the 1926 strike, the hardships of widespread unemployment, over a prolonged period, had been to an extent alleviated by the cooperation of local business people who were generous in extending credit to the jobless for necessary food and clothing. Nearly twenty years later in 1943, a number of local businessmen still voiced strong approval of the independent miners. They pointed out that the local area had been bypassed by defense plants, that formerly there had been fifteen large collieries within eight miles of Shamokin, and that the one remaining colliery still in operation could not provide employment for the miners of the town (Greater Shamokin Centennial Committee 1964, 58, 67). All this is evidence of considerable support and approval for the miners from the business merchant class.

Entry of the United States into World War II interrupted this conflict between the miners and the coal companies and drained away a quarter of the region's labor force; nearly every independent miner was drafted or enlisted into military service or found a job in the defense industry. In the southern anthracite region, local draft boards filled their induction quotas with independent miners, since miners employed by the coal companies were exempt because mining was considered necessary to the war effort. But in October 1943, the independent miners refused to comply with the ultimatum of the State Anthracite Committee to close down their mine because from their point of view they were carrying out legitimate mining. Subsequently local government found ways of leasing them land to mine (Kozura 1996, 224).

In the end, the miners won the struggle. Independent mining was legalized in 1953 and brought under the jurisdiction of the Pennsylvania Department of

Mines. Since then the small-mines industry has been subject to state inspection and safety regulations. These miners take out legitimate leases, pay royalties to the company on the coal they mine (twenty-five cents a ton), and are subject to state and federal taxes.

To sum up, the economy of favors helped sustain mining families with a near self-sufficient provision of food to support them in these episodes of staunch and determined resistance to the coal and railroad companies and the government. Families also depended all along on the factory work of miners' wives and daughters to help them to survive the difficulties and uncertainties of mining and the long months of strife. The network of personal relationships through which the economy of favors functioned provided not only means to live on in the union strikes but also the network structure for the rapid communication and mutual reliance which the independent miners' union needed to mobilize and organize protests that were so massive and so rapidly executed that they were unstoppable and eventually brought them success.

Between 1947 and 1965, independent mining from deep- and strip-mines in Coal Township produced a total tonnage of 19.2 million tons. In this later period, after World War II, the international politics of the Cold War extended down into the Coal Region, with beneficial effect for the remaining mining industry: the stationing of American troops in Germany created a market for anthracite coal to heat their barracks. The only closer source of anthracite was Russia, but it was impossible to import from the Russians because they were the Cold War enemy.

The figures in table 5.1 show that as demand increased so did the number of mines and miners up to 1955, but then as the use of oil and gas increased and the demand for coal decreased, the numbers dropped.[16]

Ed Narcavage, the Lithuanian whose history appears in chapter 3, owned one of the bigger independent mines in the postwar period. In the 1950s when the collieries were all going out of business, as the companies went down there were people who took out a lease, opened up their own mines and sold the coal to independent breakers. He had eight men working for

Table 5.1. Rise and Decline of Independent Mining

	Mines	*Miners*
1947	265	1,216
1955	435	1,701
1965	244	930

Source: Harold Shomper Report, *Coal Township 150 Anniversary 1837–1987*, p. 43.

him and they produced about 100 thousand tons a year. The mine was close to 1,800 feet deep—the Glen Burn was more than 2,600 feet. They had a good group who had come out of the army and were all the same age, and they had the mine for about ten years. At that time there was still a lot of local trade to be had since people were still burning coal for heat but a lot of the coal went up to New York to be shipped to heat the army barracks in Germany.

After 1955, the number of mines and production of coal dropped because demand decreased; miners and truckers alike were all overtaken by the discovery and technological development of the new fuels of oil and gas. But since coal supplying the Cold War demand was shipped out by rail, not by truck, the demand for trucking went into decline sooner than it did for coal. Shamokin city directories (see table 5.2) show the rapid rise and decline of trucking and teaming enterprises over the years as follows:

In the *Centennial Issue* of the *Shamokin Citizen* daily newspaper there is a statement that reads like a sad epitaph from the Independent Miners, Breakmen and Truckers Association: "We made jobs when there were none to be found. We are proud to have had a part in keeping our town alive. Now we find that people are letting us down by turning to other fuel." There were instances where this feeling of being let down turned to action with a rock through the window of a family heating with oil.[17]

As described in chapter 1, the northern and middle coal fields present a contrasting situation in which local capitalists retained their preeminence in local affairs. In the southern anthracite fields, the absence of a class of big local coal capitalists resulted in an elite largely made up of petty entrepreneurs, professionals, politicians and local P&RC&I officials, but their system of influence and patronage collapsed when the mines went down. The independent miners translated their community support into political power at the polling booths and the balance of power shifted as they elected sympathetic

Table 5.2. Rise and Decline of Trucking and Teaming Enterprises

	Number of Trucking/Teaming Companies
1936–1937	18
1941	125
1948	47
1950	37
1957	19

Source: Shamokin City Directories

judges, county commissioners and legislators. In the northern and middle fields, the power of local capitalists had easily offset the political influence of miners. In the south, "What the companies branded 'a breakdown of law and order' had actually been a shift in power that put local government in the hands of the people" (Kozura 1996, 217).

To conclude, this account of the history of the miners' resistance has shown the rise of working class consciousness in the Coal Region. Ethnic interests faded as strikes and demonstrations furthered the common interests of all miners. Their economy of favors not only helped the miners and their families to endure the conditions of work and of the mining life, it also enabled them to hold out in strikes and frequent periods out of work for longer than if they had had no other resources to live on than their wages. The networks established in this economy provided a means for the rapid communications, trust, and mutual reliance which the independent miners' union needed to mobilize and organize protests for their subsequent unstoppable challenge to the power of the state and corporate capitalism. By these means, they achieved the right to operate independently of the coal companies.

This struggle of the unions is part of the anthracite heritage which the people of Shamokin/Coal Township celebrate with pride, and is a strong element in their sense of place. It is a heritage that they draw upon today as they try to restore the sense of community of their town in their efforts to recover from economic decline, population loss and the diminishing salience of ethnicity of the latter half of the twentieth century. The next three chapters detail some of these efforts.

Notes

1. Hugh A. Jones (1978) gives a list of mostly Welsh names and a number of German ones. The breaker of the German brothers William and C. P. Helfenstein of Shamokin was burned in 1875 (Wolfgang n.d.).

2. Much has been written about the Molly Maguire era and its events are well known; a brief account will suffice here. For more details see Broehl 1964; Kenny 1998; or the shorter version of Miller and Sharpless 1985, chap. 5.

3. Founded in 1888 (McCafferty 1929, 39).

4. Law and practice varied from one region to another in Ireland, but most small farmers had at best a yearly lease and could be ejected on short notice. The problem was worse in Mayo and Donegal where *rundale* was practiced and land was divided into small pieces for each heir of each of the different grades of land on the holding (Broehl 1964, 6-7).

5. Casey McCracken, July 11, 2006.

6. By various underhand strategies since it was illegal for the company to purchase land. See Broehl 1964, 122.

7. Stella Chesnay, November 11, 2003.

8. Dave Kinder, May 10, 2006.

9. Phone interview with George Shroyer, co-owner, on February 20, 2002; *Centennial Issue, Shamokin Citizen.*

10. George Pollyniak, January 30, 2002. After the death or illness of all the brothers, a nephew took over the factory, but eventually had to close it down because of ill-health. The factory was still standing in 2006, but scheduled for demolition because of a leaky roof.

11. Delores Derk, April 9, 2003. This also echoes the bragging about the undermining of the powerful that is found in villagers' perspectives on social manipulation in the Auvergne reported by Reed-Danahay (1993, 224).

12. Eleanor Kuhns, February 13, 2002.

13. Chuck Yoder, April 8, 2003.

14. John Kwasnoski interviews on April 1, 2003 and January 19, 2004.

15. Dan Strausser, October 30, 2003.

16. Harold Shomper, miner and mine inspector, was of Pennsylvania German descent from Lykens. He was a meticulous historian of the local coal industry with an encyclopedic knowledge of its history. Sets of his superbly detailed maps, reports, and voluminous records of the Western Middle Field are in Mt. Carmel and Shamokin public libraries.

17. In the millennium, the Reading Coal and Iron Company make money by fencing their land and charging $100 for an annual permit for all-terrain vehicles (ATVs) for hunting and using the land. Former owners of independent mines are vocal in their resentment against this closure of access for them.

CHAPTER SIX

Prosperity and Decline

Shamokin's Diamond Jubilee took place over a week in 1939. Like the Ukrainian parade of 1904, this event seems diagnostic of the town at a particular period of its history. The Jubilee was a weeklong celebration of the vibrant life of the town when the economy had emerged from the Great Depression and it was again prospering with the garment industry at its peak. People came in great numbers to shop in the town because of the fine clothing produced by its factories, and because of the town's many leisure opportunities. Shamokin became a shopping Mecca with twenty-eight trains coming in every day bringing crowds of shoppers from nearby towns and even from as far away as New York and Philadelphia. The excellent transportation system made it possible to import a great variety and amount of merchandise to be sold in addition to the fine clothing made locally, and local businesses were flourishing. This was the brief golden age for the town on which people look back with nostalgia today.

This Jubilee Celebration of the years 1864–1939 consisted of a week of parades and celebrations. Great throngs of people patronized the stores and watched the parades: the event attracted 50,000 people to the town, including 6,000 former residents, friends, and relations of the townspeople. There was a different theme for each day to which the parade of that day corresponded: one was a religious day, others were for the town forefathers, industry, schools, firemen, youth, and veterans. Each daily parade had up to thirty two floats, and included several marching bands, and every evening people danced in the streets to broadcast music (Toscano 2000, 108–13).

A film of this event, found when the Victoria Theatre was torn down was made into a video called "Our Hometown." It is run at town events today and copies of it are in great demand. It shows the town as it was and reminds people of their pride in their past. In the video, crowds of people are on the sidewalks and going into stores; it walks you in after them and shows the finery displayed for sale, going into the dress shops where women try on elegant clothes, into Ben's Fur Shop, and some of the four men's clothing stores. The camera shows Liachowitz's family jewelry store, Hirsch's shoe store, Henry Lark's Hosiery Mill, and the Walnut Hosiery Mill. The floats of the huge parades are interspersed with many community groups of all kinds carrying flags and banners as they pass down the main street, and with large uniformed bands impressive in their numbers and the quality of their playing; crowds five deep line the sidewalks to watch. The elaborately decorated floats include ones for the Boy Scouts, the Odd Fellows, the Moose, the Patriotic Sons of America, the Eagle Silk Mill, the F & S Brewery, Reed's Dairy, Yoch's Bread, the Roaring Creek Water Company, the National Ticket Company, the AFL-CIO Local 689, the many fire companies, and a great variety of others.

Besides the video, other details of the successful past life of the town appear in the advertisements taken out in the books and booklets put out by the municipality, and by different churches celebrating this and other lesser jubilees and centennials in these years of prosperity. Their numerous photographs of societies and organizations with large memberships, sports teams, and commemorative events, advertisements for stores and businesses of all kinds, for lists of sponsors, boards and committee members showing many people involved in the town's activities and organizations, and the participation of plenty of successful business and commercial interests among them. All indicate the prosperity and liveliness of this era of the town's history.

It is this memory of past economic prosperity, of their ethnic heritage, and of pride in their militant history during the labor struggle that is behind the efforts of the townspeople to try and rebuild the sense of community as well as the economy of the town today. This chapter looks at the era of prosperity brought about by the garment trade, the effects on the town of World War II, then at the decline of the coal industry, the changed politics and class system of the twentieth century with the collapse of the economy, the loss of jobs when the garment industries closed, and the effect of all this on ethnicity and religion.

Shamokin as a Shoppers' Paradise

By the late 1920s, the garment industry (known as *the rag trade*) was bringing the prosperity for Shamokin/Coal Township that was to revive and bloom after the Depression and make the town a draw for the fine clothing it produced. At the end of the 1930s, the town had emerged from the hard times of the labor strife of the 1920s and the Depression of the 1930s. Shoppers were able to come from far away because the area was served by five railroads the Lehigh Valley, the Reading, the New York Central, the Pennsylvania and Erie, and the Lackawanna, and in addition had good bus and trolley services. People would tell how the streets were jammed: "on Friday and Saturday nights it was shoulder to shoulder in the streets." They would get all dressed up and go downtown to shop, talk and get ice cream. "Everybody was there, there were all these places where people could eat and drink or whatever, and the trains would come through." Such comments were often to be heard.

The sense of community of the time is reflected in those words "Everybody was there," a sense that everybody felt they knew everybody and were in some way connected to them. Today, one way people are trying to deal with the economic downturn and demographic decline is by attempting to rebuild such sense of community.

The production of fine clothes by the garment factories, the availability of other goods brought in by the ease of freight access by rail, and the many leisure opportunities of the town are what people today remember and are eager to talk about: there were four or five women's dress stores, including Locket's clothes for women (Louis Locket would go to New York if you needed a special coat or dress and bring back a couple from which you could choose), James' Fashion and Bridal, Shaner's Hats (where a little old lady fitted and decorated them how you liked), stores for children's clothes, five to six men's stores with fine clothes, ten or more shoe stores, jewelry stores and candy shops, furniture stores, and Moser's dry goods store where you were waited on by assistants all dressed neatly in black. There were thirteen banks, none of which failed in the Depression.

The Edgewood amusement park at the Western end of town, developed by Monroe Kulp, was a major focal point of the community of this time. It was a place where people played sports on the weekends; where churches, the fire companies, choirs, the Elks and many other organizations held picnics; and families and schools their reunions. It had a lake with a roller coaster over it, ice and roller skating, tennis courts and a pavilion for ballroom dancing (in 1926 a Carnival Dance here was attended by 300 couples). In addition to this park, the town supported three movie theatres.

This economic and social vigor was to continue after World War II. As one resident described it: "In the sixties, Friday and Saturday nights were like a parade or a fairground on Independence Street—shopping and theaters, lots of stores. It was like little Las Vegas, kids cruising up and down the streets." Another said: "We were very bustling, in Mt. Carmel, Kulpmont or Shamokin, Friday and Saturday night it was shoulder to shoulder in the streets with people shopping."

The Effects of the Decline of Coal and World War II

After the Depression of the 1930s and the revival of the town's economy, in the early years of World War II the demand for anthracite increased; the need for coal was such that the government offered draft deferments to miners to stabilize the mine labor force. Mining families had steadier incomes during the war than previously. But in 1942, a wildcat strike immobilized the anthracite industry, even though only 15–25 thousand of the workforce of 80 thousand joined the strike. At the outset, miners were reacting to John Lewis' ineffective leadership of the UMWA, but they were also angry at the government for wage restrictions to halt inflation being imposed unfairly: one strike leader complained that he cleared only fifty four dollars in two weeks, "show me," he commented, "anyone working for twenty-seven dollars a week in the defense industry nowadays" (Sperry 1973, 294–95).

But following the downward trend in the coal industry that began in the 1920s, the wartime economic boom effectively bypassed the anthracite region. In 1949 after the war, the coal market collapsed again and declined by nearly a quarter from the previous annual production of 59 million tons to less than 45 million tons. By 1953 it was a little over 30 million tons, as the industry lost out to bituminous coal in industry and to fuel oil, natural gas and electricity for home heating (Dublin 1998, 9–10); by 1957 coal was providing barely one quarter of all fuel energy used by Americans, although eleven years earlier it had been providing nearly one-half (Rottenburg 2003, 18).

The G.I. Bill: Social and Economic Mobility

World War II reached into the Coal Region and took many people away from its towns. Patriotic feelings ran high among the citizens of the area and many joined the war effort. For everyone the big thing was to go into the services, and beyond that to go overseas.

Many miners did not want their sons to work in the mines and World War II was instrumental in helping miners to realize this aim through the technical training many acquired in the services and after it through further education. If they survived and returned home their horizons had been widened and many had learned specialized skills. In 1944, the G.I. Bill was passed to provide college or vocational education for returning servicemen, one year of unemployment compensation, and loans for buying homes and starting businesses. It opened up a range of jobs and life opportunities of which many in the coal towns took advantage. The son of a miner (who had been disabled at twenty-three years of age with five children) describes the opportunity he found: "There was no way I could go to college. Then I got into the navy and saw a lot of the world. I got back here and applied to college in 1946. I studied business at St. Joseph's College in Philadelphia on the G.I. Bill: tuition, books, fees, and sixty dollars a month spending money. War made opportunities for everyone."[1]

Two examples of professional careers that resulted from the war follow: the first is Sam Greco of Mt. Carmel, who started his education at college on the G.I. Bill. He went on to get a master's in business, an engineering degree and two doctorates. He talked of how his wartime experience broadened his horizons. Roosevelt had declared war on Germany and Japan which got them out of Mt. Carmel at just about at the end of the Depression and brought an opportunity to see what was going on around the country. After he got out of the air force he went to airplane mechanic and specialist electrical school. Then he went overseas, the start of a trip around the world to Australia and India at the expense of the government. When the war ended, he was discharged and went back to Mt. Carmel. He described it as "a great experience."

He had a second stint in the service, and then after he got out worked on jet engines in the defense business with Westinghouse, and afterwards with the Bell Aircraft Co. on rocket engines. He eventually went to work for the corps of engineers in Philadelphia repairing dredgers. Their government contracts ran out and he moved into public administration and eventually ended up back with the corps of engineers. His final job was in research and development with Boeing in St. Louis. He was happy there, got a doctorate, and stayed until ill health struck and he retired to Mt. Carmel.

The second example is a son of a very poor mining family who became editor of the local newspaper after getting an education on the G.I. Bill. Harry Dietz credits his time in the service for motivating him to go back, finish school and make something of himself. His father died when he was very young and his mother supported her six children by cleaning and washing clothes. Harry joined the army in World War II where he was a photographer in a special engineer construction battalion. This posting taught him a lot about photography and laid the groundwork for a successful career in newspapers. He went to Temple University in Philadelphia and studied journalism on the G.I. Bill, and afterwards got a job with the Philadelphia Inquirer. However, he did not like the city and moved to Harrisburg to the Harrisburg Patriot News where he became Managing Editor. He moved back to Shamokin because of his grandmother's and mother's illness, and went to work at the Shamokin Citizen. He did some correspondence courses with Columbia University and with the newspaper institute of America and the American Press Institute and progressed from being a reporter to being City Editor. In the course of his fifty-year career he won fifteen awards and had several pictures published in leading magazines, among them Newsweek, Life, and the Saturday Evening Post.

These opportunities for jobs could include getting good pensions and medical benefits. Ed, the son of a Polish immigrant to Mt. Carmel who was killed in the mines in 1935 when Ed was in 8th grade, went into the air force, flew twenty-five sorties over Germany in a B54, and at the end of the war got a job in an airplane corporation; his youngest brother went to Penn State on the Pennsylvania Bill of Rights and got a job making rocket engines in Texas; Ed himself worked at building airplanes for Lockheed Martin, then left to serve in the navy for four years, and after the war, the company took him back and gave him credit for the four years. After forty-seven years he retired in Baltimore with a good pension and medical plans. He is one of those who though living elsewhere often comes back to Mt. Carmel for celebrations at the Polish Cultural Club.[2]

The G.I. bill provided the means for many people to move up to other jobs than mining and to be very successful. One Shamokin high school teacher commented: "When I went to Bloomsburg University on the G.I. Bill in the late fifties, over half of the people who were commuting were there on it. I think half of the teaching staff in New Jersey and Southeast Pennsylvania, including my brother and several others of my class, came from the Coal Region." New Jersey was growing rapidly and so was Philadelphia. In the 1960s a lot of people went down to the Pottstown area and a lot to Jersey and never returned.[3] Many went to Maryland and Connecticut too. They felt it was a way out of the mines and that they were the first generation who could choose right out. Fighting in the battles of World War II in units in which soldiers of different ethnic backgrounds mingled and shared common dangers, hardships and losses, also broke down ethnic barriers. "That war changed everything in the Coal Region: a lot of people left, the coal industry went down, people mingled in army units fighting under the American flag, and barriers started to really break down. It was a major changing point for this area."[4]

But the negative effects on the town were that many young people left to join the services, and many of those who survived the battles of the war did not return but found jobs in the wider world of better opportunities. The number leaving hugely increased after the war as unemployment soared with the closing of the mines reaching 17–18 percent in major mining districts (Dublin 1998, 8–10). Thus the war brought opportunities to many individuals of Shamokin/Coal Township but the result for the town was further population loss.

There were additional consequences of this out-migration in search of jobs. It dispersed families as members moved away to better opportunities as a result of the war. The eight-generation family history of Ruth Schrader's mother's family is an example (below). It shows a family, founded by a German immigrant who came over to farm in the early nineteenth century, which over four generations formed a big extended farming and mining family and was then dispersed by the two world wars.

The History of a Family Dispersed by the War[5]

Generation 1. The family was founded in America by Friedrich Wilhelm Kaseman from Nassau-Dilburn, just north of the Palatinate region of Germany. He came over at the age of nineteen as an indentured farm worker in order to pay his passage, and worked for twelve years to pay off his debt, being taught to read and write as part of the deal, and in 1815 bought fifty acres for his own farm in Irish Valley, near Shamokin. Typically for Germans, he and his three sons in *generation* 2 were all farmers.

In *generation* 3, Joseph, grandson of Friedrich Wilhelm, married to another German, moved into town and bought a house on Academy Hill in Shamokin, where family members of succeeding generations were to live. Ruth's maternal great uncle Nathan joined the Union Army. Afterwards he was a miner, a railroad worker, a store clerk and finally a colliery watchman. In these first three generations, the men were farmers and miners or other unskilled workers and most spouses of men and women of the family were German.

In *generation* 4, George Kaseman and Sarah Moser were Ruth's maternal grandparents. George was a miner, who, like so many others, was injured in a bad accident.

In *generation* 5, Ruth's mother, Florence, worked in the Eagle Mill. Her father, Charles Alexander, died young; so her mother took Ruth and they lived with the family in the Academy Hill house. None of Ruth's family got educated on the G.I. Bill, but Marlin, one of her mother's brothers, moved away to farm in California after he came out of the service; Ruth exchanges letters with his descendants and is invited to visit but does not like to fly. They are gone for her. The other brothers who stayed in Shamokin found only various unskilled jobs, a mailman, a delivery man.

Generation 6, dispersed even more widely, the men were overseas in the service and they wanted to go away again, some moved to white collar jobs: work for the government in Washington or in Lancaster, for the electric company in New Jersey; another to the shipyards in Baltimore.

Children in *generations 7 and* 8 are going to college and away. Ruth is out of touch with them.

Ruth commented that in the fourth generation and previous ones, the whole big extended family was very close and used to have picnics at the annual Folk Days at Edgewood Park, as many as fifty of them would come. "Everybody came, all your cousins that you never saw, second cousins and kissing cousins."[6] Three families lived within two blocks of each other on Academy Hill. But the family solidarity was greatly affected by the wars: "when World War I came, my mother went off to Philadelphia to work in a munitions factory and my uncles went in the services. Once the guys go in the service and go overseas, they aren't the same when they come home. The war changed things and we weren't as close."

Politics and Class in the Twentieth Century

As noted in chapter 1, the dominant families of the Southern regions of the coalfields, unlike the Northern, did not form dynasties that persisted from the nineteenth into the twentieth centuries. Most local wealthy industrialists moved elsewhere with the decline of the coal and garment industries.[7] Holding political office has run in some families of the twentieth and twenty-first centuries, however, so a few families have retained prominence in the town over two to three generations. Jim Kelley Sr. was first elected as County Commissioner in 1971 and was reelected for five terms, his father served two terms in the 1940s, and his son is following him in politics and is now coroner; three generations of the Dietrick family were commissioners; and so were Lawton Shroyer and his father of the garment factory owning family.

During much of the twentieth century, from the mid-1930s through the mid-1970s, the town was dominated by the powerful Henry Lark who headed a strong Republican political machine. His family was of Swiss ancestry, economically dominant in the town and connected to others of wealth and influence.[8]

The Lark Political Machine

The Larks were Protestants and members of St. John's United Church of Christ (see chapter 4). They had made their money in coal, and owned the Lark Coal Company. H. Wilson Lark, President of the National Dime Bank, built the family fortune. Frederick Lark became the President of the National Bank (later combined with the bank that was to be the Dime Bank) at the same time that Henry Lark was its vice president. The Lark Dress Company that made women's dresses was founded in 1932 by Thomas and Blanche Lark and run by several members of the family. It employed ninety people in 1964. In the Lark family, which became wealthy from patenting a cough syrup, Henry Lark was the politician, his father was a banker, his brother an attorney, his brother-in-law a judge. The basis of Henry Lark's wealth and political power were coal mines in Pennsylvania, West Virginia and Virginia, his ownership of a women's stocking factory, and a wire rope business (*News Item*, Achievers Series 35). He was chairman of the local branch of the Republican Party after the Depression until he resigned in 1974, having held the post for over thirty-five years, 1939–1974.

A longtime local politician described the power of this family and of the political machine of Henry Lark as follows.

> The Republicans ran the County from 1900 to the late '60s. Only then did we get a Democratic Commissioner when they broke the Lark machine and the democrats got elected. The Larks controlled the jobs. Henry Lark took a strong position, he made the decisions. I'm telling you from stories I heard from guys that were Republican and had nothing to hide, about how before they could get the job, they had to go in to see Mr. Lark, they had to register Republican, and their families had to register Republican. And that's how it worked. And they said a lot of state jobs were controlled by Mr. Lark. He had the connections in Harrisburg too. And then he controlled the county, he made the decisions about the jobs in the county. But in that process, from what I understand, and I believe it is true he did make these decisions, he was building a strong organization. If you produced for the party, you were taken care of as far as having a job. And that worked out well for the party and it worked out well for a lot of individuals who ended up with a decent job. Nobody ever got rich working for the government but they had a job. And during those years [of the Depression] you had a decline of coal. The Republicans with the Lark political machine controlled all appointments to WPA (Works Progress Administration), even in a Democratic administration, but you had to be a Protestant to get a job in the school system. Republican bosses like Henry Lark usually came from a powerful family. It was said he could rig any election. He was a political boss in the era of political bosses.

Another comment on the Lark machine focuses on the class, ethnic and religious divisions that persisted for the first half of the twentieth century into the 1960s in the town.

> You needed political connections to get anywhere. Henry Lark was the ruler of Northumberland Co. for thirty years in the '40s, '50s and '60s. Money, commercial success, connection to the railroads, and the ability to make things happen locally got the Republicans political influence. "You join and follow us and do what we direct and you are OK—if not, you are out." But we are now living with some of the stupid things that they did. The idea of 'keep

> the immigrant[9] out and don't cross the tracks' was perpetuated and there was much distrust between groups. Henry Lark fostered this distrust and the lack of communication in order to divide and rule. He would just put out fires rather than planning and cooperating. There was really class and ethnic warfare. You did not, if you were an immigrant, go up on Academy or Bunker Hill. There were no Catholic churches up there; they were in the 5th Ward and in Coal Township.[10] (See figure 4.2.)

Connections by marriage existed between prominent families in the twentieth century as they did between members of the dominant families of the nineteenth century. Henry Lark's brother-in-law was Judge William Troutman, a multimillionaire in the garment industry and a member of St. John's United Church of Christ; the Twiggars another influential family, married into the Lark family, as did the Shroyers, owners of the garment factory; Harold Barlow, the District Attorney, a graduate of Lehigh University hired by the Eagle Silk Mill to go and buy silk for them in Canton, was married to a daughter of Judge Moser. The judge and the McConnells and H. Wilson Lark lived next door to each other, and with the Twiggars had a cabin that they took their families to in the summers. They were all people of influence and money, on the School Board, and so on. In the words of one influential citizen "This was the way the place was run for years."

The way the Lark machine worked was that the Larks would pay people for working the primaries. There were thirteen wards (numbers seven, four and five were split) and they paid poll watchers and people working the polls about $10 a day ($26 a week). Wages paid by the Larks would have been about $25 a week, quite a lot of money at that time. These workers collected registrations for the party then, on Election Day, they would contact these people and bring them to the polling place. They would check off names on a list and fetch absentees to make sure they voted. The coal companies actually gave money of two dollars a vote.[11]

The career of Dan Strausser illustrates Henry Lark's power and influence for getting an individual into politics and a start on the road to becoming politically powerful thereafter. After serving in the army in World War II, Dan worked in the construction business and, as he said, "got into politics by being a henchman of Henry Lark." Thereafter, he became chairman of the local Republican Party, served as Mayor of Shamokin, was a Councilman for twelve years, and served as Executive Secretary of the Redevelopment Authority. He was also president and vice-president of the West End Fire Company.[12] Though not of great wealth, he is considered to have been very powerful. His power was built on his association with Henry Lark.

A Nickname in Politics

In connection with Henry Lark, a use of the nicknames that were so prevalent in the town (described in chapter 4) appears as a power device in politics. In this case, a nickname bestowed by a powerful politician is assumed to ensure the political success of an individual running for office. Jim Kelley, one of Shamokin's influential men, now deceased, recounted how Henry Lark did him a favor because he called him 'the bear in the cage' at the Market Street Bank—he worked there at the time—the bank looked like a cage, it had bars. He said they had laughed about it. Henry Lark asked why? And Jim said, "Well the first thing I was told after you made that statement was that I was going to win. And you got to remember that I was the candidate that never ran for county office before, and you had the sheriff that was very popular, and the commissioners Shroyer and Rumberger that were very popular; I was the fourth guy there." So Jim asked the guy who said he was going to win, how he knew that? And he was told that it was because he'd been given a nickname, and anybody who gets a nickname would win the election.[13]

This sort of nickname, conferred by a powerful person, appears to have acted as a seal of approval considered to help to carry the voters. That it could be used as an instrument of power, and was recognized as such by those in, or close to, the power structure is evident in the immediate comment on the bestowing of the nickname on Jim Kelley.

Associations and Clubs: "The Men Who Ran the Town"

Ethnic associations died out in the second half of the twentieth century. The clubs that dominated in the town thereafter, reflected and perpetuated the class structure. Members of them became social friends who met up several nights a week. People say it used to be almost a necessity to belong to them, and membership in them, along with political affiliation marked social status in the latter half of the twentieth century. After World War II, the elite were still primarily English, Welsh, Scots, and Germans, and were Protestant and Republican; the Irish, Lithuanians, Ukrainians, Polish, and Italians were Catholic and Democratic.

The big Protestant social clubs were the Elks and the Civic Club. All the prominent people in town belonged to the Elks Club. It was the place where the elite met up with each other, and English, Welsh, Scots and Germans dominated the membership. The Shamokin Elks had a fine, well-appointed building and members would have dinner and drink together there. There was one table where the same group would sit every night: they were expected at eight o'clock and nobody else would sit there; as one member commented, "They were the men who ran the town." They were industrialists, big merchants, members of the Water Company, doctors and lawyers. Members could also go to the Elks Clubs in other towns, socialize and have dinner. The club thus facilitated forging social and business connections and making the useful contacts through which the political system functioned. The Elks Club was connected to politics:

"The Elks were really powerful fifty years ago . . . you got in through your father, not because you were wealthy, plenty were not. This continued into the forties. They were a social group—you did not need wealth to belong, and a way for politicians to get control."[14]

The Elks had a hierarchy of internal organization, each level with an initiation ritual, with a parallel organization for women when they were finally allowed to join. In the early years, the Elks had only Protestant members, not Catholics or Jews. New members had to be voted in and if you got two blackballs you were not admitted; it depended on your reputation and abilities and being a good athlete helped. But later this changed as the economy declined and the locus of power and influence shifted to the cities.

The Masons were also Protestant but membership conferred lower social status than did belonging to the Elks.

The Knights of Columbus, a national order for Catholic men, was established in Shamokin in October 1899. It raised money for Our Lady of Lourdes High School and for survivors of World War II and their children. In 1959, the Knights moved into a building on North Shamokin St. and in 1962, held a testimonial dinner in honor of the Grand Knight attended by several hundred members and their wives (Shamokin Centennial Book). This impressive number is a measure of the vigor and importance of this Catholic organization in the town. It has remained very active.

The Moose was the working class club. They supported the baseball league, bought uniforms and bats for the kids, balls, masks, gloves, transportation. They made money through slot machines and gave to the Red Cross, the Salvation Army and the hospital. They had a program of sickness and death benefits for members, and ran homes for orphans and the elderly. The Lodges used to meet once a month.

Change in religious and ethnic background appeared among those of wealth and influence in the last half of the twentieth century. Two examples both Catholic and in the coal business are the Italian Rosini family and Senator Helfrick and his partner Bob Kerris (of Polish extraction).

Anthony J. Rosini emigrated from northern Italy in the early years of 1900 and after a few construction jobs in New York City came to work as a miner in the Shamokin area. After twenty-five years in the mines, he developed a produce business in which he was assisted, as they grew by his seven sons. The older boys went into independent coal trucking and mining and in 1939, Evoldo, Reno and Odone established the Rosini Coal Company and eventually branched out into strip mining. This company became an important industry in the town. Sons Don and William Rosini formed the Shamokin Filler Company which pulverizes coal, and produces specialty anthracite products (Shomper, 1987, 41). Don is today very prominent in community affairs.

Senator Edward W. Helfrick (elected to the state senate in 1980) and his partner Bob Kerris are in the coal industry. Their business had the federal contract to put out underground mine fires and they were able to mine all the coal that was not on fire. They bought all the coal lands back of Kulpmont as well as mines such as the Glen Burn in the declining years of coal. They eventually sold out all their very extensive holdings to a group of men who had worked for them.

The Loss of the Garment Trade

In the 1970s–1980s the town economy was devastated again. The garment factories in Shamokin/Coal Township and the rest of the Coal Region closed one after another as the industry moved south and then overseas in search of cheaper, nonunionized labor.[15] Thousands of jobs were lost in the Region and there was another huge population exodus from Shamokin as people left for the big cities and towns to look for work (see table 1.3). The unions fought against this development. A union organizer gives an account of her life and her participation in the struggle.

The Story of a Union Organizer

Eleanor Kuhns was a worker in the Arrow factory and a union organizer in the 1960s–1980s. She came from a typical poor mining family. Her father was of the generation of miners in which many were illiterate because they went to work in the coal breakers as young children. Her mother, born in 1895, came to New York in 1912 and worked in a garment factory there. They had seven children. After the collieries shut down in the thirties, her father lost his job at the age of forty; the family was desperately poor. The children picked coal for the winter, and gathered wild foods in the woods to eat. Her mother took in washing and ironing for a lot of people and did cleaning jobs. Her father never got another job. He had heart problems and black lung from working in the mines from childhood.

Ellie (as she was always called) completed high school and through the school got a job in the reading rooms of the Library of Congress and went to Washington. There she worked in the copyright office. She applied and was accepted to train at their expense to be a cataloger in the Library of Congress, an excellent job, but by then had met her husband to be and in 1954, after the war, he wanted to return to Shamokin. The illness and death of her parents and a sister followed; like others, she gave up a career because she was married and was needed at home to help.

She commented: "The coal barons got so rich and treated the miners so shabby. But, thank God, the union came in and they started to get better wages." She went to work as a quality inspector at the Arrow factory and became a union organizer to fight the discrimination against women in wages from the day when she discovered that the women factory workers had only been given a thirty-five-cent raise while the men got forty-five cents. She became a union steward and finally got to work for the Union in 1968; they were successful in getting the factory workers a little more money, vacations, and, in 1976, a pension plan.

The Unions organized to try and resist the threat to the workers' jobs as the factories began to move overseas for cheaper labor. As the factories began closing, she took part in the union's intense efforts to stem job losses and prevent the closures. She describes what it was like to live through this devastating blow to the town's economy and the consequences for the town and for the factory workers of this hopeless struggle.

She carried on the militant tradition of the coal workers with the textile workers. When she discovered that bigger pay raises were given to men than to women, she was so angry that she ended up in charge of the picket line down at the warehouse, and was nearly killed when a big truck tried to run through the line. After that she decided to get to know what was really happening and had, as she said, the "best Union attendance you ever saw," became a Union steward, and finally got to work for the Union in 1968. It was Local 21C of the Amalgamated Clothing and Textiles Union which had six or more shops in the area. The union was successful in getting the factory workers a little bit more money, vacations and, in 1976, a pension plan.

The unions organized to resist the threat to the workers' jobs as the factories began to move overseas where they could find cheaper labor. Ellie spoke of how hard they tried to save those plants, all those marches, all those buses to Washington. Arrow had more than one thousand people employed between the warehouse and the manufacturing plant. But the factories kept closing, one by one. The jobs just went and Arrow closed in April 1985. So there is not even one union factory around today; there are two that are nonunion, but all the union shops are gone.[16]

By the mid-1980s, the severe economic decline from the closing of the textile factories set in. The consequences of the closing of these factories were disastrous, not only economically but also culturally: there were no longer enough people to sustain the traditions, festivals and activities of the different ethnic groups. Population loss as people left in search of jobs was compounded by the national decline in interest in religion and dwindling membership for the churches that had played such an important part in maintaining ethnic traditions.

The Decline of Religion and Ethnicity

World War II and the population drop thereafter had major consequences for the town. They weakened the relative strengths of religion and ethnicity, and class distinctions became more relevant in the town in the last half of the twentieth century and into the millennium. The effect of the drastic loss of population on life in the town was compounded by the gradually declining interest of many young people in ethnic traditions and in religion, a nationwide trend. Religious institutions and observances had been to a large extent responsible for preserving and reproducing ethnic traditions in the Coal Region, as Catholics used to be taught ethnic traditions in the parochial schools of their churches. This basically depended on the teacher, who was usually a nun. Depending on how strongly she felt about passing on culture, students got history, would celebrate holidays, and learn about saints who were important. But there was no teaching of the language, it was no longer useful to anyone—not in business. "It was after World War II, in the 1950s, that this teaching of traditions stopped. Before World War II it was in place, like cement. Then World War II changed everything."[17]

Other important factors related to this change, and also connected with population loss, were the gradual relaxation of the disapproval of ethnic and religious intermarriage and the mingling of people in what had formerly been distinct ethnic neighborhoods.

Intermarriage: Mingling Religions and Neighborhoods

For the first immigrant generations, it was expected that people marry within their ethnic group and intermarriage was disapproved. A Protestant pastor captured the essence of the problem, of just what marriage within their ethnic group meant for people. He said that it was a big deal for someone who was a Polish Catholic to marry an Italian Catholic, that it was almost like a mixed marriage because of all of the cultural baggage that went with all of the prejudices; "you know, we're not one of those kind of people." Someone on the outside would say, "You are all Catholic, what's the big deal?" But someone on the inside would say, "Whoa, it IS a big deal." In a multigenerational family there are even stronger bonds, because of the grandparents who have stronger memories and stronger ties to the cultural roots. "They get very upset when a grandchild marries out of the faith or out of the culture or whatever. Back in the past, there were semiarranged marriages, chosen because they looked like us; they had the same values, culture, understanding of life and maybe the same career, because that was who they were."

The ethnic parochial schools with their efforts to preserve the language, the observance of religious and cultural traditions, and ethnic social life had all worked to preserve marriage within the group, but the strong sense of ethnic identity and the part it played in community life changed as the economy declined, the population dropped, these schools were closed, and intermarriage became general.

There had always, in fact, been some instances of interethnic marriage despite the disapproval, but after World War II this intermarriage greatly increased and by the seventies, disapproval of dating and marriage between groups had disappeared. Intermarriage became accepted and ceased to be a problem and well-defined ethnic neighborhoods became a thing of the past. Thus, by the last quarter of the twentieth century, ethnicity was no longer based on membership of an in-marrying ethnic community and its importance in life had dwindled. One pastor commented: "Most of the younger people don't care so much. The barriers may be there theoretically but they are just not important anymore."[18] Nevertheless, as the next chapter will show, although ethnicity is manifested in different ways than in the past and no longer divides or unites people in the way it did formerly, it still has some significance and some people still feel deeply about it.

Accommodations have to be made in a marriage of mixed ethnicity and mixed religion and the dominant parent usually determines the ethnic background of the children. It is thought that the marriage should take place in the bride's church, but then afterwards the pair go to the husband's church and raise their children in his church. But there is plenty of variation. Ethnic traditions may still be observed from both father's and mother's sides but one side is more likely to be dominant. One woman who considers herself Italian says: "I was raised in Italian traditions though my Mom was not Italian. My Dad told us that when they got married she learned how to cook and carry on from his mother and father. So there was a heavy Italian influence in my family. I went to the Italian Catholic school and the Italian church."[19] Sometimes, it may be influenced by which food traditions you prefer. A man who has a Polish father, an Italian mother, and a Ukrainian wife ("we are a kind of hodge-podge") says that for Ukrainian Christmas dinner everything is bland: sauerkraut, dough strings, mushroom soup, peas, no meat. On the Italian side (he had been raised in an Italian household), "You had mackerel, cod, flounder, with sea bass and shark, and it was all cooked expertly with side orders of spaghetti. It was a feast. On the Ukrainian side it was very, very bland, almost like a Passover meal, and on the Italian side a very rich meal. So I always went to the good food.[20]

In many cases, however, intermarriage was extremely problematic. In the early 1960s, a Ukrainian father felt so strongly about it that when his daughter married a Protestant, she could not come home any more. In another case, a German related that his mother was Catholic and his father Protestant. His father's people hated his mother because she was Catholic and she eventually divorced her husband and remarried; the marriage could not survive the bitterness it caused. In other cases, it resulted in no interaction between the families involved: one Irishman's father's brother married a Protestant girl from Trevorton whose father was a mine boss at the colliery. The Irish family was a mine family from Bear Valley, a few miles away. The animosity was intensified by the fact that the girl was not just a Protestant but also that her father was a mine boss, so the religious difference was exacerbated by class difference. Although their son recalled going to see his father's mother in town, there was really no interaction between the families.

Religious intermarriage could also affect inheritance. One Irish Catholic was so angry at his daughter for turning Protestant when she married, that when he died, he left her only a pittance of $50 whereas he left $500 each to the priests who were his pall bearers. In a Protestant German family, the son married a Catholic girl in the early 1960s and, as was always demanded by the Catholic Church, had to sign a paper that the children would be raised Catholic. The shock and disappointment this aroused in the Protestant family was because the children and grandchildren would be brought up Catholics. Protestant resentment of this has carried over for several generations. One reason that this is not as prevalent as it was, however, is because for the last two generations there has been a national decline in religion; people have tended to participate less actively in their churches and are not so likely to be churchgoers.

Some people, however, managed to come to terms with religious intermarriage and were able to bring themselves to accept it or accommodate the differences. One example was a German elder of the Presbyterian church. When one of his daughters married an Irish Roman Catholic it caused quite an upset in the family, but after she married, she had two children and they used to come and see their grandfather every Sunday morning. Another example was a mixed Ukrainian and Irish/English/Welsh marriage, the Protestant wife converted to Catholicism and they celebrate two Christmases: "One at home for our girls and family, and one for his Christmas," she said (the Ukrainian church celebrates Christmas on January 7).

Intermarriage has consequences for how ethnic descent is claimed today when it is not obviously ascribed as in the past when both parents were of the same ethnicity. In a mixed Protestant Catholic marriage the Protestant parent must agree that the children will be brought up Catholic. If this is not agreed, the Catholic parent abandons the Catholic faith. But sometimes ethnicity is claimed through ancestors two or even three generations back, through upbringing, and even through church membership and participation in church community activities.

In the early years of the Welsh in America, for example, having two Welsh parents defined you as Welsh. But a Welsh woman in Shamokin/Coal Township emphasized the sufficiency nowadays to claim Welsh identity on the basis of ancestry on one side of the family only—even if it is two generations back. On St. David's Day, the choir is there, and they are all people from the community. She said, "A lot of people are Welsh but a lot of them are only partly Welsh—they'll tell you, I'm part Welsh. But nowadays, we just say we're Welsh. I don't deny that I'm also German, but I was brought up so Welsh that I'm Welsh. And my kids believe they're Welsh."

Here part-Welsh ancestry is being given as sufficient to claim Welsh identity: having one Welsh parent and an upbringing in which Welsh identity is paramount, is sufficient to claim that identity. But such a claim is even possible without ancestry: she gave an example of a family in the church who gained its Welsh ethnic affiliation entirely through church membership and their participation in the choir.

A Welsh woman recounted how they even have some people who go to their church called Romanoski. "They come because when the wife's parents wanted to get married, they did not have anybody to marry them because it was back in the 1930s when Protestant and Catholic didn't marry and her father was Polish and Catholic." The Assistant Minister at the time (the first woman minister in Pennsylvania), was willing to marry them. "So they started coming to our church. Well, their children perceive themselves as Welsh. The daughter played the piano and has taught Sunday School for years, and her name is Romanoski but she will say they are Welsh when she is asked, because she was born and raised in the Welsh church." She thought that her mother had some relative that was allegedly Welsh. "But that was not really why she says she is Welsh, she says it because she belongs to the church community. Her mother (who had recently passed away) had made Welsh cookies in the church for St. David's Day, and sang alto in the choir every week."

Intermarriage has meant that people of all faiths and ethnic backgrounds gradually came to be together in their daily lives rather than having the separate existences described in chapter 4. The loss of European languages and the change from parochial to public schools compounded the effects of this change so that the salience of ethnicity has gradually declined and it is no longer an important feature of town life.

Languages: Decline and Attempts at Revival

The languages of the different groups persisted into the 1930s and 1940s, and it was common for both men and women of first generation immigrants who lived in the Coal Region to speak several languages. Names were often Anglicized by the immigration office when entering the country. For example, the spelling of the Polish names *Mieszkiewicz* became Miscavage, *Szczesny*/Chesnay, *Saviski*/Savitt, *Kerisavage*/Kerris, and *Pavajinski*/Parker. But by the next generation people were no longer multilingual. A Lithuanian of St. Clair said her father, who was illiterate, spoke seven languages which he had learned from his fellow miners as he worked with them. She remembers him sitting in the swing on the front porch and talking with anyone who went by. He was fluent in Polish, Ukrainian, Russian, German, English, as well as Lithuanian, and he spoke some Italian and French. But parents encouraged their children to Americanize and many insisted they learn to speak English. "A lot of people had the philosophy that we are here in this country and now we are going to speak English."[21]

At first the parochial schools helped to maintain the national languages. In the Mt. Carmel Polish school classes were in Polish in the morning, English in the afternoon. But by the second generation, this was no longer the case. Bob Chesnay, a third generation Pole, says: "Our parents were Americanized. Their parents told them they had to become Americanized and speak the language; when we were born obviously they didn't speak to us in that language and so it was lost." His son, Vince, whose mother's family is Ukrainian, adds: "By the time I was in school, myself and my brothers, we would have a weekly Ukrainian class (I was in Transfiguration School) and occasionally a Polish priest here at St. Casimir's Church when I was growing up, would throw in some Polish—that was the extent of it." So it went from Vince's grandparents' generation when the morning classes were all in Polish, in two generations to just one lesson a week. Although when he went to Transfiguration School, he would go to morning mass before school which was in Ukrainian, so he knew the Ukrainian Old Slavonic of the church. The mass in church would be in both Ukrainian and English.[22]

The Lithuanian grade school tried to teach Lithuanian as a second language. Today very few Lithuanians still speak their language fluently. One, who does, gave a reason for its rapid decline: The immigrants' children all said they didn't speak it when they were growing up, so they didn't bother to learn it. Now, she said, they wish they had. "But you know, we were kind of laughed at if we spoke a foreign language. They'd say, 'this is America, speak American.' So nobody really wanted to speak their own language; they weren't proud of it. Now people are proud to have an ethnic background."[23]

Those who speak Lithuanian today are second generation immigrants. Their parents, born in the home country spoke it at home, but they did not teach it to their children. Very few born after World War II speak it.

A Welsh woman with a German grandfather likewise said it was hard to keep the Welsh language because people were trying to be American: "We didn't learn the Welsh language itself, we learned expressions from our grandparents. We also learned songs but in English. My grandparents' children did not speak Welsh, they weren't taught it. But they all were taught the love of music and they were all very talented." They learned to sing a different part or to play a different instrument: today members of the congregation routinely sing tenor and alto.[24] Thus, the church holds people together in knowledge of music and sometimes in singing in Welsh: at festivals such as the *gymanfa ganu*, some of the hymns are sung in Welsh.

As intermarriage between ethnic groups increased during and after World War II, it constituted a further blow to the effort to preserve the languages that were rapidly dying out in the younger generations. People's pride in their ethnic heritage, however, revived in the late 1960s[25] and aroused the interest of people in learning the language of that heritage: in Frackville, they made requests that the Vocational Technical school offer language teaching of Lithuanian and Ukrainian (two principal ethnic groups of the town); in 2001 in Mt. Carmel, the revival of interest in learning Polish resulted in evening classes that enrolled ten people a year later.

Attempts at reviving languages are beset with difficulty. Lois Huffines emphasizes that language maintenance efforts can only be successful if they create or preserve domains for the language. Her study of the Pennsylvania German dialect concludes that as social, educational and occupational concerns independent of their ethnic group have drawn German-Americans into mainstream America and their ethnic affiliation has declined, the functions previously allocated to German have disappeared, which seems to doom to failure a revival of this dialect of the language. Once ethnic communities arrive at a threshold of contact with the dominant society beyond which retaining the ethnic language becomes impossible, they change rapidly: school systems do not uphold the mother tongue of children raised speaking another language; churches must appeal to younger generations who cannot any more follow teachings in a non-English language, as must the ethnic press; and ethnic clubs are no longer relevant to those who are assimilated into mainstream America and its values (Huffines 1985, 249). All these problems have confronted the efforts to revive languages in the coal towns.

Ethnicity was in decline in the last half of the century because of all these factors, but many saw the final blow to it to have been the merging of the ethnic Catholic churches in 1995.[26] Protestant parishes suffered from declining membership too, but the different Protestant denominations have had varying solutions to the problem, to be detailed below, which were not imposed upon them from above. As in the Protestant parishes, the Catholic bishop of Allentown did not insist on mergers of the ethnic churches of his diocese, which includes the northern part of the Coal Region, but has left them to work out solutions for themselves to the decline in membership of their ethnic churches, as we will see in one example.

The Merging of the Churches

In the years of the great influx of immigrants into the United States from Eastern and Southern Europe to work in the mines in the late nineteenth century, the hierarchy of the Roman Catholic Church had made the decision to create ethnic parishes. These continued to exist until 1995, when the ethnic Catholic churches of the diocese of Harrisburg in the Coal Region were asked by the bishop, on instruction from Rome, to merge into a smaller number. This meant that people had to go to a strange church rather than the one that they and their forebears had gone to and even built, and caused great distress; many people felt deeply resentful and upset that their parish was being taken over by people of another ethnic group.

In Shamokin/Coal Township, Mt. Carmel and Kulpmont: "One of the biggest things that was devastating to this whole area, was when the Catholic Church consolidated all the churches," was a frequently expressed view. A lot of the older people who had been baptized, received communion, and been confirmed in a church, wanted to be buried in that same church, and the action of Rome and the bishop seemed unendurably high-handed: "No Italian bishop is going to tell this Polish that he has to go to the Irish church" (i.e., from St. Stanislaus to St. Edwards/Mother Cabrini) was one instant reaction. Some parishioners stopped attending church regularly; some went to churches in other towns. Many people felt after the mergers that "There is no ethnicity any more, they are just Catholic churches. Ethnicity is now cultural, not religious."

In Shamokin/Coal Township, seven Catholic churches were merged into two (see figure 4.2). In the East end of town, Mother Cabrini Church was created from the merger of five: the original church, St. Edward's, (primarily Irish, Italian and German, though all their pastors were Irish), was merged with St. Michael's (Lithuanian), St. Mary's (Slovak), St. Stanislaus (Polish), and St. Anthony's in Ranshaw, an outlier to the east of Shamokin (predominantly Polish). The Franciscan order that had been running St. Stanislaus was put in charge of the new church, which took over the former St. Edward's building. In the West End of town, Our Lady of Hope was created from St. Stephen's (Polish) and St. Joseph's (Irish, German, and Italian). In contrast, the Ukrainian Greek Catholic Church of the Transfiguration in Shamokin, which is in the diocese of Philadelphia not of Harrisburg, has not had to merge, and has remained a viable, cohesive and active congregation.

It was the same for the other two towns. In Mt. Carmel five churches were merged into two. In Kulpmont, St. Casimir's Church was Polish. This congregation and Holy Cross in Mt. Carmel mounted a big struggle to keep their churches open and were very antagonistic to the bishop for closing both: St. Casimir's had just been renovated; Holy Cross was not in decline and the priest was very popular.

Thus in Shamokin/Coal Township, the decline of the economy, the departure of many of the young people to bigger towns and cities, the decrease in church attendance that was taking place nationwide, and a shortage of priests, all played a part in the drop in membership of the ethnic churches that led to the mergers, and to a decline in ethnic based activities. For example, in the thirties Ukrainian High School graduates had had a dance group that performed at graduation; it died out after the war. Choirs had the same problem: the Ukrainians tried reviving their choir with a director from the Hazleton monastery, but there were not enough young people left who were interested enough to make up the number they needed. The last public performance of the choir was in the early 1950s. Attempts to revive it in 1964 could not attract sufficient numbers.[27] It was the same story with the Welsh choir. These and other ethnic traditions and organizations, strong before the war, faded away after it. They continued in gradually diminishing form into the sixties, when people still remember different languages spoken in the streets and *babushka* (grandmothers) in black headscarves, but by the seventies most ethnic traditions had faded completely or existed only in greatly diminished form.

Nevertheless, the sense of ethnicity remained strong enough for members of congregations to be very upset by the closing of their churches in 1995. Some even abandoned their Catholic religion and went to a Protestant church. In one case, in an outlying part of the city some distance away, members of a Catholic church who had formerly come into town every Sunday joined the local Methodist church near their homes when their Catholic church merged. It was much easier for them not to have to go into town, and changing their religious affiliation seemed less difficult than joining with Catholics of a different ethnicity.

A leading member of St. Michael's, the Lithuanian church in Coal Township, explains why their merger was so painful.[28] The leaders of the parish consulted with a number of people from the church, with reports and discussions. But nevertheless, what so distressed them was that many of them or their fathers and mothers were the founders of that church. "It was a major blow because they saw their heritage, the singing of their hymns in the church in Lithuanian, the windows with Lithuanian decoration and dedications to certain Lithuanian families, all just disappear. It was a blow to them that many of those windows were sold and dispersed." But they suffered an additional loss. It was not only the loss of religious customs and the building their ancestors had constructed and to whom there were specific commemorations, and the continuity this represented for them and profoundly rooted them, but it was also that the merger was so destructive to the Lithuanian community based on that church.

The church was an important center of peoples' lives in terms of religion, of events, of getting together. There were Christmas plays, Easter plays, and other events to which everyone came, so the merger has had major impact. The church leader thought there was more of a unity before the merger with about 125 to 150 people who had that common heritage: "They did not all go to one particular church but have spread out to about four different ones in the area, so that there is no commonality; the people have dispersed themselves." The mergers weakened ethnic church communities, the core groups that had still been holding on to what was left of the ethnic culture and ethnic identity in the Coal Region. So the church in Shamokin/Coal Township and in Mt. Carmel which has been a major factor in the Lithuanian community for a hundred years is gone. It is a major blow, he laments: "what do you turn to, and how do you celebrate?" As one Welsh woman put it: "When you look at some of those churches and how much the dollar was worth when they built them . . . you couldn't believe that they took it away. It was like a knife in the back"[29] Such statements are revealing of the strength of the sense of religious and ethnic community of the past and their significance to people in the present; they are part of a sense of community that the townspeople actively want to regain and retain.

For some people, the merged church cannot compensate. A Czechoslovakian woman from St. Mary's, the Slovak church in Coal Township, spoke vividly of the isolation that the loss of church community meant when they merged into Mother Cabrini Church. "Before, everybody knew everybody in the church: they sat in the same place, and talked together after church. They were like one big family." Christmas for her was the midnight meal: family and friends from church would always come to her house after mass for ham. "But at Mother Cabrini it is not like that, most people are strangers. People are just for themselves." She voices the wish to keep the sense of community; that was the legacy and heritage of the past.

Such intense distress from the mergers is however gradually dying down for at least some people who have been able to accept the merging of their church into another and felt that it was working out all right. In Mother Cabrini, the priest took whatever he could from the churches that were joined, and put them all together to make a church in which everybody had things from their own church. This process of constructing a church to suit several ethnic groups shows how the religious distinctiveness of a particular group was represented in symbolic and decorative objects that were created and endowed with connections to particular religious events, places, artists, and symbols specific to the history of the church of each group; it is this which gave them their significance and value.

These connections are very evident in a pamphlet available to visitors in Mother Cabrini church which explains the history of the items taken from each church. The altars are the original anthracite coal altars commissioned for St. Edward's church (Irish, Italian and German) in 1972 as tribute to the mining heritage of the people of the area, and the coal lectern has the original altar rail gates of that church from pre-Vatican II. Murals from St. Mary's (Slovak), over one hundred years old are on the rear walls of Mother Cabrini. Statues of Sts. Peter and Paul flank both sides of the center doors and one of the Sacred Heart of Jesus stands in the sanctuary; these statues, purchased in the 1920s, had been part of the high altar of St. Michael's (Lithuanian) for many years. The statues of Mary and Joseph on the right side of the sanctuary came from St. Mary's, where they had been purchased in 1953 by the Marcinek siblings in memory of their parents. The crucifix behind the altar and the font are from St. Stanislaus Church (Polish); both are more than one hundred years old. A Venetian tiled mosaic from St. Anthony's (predominately Polish) hangs over the tabernacle. Each is of course, only one of many such objects which graced the original churches and gave them special meaning. Collectively with other items in their original churches they were elements of the group's identity.

As well as symbolic items, religious traditions of different groups are celebrated by all in the merged church. Mother Cabrini has the ceremony of the Blessing of the Baskets of food for the Easter breakfast on the day before Easter from the Slavic European tradition, and the non-Slavic members of the congregation have learned to do it too. A Polish couple who had been in the Polish Church of Coal Township, St. Stephen's, which joined with St. Joseph's, an Italian-Irish church, appreciated the priest's efforts to make them feel at home: "The priest was nice enough to keep some of the Polish traditions. They never had these in their church, they never gave out the Christmas wafers, but we have had them ever since then." The bishop gave them a list of things to pick what they wanted the new church to be. "Anyway, now it is called Our Lady of Hope, and it's nice." He and his wife both said it was working out well, though acknowledging that "some people were really, really bitter."

The use of at least some ethnic religious traditions of others seems to parallel the way in which everyone now enjoys everyone else's ethnic foods at all festivals, in the mingling of food traditions that has developed in the towns.

Some of the clergy of the town, both Protestant and Catholic, were optimistic about recent encouraging signs of growth in new and younger members of their churches, and of the number of younger ones waiting in the wings and getting training in how things worked against the days when they would be needed to run the smaller number of, but still enthusiastically supported, church and ethnic festivals (see chapter 7) that continue to be a strong feature of Coal Region life.

The same problems of coping with population loss exist for Protestant churches as for Catholic ones. Most Protestant churches are not ethnic churches, but some of them have so few members they can no longer afford a full time pastor. Thus the Protestants face the same problems of drastically declining membership as do the Catholics, but the extreme shortage of priests of the latter is not a factor. They have, however, been allowed to make their own decisions on how to deal with their problems rather than having a solution imposed from above. In the big German church in Mt. Carmel, the stained glass windows need their frames renewed: that alone will cost $40–50 thousand. Everybody realizes what will inevitably happen.

Some Protestant churches merged earlier than did the Catholics: in the mid-1980s four Methodist churches merged into one. The Lutheran churches of Grace/St. Paul and Trinity Church have been doing what is called a Lutheran Community cooperative for the last three years. St. John's United Church of

Christ is the largest Protestant church in town and has so far been able to exist on money from some very rich families in its early years. They are currently trying to assess their prospects for the future as this money dwindles.[30]

The intensity of the reactions to the merger seems to indicate that a continuing sense of ethnicity and ethnic community existed into the 1990s, well after the 1960s and 1970s when endogamy, ethnic neighborhoods, and many cultural traditional events had effectively ended. These reactions are revealing of the degree of identification of ethnicity and religion.

Opinions thus vary on the decline of ethnicity and the effects of these mergers: for some closing their church was a loss in a fundamental sense of who they were, because their identity was so strongly rooted in their religion, their ethnicity, and their church; for others, especially the younger generation, this destruction was not so strongly felt because religion and ethnicity were already for them a part of the past, or they felt that people had changed after the mergers and were more accepting of other ethnic groups.

Ethnicity in these towns has included these changing strengths and emphases over time; today it exists primarily as an element of people's identities of varying strength. This account of responses to changing circumstances adds to the understanding of it as a process. The chapter concludes with an account by a Catholic priest in Mahanoy City (see figure 1.1), of the combining of two parishes with a successful adaptation, invention and continuity of ethnic religious traditions.

The Polish church of St. Casimir's in Mahanoy City is in the diocese of Allentown where the bishop did not ask that the churches merge. Father Bukaty the priest there was able to deal with the declining membership of his church and a Slovak church in a different way. His account of what he did reveals in the continuing change, adaptation, practical adjustments, invention and transmission of some ethnic traditions how ethnicity is a process. His fluency in Polish and expertise in music, and his intense efforts to preserve religious tradition and national culture, have been a solution to the problem of combining the two Catholic churches to which he ministers and are also a help to other churches and organizations in the region.

Ethnicity as Process: Adapting Religious Tradition in Mahanoy City

The population of Mahanoy City, northeast of Shamokin/Coal Township, was at one time more than 13,000; it is now closer to 4,000. But it still has six churches. They are in the Diocese of Allentown and do not have to merge so long as they are self-supporting. A parish continues unless it dies a natural death or decides to join with another parish. In St. Casimir's, the Polish parish, not one of the parishioners was born in Poland; the old timers are all third generation, but it is still thought of as the Polish parish. Father Bukaty[31] is the priest for the joined Polish and Slovak parishes and sees them as one culture. He says: "We have the same culture and traditions, we are the same blood, we are Slavic." He was born in America, of parents fluent in Polish. He was raised in a Polish speaking neighborhood in Kansas City and belonged to the Polish parish. He studied theology over four years in Poland and was ordained there, and his love and knowledge of the language and culture comes from this background. He is the last priest that will speak Polish, because today there are no boys who speak the language or know the culture who are becoming priests in America, and it is not clear that the Bishop would accept one from Poland.

He related the traditions and culture that he was giving his parishioners. He has invented some new traditions, adapted old ones so that they will work in American culture and stay alive, and promotes some use and understanding of the Polish language in order to preserve it to a minimal degree. He appreciates the qualities of the people to whom he ministers, while persuading them to essential transformations of outlook, attitudes and practices that can give their descendants a better prospect of maintaining some of their Polish identity and heritage.

There are many Polish parishes in the coal region, but most of the pastors are, like him, Polish-American. They do not know the language, but they have Polish names and do celebrate cultural things as best as they can, but with the shortage of priests, there are areas of the diocese where there are not Polish priests in Polish parishes. Father Bukaty said that he would have to be a fool to be preaching in Polish on Sunday: "my people would be looking at the wall. Although the first year I had it all in Polish, I saw they did not understand. So then I prepared new booklets, one verse in Polish, one in English. I preach only one sermon, but I go back and forth in English and Polish." So everybody understands the gist of what he is saying, and often his audiences are mixed.

He uses Polish for the Lenten Devotions and is the only priest in the area who can do this. When a new pastor came to St. Casimir's church in Shenandoah, they made a pact. Father Bukaty would play the organ for it because he knew the music. Musically it is very difficult to play and that is why no organist plays it and nobody knows it any more. So he played the organ for the Devotions and his priest friends came in to celebrate it. They didn't have to do anything in Polish, he did everything from the choir through the microphone. "So I keep it alive," he says, "the people sing, I am playing the organ, the priest does the part he has to do, and we keep the whole thing going. But it only happens because I am a musician as well as a priest."

He is involved in the Polish clubs in Mt. Carmel and in Allentown, and with the Polish National Alliance in the Lehigh valley, a fraternal organization in which he is very active when they put on celebrations. When it began, ten or twelve years ago, it was all in Polish, but as he began to see more and more Polish-Americans and people who did not speak Polish at all but were Polish, he took the liturgy and had it in both languages, one reading in Polish and one reading in English—for gospel reading, songs, sermon, one in each language. He says: "This keeps everybody happy and everybody coming because there is something there for everyone. A polka orchestra plays for the mass, and as soon as the mass is over the dancing begins and we have eight hours of it."

According to Father Bukaty, ethnic groups still hold in Mahanoy City. They are very proud of their parishes and when the families come home for the holidays, they are all back to their ethnic church. There is Christmas and Easter, those are the big family celebrations, also Thanksgiving Day, an American holiday. He recounts how "We have a tradition here on that day, I bless bread. I have little bread loaves baked: I order about 100–150, we bless them at the mass, everyone comes up and I give them a blessed loaf that they take home to share at the Thanksgiving table. That is one of our traditions here." The little loaves are a new Polish tradition in a lot of parishes now that has been picked up because, he says, it is a beautiful tradition. And with the blessing of the Easter baskets—"Why are they doing that at the Irish church? That's not their tradition, but everybody is doing it."

His parish started the three-day festivals in the town and was the first to have carnivals at which the biggest draw was always the music and the ethnic food. The homemade Polish sausage, fresh and smoked, homemade sauerkraut, *halushki* (cabbage and noodles of homemade dough), homemade Polish hamburgers (not just beef, but with bread, onions, pepper, seasoning, and eggs, called *granati* in Polish because they looked like hand-grenades, soups (the red beet soup called *ascht)*, bean soup, chicken soup, homemade Polish vegetable soup, tripe soup), *bigos* (hunter's stew). They all brought in a lot of money.

Father Bukaty recounts how in the past people did not drive but walked to mass. They walked from all the coal patches around in the woods along walking paths. They would leave at 5:30 a.m. in the morning to come to 7 or 8 o'clock mass. They never missed mass, the whole family came. This was their social life. Today it is the sacramental life of the family for which they come back: baptisms, weddings, funerals. People come who are in driving distance of two to three hours. The church is usually full on Christmas Day. They have one or two carols in Polish and young people come. The members of the Mt. Carmel Polish Cultural Club, when the weather allows, come to celebrations here. "We have a beautiful attendance on Memorial Day, Labor Day, Fourth of July, with a morning mass at 9:00 a.m., not too early. I have the procession on Easter Sunday at the 10:30 mass. In Poland, it is celebrated at 5:00 a.m. Of course, if I had it here at 5:00 a.m. I'd be singing to myself, so I have it at 10:30 a.m.[32]

Father Bukaty's strong emphases on some minimal degree of use of the Polish language, his strategies to enable his congregation to use and follow it a little, preserve it as a significant element of the essence of being Polish. His efforts are valued by Polish American priests in the area, who do not have the language and who elicit his help in introducing something of it into their own services and celebrations, and by other local Polish organizations. As well as his fluent Polish, his musical abilities are key factors in what he does. He makes it clear that where the language and music have died out, the retention of religious culture is very difficult. This underscores the importance of both language and music, even in greatly modified use, as part of Polish ethnic identity. Their continuation to some degree in Mahanoy City lies behind his claim that "the ethnic groups still hold in Mahanoy City"; they have not changed so much in this part of the region as they have in Shamokin/Coal Township. The polka bands and music beloved of Eastern

Figure 6.1. Blessing the Easter Baskets at Transfiguration Church on the Saturday before Easter

Figure 6.2. Displaying the Baskets and Their Contents

European—and other—Americans are another continuing and modified element of Polish tradition. They are a part of the cultural musical repertoire Polish people enjoy in their lives.

The newly invented tradition of the little bread loaves that are blessed and given to people to take home at Thanksgiving, as well as the ancient ones of Blessing the Easter Baskets (see figures 6.1 and 6.2) and the Christmas Wafer (formerly only used in the Lithuanian, Polish and Slavic churches), are now being used in many other parishes in the area which have specifically requested them.

These traditions are spreading which indicates that their observance is not dependent on one particular priest. This spread of religious tradition is adding to the multiethnic traditions of the Coal Region today, where also the ethnic foods of each tradition are now eaten and valued by all.

Conclusion: Part Two

Part Two has shown how the shift from local to national to global power relations and the changes in the economy affected the process of ethnicity and the life of the town in the twentieth century. In Shamokin/Coal Township as in other coal towns, with the rise of organized labor class solidarity developed among miners and factory workers, and working class interests came to dominate over the divisive interests of the ethnic groups of these workers. This change combined with national and global economic and political events and technological and demographic changes to bring about a substantial transformation of life in the town, and ethnic celebrations, languages, associations, endogamy and culture declined significantly.

The *Diamond Jubilee* video of 1939, described in the opening section of this chapter, pictures the height of prosperity of Shamokin/Coal Township in the forties and fifties and contrasts with its economy today. The closed stores and the shortage of good jobs to attract the young and educated are consequences of technological change, of the effects of World War II and of the globalization of capital. The skills, further education, and broader perspectives gained in the war resulted in social and economic mobility for many who returned from it, but the jobs they needed were not near to home. They left for the better opportunities of bigger towns and cities. The adverse effects of the decline of the coal and garment industries and the population exodus on the town's economy, on religion and the churches, and on the maintenance of ethnic traditions, have profoundly transformed the manifestations of ethnicity in the social and economic life of the anthracite towns, but, as shown here, they have not entirely done away with them. Theories of the "Melting Pot" and the expectation that ethnicity will inevitably disappear do not seem to hold here.

In Part Three, chapter 7 will document that ethnicity still matters but that its significance in people's lives and in the town is quite different today from what it was in the first century of the town's history. Chapter 8 details the strong sense of place and the pride of the townspeople in their past prosperity and in their ethnic and mining heritage, and describes how they draw on this heritage today in an attempt to restore some of the sense of community of the past as they adapt to economic problems and population loss. It emphasizes the significance for the economy of the town of some former residents who have moved to the big towns and cities but who remain connected by this sense of place, heritage and feeling of belonging. Some often return to visit the town and potentially may retire there. This wider community is significant in the efforts to rebuild town life after its demographic and economic losses. The chapter ends with a look at recent political change and some of the attempts to rejuvenate the economy.

Notes

1. Catholic Deacon, Bob Mack, April 1, 2003.
2. Ed Yodzis, June 24, 2003.

3. Walter Neary, January 22, 2004.
4. Dave Kinder, May 10, 2006, by permission.
5. Ruth Schrader, January 23, 2003.
6. David M. Schneider defines these as relatives seen only rarely on special or ceremonial occasions (1968, 72).
7. Judge Troutman who became a multimillionaire in the garment industry is one exception.
8. Switzerland was the home of the German Reformed Church. Soon after this church was founded and as it spread, its members came under persecution from which many Germans and Swiss fled to America in the mid-eighteenth century seeking freedom of religion (Shawda and Meyer n.d., 5).
9. The Catholic immigrants, Irish, Polish, Ukrainian, Lithuanian and Italian. This was a class as well as a religious and ethnic distinction.
10. Dave Kinder, by permission.
11. Mel Farrow, February 24, 2004.
12. Dan Strausser, October 20, 2003.
13. Jim Kelley Sr., May 6, 2004.
14. Fritz Reed, March 19, 2002.
15. In Shamokin, a shoe factory closed too for the same reason.
16. Eleanor Kuhns, January 14, 2002 and February 13, 2002. Eleanor retired in 1988, went into politics and became a County Commissioner. Details of her political career follow in chap. 8.
17. Dave Kinder, May 10, 2006.
18. Richard Wilcock, April 28, 2003.
19. Marianne Kinder, January 5, 2005.
20. Frank Sawicki, in group discussion on December 15, 2003.
21. Ann Wargo, December 29, 2004.
22. Bob and Vince Chesnay, February 25, 2003. At all major festivals this church has some hymns in Ukrainian.
23. Eleanor Vaicaitis, Frackville, June 18, 2004.
24. Jane Kearney, November 5, 2004.
25. The publication of Alex Haley's *Roots* in 1976 appears to have had a part in starting this revival. Fritz Read, former Recorder of Wills, says there has been a great increase in interest in genealogies since its 1976 publication.
26. The mergers took place primarily in the Coal Region, but also in Lebanon and Steelton, to the East of Harrisburg, (see figure 1.1) which were similar to this region economically and also had ethnic parishes.
27. George Pollyniak, October 23, 2003.
28. Robert Wislock, April 28, 2003.
29. Jane Kearney, November 5, 2004.
30. One Protestant and two Methodist churches have merged in Mt. Carmel.
31. Later to become Monsignor Bukaty.
32. Father Bukaty, February 13, 2003.

PART III

RECOVERING HERITAGE AND COMMUNITY

CHAPTER SEVEN

Ethnicity in the Twenty-first Century

Ethnicity has greatly declined in significance in Shamokin/Coal Township and the strong manifestation of ethnic groups in the nineteenth century have been transformed so that in the twenty-first century it no longer structures people's lives. People in the town today are interested in seeking out their relatives in Europe, visiting the homeland of their ancestors, and in raising large sums of money through sale of traditional ethnic foods, today eaten with appreciation by everyone regardless of ethnicity, to support charitable causes, churches or seminaries. Formerly associated with belonging to a group, ethnicity today is, to varying degrees, an identity. In the town, it finds occasional expression in public celebrations and religious festivals, though in greatly modified form from what they used to be in the past, and it provides meaning for the cultural items displayed in homes. The expressions of ethnicity today fit J. Lorand Matory's formulation of modern ethnicity as "a geographical focus, an identity option, and a context of meaning making, rather than a uniquely bounded, or over determining thing" (2005, 273–74).

These identifiers frame the continuing account in this chapter of ethnicity as a process changing over time. The chapter first looks at ethnicity today as an identity option and shows how the forms this takes varies between different groups and incorporates a wide range of criteria. Despite its loss of significance in town life, ethnicity still has economic content in the large amounts of money produced by fundraising events in which tradition is commoditized by the sale of ethnic foods and of the arts and crafts bought to decorate people's homes today, and by attendance at performances of paid dance and music groups rather than by local talent as in the past. The chapter concludes with details of the ethnic newspapers to which people continue to subscribe and through which they connect to their wider national ethnic communities.

Ethnicity as Identity

Today considerable variation exists in the various ethnic identities available to people. The priest of the Greek Catholic Ukrainian church commented that the Italians were very cohesive and spoke Italian among themselves though they were not organized. He viewed them as a distinct element in this community. They are not organized by the church, but they still maintain identity and customs like the Ukrainians who are a church based group. He noted that the Welsh do not seem to talk of their identity, and that the Irish have more identity but it is not manifested in anything much except the idea of it. This was a different sort of identity from the Ukrainians, who did not even Americanize the holidays. (They continue to celebrate Christmas in January, for example.)[1]

Others emphasize that with the changes that have taken place, "some things are lost, but some things stay pretty strong." A Catholic sister said: "There is a continuity that seems to be nourished by cultural and ethnic identities that are still in place that people don't let go of. When people leave, they don't know what to do without certain foods; they are expressions of home that don't exist elsewhere. They can't believe what you can't get out in the rest of the world."

This sister, who moved into the area in the 1990s, notices as a distinctive feature of the region today the continuing strength of ethnic identity. "You speak to people for a while and they are always referring to it: 'You know how it is, we Polish people, we do this, that, or the other.' They say, 'I'm Ukrainian,' or 'I'm Slovak.'" It seems that individuals still think readily of themselves and of others as being of a particular ethnicity, but they also consider that this identity is no longer significant in life in the town. Others are not so definite: a German woman stated that she was aware of ethnicity but in a distant way: "People say, so and so's wife is Polish, but it doesn't mean anything." And there are some who think that ethnic and religious differences no longer matter at all: in the opinion of the Welsh Mayor of Mt. Carmel in 2002, "Nobody really cares about either any longer, though religion is more important than ethnicity."[2]

A Lithuanian woman and her son commented on the celebration of Lithuanian Day, formerly a major event for the whole Coal Region, and how it is different today than it was in the past. She described this Day as it used to be. Their different comments are revealing of the change that has taken place. As she put it:

> It was really the busiest day of the year. I would compare it to Christmas. We walked around looking for people we knew and greeting them. It was wonderful. For me it was just one big party, all day long, it was like one big family affair. I can remember as a child coming to a table and hugging and kissing everyone, especially if they came from the same section of Lithuania that I did. They weren't relatives but acted like they were.

Her son however, noted that in the past on Lithuanian day, the park had concession stands, but not for the sale of ethnic foods as is done today, because everybody brought their own. But the foods that are for sale today consist of the same dishes that in the past used to be cooked by women for their families and brought to be eaten at the event. Preparations began a week beforehand. "The big difference is that today, and even when I was growing up, it has become more of a day of remembrance: before, you lived the Lithuanian culture every day, so you didn't go to Lithuanian Day to be Lithuanian, whereas today you do. Now you are American 364 days out of the year and you want that one day to remember you are a Lithuanian." He emphasized that in the old days his mother was not celebrating being Lithuanian, it was just Lithuanian Day, the day when everybody they knew got together, and that now, it is not so much Lithuanian Day as a Lithuanian bake sale; they call it Lithuanian Day, but that's what it comes down to, and he asserts that it is not really the same.

This account marks an acute awareness of the difference of identity in the present and the past. Today Lithuanian identity is an option and is celebrated in this public event but American identity is seen as primary. The accounts of Lithuanian Day by mother and son strongly mark the difference between second and third generations. In the early days identity was not something you thought about: you *were* Lithuanian. But today it is an option and Lithuanian Day has become a food fest to mark it.[3]

What ethnic identity means to people and how it is expressed varies considerably for both individuals and groups. For the Welsh, the *gymanfa ganu*, or annual hymn sing, is the only activity of the local St. David's Society in Shamokin.[4] It is held on St. David's Day in the Mt. Zion, Welsh Congregational United Church of Christ, a tiny little church built on a corner lot, and is followed by a Welsh Tea in the basement hall, including Welsh cakes (a kind of cookie) and the strong steeped tea favored all over Britain. The little church was nearly filled for this event in both 2002 and 2004 with 90–100 people, a majority from out of town and a number of them not Welsh. In 2004, relatives of one prominent Welshman had driven all the way from Washington, D.C. This event, and their family connection here, was significant enough for them to warrant driving such a distance.

Geraint Wilkes, a professional singer born in Wales and a Welsh speaker who officiates at these hymn sings all over the United States and Canada, has conducted the event for four years. He sings some solos and coaches the congregation in singing some verses of the hymns in Welsh, and the St. David's Chorus of nine women and seven men sing some hymns on their own.

But a Welsh woman resident in the town expands on what singing really means as an expression of being Welsh:

> The first time that we went to a National [hymn sing] was twenty five years ago. It was in Niagara Falls. We had a whole busload going from Shamokin. Our church took buses up there for about five years. And there was a lot of people that went—all either Welsh or with some connection. I had been to Wales when I was in college. But talk about a jolt to your psyche—as a Welsh person. It was wonderful. They sang from Thursday to Monday morning. I have never had a voice coming back from there, couldn't talk, because you're singing; they had you psyched up so you were really singing.

But she emphasized the importance of singing and music in what it means to be Welsh, all the time and not just at the *gymanfa* (the annual hymn sing).

> After the *gymanfa* at our church, we have for years and years gone to someone's house, just the choir and the committee that have done things in the church. There can be forty five people. And we'd start over on page one of the hymn leaflet and sing all of those hymns. Then pretty soon someone would bring out the crates of music, and you'd want to sing again "There is a balm in Gilead" that you'd sung two years ago, and that happened. That's just the way it is. That stuff to my children and to my friends' children will still carry on the idea of what it means to be Welsh. A lot of people that come to that aren't even at the *gymanfa*.

She also commented that on just an ordinary Sunday, there would be thirty-five people in church and everybody singing but singing in parts. The other ethnic groups, she noted, have their Block Parties (formerly in ethnic neighborhoods but now an ethnic or other celebration put on for everyone in town) to pull them together, but for the Welsh it is their music. In her family, when her parents were children, they were all socialized into this and taught the love of music, and they were all very talented. They learned to sing a different part or to play a different instrument.

This account shows how powerful singing is as an expression of ethnic identity for the Welsh. It is expertise that is distinguishing here: the singing of hymns in parts by the congregation in church still today, and the early miners doing the same as they walked over the mountain to work, as noted in chapter 2, is a mark of musical skill.

For one Irishman who says he was always self-consciously Irish but who cannot claim pure Irish heritage by blood and was not raised in an Irish community, it was his name and the notion of heritage, of which pride was one element, that gave him his Irish identity: "It was always the sense that our name was Irish, that we were descended from Irish people."[5] For others it is the closeness of the family that particularly makes them feel Irish. Another Irishman in Shamokin said his pride in his Irish heritage started for him about eighteen years ago when his large extended family began having reunions at which 130 to 140 people gather. They are now a huge, self-consciously Irish family, which holds reunions up in Kulpmont and will get together for special birthdays at a local restaurant, pub, or grill.[6]

The Ukrainians are the strongest, most clearly identifiable, ethnic group existing in Shamokin/Coal Township today. They are a church based group with a church that did not have to merge, so it has remained independent with its own parochial school and this defines Ukrainian identity. In one case, for example, the Polish church refused to baptize a baby girl with a Polish mother and a Ukrainian father, so she was baptized in the Ukrainian church, went to the Ukrainian school and thinks of herself as Ukrainian. Religion and church membership are the strong identifiers of being Ukrainian in this town.

> We have no new immigrants here but we are surviving strongly. There is a strong sense of identity and of community. We do have an out-migration of young people leaving . . . but they always come back: for special Christmas service, for Easter—for the Easter Morning sunrise procession, for the block party, for Memorial Day.[7]

An Italian, asked what it meant to her to be Italian today, answered:

> "Food: that in and of itself is really pretty much what it is all about. Since my parents died, I know my sisters and I are really struggling to maintain our heritage, and it really is a struggle. It was so natural for my parents." Even over this Christmas, she said, it seemed like work, trying to repeat the same things her Mom and Dad did, with the cooking and the baking. She also emphasized the spiritual side of the Catholic Church and participation in all their activities, and she wants her daughter to do the same, rather than have the generic sort of family. She and her Lithuanian husband always talk to her about the Lithuanian and the Italian.[8]

She emphasizes food but she also stresses the importance of the Catholic Church and of the dual ethnic heritage for her daughter.

In mixed ancestral ethnicity of an individual, it was often the case that the ethnic identity of the strongest parent was passed on to the children. These examples, however, show that the criteria for claiming and allocating modern ethnicity have changed very considerably. Not only do they no longer indicate bounded groups. Unlike in the late nineteenth and early twentieth century, there are many possibilities of choice: with intermarriage between groups there is the possibility of choice in religion and between parental or more distant ancestral ethnic identity and tradition; ethnic foods are no longer eaten only by particular groups but relished by everyone; and the "Welsh Church" includes many with no claims to Welsh identity among its members. Such changes in the criteria for ethnic identity reinforce the concept of it as a process that changes over different historical time periods. The variation between different groups reflects the course of their history.

A Context of Meaning

Ethnicity provides a context of meaning for association and event celebrations in the Coal Region towns today. These festivities may occur annually, or persist for a while and then be discontinued or change in response to political and economic circumstances. Groups will be described in turn for comparison on this aspect of their ethnicity today.

Parades, Associations and Festivals

In the United States, since the 1960s, there has been a widespread revival of Irish culture and pride in Irish identity; part of this has been the revival of the Ancient Order of Hibernians (AOH). As one Irish resident of Mt. Carmel put it, for years after the Mollie Maguires there was just silence, a murkiness, about the AOH. Now it has been reorganized. "We are all Hibernians and that shows we are proud of the Irish identity," says one member.

Irish identity is not manifested in foods so much as in parades and celebrations in the Coal Region towns that are associated with being Irish. Shamokin is not such a town, but Coal Township is, and others include Girardville, Heckshersville, Jim Thorpe (formerly Mauch Chunk), and Pottsville. Shamokin/Coal Township started having an Irish festival and organized it for six years. They got the Irish bands in and played Irish music all day, and they had some step dancers from the school of dancing in Pottsville, which were a big drawing, with their dancing and their embroidered outfits. People came from Hazelton, Wilkes Barre, some from New Jersey. One thousand dollars of the proceeds went to Lourdes Catholic High School scholarship fund every year. However, the sixth year they lost money after they had paid the costs of the bands and step-dancers, and so they stopped having the Festival in 2004.[9]

But that same year, the small mining town of Girardville (see figure 1.1), known as one of the strongest and most consciously Irish communities with families interconnected through marriage, started holding an annual St. Patrick's Day parade in March which has been very successful. In 2006, this event at Girardville drew a huge crowd, some from as far away as New Jersey. Many of the houses were decorated and bright green hats, and clothing, feathers, necklaces, shamrocks, and so on, were everywhere in evidence.

The parade, sponsored by the local Ancient Order of Hibernians (AOH) was impressively long: it took about two hours to go by. It was led by two young men from Mt. Carmel wearing kilts and bearing an AOH banner, with six flag bearers behind them; many branches of the Order from nearby towns with banners and flags, some in decorated trucks; eight or more pipe and drum bands, resplendent in kilts and plaids (see figure 7.1); high school bands; and fire equipment from the nearby towns; local representatives to congress, state politicians and the national president of the AOH, waving and stopping to shake hands and have a word with the onlookers,

Figure 7.1. A Pipe and Drum Band in the Irish parade in Girardville, 2006

and Catholic priests mingling with the crowd. The Grand Marshalls of the parade were clergy and rode in a car.

As the parade drew to a close, people serious about being Irish hastened to the tavern formerly owned by "Black Jack" Kehoe (a leader of the Mollie Maguires and one of those executed), which today is still run by his grandson, in order to get inside while it was still possible to do so. A mural of miners decorates the wall of the staircase at the back of the house, and a door in the house is said to be the actual door of Jack Kehoe's prison cell. The tavern was very soon packed tight with people, with two pipers playing in the bar and everyone else starting on the drinking and partying that was to go on until the small hours. By 3:00 p.m., a group of about thirty pipers from the bands, and others as well, had gathered in a huge circle outside with six to eight drummers, and were playing Irish music, to the delight and fervor of the large crowd packed densely around them (see figure 7.2). The trophies for the pipe bands in the parade were presented after this event.

For the parade and the gathering at the tavern, the context of meaning was the history of the Irish in the Coal Region; the part played in it by the Mollie Maguires in their struggle against the oppression of the coal companies and what that means for the Irish; the loyalty of these Irish to the AOH; and the importance of music as a prime element of Irish identity today. The

Figure 7.2. Outside the Packed Jack Kehoe Tavern after the Parade

parade was followed by an assertion of Irishness in a good time of partying, eating, drinking and music. For this, some of the people of the town spontaneously opened up their houses for buffet meals they had prepared for friends and friends of friends, and for strangers they welcomed in, and the good time spread through the town. For this Irish occasion, and in accordance with custom in the Coal Region today, the food in the house to which I was invited included dishes from several ethnic traditions as well as American food.

The parade was initially organized by four people, three of them from towns other than Girardville (Centralia, Mahanoy City, and Mt. Carmel), reflecting the broad base of this event among the Region's Irish residents.[10] In the second year of the parade, the people of Girardville opened themselves up and invited people into their homes. The organizers felt that this opening up of the town's houses for the public that continued in the years that followed, has been a crucial factor in the success of the parade.

This parade shows the building of a tradition to express and celebrate Irish identity by Irish people. Its success, shown in the spontaneous participation of the townsfolk and in the large crowds that gathered and came to the event from all over the Coal Region, indicates the vitality and strength of Irish identity still in the Region today.

The Area Polish Cultural Club is a flourishing ethnic association. It came into being in Mt. Carmel much later than the ethnic beneficial associations of the days of the mining era, such as the Jan Sobieski, the Polish Cadets and the Sons of Poland, which are all now social clubs to which anyone can belong. Organized in 1978 so that people of Polish descent could learn about their heritage, the club preserves and maintains Polish heritage in the area by holding festivals, celebrations, and other events, raising funds, and sending out a regular newsletter. Membership in 2003 was 240.

Polish traditional celebrations are held in the club and it displays emblems of Polish ethnicity: a Polish flag and glass cases full of Polish crafts, including embroidered blouses, beaded vests for children, and dolls in regional Polish costume; photos of the Pope, of the club's various events, and of groups hang on the walls. In the basement is a dining hall and kitchen. Here they hold food fairs each month to sell Polish foods. They sell pigeons, *haluskis*, *pirogies*, potato cake batter, (and formerly soups, which always sold out but were discontinued because they were too much work), and Polish arts and crafts. People who have moved away return to attend events at the club. Some come back again and again. Victor Greene considered in 1980 that regional and national associations were particularly strong among the Poles and that they represent a major aspect of ethnic life, despite a drop in membership over the years (Greene 1980:793).[11]

The club has a program and meeting once a month. In 2003, it celebrated its twenty-fifth anniversary with a banquet at Lazarski's Banquet Hall in Mt. Carmel. The announcement sent round was emblazoned with the Polish Eagle from the coat of arms of Poland. The hall was decorated with the red and white Polish colors. A good number of the 200 or so present were in Polish dress (see figure 7.3) or wearing something white and red. Note the Polish Eagle on the necktie in the photo.

The banquet was preceded by a mass the day before, (a prerequisite of any significant ethnic celebration) attended by 150 people. It began with the American and Polish national anthems. Those at the banquet included quite a number of young people, some non-Poles, and members of another Polish Club from Hazelton. Most of those attending seemed to be from Coal Region towns but there were some people there from neighboring states.

After the banquet (which did not include Polish dishes, though some were included in a buffet later in the program), the National President of the American Council for Polish Culture, the featured speaker, spoke of the desire of Polish Americans to succeed, the contributions they made to this country, and great Poles in world history and the arts. It was a speech boosting pride in the Polish heritage. At the end the priest closed the event with a blessing, repeated in Polish, which was also used several other times

Figure 7.3. A Couple in Polish Dress at the Banquet of the Polish Club

Figure 7.4. The Polish Dance Ensemble Who Performed Dances at the Banquet

in the course of the program. Twelve dancers of the Janosek Polish Dance Ensemble, from Willow Grove, near Philadelphia, performed regional dances from Poland, each couple wearing different regional costumes. The Polish Family Band provided music all evening.

This event asserted Polish ethnicity through some use of the language and national costume, decorations in the Polish colors, the dance performance, the coming together of Poles from near and far, and a speech extolling the historical contributions of Poles. The event was more programmed than the Irish celebration in Girardville and the emphases were different, but in both cases ethnicity was celebrated and its meaning and value to each group affirmed.

Formerly each group celebrated its annual national day at Lakewood Park near Barnesville (see figure 1.1), until it closed in 1984. Polish Day was an exception: members of the club would be taken by bus every year for a picnic held in the grounds of the club's former President's house on a Lake near Hazleton. Today only Lithuanians, Ukrainians and Italians hold such festivals and they are on a very much smaller scale. Accounts of each follow to show how these ethnic celebrations in the Coal Region are continued in the twenty-first century.

Many Lithuanians who left in search of jobs kept returning for many years for Lithuanian Day, the huge event which was attended by many thousands of people from the Coal Region and beyond in the past (as described in chapter 3). Today, traditional foods, music, dance, costumes, arts and crafts are all still components of Lithuanian Day. It now takes place over two days on the weekend closest to the Holy Day of the Assumption in August, in the Schuylkill Mall outside Frackville. But it is a very much modified and smaller affair than it used to be. Several hundred Lithuanians and non-Lithuanians from throughout the Coal Region, including Shamokin/Coal Township, go to it each year.

On August 6, 2005 for the ninety-first Lithuanian Day two accordion players and a singer came up from Philadelphia. The latter gave a speech and directed the singing of patriotic Lithuanian songs from a stage with a huge shield on each side with a knight on a white horse, the state emblem of Lithuania and of the Knights of Lithuania in America. A Lithuanian dance group of costumed dancers from Philadelphia performed at intervals during the day (see figure 7.5). The crowd wandered round the stalls of Lithuanian arts, crafts, amber jewelry from the Baltic coast, clothing, and books on Lithuanian history and religious life or children's stories.

At one table, two college age daughters of the Luschas family-owned enterprise, Lithuanian Straw Art, were demonstrating the making of decorated eggs and straw ornaments, both wearing Lithuanian costumes (see figure 7.6).

Figure 7.5. Lithuanian Dancers for Lithuanian Day in Frackville, 2005

Figure 7.6. Lithuanian Straw Art, Made, Displayed, and Sold at a Booth on Lithuanian Day

The foods that were brought from home in the past for family consumption are now sold all day on both days of the event. In 2005, they included dishes particular to Lithuania: potato sausages (*bulvinia desros*); potatoes with eggs, onion, milk, and bacon (*kugeli*); red beet soup (*salterbersiai*); green leaf soup of spinach, sorrel, and beet tops (*lapieni*). All proceeds from this event go to aid to Lithuania.

A new feature on the program of Lithuanian Day in 2005 was the presence of the Lithuanian Partisans Living History unit from Baltimore. A group in military uniforms set up an exhibit of photographs and artifacts, tents, weapons, and the like, and recounted the struggle by the partisans after World War II against the Soviet army in Lithuania for over nine years. This new addition to the events reflects the interest of Lithuanian-Americans in the struggle of their country to achieve independence from Russia in the 1990s, and their desire to help its people today by raising money to send to them to alleviate the difficult circumstances in which many of them live.

Ukrainian Day, like Lithuanian Day, is now also a much smaller event. It is known as the Primrose Picnic, to which Shamokin/Coal Township Ukrainians and busloads of Ukrainians from the nine parishes of the deanery go every year. On the last Saturday in July in the village of Primrose, near Minersville (see figure 1.1), they combine to raise money for their seminary in Washington. At the 2002 picnic, as with all ethnic Catholic festivals, the day started with Mass. Then the program began with a concert of Eastern Byzantine-rite music followed by a meal including Eastern European dishes, *pirogies*, cabbage rolls (*halupki*) (noodles with cabbage (*haluski*), kielbasa sausage, and potato pancakes, cooked and sold by members of the nine different parishes that make up the Deanery. A large hall had a big art display of embroidery, woodwork, icons, decorated eggs, and ceramics painted with traditional designs, which vary according to the regions of Ukraine. Outside, booths sold similar commercial items of lesser quality, including embroidered shirts, runners and pillow covers, candles with painted designs, books on egg decorating and embroidery, religious books and icons, children's books with Ukrainian illustrations, mugs and glassware, tapes and CDs for children and adults of the liturgy and traditional songs.

In the afternoon, the Kazka Ukrainian Dance Troupe danced and sang folk songs on an outdoor stage, with musicians at the back. This dance group regularly performs dances from different regions of the Ukraine at the Primrose Picnic, the men costumed in embroidered shirts, sashes, and voluminous blue pants tucked into red boots, and women in embroidered blouses, full skirts, and flower headdresses with long ribbons down the back (see figure 7.7). The director of the group explained each dance to the audience.

Figure 7.7. The Kazka Ukrainian Dance Troupe at the Ukrainian Picnic Celebrated Annually for Ukrainian Day in the Village of Primrose, near Minersville, 2002

As in Poland and Lithuania, traditionally each region of Ukraine had its own dances, songs, costumes and music. The performance was followed by a polka band concert, a prominent feature of cultural events for all three Eastern European groups. The whole event is a reaffirmation of pride in ethnic heritage, and many Ukrainians from Shamokin/Coal Township attend and speak of it with great enthusiasm. Each year it is successful in raising $20–27 thousand in one day.

The revival of interest in the heritage of Italians has taken the form of a service club, sponsoring fundraising activities and holding an Italian Festival every year in Scranton, to which Shamokin/Coal Township Italians go. This club, Unity, Neighborliness, Integrity, Charity and Opportunity (UNICO), founded in 1976 is a newer association than the original ethnic club, the Sons of Italy, which has now become just a social club to which anyone can belong. UNICO is open to anyone with an Italian connection of birth, heritage or marriage. In 1976, Italian communities nationwide were celebrating Italy's 200th birthday, and the Scranton *fiesta* was patterned on Italian ones.[12] The 342 members of the Scranton chapter make it the largest in the UNICO national chain. It provides scholarships to needy students who attend local colleges and universities, contributes to the Boys and Girls Club of Scranton and to many other local charitable organizations, as well as donating to UNICO national causes. It sponsors three major activities each year as fundraisers: the annual Charity Ball, a soccer tournament for boys and girls who are high school seniors, and, its biggest event, *La Fiesta Italiana* held every Labor Day weekend in the central square of downtown Scranton.

In this *fiesta*, we see the reinvention of an Italian tradition as it is adapted to American culture. In Italy, a traditional *fiesta* is characteristically associated with a particular saint. It always begins with a religious procession and is followed by a celebration of Mass. In America this emphasis on religion has diminished. A study of an Italian *fiesta* in Hartford, Connecticut showed that over succeeding generations religious observances have receded in importance and nontraditional activities that are part of American life have succeeded them, such as carnival rides, vendors of food and goods, and sporting events. Food used to be part of *fiestas* only after the completion of the core events, but as time went on, the *fiesta* became an urban celebration of eating and drinking with a growing number of non-Italian participants (Rauche 1988, 206). In Scranton today, the venue and the socializing and entertainment of the *fiesta* are traditionally Italian, but the religious element does not dominate as it does in Italy.

In 2005, *La Fiesta Italiana*'s thirtieth year, as in all Catholic ethnic festivals, mass was celebrated. It was in Italian in St. Peter's Cathedral at 12:15 p.m.

Labor Day Sunday, for which banners from Italian towns were carried in procession. But it was in Scranton's central square on all three days of the festival that "Pennsylvania's largest celebration of Italian culture and cuisine" was in full swing (Supplement to *The Times Tribune*, August 31, 2005). The main feature of *La Fiesta* was the sale of Italian foods. Some eighty vendors offered a variety of foods on the four streets of the square selling pizza, stromboli, porchetta (pork) sandwiches, gelato ice cream, Italian pastries, and a wide range of other classic Italian specialties. There was also a variety of American and Greek foods, and on one stall, in keeping with today's multiethnic food tradition at such events in the Region, I saw Welsh cakes for sale (see figure 7.8).

Vendors were selling crafts, jewelry and a variety of other goods in the central building, but none were specifically Italian. There was continuous live entertainment of orchestras, bands, and dance troupes on a stage, with benches and chairs for the audience, as well as strolling musicians. On Monday evening there were fireworks. This festival attracts thousands of visitors, including plenty of non-Italians, both local and from out of town; some of Shamokin/Coal Township's Italians attend it regularly.

Comparison of these groups shows marked differences between their celebrations. Of the three annual ones, the Ukrainian is the most ethnic, reflecting the comparative strength of local Ukrainian ethnicity. It raises impressively large amounts of money for the Ukrainian seminary in Wash-

Figure 7.8. Food Stalls at *La Fiesta* in Scranton, 2005

ington, D.C., reflecting the strong religious base of some of the local Ukrainian communities. The Italian festival in Scranton is the largest of all, attracts the most people and is the most appealing to lots of people besides Italians; its chief ethnic element is the array of Italian foods and the Italian aspects of the mass. Italian food is the strong marker of Italian American culture today and this festival lacks the ethnic arts and crafts of the other two. The Lithuanian event, the smallest, has the greatest variety of their own special foods, the most varied display of traditional culture and also emphasizes recent history of the home country, reflecting the long involvement of Lithuanians in the events there and their early and longstanding sense of national identity.

Ethnic Catholic Religious Celebrations

The major festivals of the churches celebrated according to ethnic tradition with family members returning from the towns and cities where they now live to gather together, are Christmas and Easter. There is "standing room only" in the churches.[13] Many Eastern European families especially come back from out of town for some or all of these events which are celebrated according to ethnic traditions by families gathered together. For these gatherings the traditional ethnic foods and rituals are still a main feature of the big meal to which they all sit down together.

Polish, Ukrainian and Lithuanian Catholics all start celebrating Christmas with the family gathered for dinner on Christmas Eve. Up until the 1950s, Polish families always celebrated this meal (*Wygilia*), with a family gathering in their homes; many still do so, especially those who are close enough to return to be with the members of the older generation. But in the twenty-first century, some find it easier to attend the communal celebration put on by the Polish Culture Club in Mt. Carmel.

In 2004, when *Wygilia* was held in the Club on the twelfth of December rather than on Christmas Eve, well over one hundred people attended (they sometimes have 150). They filled eight tables in the club basement. No meat is served because Christmas Eve is a strict fast. Polish elements were the red and white drapes embroidered with a scarlet Polish eagle, a painting on the wall of the death of General Pulaski (the famous Pole known as "Father of the American cavalry"), four or five women wearing black, colorfully embroidered vests, made I was told, by gypsies from the Carpathian Mts. and bought on commission by people visiting Poland, and one man's sweatshirt bought in Poland with Happy Christmas in Polish on it.

As at the banquet, efforts were made in this event to continue using the Polish language: *Wygilia* began with lighting of table candles with the lights turned down, and a greeting in Polish read from a card at each table; all then sang a carol in Polish from a leaflet on the table (but there was also a reading in English that described this traditional meatless meal and all its dishes, recognizing the lack of Polish speakers in such gatherings today.) This feast of Polish foods, started with a mushroom soup, then a buffet of other traditional dishes, including pickled herrings, dried fruit compote, *pirogies*, deep fried smelts, fish patties, cheese potatoes (*babka*), carrots in a clear sauce served cold, sauerkraut with peas, and beets. It was followed by desserts, including poppy seed roll (plum and nut rolls are also traditional) and *chrusty* (the women of the club had made eleven dozen of these crispy convoluted shapes heavily dusted with powdered sugar). The use of food in fostering ethnic community ties and identity was borne out again by the way everybody at the table I was at was reminiscing about their mother's cooking: potato dumplings, carrot soup, duck soup, and the like.

The Ukrainian Christmas falls on January 7, with the Holy Supper the evening before. The whole family assembles and spouses visit the celebrations of both families. Brothers, sisters, and children come back to the parental home. In the days of the second generation, everybody came, from the cities as well as those living locally, and including nephews and nieces. It continues to be a very important day. Traditionally, Ukrainians have twelve meatless dishes for the twelve Apostles at Holy Supper. Christmas dinner next day is likely to be turkey and other American foods, but preferred desserts are traditional poppy seed and nut rolls. In 2002, one family had twenty five for Christmas Eve and twenty one for dinner on Christmas Day. One woman has ten grandchildren of school and college age; they all come for the blessing of the baskets at Easter and for holiday meals, and her sister and her husband's brother come up from Philadelphia. Another woman has two sons and two daughters and nine grandchildren; all live locally and all gather for Christmas, Easter and Thanksgiving.

Lithuanians celebrate traditional meals adapted to provide what is palatable to the new Americanized generation who were not raised on the peasant foods of their forebears. For Christmas Eve dinner they always have fish, potatoes and some kind of vegetable. Dried peas were customary but now they use frozen ones. For dessert they have fruit compote made from dried fruit and little biscuits that were baked and served with poppy seed milk. It was the job of the eldest girl to grind the poppy seed. They serve it still but buy the poppy seed cake filling and stir in a can of condensed milk. No one wants to grind it and would not eat it if it was just mixed with water as it used to be. For meat on Christmas Day they have chicken, duck or goose.[14]

They baked cookies on Christmas day and made *pirogies* too, with mashed potato or cottage or farmer's cheese or ground up ham for filling. Christmas Eve dinner dishes could be devilled crab, orange roughy fish, mushrooms (a must), dried peas (a must), *pirogies*, boiled potatoes (traditional), sauerkraut, breads, cookies, shrimp (not traditional), oatmeal pudding ("a horrible tradition so it is not made, nor are the hard biscuits dipped in poppy seed milk"), herring (not likely to be palatable either, though there was always a barrel of salt herrings for Lent).[15]

The changes in these meals adapt the traditional Christmas Eve dishes of poor peasant farmers to conform to American tastes, and the Catholic Church encourages them. One Lithuanian priest told a parishioner, "It is not what you eat, but continuing the tradition that is what matters." These traditional ethnic foods celebrate ethnic heritage; it is the ethnic context and meaning of this occasion that is significant in marking the continuity of these families over generations, and it is a reminder of the far distant country of the homeland.

There are also celebrations in the Easter season. The Polish service of Bitter Lamentations (*Goszkedzaly*) is celebrated during Lent and consists of the chanting of the passion story in Polish, a sermon in English, and hymns. It is followed by a meal of traditional Polish dishes. Another tradition for Easter Saturday morning for both Poles and Ukrainians is the ceremony of the Blessing of the Baskets. This is an Eastern European tradition that is even spreading to other groups. Families take all the traditional foods for the family breakfast on Easter Sunday in a decorated basket to the church hall where they are laid out on tables and blessed by the priest. At Transfiguration Ukrainian Catholic Church there are three such ceremonies in the course of the day. At Mother Cabrini Church in Shamokin/Coal Township, into which the Polish Church was merged, the priest continues to perform this tradition and the Italian members of the congregation enthusiastically join the Eastern Europeans and bring their baskets of Easter food to be blessed. On Easter Sunday, Ukrainians hold a Sunrise Procession and service which begins at 6 a.m. with the congregation parading around the church. They then return home for the Easter breakfast with their assembled families. Traditional foods and family gatherings are the common elements of these occasions.

Ukrainian family members will come back to the town for Easter and Christmas, for the block party, and also for Memorial Day. Memorial Day weekend has always been a great occasion for the people of a parish to gather and for families to reunite. Despite a marked decline of the significance of ethnicity and religion in the life of the town in general, these Eastern European traditions still sustain a sufficiently strong element of meaning and bestowing of identity with enough people for this quite considerable number of traditional events to be held in the town's Catholic churches every year.

Roots in the European Homeland: A Geographical Focus

The geographic focus of ethnicity today appears in the strength of connections to the home country. They vary considerably from one group to another, however. Poles and Lithuanians are particularly involved in connections with their European homeland, as seen in some examples of efforts to track down relatives there and to send support in the form of money, medical supplies, household goods and clothing. Len Oszko's[16] account of the efforts he made in searching for his relatives in Poland reveals how powerful the geographical focus of ethnic identity can be and how strong are these roots in the ancestral homeland. The persistence Len needed and the experiences he went through to eventually find his relatives make a vivid tale. It follows as he told it.

> In 1988, my brother-in-law and my sister and I, we took a tour to Poland. He was looking for his relation and he had the name of the village from an old address. He found his father's relations, long lost cousins. So I thought that seemed pretty easy and I'd like to find my Dad's relations too. In my Dad's army discharge paper, his name was spelled Oshko (the phonetic spelling), but in Polish it is Osko. And then it gave the place in Poland, Worokow. So I thought I had the name and the village, no problem. So from 1988 to 1996 I actually made six trips and eventually found there is no such town as Worokow. It was all a little more difficult than what I figured on.
>
> So I started in the courthouse looking at all the naturalization papers. I spent about three days there and must have looked through about 1500. But simply by dumb luck I wrote to the National Archives in Washington, and gave his name, and I'd found out from the records that my Dad come through in 1914. Always figured he was born in 1899 or 1898. They said no such record, but then from Ellis Island in 1914, they found a Jan Osko from Mrokow had come through. The reason for the misunderstanding of the village name was the result of it having been spelt according to Russian phonetics as Worokow.
>
> So my Dad came over and he was visiting a cousin in St. Paul, Minnesota. Everything started meshing together. I wrote to the church there and got no answer. So I took a month off and went there. I went to Mrokow village in 1996 to look for my dad's relations. At that time, I didn't know if there were any.
>
> At this time, we were sending parcels of new and used clothing, jackets, boots, through a travel agent in Philadelphia. He had a friend in Warsaw who

was a taxi driver, and I got a hotel to stay there. I had an arrangement to go to see this village the next day. The way that it happened that I went at that particular time, my son was working for United Airlines as a machinist, and he was allowed two free passes for a family member. On the flight to Frankfurt, Germany, it was business class on Lufthansa with white linen and personal service and all. From there I flew to Warsaw. The taxi driver met me. The taxi driver suggested that instead of the $80 hotel, I might like to come to his house for $30 for the night. His daughter could speak a bit of English.

The next day, the driver took me to Mrokow. We met a guy on the outskirts outside his house, pretty nice with a fence around it, and we said we were looking for someone, name of Oszko, so he sent us down a road to a dumpy looking place, windows out and boarded up, yard a mess, barn with a broken down roof and a couple of pigs in it, and nobody there. So we were looking around, wondering if this was the right place, and the man that sent us came down and said, yes, this was John Oszko's. So he was out working somewhere. So we went back to the house and started explaining how we were looking for the family, and the taxi driver made a deal that I was looking for a place to stay. They talked in Polish and I could understand a little. The next thing I knew, the guy went into the house to talk to his wife, and they made a deal that I could stay there for eight days at twenty five dollars a day room and board.

I was able to speak Polish a little, because after my first visit in 1988, I found I could understand only a word here and there and couldn't answer or read anything. So, on my return home I took a Polish language course. I did this for two years and finally I could understand about 80 percent and carry on a conversation. So by the time I got to Poland in 1996, I could do quite well.

So we went looking for civil records at the District office and church records in the local church. When I got back to the village that first evening, there was a lady, a *babushka* [grandmother] with a young girl, sitting there. This woman had a picture and said she was related to the Oszkos. It ended up that she showed me this picture—and there was a picture of my dad with hair! I had never known him with hair, he was prematurely bald. Then I knew for sure I had the right party. She had another picture too. It turned out she was the oldest daughter of my dad's younger sister. She still lives where her family lived, mud and wood walls, and a thatched roof. So we hugged each other and got to know each other.[17]

Len heard from them many family stories of his ancestors who were very poor people. Since then, Len has been sending clothes and money to his father's family and others as well.

Other Poles in the Coal Region have also long been in regular contact with relatives back in Poland. They send checks, packages and may go regularly to visit. These activities preserve family ties between dispersed members and additionally provide considerable assistance to those back in Poland as well.

Lithuanians have been very actively involved in assistance to their homeland. The Knights of Lithuania today is divided into five districts and then into 150 numbered councils. The hard coal region forms The Knights of Lithuania Anthracite Council #144 of the Amber District. It today totals about 700 paid up members. The number of members nationwide today is five to six thousand.

In the past, members smuggled information (such as bibles and history books), medical supplies (medicines have been scarce), and clothing into Lithuania through an underground organization. The history books were to offset the inaccurate histories put out by the Soviets, and before 1988 when Gorbachev was imposing religious restraints, bibles were needed too. Clothing sent by mail would only be released by the post office after the payment of the equivalent of a month's pay (*Pottsville Republican*, January 17, 1990).

Money raised on Lithuanian Day now goes through the Humanitarian Aid Committee to various causes in Lithuania, after expenses are paid. In 2006, the whole event cleared $5 thousand. The largest amount from this money was $1 thousand given to the Lithuanian Pontifical College seminary. Before that, in 2003, the committee gave a donation to an agricultural school for teaching the use of modern equipment, and they will do this again. They have also adopted a rural village school to which they send as much as seven hundred pounds of winter clothing, medications, school supplies, goodies, and toys for Christmas. The money that they raise goes to the poorest in Lithuania. "In the cities they are doing OK but in the rural areas it is still very bad, so we have been sending food and clothing. We clothe the children in several schools and send boots for the winter—boots for the whole school. And books and school supplies, all those things."[18]

These are the ways Lithuanians focus on their country of origin and affirm solidarity with their disadvantaged countrymen and women. Their biggest other local fundraisers after Lithuanian Day include flea markets, raffles and dances, for which they may pay for the cultural attraction of a performance by a Lithuanian dance group.

The main focus of the Knights of Lithuania in the twenty-first century is charity rather than by keeping in touch with relatives or direct participation in affairs in the home country as formerly. Charitable activities are especially directed towards raising aid to Lithuania, including scholarships for Lithuanian students to go to America. This aid has totaled $72 million dollars over the years, of which amount the Coal Region Amber District has contributed $100 thousand for scholarships. They also have had a big part in helping a hospice over there. Contributions to Aid to Lithuania, Inc. was established in 1990 at the national conventions, shortly after Lithuania again declared its independence, and in 1996 the Knights sent forty containers of medicine and medical supplies to Lithuania worth $35 million. The members raise money for this assistance. These massive amounts of money reflect the very considerable interest in, and commitment to, their home country of many Lithuanians.

Connections with the homeland have varied with the political circumstances of different countries. In the early 1930s Ukrainians used to write letters to family back in Ukraine, but with the onset of World War II they no longer received any replies. Some could send things to relatives before World War II, but after the war the displaced persons who immigrated told them packages would never arrive and that people who received money were accused of spying. The Stalin regime made continued connections more difficult for Ukrainians than for other groups, though a few people have nevertheless managed to maintain them and do go back and forth.

Commoditizing Tradition: The Economic Content of Ethnicity Today

In the early years, the different food traditions of ethnic groups made up the daily diet of people in the town, and traditional dishes cooked in the home were diacritical markers of the different groups. Today ethnicity no longer structures town life. Intermarriage, the disappearance of ethnic neighborhoods, and the merging of churches means that distinct ethnic groups no longer exist, so traditional foods no longer mark them. However, these foods remain a distinctive feature of life in the town; the difference is that they are all eaten by everyone.[19] But people no longer cook them daily, although they will be cooked for family celebrations and for family members who have moved away but who return on visits. They are primarily made on a large scale for sale at fundraising events. These foods have been commoditized and are sold to the public and are not only cooked for occasional family consumption.

Igor Kopytoff notes that commoditization is a process, best looked upon as "a process of becoming" (1986, 73). In this process, the various food traditions of the Coal Region are modified and adapted as necessary to conform to the tastes of present day America. Crafts are going through the same process; they are now marketed through shops or on the internet, or by vendors at festivals. Their forms have changed from decorated and beautified objects of everyday use, to ornamental and artistic objects for display on shelves or in glass fronted cabinets. Today, with some exceptions such as those described for the Welsh and Irish, traditional forms of dance and music are not spontaneous performances, but formal ones by a trained group and paid for in set fees at public celebrations and festivals.

As the salience of ethnicity has diminished and many ethnic markers of the past have disappeared, those that remain and are sold serve to intensify the sense of place and the awareness of the multiethnic heritage of the inhabitants of the town. People especially value and relish traditional foods so that large amounts of money are raised by selling them: to those who are residents in the town and to those who have moved away but still want to get them whenever they can, and the latter even find a market in their friends and neighbors to expand sales.

Ethnic Foods as Fundraisers

Msgr. Fedorovich of the Ukrainian Church made the perceptive comment that "all community building is centered on food; everyone helping to prepare it forges the community bond." This section gives details of how in the Coal Region, production and sale of ethnic foods constitutes a major means of fundraising to support churches, associations, charitable organizations and seminaries, and, for some groups, aid to the homeland, and in so doing, constructs bonds of community and identity. Small groups of members of churches or other organizations produce these foods on an impressively large scale today. Not only do the considerable amounts of money they raise give ethnicity a significant economic content despite its decline in social life today, but also the mass purchases of ingredients for making these foods boost the local businesses who supply them. The section ends with a look at cook books, including or focusing on ethnic recipes and compiled and sold by different organizations as popular fundraisers.

The array of ethnic foods sold at festivals and celebrations has become a characteristic of the Coal Region, and everyone today enjoys the foods of all the different ethnic traditions. The most persistent usage of the vocabulary of national languages in the towns is for the different dishes of ethnic foods appearing at most of its events today. This usage reflects a multiethnic food tradition that has appeared as part of the town's various celebrations and festivals and continues to give these events ethnic content long after the decline of the importance of ethnic groups in town life.

This economic aspect of ethnicity today consisting of the large sums of money raised by the sale of ethnic foods depends in part on the wider community of former residents. In the first example presented here, a network of personal connections operates to market *pirogies*, a favorite ethnic food in the town and its wider community, to raise funds for maintaining the school of an ethnic church. This network operates through family, friendship, neighborhood and workplace ties, both from the locals and from those who have moved away but are still eager to get *pirogies*, with the consequence that money is being returned to the community by the upwardly mobile who have left in search of jobs and good careers. Thus the large scale purchases of *pirogies*, an ethnic food that is appreciated and much sought after because of its quality by those who have left for the nearby towns and cities, contribute to the survival of a town institution.

The Welsh, German, and Irish events have fewer of their own particular foods featured for special occasions than do the Eastern and Southern Europeans. In the case of the Irish, this seems to be a matter of their circumstances prior to immigration, with their extreme poverty and oppression in Ireland; for the Germans, it was their need to disassociate themselves from their culture because of the world wars; and the assimilation of the Welsh and their unease following the resentment of their superior position in the town hierarchy, is lately forgotten so that efforts are being made to revive some culinary specialties identifiably Welsh. Particular foods were shared by the Eastern European groups whose homelands were contiguous; Poles, Ukrainians, and Lithuanians had various traditional foods in common, such as *pirogies* for example, but there were other dishes unique to each of these groups. For Italians, as shown in chapter 3, foods and family celebrations have long dominated as markers of their ethnicity.

Details of the group of *pirogy* makers at the Ukrainian Greek Catholic Church of the Transfiguration in Coal Township bear out Monsignor's comment. The group works most of the year cooking huge quantities of *pirogies*, and, before festivals, other traditional Ukrainian foods as well, to raise money for their church and parochial school. It is evident that members of the group look forward to and enjoy socializing at this weekly activity. One worker commented: "*Pirogy* making is therapeutic, I love it. These are great people." During the research period, their efforts were contributing an impressive one-third to one-half of the school's annual budget.

This group consists of one to two dozen or more women and four to six men. They make *pirogies* every Thursday for most of the year (with a break in June and at Christmas). Some of them have been doing this for as long as fifty years. They work in the Parish kitchen adjacent to the church hall, each taking on the same task each week. I participated in this activity at different times during my research. The quantities of materials used and the huge amount of *pirogies* and other foods produced and how they were made, give some idea of the effort that is expended and the extent of the demand for them.

These workers make up three to four fifty pound bags of potatoes for the *pirogy* filling each session, depending on the number of orders. One of the men does the potatoes, peeling and mashing them in machines. He starts at

1:30 a.m. and the potato ball makers for the filling come at 4:00 a.m., the rest of the workers any time from 6:00 a.m. on. Other men have the tasks of kneading the dough by hand, rolling it out through a machine, and cutting it into rounds at one end of the big table at which a group of about a dozen women sit and work as they are tossed the rounds of dough. They fill these with the potato balls and pinch the edges closed, laying them out on big trays. The *pirogies* are then boiled in huge pots of water till they rise to the surface and are lifted out with slotted spoons, rinsed with cold water and laid out to dry. Finally, they are bagged, a dozen to a bag.

The number of potato-filled *pirogies* made at different sessions ranged from 134 dozen to as much as 300 dozen, together with from thirty-seven to forty-seven dozen cheese filled ones. In 2003, they were sold for $4.00 a dozen for potato filled ones, $5.00 for cheese filled. They first filled the orders that had been telephoned in, and then prepared the ones for the school lunches in the church hall. Each week the children from the school came to sit in the hall and have *pirogies* for their lunch, for which orders would have been taken by the teachers. They thus developed a taste for this ethnic food (paid for by the parents). At the end of the cooking session, lunch was provided for the group of *pirogy* makers, provided by one of the women with contributions from others, making it a social occasion enjoyed by all. After lunch, a few

Figure 7.9. Making *Pirogies* at Transfiguration Church

Figure 7.10. Boiling *Pirogies*

people stayed on to finish bagging, and to take in the money from the people who come to buy them or to pick up orders.

These sessions were enlivened on the occasion of a birthday of someone in the group by a birthday cake and the singing of "Happy Birthday to You," first in English, then with "May the dear Lord bless you" sung three times and followed by the Happy Birthday refrain, and finally for the third time in Ukrainian which repeated "Many Happy Years" three times. This little event marks the blending of American, religious and Ukrainian elements found in this group.

The orders they receive can be for as many as 100 dozen per order, which will be distributed to family, or sold to friends or coworkers of the purchasers or frozen in home freezers. These orders come not just from the local townsfolk, but from relatives who come home to visit for weddings, baptisms, funerals, or religious holidays, or from relatives or friends who live and work in local towns and also out of state. The workers say their *pirogies* are distributed all over the country to many of the Ukrainians who have moved away but come back at various times and order them. They sell them to friends, neighbors and coworkers in the towns they live in, keeping plenty for their own freezers. One week, for example, there was an order from Chicago; another, an order of twenty-seven dozen from coworkers of a church member in a local government office; and at other times, a man who lives in Phoenixville, near Philadelphia, takes ten dozen of each kind of *pirogy* back home, where his brother sells them to workers in his computer firm, or his brother-in-law, who lives in Williamsport, will come and take ten dozen back to his workplace. They are enjoyed also by many others besides Ukrainians who live in the town or return to visit: for example, an Irish family's son takes back six dozen when he comes home to visit. They are an example of the way some ethnic foods are today enjoyed by all and serve as markers of Coal Region rather than ethnic identity.

The economic aspect of ethnicity can only be perceived if such ties to the wider community are taken into account. These purchases show that some ethnic foods are today appreciated and bought by many in the wider as well as the local community. A network of personal connections in the town operates to market a product within and outside it to raise funds for maintaining the school of an ethnic church. This network operates primarily through family ties, but includes also friendship, neighborhood and workplace ties. The economic aspect of ethnic loyalty and identity in this church-based community is that considerable monetary resources are not only being supplied by church members and town residents but are also being returned to the community by the upwardly mobile, who have left the town in search of jobs and good careers. Those who are dispersed and live elsewhere are thus contributing to the town economy by their purchases of ethnic foods.

Other churches, Mother Cabrini (once a month) and Our Lady of Hope, also make *pirogies* but not with such sustained regularity and quantity. A group of women from Mother Cabrini have maintained the fifty-year tradition of a food stand at Bloomsburg's annual fair of St. Mary's, one of the churches that merged with it. The stand sells Polish specialties, including *pirogies*.[20] Ukrainian churches in other towns also make *pirogies* to raise money: in Mt. Carmel at St. Peter and Paul's Ukrainian Catholic Church, they make them once a month with fifteen to twenty helpers or more, making 400 dozen at a time; the church in Marion Heights makes them about every two months; and St. Michael's in Shenandoah also raises money this way. *Pirogies* are a food tradition of other Eastern European peoples besides Ukrainians: they are also made and sold by Lithuanians in St. Clair, and the Polish Culture Club of Mt. Carmel raises money by selling them with other favorite Polish foods at monthly food fairs. $450 was raised at one of these fairs by the sale of *pirogies*, several kinds of soups (some traditionally Polish), Easter eggs, and *haluskis* (noodles and cabbage). This is not a church based activity, since the Polish church in the town had to merge, as described in the last chapter.

Sale of ethnic baked goods similarly raises large amounts of money. The Transfiguration Church group used to make Easter breads (*paska,*), which were their biggest money maker until 2004 when they stopped making them because it was too much work. These loaves were made before Easter every spring on Mondays and Tuesdays. This bread was especially favored by Ukrainians. The loaves were formed from an egg dough, some with raisins, some plain, decorated with braids of dough, and sometimes with a three barred cross fashioned from strips of dough. They were so popular that it was impossible to get sufficient help to make enough to fill the demand. Ukrainians and others bought them in quantities for their families and to give away to friends and neighbors. One Ukrainian who lives in Kulpmont bought 100 loaves every year for this gifting. The workers would usually make as many as 300 loaves at a time in the past when they had enough helpers.

In Kulpmont, the nuns at the Carmelite convent make good money throughout the year selling ethnic baked goods: Christmas cakes, poppy seed cakes, sugar loaves and Easter breads. The big orders come from local people's coworkers, friends and neighbors, and from relatives in nearby towns, who are eager to get these wonderful foods. The nuns are reported to have had one $1,800 order for Christmas for these baked delicacies, and, at different times, other orders of as much as $700 and $400. The Ukrainian Orthodox Church in Minersville, made 300 nut cakes and 800 *paska* in 2003.

Mother Cabrini's other great fundraiser is chocolate covered Easter eggs, not an ethnic item, made every year on a huge scale by a group of about fifteen women. In 2000, they reportedly made $36,000. These eggs are popular in the Coal Region, and the fire companies as well as churches make them for fundraising. Transfiguration Church members additionally make potato pancake batter. It is mixed on Mondays and sold by the quart and any they have left at the end of the day is stored in the freezer. They make up maybe two fifty-pound bags of potatoes at a time. The amounts made range from 119 to 164 pints for a morning's work.

Ukrainian foods are also a major component of a big fundraiser for Transfiguration church on a weekend at the beginning of August, the annual block party.[21] The proceeds go to the church and the church school. Others join the regular weekly group of *pirogy* makers to help put on this event and make the enormous quantities of ethnic foods that the townsfolk come to buy and consume on this occasion. These workers cook for two weeks beforehand. The block party is a big event to which not only many townsfolk turn out: former residents come from all the towns around and even come home from out of state to attend, from California, Virginia, New Jersey, New York, Delaware. In the evening a band performs and a big crowd will be present.

This event is held in the school yard on Saturday and Sunday, using both the church and the school's kitchens. The helpers include some younger family members of the usual weekday workers, who are at work during the week. Tables and benches are set up for eating and music plays all day.

During the period of my research, these block parties were making $21–22 thousand each year (after expenses). The money goes to the church and its school. The workers prepared huge quantities of food to achieve this amount of money. For the 2004 party, they made 600 dozen *pirogies*, 1,200 pigeons, 450 hamburgers (the meat was donated by a local meat market), 200 sausages with sweet pepper and onion sauce, twenty-five ten-gallon buckets of potato pancake batter (for which they used forty fifty-pound bags of potatoes), *haluski* dough (a lot of work as it has to be cut into little strips), and bean soup. Everything they make sells out. Purchase of the ingredients for all this benefits the local merchants from whom they buy.

Lithuanians also make ethnic foods throughout the year for fundraising. The Lithuanian church of Coal Township had to merge into Mother Cabrini, but independent Lithuanian churches in other coal towns continue to raise funds by selling traditional foods. St. Casimir's, the Lithuanian church in St. Clair, raises funds for their Diocesan Assessments which keep the Catholic Schools open. They make *pirogies* every week, freezing them, then boiling them and selling them hot on the first Friday of each month except the two summer ones. They make an average of one thousand dollars each time.

Selling ethnic foods is important for fundraising in Protestant churches also. Pastor Sally Dries of Salem United Church of Christ, the German Protestant church in Coal Township, said that besides the usual German ethnic foods of pies, cakes, sauerkraut and pork, there are also other special German items, such as molasses, sugar cookies and doughnuts. "We now make *pirogies*, and we say 'how can there be Protestant *pirogies*?" They also make lasagna, and have their peach festival, but they do not make *soupis* or Italian Wedding soup. They do have pot pies, beef or chicken, which is Pennsylvania Dutch. In Shamokin the Germans are Pennsylvania Dutch and follow their food traditions. She comments, "I have not seen the Catholics doing sauerkraut; it is the Protestants who have usurped other groups' foods!"

In 2002, Salem Church was renovated and expanded, which meant that services were held in the basement for five months. The fundraising events into which they put so much effort paid the $27 thousand for this renovation. Salem can raise $8–9 thousand in one day at their Peach Festival; it is their major fundraiser. It is mostly people from the community who come, that is from Coal Township and Shamokin, but some also come from Elysburg, Mt. Carmel, and other nearby towns. Some Salem families make a kind of reunion out of it for which all the kids come home. They plan around the festival and stay on for the weekend.[22]

The menu for the Peach Festival is a fine example of the mingling of food traditions that is found today in all the festivals and block parties of churches of the different denominations. It consists of peach pie with vanilla ice cream, funnel cake and angel food cake; traditional German shoofly, lemon sponge, apple, and coconut cream pies; Eastern European *pirogies*, potato cakes, *haluskis*, and pigeons; hot Italian sausage and pizza; and hamburgers, hot dogs and devilled crabs. Besides selling food at the Peach Festival, they have raffles and a stage set up for entertainment. They start to prepare for it in June, and continue through July until the tenth or eleventh of August. They make the *haluskis*, in the evening so the younger people can help; the 14th–15th of August they make peach pies all day, 325 large peach pies and eighty small (six-inch) ones; then, on the evening of the fourteenth, potato cake batter, that favorite Eastern European food.

The quantity of food made for these events and other fundraising efforts is as impressive for the amount of very hard work it represents as for the amounts of money it raises. It reflects the great loyalty of the people involved to their church and church community, strengthens their community bonds in all these work sessions, and maintains the continuing significance of their ethnic heritage in the town. Salem has other money raisers, which do not emphasize any German food tradition. But in November for Election Day they do make the meat and chicken pot pies (potatoes, meat and vegetables in a crust) of traditional German cooking; Trinity Lutheran and the Methodist church follow German tradition and sell sauerkraut and pork for election day also. In the Spring Salem makes crab cakes for sale on Ash Wednesday and also puts on a spaghetti or lasagna dinner. They also have sales of homemade soup. I helped out at the crab cake making in the basement of the church hall in 2003 for the Ash Wednesday sale, where twenty or more women and six men ("a good turnout") worked to make 2,000 crab cakes. They take orders ahead of time and clear about $1.5 thousand. Besides food money raisers, they have bingo games. At these games they serve suppers which must be bought in addition to the entry ticket, and for which they have hamburgers and hot dogs, and *pirogies* and *haluskis* of Eastern European tradition. So for this church, German mingles with Eastern European, Italian and American foods.

The importance of the multiethnic food tradition of the Coal Region today is manifested in the popularity of the compilation and sale of cookbooks as fundraisers. I came across several put out by churches, by ethnic organizations, and by the Chamber of Commerce.

A pastor's wife, active in the cookbook fundraiser, after a discussion on the decline of ethnicity and its primary manifestation today in food, made the following pertinent comments:

> I think the cookbooks that our church has been doing sell so well because some of the recipes, pies, cakes, sauerkraut and pork, are what people remember from their youth. Once you made them and never paid any attention to recipes, and the person in the family who always made it is gone. So now they are looking for recipes for these ethnic foods, which they may not see so much as ethnic but as a family tradition. . . . I put in a number of my mother's recipes and a lot of them are Jewish and they're family recipes but each one has a distinct holiday remembrance that goes with it, and yet other people wouldn't look at it that way. So they are categorized like appetizers, soups, meat, vegetables, and yet if you really look at them, you can tell that there is a definite ethnicity in a lot of the background.

This comment illuminates the continuing intersection of ethnicity and family in that family reinforces and upholds ethnicity through family gatherings for festivals and the continuing cooking of ethnic specialties for these occasions.

This *Keepsake Cookbook: In Grandma's Kitchen*,[23] announced on the title page as "featuring family heirloom recipes of the Anthracite Coal Region of Pennsylvania," is divided up into the usual cookbook categories and includes recipes for a broad array of ethnic specialties, as shown in the box.

There are also cookbooks for fundraising that are specifically ethnic. "Gather Around the Table: a Collection of Recipes by the Ladies of UNICO, Their Families and Friends, Scranton, PA"[24] is specifically an Italian cookbook, and at the Primrose Ukrainian picnic there were Ukrainian cookbooks for sale. One promotes Ukrainian traditions by including a list of North

> Red beet eggs, *bruschetta* (with the suggestion of adding basil if you want "a more Italian flair"), Depression *faggots*, Irish potato soup, Easter *kielbasa* in brioche, *schnitzem knepp* (dried apples, ham, and dumplings), Hungarian *goulash*, *haluski* and cabbage, Pennsylvania Dutch filling, *Acini de pepe* with tomato-pepper (an Italian side dish), Jewish noodle casserole, Irish buttermilk and Irish soda bread, crisp Italian bread, *challah*, funnel cakes (a Pennsylvania Dutch favorite), *Sfingis:* Italian Donuts, Romanian nut roll (a family recipe from 1925), *pwdin efa* (Eve's Pudding, a Saint David's Day Welsh recipe), *shoo fly* cake, *hamentashen* (served at *Purim*, the Jewish Feast of Esther), Swedish tea cookies. It also has one recipe from a particular ethnic church (Lithuanian): St. Michael's Cream of Crab Soup (a parish favorite).

American Ukrainian cultural sites to visit, and a brief account of the history of egg decoration and Ukrainian designs.

Music and Dance, Arts and Crafts

Dance groups, bands and choirs formerly made up of members of the ethnic groups of the town are now rare; they exist only in some parts of the Coal Region, members are not just locals, and they are in demand to perform at events, for which they charge fees. That dance and music are considered important components of cultural heritage is indicated by the inclusion of dance performances and pipe bands at cultural events, even though they are the highest of the expenses incurred.

Certain arts and crafts and items of traditional dress and ornaments and household items formerly made by members of the different groups for their own use are now sold at stalls at fundraising events, and in ethnic arts and craft stores in the region. New items adapted to American life have been added to the traditional ones.

Music, dancing and the oral literature of storytellers in earlier times had always played a prominent role in Irish rural life (Miller 1985, 72). In the early nineteenth century, this music acquired cultural and political significance when antiquarian collectors incorporated it into their mythological image of a Gaelic Ireland. The young in Ireland incorporated cultural activities into the struggle for political independence and in the Gaelic revival movement of the turn of the century with two organizations: the Gaelic League preserving the Irish language and promoting cultural nationalism with music and dance, and the Gaelic Athletic Association, a militant radical nationalist Catholic organization with a cultural focus, including, by 1897, pipe bands with national costume and regalia.[25]

Irishmen in the United States have played a large part in not merely preserving the genre of Irish traditional music, but in reconstructing its meanings to enable it to speak to a broad constituency in and out of Ireland (G. Smith 1994). Msgr. Fedorovich commented: "I know the influence of the Celtic and that is coming back strong, not the green beret and getting drunk on St. Patrick's Day, but the whole Celtic spirituality and music, and that is enriching America."

In the last half of the twentieth century, a change in what it meant to be Irish took place in terms of music and this has been a major element in the cultural revival and pride in Irish identity and heritage in the Coal Region, noted earlier in this chapter. In the sixties, with its folk music movement, the Clancy Bothers were living in Greenwich Village. These three brothers, all born in Ireland, took Irish songs—not sentimental American songs written about the

Irish—and began to sing them. These songs were taken from the period of the Risings of 1798. They were part of a powerful movement which had remained very familiar in Ireland. The Clancy Brothers also sang Gaelic songs and laments of the ancient musical tradition of Ireland, drinking songs, and Dublin music hall songs.[26] When they appeared on the Ed Sullivan Show for St. Patrick's Day, the Irish became an overnight sensation and the brothers became a big part of the revival of traditional Irish music in America. Irish bands and groups have taken up performing this music for Irish festivals and gatherings.

Ukrainians used to have dance groups and choirs in every parish, and dancing for Shamokin Ukrainians in the first half of the twentieth century was part of their way of life. Up to World War II, they had an adult choir of sixty and a junior choir of thirty. The situation is very different today: there is no longer any choir and dance takes place in paid performances.

Today the *Kazka* dance group that performs at the Primrose picnic, near Minersville (see figure 1.1), regularly attended by many Shamokin/Coal Township Ukrainians, has adapted traditional Ukrainian folk dances for performance. The group is funded as a rural art in Pennsylvania[27] and is based in the northeastern part of the Coal Region. The director and the dancers consider their primary identity to be Ukrainian not American and they are not church affiliated. The dancers are recent immigrants and come from as far as Philadelphia and from the Scranton and the Shamokin area and the twenty nine adults and thirty children meet for weekly rehearsal in Allentown. They speak Ukrainian to a greater or lesser extent; from a few words to fluency, and parents encourage learning the language.[28]

The dance forms of this group evolved from Ukrainian dance tradition and were modified to fit American society. Costumes, music and dance varied regionally in Ukraine. In the villages of the homeland, people danced at weddings and parties, at harvest time, at private celebrations, and in the special dances for Easter. They had line or figure dances which are still used as polka dances. But such dancing is too repetitive for performance. The *Kazka* director's dance trainer came to the United States after World War II, having previously been a professional dancer in Europe. He brought with him the dance styles of the 1930s and 1940s in Ukraine and in the dance he teaches there are now more modern influences from current Ukrainian dance which include ballet training and dancing. In the United States they have adapted tradition to include elements of ballet and they exercise at a bar.[29]

These dancers perform at the Primrose picnic for a fee and are the highlight for the day of the Ukrainian audiences for whom this dancing seems to be a symbol and public representation of their culture and identity. But as an expression of ethnic tradition, it is a long way from the first half of the twentieth century in Shamokin/Coal Township when 90 percent of the men knew how to do the very athletic fast dancing and would roll back the rugs to do it spontaneously of a Saturday evening (as reported by George Pollyniak in chapter 3).

Great efforts were made to sustain Lithuanian music and dance in the Coal Region. Before World War II, there were bands, choirs and dance groups from different churches on the program at Lithuanian Day, which were all local. But since the war, with the exodus of people from the region, there has no longer been enough local talent to provide the cultural entertainments of earlier years for their national Day, and bands and dance groups have been brought in, and paid for, from the big cities: Baltimore, Philadelphia or Boston.[30]

The county choir of the Knights of Lithuania persisted until the 1980s but now, like bands and dance groups, choirs are no longer sustainable in the local community and are brought from outside the region to the annual event of Lithuanian Day.

Lithuanian traditional culture is also preserved now in The Lithuanian Cultural Center museum, established in Frackville in 1982 by a small group who wanted to maintain their heritage. It displays a wide range of arts and crafts: cloth woven from flax, carved wooden boxes, elaborately decorated Easter eggs, embroidery, amber jewelry, woven straw baskets and mats, doll dancers, pictures made of straw, and carved wooden crosses from wayside shrines (these shrines used to stand at the entrance to every village in the 1920s). Eleanor Vaicaitis, my guide to the museum whose parents were small farmers from western Lithuania, explained how craft making used to be done at home by immigrants: "The Lithuanian people brought a lot of crafts with them. My mother brought a blanket: she raised the sheep, spun the thread and dyed and wove it. They could do all that you know. They had to be self-sufficient. She did a lot of crotchet and tatting and taught us three girls."

Lithuanians in the Coal Region maintain old, new and invented craft traditions. Lithuanian priests started craft production in America and craft displays have always been a part of Lithuanian Day. Crafts include hand-woven linen and carved wooden items, decorated eggs, costumed dolls, and silver and amber jewelry, and they decorate Lithuanian houses.

The Christmas tree at the Lithuanian church is traditionally decorated each year entirely with ornaments made of straw.[31] But this is quite a new tradition: Christmas trees were not popular in Lithuania until the early twentieth century. Straw ornaments for decorating them became popular pre-World War I and spread from the cities to the countryside.[32] Lithuanians, like other Eastern Europeans, decorate eggs for Easter.

Ukrainians arts and crafts originating in the peasant culture of the homeland, have been selected and adapted in America today to fit the Ukrainian-American lifestyle, such as ceramic statues, lamps, bowls, vases, candles and

Figure 7.11. Lithuanian Crafts Decorating a Home

candlesticks painted with Ukrainian motifs; embroidered cloths; lacquer bowls, beakers and ladles; wood carvings; and collections of exquisitely decorated eggs (*pysanky*).

Polish arts and crafts are displayed in the Polish Cultural Club in cases around the walls and in Polish homes: crystal and wooden carved items such as inlaid platters, dolls in regional costumes, straw pictures, and decorated eggs. Some are sold at the Polish Club's food fairs held every month to raise money. Pride in being Irish appears in a Waterford glass Celtic cross; ceramics such as green tiles ornamented with a Celtic knot and others painted with shamrocks; a door knocker in the form of a *claddagh* (a crown and two hands holding a heart, a Celtic symbol often reproduced in jewelry) (see figure 7.12).

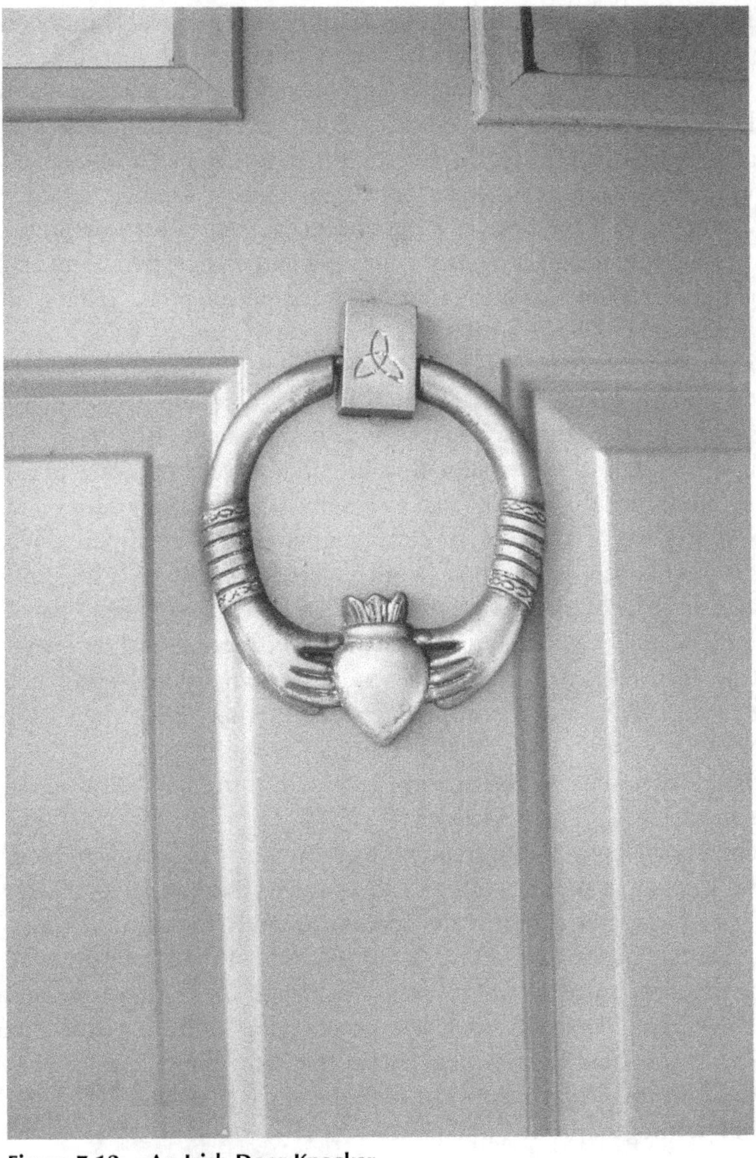

Figure 7.12. An Irish Door Knocker

These traditions of music and dance and arts and crafts have a market because they help sustain a continuing sense of ethnic identity in a new way of life, although their use no longer forms an integral part of life as it did in the old days in the homeland and in the early years of settlement in America.

Ethnic Newspapers: Imagining the National Community

Ethnic newspapers subscribed to in the Coal Region put people in touch with their national ethnic communities. Benedict Anderson considers that one way 'imagined' communities are united is by printed texts in the vernacular which enable people to imagine themselves as a face-to-face community and share experiences with people they have never met (Anderson 1991, 44–46, 60–65). Anthony Smith suggests the term "print communities" for them (A. D. Smith 1991, 361). In the Coal Region, ethnic newspapers include to varying extent, pieces in the vernacular, and reports on the activities, experiences and cultural celebrations in different states of the Union of people of the same ethnicity. The occasional use of the language in these newspapers has value because the languages of many groups are fading in the later generations of immigrants.

Accounts of events elsewhere help people of common national ethnic background to share the experiences of men and women who have the same ethnic traditions as they do but with whom they have never come in contact. Matory points out that nation-states are not the only communities united in this way. Reports of ritual and musical practices shared by dispersed national populations likewise enable unacquainted parties to powerfully imagine communally shared experiences (Matory 2005, 71). As people who participate in the music, dance, craft, and specialty food production of their own ethnic tradition in the Coal Region read about these traditional observances in other parts of the country in ethnic newspapers, they renew their awareness and celebration of their nationwide ethnic heritage.

I found subscribers to the newspapers listed in the box below among my informants.

German newspapers were among the earliest to be published in Northumberland County in the mid-nineteenth century (Burrows 1930, 73–75). All were very Democratic. These newspapers formerly found in all the towns had ceased publication by World War I, because of the strong anti-German feeling that developed before this war (see chapter 2). The greater number of Welsh events advertised in *Ninnau* for other regions of the country compared to those in the Coal Region would seem to reflect the particular history of the Welsh in the Coal Region and the reluctance they have had to emphasize their heritage, as noted in chapter 2.

The National Hibernian Digest, Irish. Published in New York. It carries news, articles and reports of events in Ireland and in America. It is primarily in English though in one issue, I found a song in Gaelic with English translation.

The Ukrainian Weekly. Published by the National Ukrainian Association, in Parsippany, New Jersey. Founded 1933. This has news articles on the Ukraine, reports on Ukrainian events and celebrations in the United States, and has a monthly calendar of events in the United States. It is almost all written in English.

The Way: Catholic Ukrainian biweekly. Published in Philadelphia. About half the paper is on religious topics and written in Ukrainian; the other half, in English, has reports on events and Ukrainian history, as well as religious articles. *The New Rusin Times* is another.

Ninnau (We Welsh): The North American Welsh Newspaper. Published monthly (except for September) in Basking Ridge, New Jersey. ("Answering the need for a stronger link between the many Welsh communities of North America.") Some letters are in Welsh. The annual *gymanfa* in Shamokin appears among a whole page of events nationwide, perhaps more than are advertised in any other ethnic newspaper. It announces also small annual scholarships for Utica given by the St. David's Society for members of the society or their close family members.

The Sons of Italy Times. Biweekly. Official organ of the Grand Lodge of Pennsylvania, mailed free to every member household.

The Jewish Daily Forward. A Jewish-American newspaper published in New York City. Founded in 1897 as a daily in Yiddish, today it is a weekly news magazine in two independent publications, one in English, one in Yiddish.

Vytis (*The Knight*). Lithuanian. This is not a newspaper but the official magazine of the Knights of Lithuania. It is published six times a year, with articles on Lithuanian culture, activities, and organizational matters.

Zogoda. All in Polish. *Post Eagle*. Bimonthly in English and Polish, published in New Jersey.

The Polish American News. Weekly. Serving southeastern Pennsylvania and New Jersey since 1925. Little in Polish, though some reports on Polish public events and celebrations in the area, including the many taking place in Philadelphia.

To conclude, will ethnic identity still persist? Parents in both a Ukrainian and in a Lithuanian family said their adult children have no allegiance to rituals or ethnicity and no interest in them, but in a Polish family and in another Lithuanian family that is not the case, their heritage is still very much valued by the new generation of adults of these families. Predicting a continuing future decline in interest in ethnic heritage does not by any means seem an obvious conclusion. In 1995, when the churches merged, although there was a tremendous diminution by that time of the strong manifestations of ethnicity of the first half of the century, the merger was nevertheless still a traumatic event not only because of people's ancestral churches closing but also because it inevitably entailed a decline in observance of ethnic traditions. That people were so upset by this merger revealed that ethnicity for a large number of people was still a powerful element of their identity. Some of the next generation certainly put a high value on their ethnic heritage, and the extraordinary amounts of money that are raised by the sale of ethnic foods and arts and crafts, and of the donations made to help people in the homeland, as well as the increasing interest in visiting it, indicate that the present manifestations of ethnicity may be quite persistent. Mary Waters notes that Americans generally have not given up their ethnic identity but retain some degree of it in the American tradition of cultural pluralism (Waters 1990, 3).

What ethnicity means today, and the form it takes, varies greatly between the principal ethnic groups of Shamokin/Coal Township and is a consequence of the different historical circumstances of each group. Those of German descent no longer hold ethnic festivals in the region, or celebrations to publicly celebrate their ethnic heritage with German foods, arts and crafts, music and dance; nor do they any longer publish newspapers giving accounts of what other Germans are doing nationwide. They have been in the country longer than the other groups and the World Wars caused them to submerge their German identity, and though still aware of it, most have merged into the American middle class. In the coal towns, the Welsh were resented for their discrimination in favor of their own in the allocation of jobs, and to a great extent abandoned their ethnic nationality. These circumstances made both groups lose much of their sense of cultural distinctiveness. The Welsh do express their ethnicity in musical celebrations, but chiefly in their church community. More recently, however, there are signs in the Coal Region that they are reasserting pride in their heritage and in expressing it as the Welsh do in other regions of the country. Ethnicity, as previously emphasized, is a changing process.

The Irish rose from their initial position in the lowest socioeconomic level in the life of the town to outlive their association with the violent protest of the small group of them involved in the activity of the Mollie Maguires, and to move into politics and the church. They have found themselves buoyed up by the Celtic revival and its music and dance of the last part of the twentieth century. Like the Welsh, their sense of heritage has grown in recent years. In both cases this stronger sense of it is not manifested in organized events, and in this town, was found in spontaneous gatherings after the main public events: by the Welsh at a singing celebration in someone's home after the *gymanfa*, and by the Irish in Girardville in an assertion of their Irishness following their parade, at the tavern owned by the descendants of a leader of the Mollies.

The Jews formed a strong religious, commercial and professional community but its economic base was completely destroyed in the towns by the economic competition of the shopping malls and the great majority of members of this community have moved away. Other groups are associated with religion in different ways, though less strongly than were the Jews in the past. As shown in chapter 6, membership in the Welsh church and participation in its activities could confer Welsh identity. The Ukrainians in the town form a strong religious and ethnic community, based on their church and its school, and are distinct by the degree to which their activities promote and support both to maintain their ethnic heritage in their lives. The Lithuanians were also closely tied to their church and were particularly hard hit by the church mergers. The Poles are very active in sustaining and promoting their heritage in their new country and in their contacts with Poland and their relatives there, and with providing aid to their homeland in general. In this they are matched by the Lithuanians who have remained intensely involved in aiding Lithuania, both in the period under Russian domination and after its independence. The Italians, like the Eastern Europeans, came later than the German, Welsh and Jewish groups. They have a strong sense of heritage that does not manifest itself much today in public events, but is rooted in the family, in the foods they eat, and in membership in the Catholic Church.

This book started with the early history of the town with ethnicity marked in well-defined groups that structured town life. Today it is not like this at all and ethnicity no longer converges with class and religion. Yet it is still significant as an identity for many people, as an interest in a specific European homeland, and as a heritage that gives meaning to still continuing ethnic festive occasions and to the cultural and historical objects that continue to be part of people's lives. This documentation of ethnicity as a process shows that, after 150 years, it is still present though transformed. The next chapter shows that it is a component of the strong sense of place and pride in the town's heritage, which is drawn upon in the effort to rebuild the sense of community of the past, and in the present of the town in its struggle to recover from economic decline and population loss.

Notes

1. Msgr. Fedorovich, January 6, 2002.
2. Kevin Jones, January 16, 2002.
3. Generally when people were asked what their primary identity was, the answer was American. I was told however, that in the northeast of the Coal Region, ethnic

identity was likely to be more dominant, and among Ukrainians near Hazleton this turned out to be the case, as reported in the section on music and dance below.

4. The national *Gymanfa Ganu* Association of the United States and Canada is the only national level association of Welsh Americans. It meets in a different American center every year on Labor Day. Its original gathering at Niagara Falls in 1929, attracted nearly 4,000 people (as reported in the Welsh Newspaper *Ninnau* 2003, vol. 28[2]).

5. Casey McCracken, December 2, 2004.

6. Ron Burns, February 4, 2003.

7. Msgr. Fedorovich, January 16, 2002.

8. Marianne Kinder, January 15, 2005.

9. Walter Neary and Joe Connolly, 2004.

10. In starting up this event in 2004, the organizers had tried to learn from the problems of other parades in the area. According to one of them, Jim Thorpe has a huge parade with a large crowd, but there is nothing besides the parade for people to focus on, besides a bar and two restaurants to which you cannot get in, and rowdy elements take over. Pottsville's parade is small and made up of the Irish of the town marching to make up a parade, nobody participates in anything, there is nobody really watching, and there is nothing to do, or to make it a real event. Clearly the Girardville parade succeeded in improving on both.

11. Now after the millennium, the Polish Cadets in Shamokin is a Polish organization but does not raise funds or send money to Poland, though individuals may do so. The St. Francis Society, also in Shamokin, is still a private club with a bar. It has social members as well as members who are of Polish descent. The Polonaise Society in Hazleton is similar to the Polish Area Club in Mt. Carmel and holds meetings, but does not have a building or cook food. The Sons of Poland in Mt. Carmel is now just a social drinking club and has nothing to do with Poland.

12. Honorary Chairman Pat Fricchione, *Times Tribune* handout.

13. This applies particularly to the ethnic Catholic churches, it is not so pronounced in the Protestant churches. Sally Dries, Pastor, Salem Church.

14. Since traditionally the Christmas Eve meal was meatless, for Christmas Day meat would be served in abundance: ham baked in sourdough rye or smoked; goose roasted with apples; duck with sauerkraut or red cabbage; turkey with prunes; roast suckling pig; leg of veal or mutton.

15. Eleanor Vaicaitis, Frackville, June 18, 2004.

16. Len Oszko's life history is given in chap. 3.

17. Len Oszko, February 28, 2002. Quoted with his permission.

18. Ann Wargo, St. Clair, February 22, 2006.

19. Typically, in 2002, the West End Fire Association announced its annual fundraising picnic's foods would include: *haluskis*, potato cakes, *pirogies*, funnel cakes, pizza, Italian ice, sausage, hoagies (*News-Item*, July 17, 2002).

20. *Susquehanna Life*, 2003 (Winter): 23–25.

21. A block party was originally a neighborhood party, but the term is still used for this event though people from the whole town come to it. Many organizations hold such events. They are also referred to as picnics or summer festivals.

22. Pastor Sally Dries, Salem Church.

23. Fundcraft Publishing and Printing, Collierville, TN: 2003.

24. Published by Morris Press Cookbooks, Kearney, NE: 2005.

25. Pipe bands are a major feature of the St. Patrick's Day parade in Girardville described in the last section.

26. *The Clancy Brothers and Tommy Makem Song Book.* 1964. New York: Tuparm Music Publishers.

27. They are funded by the Pennsylvania Council for the Arts, the Pennsylvania Humanities Council, and Schuylkill County, under the category of rural arts. They perform up to fifteen shows a year, at least one a month except in Lent, and have given dance performances in Baltimore, Pittsburgh, New York, and New Jersey, and in the Ukraine in 1992.

28. A high percentage of young Ukrainian Americans nationwide are fluent in Ukrainian. One study shows 86 percent of children of recent immigrants speak it at home. In the twenty years after the influx in 1945, the number of Ukrainian speakers in the United States more than tripled (Magocsi 1980, 1004).

29. Paula Holoviak, March 25, 2004.

30. Ann Wargo, St. Clair, February 22, 2006.

31. This is a craft that is widespread in Europe.

32. A more ancient tradition was the wedding tree, or "bride's tree," for a wedding decoration, symbolizing youth and fertility, decorated with these straw ornaments and hung above the bride and groom at the wedding feast.

CHAPTER EIGHT

Community, Sense of Place, and Changes in Economics and Politics Today

The third community event highlighted as diagnostic of a particular period is the Anthracite Festival of the Arts in Shamokin/Coal Township. This revival and modification of an old festival that died out in the early nineties for lack of interest and funds is part of the efforts by people of the town to confront the downturn of the economy and the loss of population by rebuilding the sense of community of the past and reinforcing the pride people have in their town and heritage. This festival, started on Memorial Day weekend in 2006, was so successful that it was expanded from one day to two and treated as an annual event, sponsored by Northumberland County Council for the Arts and Humanities, advertised at all the Welcome Centers in Pennsylvania, in several statewide publications, and in American Profile Magazine, and pronounced by Susquehanna's Visitors Bureau to be one of the five best events in the state to visit.

The townspeople praised the festival for reviving the parades that were such a major feature of town celebrations of the past[1] and for changing the despondent attitude of the community to the former Anthracite Heritage Festival to one of enthusiastic participation. The event began on the Friday evening with a short opening parade, followed by a luminary service, with white candle lights lining Lincoln Street, the site of the town's war memorials, at which the names of the honored dead were read aloud. This recall of the sacrifices of the lives of past members drew the community together, and the evening ended with celebration in a display of fireworks.

Saturday began with church bells at 8:50 a.m. and a blast from the Cameron Colliery whistle at 9:00 a.m., and Sunday with an ecumenical service. These referenced two powerful features of heritage: religion and the mines. In 2007, an estimated 5,000 people had lined the street to see the Saturday parade. It lasted thirty minutes, and included the Commonwealth String Band, marching bands from the town, antique cars and bikes, and the city's fire trucks at the end; the *News Item* reported a total of twenty-three participating bands and organizations. In 2008, the parade had expanded to a total of fifty-seven bands, floats, and marchers representing various groups with entries in three divisions, and had an even bigger crowd watching it. The emphasis of the festival was the town's heritage: the parade was called "Heritage through the Ages," and it was acclaimed as "the best thing that's happened to Shamokin in decades" (*News Item*, May 25, 2008).

The differences between the Anthracite Festival of the Arts in 2008 and the previous Anthracite Heritage festival of 1982 (as reported in the Heritage Supplement of the *News Item*, Friday, June 13, 1982) reflect the final decline of the coal industry and of the significance of ethnicity in the life of the town that have taken place in the intervening twenty-six years. Many features were the same: fire companies and bands in the parades; the representation of churches; and antique cars. But notably different was the representation in the 1982 parade of the coal companies, marching retired miners, and UMWA representatives; and the ethnic organizations of the Frackville Ukrainian Dancers, the Lithuanian Club float and the Tony Kaminski Polka Dancers. None of these appeared in 2008. But the success for the town of the reinvented festival of today was marked by the number of entries in the parade: it was still fifty-seven the same as in 1982 despite the economic and population changes.

The new events of the festival in 2008 focused on the history of the town, building community by an emphasis on heritage. They consisted of horse drawn carriage and trolley tours, accompanied by narration of the town's history; tours of the town cemetery on Saturday, three in 2007, two in 2008, which drew large groups of more than fifty people at a time; and stories of mining history told by a member of the Breaker Boys reenactment troop. The cemetery tours, guided by Fritz Reed, a former mayor and a local historian reaffirmed town pride and sense of community with their focus on upstanding citizens of the past who had built the wealth of the town. They were enlivened with costumed actors representing some of the historic residents whose grave stones were stopping points in the course of the tour.

In addition, the town Career and Arts Center had photographic exhibits which attracted crowds of viewers. These also emphasized the town's history and anthracite heritage. They included an exhibit of over 200 photographs of life in Shamokin in the past for over sixty years, another one of photos of coal miners commemorating the 110th anniversary of the Latimer Massacre titled "Work the Black Seam," and videos of the Diamond Jubilee Parade and other historic events. Prints of paintings by local painters of Shamokin as it used to be, and of miners, were for sale.

The six churches opened for self-guided tours and six more with booths reflected the dominance of religion in the town in the past and its role in the town's heritage, and there were food vendors of ethnic specialties, such as *soupies* and funnel cakes. The festival served to reinforce the sense of place and of community of past and present residents and their pride in the town.

People emphasized that the choice of Memorial Day weekend for the festival instead of a weekend in late summer was critical: it is a very popular weekend for people to return to the town for high school class reunions. Since the population exodus, the town has drawn upon the feelings of identity and belonging of a wider extended community of former residents who live in the towns and cities and come back for events like this. They boost the sense of community of the town, and provide continuing economic support through their purchases of ethnic foods and their participation in and contributions to celebrations and other events. That the festival reinforced a sense of community and place is voiced in one reported comment: "It's what our town needs. We need to bring back the spirit of the Coal Region and our heritage and where we came from" (*News Item*, Sunday, May 25, 2008).

The conceptualization of community in anthropology has shifted away from "community as an actualized social form to an emphasis on community as an idea or quality . . . associated with collective identity rather than interaction" (Amit 2002, 3). This fits the reconstruction of the sense of community in Shamokin/Coal Township which builds upon the community pride and strong sense of place of the people of the town and also of the past residents who keep returning and retain a great loyalty to their hometown; all share a collective identity in community as an idea or quality. Karen Fog Olwig emphasizes that:

> From a modern global point of view, place is therefore not only a geographically delimited space where people live their lives and to which they therefore attribute particular meanings. It has also become an anchoring point where modern mobile people can find a source of identification across appreciable distances in a changeable world. (Olwig 2003, 60)

This is the case for the town and its wider community of those former residents who have moved away but remain deeply rooted in it. The last chapter showed how the connection to former residents who have moved to find good jobs in the cities extends the local community and brings in contributions to its economy. These extended networks make up a "wider community of belonging and identity" for the town, based on sense of place and community. Olwig uses the term wider community for the global fields of family relations of West Indians living in Britain, whose widely dispersed family networks reflect common background in the Caribbean where the family home and various contexts in which individuals are situated are located (Olwig 2002, 143). The networks of this wider community of Shamokin/Coal Township and of other coal towns exist in the larger towns and cities outside the Coal Region as well as those in the Region itself to which people commute to work, like Harrisburg, Reading, Allentown and Scranton (see figure 1.1).

The chapter begins with an account of community pride. This is shown in the intense involvement and support for the area high school football team from all three towns and from their wider community of former residents, numbers of whom return to attend their games; in the public art, monuments and museums of Coal Region towns and in other less tangible expressions of pride; and in the attendance by local and former residents in large numbers at major religious festivals at the fine churches of the town and region despite the nationwide decline in religion. These manifestations of pride are one way the town functions as an identity anchor for its wider community in the big towns, which is fostered by institutions that provide feelings of belonging and identity for both present and former residents who return to visit. Details of the strong sense of place of the people of the town and of the institutions that sustain it, show how "specific expressive practices and performances imbued acts, events and objects with significance, thus illuminating different ways in which place is voiced and experienced" (Feld and Basso 1996, 8). Former residents return to visit, and make an economic contribution to the town through their purchases of the ethnic foods produced in abundance, as detailed in the last chapter, and through their participation in events such as the festival described above. The last section describes economic, political and demographic changes that are taking place, including the economic content of the attenuated ethnicity of today, and some new shifts in power and class relations.

Sense of Community and Town Pride

The Importance of Sports

People are quick to tell you that if you are interested in the town, you had better be interested in football. Pride in the success and high quality of the Mt. Carmel Area and the Shamokin high school football teams and pressure to support them, has united all social levels of the towns through the years, and reinforces ties of identity with the region for those who have moved away. This pride is a strong element in the sense of community of the town. As the football coach described it in 2003:

> You walk around here during the football season and it is unbelievable, everybody is up in the Mt. Carmel area to the football game, and they follow the teams. Up in Kulpmont the whole town closes. They used to play Saturday afternoon, then before it switched to Friday night, everything would physically close because everybody was at the game, and if you weren't at the game, then they wanted to know why. When the teams are winning you can feel the difference, the whole atmosphere shows it.[2]

This participation is what a sense of community means in these Coal Region towns: everybody is expected to be at these games and the support for the team and enthusiasm for the game unites the town and is a source of conversation that bridges social and economic divisions.

This enthusiasm has historical roots in the Coal Region from the time of the miners' sports teams, as they played football after their workday in the mines and there were eight to ten basketball teams of the fire companies and mining patches until after World War II and into the 1950s. It carried over to the High School football, wrestling and basketball teams with the strong winning traditions and legendary coaches of the Region. Shamokin was known for its good football, basketball and wrestling teams. Their wrestlers dominated in the 1930s, with fifty-eight victories and eight losses (Toscano 2000, 101). The football program at Mt. Carmel High School started in 1893.[3] The school combined with Kulpmont High School in 1965 and the football team is known today as the Mt. Carmel Area Red Tornadoes or "The Big Red," and leads the state of Pennsylvania in 697 all-time wins. These football games between opposing teams of the different towns and at the state divisional championships are major events at which the whole town is unified behind its team and through which it presents itself to the outside world.

In 1936, as the Depression faded, Shamokin High School had an undefeated football season and got a lot of attention. The final Thanksgiving Day game of the season in that year against Mt. Carmel got over 11,000 spectators (Toscano 2000, 101). Banker Charles Yoder's comment on the tradition of this game, known as The Turkey Game, shows it as an annual feature of town life unifying family and community. He looks back on it nostalgically[4]:

> For a number of years, Shamokin and Mt. Carmel Area played each other on Thanksgiving Day. That was a very big family day, not only did you have Thanksgiving at home but you went to that game first, and then came home

and ate your Thanksgiving dinner afterwards. That was a real big social event. That was what you did on Thanksgiving Day. It wasn't that you stayed home: you went to that game and then you came home and had your Thanksgiving. I don't know how long that game went back, but it went pretty far back as far as tradition went; it was a pretty hot and highly contested ball game. I would say it was one of the things that everybody looked forward to, coming back from school for the holiday, families coming in, and everyone making sure they got tickets. It was something to look forward to, and that's not there anymore. It's gone. It ended 1974–1975.[5]

But the football team still symbolizes the unity of the town and the town's prestige is measured by the success of the team. Outsiders are impressed and astonished by the degree of Coal Region enthusiasm for football. When Charles Yoder was at Susquehanna University he would come home on weekends with a lot of his friends in the 1970s and early 1980s.

> In this area football is the big event; it is one of the biggest events going on. Everyone went to the football game Friday night, that was like your social event, you'd see a lot of friends, people coming in from school, and that was the thing to do. I can remember, I think it was in my sophomore year, the Mt. Carmel Area team was playing to win the game that would take them to the Southern Division Championship, and I brought four guys from school. They were from New Jersey and New York and they couldn't believe it. There were over 8,000 people at this high school game: it was packed. They just could not believe the interest and they were really impressed with how good our high school football was. They always told me about that. We were proud that being from the Coal Region we had good kids and were well-representative of high school football, so that was pretty important for us. That was pretty neat that they enjoyed it. The high schools they went to, it was not that big of a deal. But to see that stadium as packed as it was—you'd go to a football game at Susquehanna University and there would not be half as many people that were at that high school game, at that time.[6]

The importance of the team to the townspeople comes out again in a player's report that after his first game when he returned to work the next day in the local hardware store, at least thirty elderly people came into the store and talked to him about football, and little kids in the street asked him for his autograph.[7]

Coach Jazz Diminick, an iconic figure of Mt. Carmel Area football, inducted into the Pennsylvania Hall of Fame in 2001, said that pride is what it is all about. "In Shamokin, you'd go downtown on a Saturday and stand on the main street because every Saturday the huge High School Band would march down. It was just like the whole town was involved: the band would start at the end of town at ten or eleven o'clock at night and parade through the town."[8]

The team holds a Pride-Night ritual the evening before the playoff, which Coach Bob Chesnay said was as important as any pregame preparation. In some years, as the team walked to the field for the playoff, the fans would chant "WE BURN COAL," and again even louder in the faces of the opposing team when they walked in.[9] They play for a coal bucket, which is filled with flowers and presented by the cheerleaders of the losing team to the cheerleaders of the winning one.

Vince, son of Coach Chesnay, commented on how in Kulpmont, the townspeople identified with the team as a part of their pride in the town and after Kulpmont High School was merged with Mt. Carmel's in 1964, they looked for ways to create their own town identity. Growing up they noticed that Mt. Carmel had its own high school, Shamokin had its own and Kulpmont did not. "That definitely stirred up pride and a sense of individuality . . . we had to create our own identity. So even growing up we would love to go to the Little League football or baseball games. They call them the Cougars—'Kulpmont Cougar Pride.'" So sports teams other than football also create town pride.

Not only does the football team serve as the internal symbol of the town's unity, it also becomes a symbol of the town in opposition to other towns, to the outside world.[10] In 2003, Bob Chesnay suggested that this enthusiasm represented something to cling to in the face of economic downturn and population loss. "It shows success when everything else has been drained from us. When we've played other teams while coaching at North Schuylkill, we'd go to play down by Gettysburg, to Havertown twice a year, even to Archbishop Carroll in Philadelphia, we probably had as many fans if not more than the home team."

The significant sport continues to be specifically football. Wrestling used to be important: Shamokin wrestlers dominated in the 1930s, with 58 victories and 8 losses (Toscano 2000, 102), but is becoming a dying sport.[11] Basketball is hot and cold. The Shamokin area teams are a little more for basketball;[12] Mt. Carmel Area is more football. The split of Shamokin/ Coal Township team when the borough divided in 1965, left bitterness and the Shamokin football team has not been so successful since then, nor is the community feeling that football creates in Shamokin as strong as in Mt. Carmel.[13] "That's still the banner that the Coal Region waves; sports are still strong," says a newspaper writer. He expands on what it means: "I know people who work in Harrisburg who say to people down there. You might have the best basketball and baseball but we have the best football up in the Coal Region. They are very proud of that, even though they are socially not so far up on the social ladder, athletically they have made it."[14]

Besides sustaining a sense of community, some people consider sports to be part of the process of social mobility. Gerald Breslin, track coach at Mt. Carmel Area High School, undefeated for thirty years in dual track competition, and elected to the Pennsylvania Hall of Fame in 1986, emphasized the connection of sports to social and economic mobility. He graduated from Bucknell University in 1926, where he was active in organizing a Catholic fraternity. He considered it difficult for Catholics to get into a fraternity, "and really only possible if you were an athlete because good athletes could attract good people to a fraternity. Sports are more intense now. The way for college kids to get a college scholarship is through being a good football player and they take a great pride in being good."[15]

A short piece entitled "Home is where the Big Red is," appeared in a column in the *News Item* after the State playoff of December 12, 1998, in Hershey stadium, written by Bob York, a Mt. Carmel Area graduate, class of 1969, and a former Tornado, who lives in West Chester. It encapsulates how these football events united the town and its former residents and, on a wider level, the whole Coal Region. It refers to both sense of community and sense of place. It is given in the box below.

Another sport that enhances pride in the town in competition with others is sledding or "coasting" down the steep streets. This used to be the king of winter sports in the coal towns and continues in modified form today. Bobsledding in particular was tremendously popular in Shamokin. "Roaring

> We were all here, 5,000 strong. . . . Movement about this red army was like a stroll down the time tunnel of life. All through the crowd were bits of my youth: guys from Little League, old neighbors and former teachers. Grade school classmates blended with ex-players. Dentists, cops, ex-miners—we were all one, one equally joined by an umbilical cord of red. . . . At the box office, the PIAA loves the Tornadoes. After all, we have brought the three largest crowds in championship history. In that sense, we never played an away game. It may be no coincidence that in our three title games, we were the home team each time. . . . The coal is gone now, but the people remain. Those dark holes in the landscape all about us forged a character; a mentality if you will that binds us together forever. We all feel that up to the last hour of our last day, we will be coal crackers. The team is in our hearts, but the region is in our soul.

down Sunbury Street on a bobsled at a speed of seventy miles an hour, from a starting point in a small grove of pine trees near the brow of Bunker Hill, supplied a never-to-be-forgotten thrill to the more daring youths of past years." Giant sleds for as many as twelve or more riders brought the owners and the fathers who built them the greatest status and popularity. Rides, however, were infrequent: it took almost an hour to haul the huge bobs back up the hill. The most famous was that of the Liberty Hose Company which carried twenty four riders and signaled its approach with a large fire gong mounted on the front (*Shamokin Centennial Booklet 1954*, 62; Marlok 1976, 51).

Bobsledding no longer takes place because of snow removal for traffic, but the street sledding tradition still continues: Mt. Carmel and the other towns today lay rival claims to having the best street sledding. One resident explains what makes this a unique feature of life of which the coal towns are proud: "there's an intensity to that experience, everybody sleds, even kids in the suburbs, but this idea of taking it to a degree of intensity within your community and then arguing with the next community over who has better sledding—'this is the best in three counties'—that kind of thing, that's different.[16]

The Anthracite Heritage

Pride in the anthracite heritage is explicit: "Heritage is the key: knowing the heritage, living the heritage, fostering and nurturing the heritage is the heart beat of the Coal Region."[17] After the terrorist attacks on the World Trade Center and the Pentagon on September 11, 2001, the mayor of Shamokin suggested that the name of the Cameron Bridge on Rte. 61 should be changed to the 'Let's Roll' Bridge after the rallying cry of the passengers who heroically took over the plane that crashed in Pennsylvania as part of these attacks, to memorialize those who died in it from Western Pennsylvania. But the idea aroused strong opposition in letters to the editor of the newspaper: "My father worked in the mines. I feel we need that name for our Cameron Bridge;" "I have a lot of relatives—father and grandfather—who worked there. . . . It is an insult to the miners who worked at the Cameron mine;" "The Cameron Bridge is precious to all in this town" (*News Item*, October 18, 2003). The bridge has always been regarded as the gateway to Shamokin/Coal Township and to the entire Coal Region. Residents wanted it to keep its historic name and remain as a memorial to the miners whose labor built the town and the industry. The idea of a new name was dropped.

In 2002, CBS ran a TV series called *The Amazing Race*. It consisted of a worldwide scavenger hunt by teams from different states of the Union. Mary Lenig and Peach Krebs, two sisters from Shamokin/Coal Township, represented Pennsylvania and took six weeks going around the world to make the film. It was shown for an hour a week on a local station opened in the Coal Region. It became enormously popular and generated an outpouring of support: people would meet in clubs and watch in groups and were fanatical about supporting the sisters although they did not necessarily know them personally—"You are the hometown girls and we are behind you." A letter of support to the editor of the local paper stated: "The entire time we watched Mary and Peach on the Amazing Race we were so proud of how well they represented the Coal Region" (*News Item*, May 11–12, 2002). But people were upset that the sisters were just announced as being from Pennsylvania and not specifically from the Coal Region.[18] The indignation they expressed at CBS for this omission reflected the strength of their pride in their mining past and their consciousness of being united in a community, in the sense of a collective identity, by their Coal Region origin. The morale boosting significance for the town of the Amazing Race was reiterated in the Anthracite Festival of the Arts with a giant scavenger hunt called the Amazing Coal Cracker Race, which ranged throughout Shamokin area. It was run by Peach Krebs, one of the sisters in the original race.

Another way this pride in the anthracite heritage is expressed is through public art and monuments, and museums. Public art takes the form of statues that have been erected to memorialize miners in several Coal Region towns

Figure 8.1. Memorial of a Miner with His Mule and a Coal Wagon

in the Southern Coal Region. They include a figure of a miner with his mule drawn wagon standing at the mock entrance to a coal tunnel in the hamlet of Buck Run north of Minersville (see figure 8.1), and an imposing statue of a miner holding his lamp aloft on the southern outskirts of this town in front of a gas station (figure 8.2).

Figure 8.2. Statue of a Miner in Minersville

Another example is a 1938 memorial to the mothers of the Coal Region, a bronze statue of a woman, replica of a painting by Whistler, towering at the head of a long stretch of Route 61 as it comes into Ashland.

Shamokin's fine little historical museum of mining was moved for a time to Knoebels Amusement Park in Elysburg, but was returned to Shamokin and open for the Anthracite Festival of the Arts. The tiny museum of the fire companies of Shamokin/Coal Township (described below) is open for visits by appointment. In Ashland, the Pennsylvania Museum of Anthracite Mining shows how the coal is mined, with a collection of tools, machinery and photographs. Nearby, visitors can take a train trip into the huge main tunnel of the Pioneer Tunnel Coal Mine and see the wet conditions and cramped spaces of the branches of its tunnels in which miners worked, and experience the darkness of the mine with only the faint glow of the miners' lamps. There used to be such a tour of the Glen Burn mine in Shamokin. Scranton has the Pennsylvania Anthracite Heritage Museum. Eckley Miners' Village in the northeast (see figure 1.1) is a museum of original miners' houses with their long garden patches out back, some still inhabited by retired miners, with a small but comprehensive museum on the material culture of how they lived and worked. And there is the small Lithuanian ethnographic museum in Frackville (described in chapter 7).

The local newspaper, the *News Item*, fosters interest in community spirit and pride. It runs periodic in-depth articles on coal mining, and other elements of the community heritage and history of the town, reflecting and maintaining this interest. A long series of articles came out on Sundays every other week in early 2006 called "The Achievers," by Dick Morgan, Garth Hall, and Reba Hirsch, on the lives of notable citizens who, in various ways in the past as well as the present, have made a difference to the town. Earlier lengthy articles in this paper appearing during the research, included a series which described still operating family coal mines, the details of *soupie* making by a local business, and a full page account of the last remaining corner grocery store and its owners. Scans of newspapers of the early nineties and before, however, did not reveal such in-depth coverage and exploration of local heritage. That this interest in the town has been intensifying as the effort to reconstruct the sense of community builds, is borne out by the success of the revival in 2006 of the transformed Anthracite Festival of the Arts, presented at the beginning of the chapter, with its focus on interest and pride in the past.

Reviving, Creating and Reinventing Tradition

Restoration of a sense of community has included reviving, transforming and inventing traditions. Coal Towns are proud of their fine churches and synagogues, and a major tradition in these towns in the past was the construction of elaborate and beautiful decorations in many churches to celebrate Christmas and Easter. People would visit the churches to view these decorations. Local historical societies in the area recently revived this tradition with sponsored tours. In 2002, the Schuylkill Saturday newspaper reported two tours. One, the third annual Shenandoah Christmas Church Tour, attracted over 100 people in three buses to be taken to seven of the town's churches, with people coming from not only Shenandoah but also Danville, Minersville, Port Carbon, Pine Grove, Pottsville and elsewhere, an indication of the appreciation of traditional celebrations of religious heritage throughout the Coal Region. The newspaper published a full page of photographs of the decorations in St. George's, Shenandoah, the oldest Lithuanian parish in the country, St. Stephen's, founded as a Slavic church in 1899, St. Casimir's, the oldest Polish Roman Catholic church in the East, St. Michael's Ukrainian Catholic Church, and two Methodist churches and a Welsh Baptist church.

The other tour, held earlier in the month in Frackville, was not specifically a Christmas tour but was for viewing the churches: seventy people participated in bus trips to five churches (three Roman Catholic and two Protestant) and a synagogue. It was sponsored by the Frackville Area Historical Society. The organizer commented: "Feedback has been extremely positive. People are just so proud of their heritage and proud of their town." This revival of tradition demonstrates a renewed sense of community pride and recognition of the heritage of the different religions of the area. It was continued in the self-guided tours of churches in Shamokin/Coal Township during the Anthracite Festival.

The Welsh have revived symbols of identity with historical origins. The red dragon of the Welsh flag was in evidence at the Shamokin *gymanfa* embroidered on the lectern frontal in the church, and on both sides of the director's shirt collar. And a large black dragon featured on the front of the program for the event in 2003. This symbol dates from the Middle Ages when it was part of the arms of the Tudor dynasty between 1485 and 1603. At that time it was not considered a national symbol, it was the administrative symbol of the Council of Wales. But in 1807, it reappeared as the royal badge for Wales and was increasingly used in the banners and badges of Welsh societies in the early nineteenth century (Morgan 1983, 90). It has been revived as a Welsh symbol in America.

A Welsh society founded in Danville, north of Shamokin (see figure 1.1), decorated a storefront window for the Danville Iron heritage Festival. The markers of Welsh identity it included were interesting in the range of historical symbols they drew upon to revive Welsh traditions. They included leeks, the three ostrich plumes of the Prince of Wales, and women's costumes with tall black hats and large cloaks. The leek was used by the Welsh as a badge dating back to Saxon times; its green and white color was associated with the Welsh princes and it was used to decorate the *eisteddfod* pavilions in the early nineteenth century. In the eighteenth century, however, the most common symbol for Wales was not the leek but the three ostrich plumes of the Prince of Wales. Welsh peasant women of the eighteenth century used to wear the hats and cloaks that were later adopted as an invented national costume (ibid., 79–90).

A dominant symbol of Ukrainian identity in the Coal Region is the three barred crosses so visible surmounting the cupolas of the Ukrainian churches in many of the coal towns and on most graves in the Ukrainian cemeteries (see figure 4.3). It is known everywhere as the Ukrainian Cross. "But in fact," Monsignor Fedorovich commented, "there is no such thing as a Ukrainian cross. In Ukraine there are these three bar crosses in the mountain areas from which the people here came, but for the most part all throughout Ukraine, there are two bar crosses." He continued to explain that some people looked down upon the churches with three bar crosses over there, though not here in Pennsylvania. He noted that there are a lot of intermarriages here and those who marry come to church and they wear, almost like a badge of honor, the three barred cross, which they show to you proudly. And they baptize their children to get them a three bar cross, whether they have a Ukrainian background or not. He said it was a trivial thing, but part of how people expressed themselves.

This cross thus reflects the need for a symbol of identity for those marrying across ethnic lines, and is the transformation of a regional symbol from the home country into a national one for Coal Region Ukrainians.

A newly created tradition is the annual *soupie* contest started in 2000. Making *soupies* and homemade wine is a part of the Italian heritage, and Italians identify with these activities, but a newly invented tradition for the town is this contest which has become extremely popular. All the townspeople participate, not just the Italians. *Soupies* have become a cherished local delicacy, and a great interest in making and eating them has developed in the last twenty years. This interest has generated this new annual tradition of a contest for making the best *soupies*. In 2003 and 2004, the winner of this new tradition was actually a non-Italian, and in 2004, even one of the judges, the mayor of Mt. Carmel, was Welsh and not Italian.

Two of the fire companies, the Forrest and the West End, now hold *soupie* contests. A Lithuanian married to an Italian tells of this food in Italy and of the new tradition it has generated in these Pennsylvania towns.

> *Soupie* contests are huge around here among the twenty-five to thirty-year-old population and they give out trophies and prizes. We are talking about a food that originated in southern Italy in the 1800s, only because the southern Italians were poor and didn't have refrigeration. But they had pigs, they had pork, and they made *soupies*, which back there is the lowest form of pork that you make. *Soupies* are very popular in Kulpmont which is six miles away. I and a friend were taught how to make them by my Italian father-in-law. The contests are only within an eight mile radius and most of the contestants are not Italian: I know they're not. And they are bought by people who have no connection whatever with southern Italy. Now there is a huge stand at the Bloomsburg fair with people fighting to get *soupie* sandwiches. And [back in Italy in the past] people considered this was the last stop before they starved—you'd get a piece of *soupie*! In the Coal Region, you can only buy *soupies* in Shamokin, Kulpmont and Mt. Carmel, but they are also sold in the Italian Market in south Philadelphia where they are called *sopra-satte*.[19]

Soupies and other ethnic foods today signify people's attachment to the Region and to their roots, but these foods are no longer markers of ethnic groups. People agree, however, that the rich variety of such foods is a distinctive Coal Region characteristic that is not found to the same extent in surrounding regions.

Sense of Place

"Don't Forget that Wherever You Go, You'll Always Have Coal Dust on Your Feet." This admonition reflects the strength of the identity bestowing attachment to this Coal Region town that is a home which defines its inhabitants as a particular people. As well as the sense of community and pride in the heritage of the town discussed above, and the black hills of coal waste of the surrounding countryside, the components of sense of place are the warmth and support of family, friends and neighbors; the family homestead where you were raised; the tastes, sounds, smells of home; the places that, people say "you must visit when you return" which are the institutions that provide the places where people meet up, socialize and celebrate; and the churches and their festivals. Sense of place also includes pride in the coal mining heritage and the struggle of the unions against the coal and railroad companies, and pride in ethnic ancestry and traditions. In these ways it is located in "the experiential and expressive ways places are known, imagined, yearned for, held, remembered, voiced, lived, contested, and struggled over" (Feld and Basso 1996, 8, 11).

The black hills of coal waste of the landscape are an essential part of this sense of place, though reactions to them are various: some deplore them as grim and unsightly and for the dirt and dust they release into the air; for others, they are places for bike riding or the enjoyment of the many wild creatures that have come to live there; for teenagers they are getaways where noisy drinking parties are not disturbed; and for those for whom the region is most deeply home no matter how far away from it they go, they are the essence of its landscape. This is an instance of Karen Blu's assertion that it is the combination of land and people together that makes the tie of sense of place so compelling (Blu 1996, 224).

Blu also notes, however, that some people move around and live and work in many places without any of them existing in their imagination or experiences to be at all important or identity bestowing (ibid., 219). This is true for some people from the Coal Region; some never do return. But the majority of the people I talked to have a strong attachment to the town and a strong sense of it as a place in which they fundamentally locate themselves, and to which they return if they have moved away, to visit or to retire, and to which they are brought back for burial.

A pivotal feature of this sense of place is the homestead, the family house in which the children were raised. It is a particular locus of home and especially draws people back to the town while their parents are still alive and living there.

The Homestead

A homestead in the Coal Region is the house in which you were raised as a child; it is your home, but is not necessarily multigenerational. Sense of place is rooted here. Family members who move away keep coming back to visit while parents are alive and living in the homestead, or may even take it to the extreme of keeping up the house after the parents die. This tie is so strong that I heard of two cases, in which the homestead has been kept so that it can be used as a place for family to stay when they visit. Upkeep is an expense, so this cannot often be an option. In one family after the widowed mother died, one of the sons bought the house instead of putting it on the market. His wife goes in to check on it and do anything that needs doing a couple of times a week, and one of the daughters who lives in town takes care of the laundry after anyone comes to visit, and makes coffee and cake for family get-togethers there. "In this way, the homestead can remain as the family remembers it, the same pictures and photos on the wall and so on."[20] Another family in Kulpmont moved away to a job but they still keep their homestead and come back periodically for a week here and there and two in the summer. They keep the home vacant and the neighbors watch it, mow the grass and remove the snow, and if the kids want to come home and visit, they have a place to stay. They are not sure about retiring and that is why they do not sell the house: they think they may come back to retire and do not want to cut off that option. "They are not interested in renting it because they want their things in it and their grandmother's face on the wall; so that when they come back it is all there."[21]

These statements give us not only the sense of the town as home but also of a community where the neighbors care enough about you that they will help you out, a strong feature of the sense of place that roots people here. But now there are people who speak sadly of how this close community spirit has changed, mostly phrased as how they never used to lock their doors but that nowadays they feel they must.

Coming Home to Visit, Retire, or be Buried

The occasions that people come back for year after year are family events (weddings, baptisms, funerals, family reunions and to visit family graves), football matches, class reunions on Memorial Day Weekend, religious festivals (Easter, Christmas and Saint's Days), and block (neighborhood) parties. The features of the town today that seem to compel those who have moved away to return again and again are family, church and community ties; the ethnic foods that enrich all events, foods which they both eat while there and purchase to take back with them; the sense of place that this town is home; pride in their ethnic and mining heritage; and the special places to which they go every time they return in order to make the visit complete. Part of it also is the ravaged landscape with its great banks of culm and pools of water. It is all this that you cannot shake along with the coal dust on your feet.

Religion is an integral part of sense of place in the Coal Region. Many people come back to be with families and go to church for major festivals of the year so that there is standing room only at Christmas and Easter services in many churches, particularly Catholic ones. Some find it essential to return to get married in these churches, and then to bring their babies to be baptized in them. Besides visits to family, these occasions also draw them back to the town. At such times, churches have an influx of young people into the usually predominantly middle-aged and elderly congregation, and three or four generations of a family will fill several pews.

People have come back for these occasions in great numbers for many years. The *Shamokin Centennial Booklet of 1964* commented that in 1938, "Adding to the gay holiday spirit around town were the countless home comers who had traveled from near and far to be with their family and friends for Christmas. Railroads and bus companies found their facilities taxed as crowds of holiday travelers sought transportation to this area. Finally it was necessary to put extra buses into operation" (Greater Shamokin Centennial Committee 1964, 62).

High school reunions are also occasions for returning. Alumnae Day coincides with Memorial Day weekend and there is a town picnic in Shamokin cemetery at which people care for the flowers, trim the grass, tend the graves and clean the stones. The Catholic churches have their own picnics. It is a home coming holiday to which families go together. As one resident commented: "They have never managed to make Memorial Day a political event."[22]

Though no longer a defining feature of ethnic groups, ethnic foods remain an essential component of the sense of home. An account from the Chesnay family shows how this strong relish for traditional ethnic foods is part of a sense of place. They relate how their friends and relatives visiting the Coal Region appreciate its ethnic food culture. Vince, their teenage son, comments that when he went to college in Maryland, he was surprised that it was not the same case there with ethnic cultures having their strong ties to food. In Maryland, the food is regional food like crab cakes, not ethnic food. "I would tell stories about the ethnic food of the Coal Region and the different cultures, and people were quite surprised that that is the case—especially when I would come back with a cooler full of home-made food from Mom and from my grandparents and everybody loved it."[23] He would bring back *haluski* and different soups, *pirogies*, potato cakes, kielbasa.

Bob noted that "Claudia's cousin, who just comes here to visit, lives in Dayton, Ohio, but his father, Claudia's mother's brother, was raised here. Every time we go to Ohio or he comes here, we fill a cooler specifically with *soupies*, kielbasa, garlic bologna, Italian cheeses, and it all goes to Ohio." These ethnic foods are seen as identifiers of home. Claudia finds that in her son's generation there is a pride in the ethnic foods: "when Bobby [Jr.] comes home, they can't wait to brag to their friends, 'you've got to come to Kulpmont' and try this food and that food. I think that's the tie to their ethnic background." She feels it is a source of pride for them that they have such a background.

This study has dwelt on food at some length and in some detail because of its importance: Claudia's comment makes it quite specifically a feature of ethnicity that remains strong today, although changed from the days of the past when each group had its own foods as a diacritical marker. Food traditions now mingle at town events.

Bob also stresses another feature that is part of the sense of place that brings people back: the community's hospitality and warmth. He stressed the amazing openness and instant hospitality: the first thing that everybody does is to offer something. "We had a couple of millionaire's kids come here, who had everything you could ever want in life, and yet the simplicity of coming to a place like this—no big fancy nightclubs and stores—you just walk around talking to people instead of going places and being entertained." He thought they really enjoyed it. He was emphatic that that is one thing that has not gone. It is one good trait that has stayed and has not been dissolved or diluted over time, like the language and the economic opportunities.

Others make the same point by contrasting the unfriendliness found on moving to other towns or cities. One young man who moved to Harrisburg in the early sixties described the difficulties of going to a new place, trying to make friends: "people never invited you to their house, and the first friend I did make, it took him weeks to invite me to his house. The Coal Region is very friendly, it don't matter who you are. In Harrisburg, it took an awful long time to make friends."[24] These feelings are shared by others. One woman has a sister who lives outside Harrisburg: "It's an area where there are nice homes, it's a nice development, and they have a small group of neighbors they get along very good with, but for the most part you don't know the guy a block away from you." The Coal Region towns are small and the perception, often voiced, that everybody knows everybody and you are expected to show up at important events is a strong feature of community in these towns.

Some young people do stay, or come back after leaving, to raise their families here because they value the community. A writer for the *News Item* felt that he was one of the fortunate ones able to find a job here. "As long as you are happy and can make living, there are a lot of intangibles about living and working in your hometown. Sometimes I regret not having the wider perspective, but in the long-run, I don't regret staying here all these years. I have a lot of pride—I see myself as a traditionalist in a lot of things."[25] Others choose to continue to live in the town and commute to work, drive to Harrisburg, York, Carlisle or Reading or other city or town every day.

People use places as anchoring points and sources of identification to enable them to both explore opportunities in the wider world and to maintain their sense of rootedness. This lasts until they decide to let go and root themselves elsewhere (Olwig 2003, 74). For some Coal Region people, their deep sense of rootedness in their home town means that this final move is returning to retire. People go away, work for thirty or thirty five years, make money and have a house "They can sell that house in the suburbs and buy a much nicer one in Shamokin/Coal Township than they could afford for the same money in the cities or their suburbs. The big expenses like taxes and real estate are less here."[26] Prices go up a little in Kulpmont and a little more in Mt. Carmel, but older people living in the area tend to have enough money to travel a lot, as shown by the number of trips organized by the different senior citizens' groups such as the Sunshine Club. Returning to retire brings them a better lifestyle and a more comfortable retirement than would be within their means in the city. This choice is frequent enough to bring benefits to the economy and tax base of Shamokin/Coal Township.

People in the town express their fears of the waning of community strength, but in fact the numbers of people returning to retire have been increasing since the early nineties, according to realtor Shirley Persing in 2003 who sold homes to many of them.

Deliberate efforts are made to maintain community when individuals move to the cities. Former Coal Region residents who live in the area to which people move are notified by friends or relations of the person or family who move. When people hear of someone leaving their Coal Region town for a job in the city, they come up with names of former residents in that city who are friends or relations, and they will call them and tell them who is coming and to whom they are connected. When those who are moving arrive, they will be called up, welcomed, and helped out. The former residents of the Coal Region in the town or city will also willingly help with connections for finding jobs. Those newly arrived in the city also seek out and find each other in the cities and stick together: "I went to the University of Pennsylvania and all of us there from here hung out together. You go to the big city where you know no one and you keep friends from here that you feel very comfortable with. Of course, you make new friends too."[27]

Institutions Sustaining Sense of Place

Specific institutions provide the places and opportunities for people to socialize on a regular basis or furnish the leisure activities and occasions which sustain the social relationships and overlapping networks of connections that are components of a sense of place. "Community is not simply a network of like-minded institutions but a network of institutions that also serve as nodes around which these interpersonal networks can cohere . . . rooted in a given physical space that draws together the diverse social circles networks and subcultures into a single holistic community" (Hunter 2007, 24–25).

The Coal Cracker Club is a new institution that fosters the wider community of the town and its former residents living elsewhere in nearby towns and cities. It is founded on the strong sense of place which remains for so many after they move away. The Club, started in 2003, is an organization made up of both town residents and of those in the wider community. They meet four times a year for lunches, sometimes in the big cities, sometimes in a Coal Region town. The Club has over 200 members (husband and wife equal one member). They are resident in many states: Delaware, Maryland, Pennsylvania, New Jersey, Ohio, New York, Florida. The first meeting was held in Knoebels Grove in Elysburg.[28] There are 150–200 people at these meetings. They have no order of business to discuss but just meet to eat together, socialize, reminisce, and keep up the ties based on the old times. The club reflects and sustains the strength of the wider community of belonging and identity.

Driving through Minersville, a sign catches the eye, in big letters on top of a building, announcing the Coal Cracker name for another organization, a Veterans detachment of the U.S. Marines (see figure 8.3 and note the miner's cap with lamp).

There are several restaurants in Shamokin/Coal Township which are icons of the home town.[29] People who live in this town go to them, in some cases almost daily, to meet and socialize and catch up on what is going on, sit down and relax and enjoy some company. Those who have left town, feel there are places to which they must go when they come back to visit. Such places "promote the community's collective identity and sense of distinctiveness" (Cnaan and Milofsky 2007, 15).

Coney Island is one that is described as "a sort of icon of the town"; it is a type of restaurant known all over the Coal Region, which serves only hot

Figure 8.3. Coal Cracker Sign for the Local Veterans' Detachment of the Marines

dogs and hamburgers with onions and their own special sauce, and it is open until very late at night. Its hours are 11:00 a.m. to 3:00 a.m. Some have the name Coney Island, as does the one in Shamokin (see figure 8.4).

Some are called by the name of the owner, for example Tony's Lunch in Girardville. They have only two things on the menu, Screamers and Growlers, and you are supposed to know that they are hamburgers and hot dogs respectively and come with a special sauce. The idea for this type of restaurant was picked up from one in Coney Island, New York and they are found in coal towns from Pottsville, to Shamokin, Hazelton and up to the northern coalfields, but not outside the region.

Coney Island in Shamokin on Independence Street is owned by the Gorant family: three brothers came over from Greece in 1918 and opened a restaurant and it has been there ever since. This small restaurant has the furniture and fittings of the 1920s, which the owner goes to great pains and expense to maintain or replace in the original Art Deco style. Every year they have a Christmas tree at the back decorated with 6,000 or more tiny bulbs. Lunchtime has its special set of customers, many of them coming every day, but it is most crowded late at night, especially when there are town events and festivals. It is a landmark of the town; one of the places where everybody who comes back to visit feel they must go.

Figure 8.4. Coney Island Lunch

The daytime crew is two women, Sharon and Lucy, who have been there twenty-six and twenty-eight years respectively: this is a longtime institution. The manager serves at night with two helpers. The customers are twenty-two to seventy years of age; younger kids go to the mall and the fast food chains. Not only do people make sure they visit Coney Island when they return to Shamokin/Coal Township, but they may bring a cooler and dry ice, have fifteen to twenty dozen hamburgers and hot dogs and sauce made up for them, and take them home and freeze them. One former resident in New York City would come in for 104 at one time whenever he came back. Someone will come in to order like this every week or so. Once they supplied a funeral dinner that the dead man had requested before he died, for which his son picked up 100 hamburgers and hot dogs.

Maurer's Ice Cream Shoppe is another of Shamokin/Coal Township's long-established special eateries, employing ten in its shop and cafe. It is famous, and has won prizes, for its bittersweet ice cream, vanilla with fine flakes of bitter chocolate, and is one of those places which must be visited by people when they return. They stop by, have a cone, and take home a gallon or more of ice cream packed in dry ice (which will keep it for fourteen hours) for their freezers.[30] Maurer's makes their own ice cream on the premises and have taken prizes for it. In summer they do big business at carnivals and they even ship ice cream packed in dry ice cross country.

Palmer's Diner on Route 61, coming from the east into town, is another family business that is a special feature of life in the town. People come for a good American breakfast, its primary offering. Some come every day, on their way to work, but many are retired and just want to spend a long time socializing with customers and staff over their breakfast. "It is something they do, they come in, meet other people, it is just like a gathering place. Coney Island is late night, Maurer's ice cream is evening, and we do breakfast," says Paul Palmitessa the diner's owner.[31] He says the diner is always full of people, and it is noticeable that there is a full line of cars outside whatever morning you drive by.

The diner was started in 1947. After a fire in 1981, the owner restored its original 1950s style, with juke boxes in several booths that are mounted to the walls and play only fifties music. Customers donate their memorabilia to help keep the theme alive. The breakfasts are excellent, and the staff know all the steady customers. Hiring arrangements with the staff are the key to the survival of the business. They are all part-time, most of them housewives and mothers, and they get the flexibility of hours they need: they are never refused a day off, and they can arrange their hours around school schedules. There are six cooks, instead of two or three, so that they can work around each other, and there's always someone there and readily available. Paul cannot afford to pay them benefits but most of them have husbands with jobs and benefits anyway. Most have worked there since High School. Some have put themselves through college and got jobs but still work at the diner on weekends to make extra money.

There are other restaurants in the town that have this quality of being town institutions: Fisher's Restaurant, Harry's Grill, and Mack's Hoagies (with its walls papered with names of different kinds of hoagies, such as "The Politician's Hoagie: A Lot of Baloney"). All these small eateries are distinctive in their contrast to today's fast food chains, of which there are several in town, because they are all small family owned enterprises and operate on the basis of personal relationships for employees and clientele alike; they have their steady customers who all know each other and the staff. They provide the places for people to meet up and socialize and keep up the networks that contribute strongly to community life, and they do this for both current residents and for those who come back to visit.

The volunteer fire companies have long been important institutions of town life. For instance, in 1939, the Jubilee celebrations marked their significance by selecting firemen as one of the themes for a day of the week of celebrations.[32]

The Shamokin Fire Bureau was founded in 1874. There are five fire companies and a rescue squad in Shamokin,[33] six companies and a rescue squad in Coal Township, two companies in Kulpmont and four in Mt. Carmel. Four of the five fire companies in Shamokin still have social clubs which are attached to the fire hall and these clubs continue to function, unlike many other social clubs that have ceased or faded in the economic decline of the town. In Shamokin, the Liberty Fire Company club is the only one that has closed with the decline in population. Through their extensive social activities, these clubs help maintain the networks of community social life and leisure activities.

In the past, volunteers of the different companies tended to be of the same ethnicity because they were set up in the town neighborhoods, a necessity in the days of horse-drawn wagons for putting out fires, and they drew volunteers from the ethnic group that predominated in each area; the Friendship was Italian and the Liberty and the West End were predominantly Polish. Now the volunteers in each company no longer live in the same neighborhood and they are called out on their pagers to come in by car when there is a fire, and it is a long time since they have been of the same ethnic background. Also formerly some of the companies restricted membership to particular religious affiliation. The Rescue and the Independence Fire

Companies used to have the unspoken though not written rule that their members be Protestant, which was strict up until the 1970s, whereas the Friendship in the "Bloody 5th" Ward used to be Catholic. Another change is that fire companies now have women members. Volunteers come from all social levels, and members of one family will stick with the same company over the generations.

The fire stations are owned by the city, and the city fire chief governs all of them. The city also now owns the equipment and pays for the fuel and the insurance on the trucks and on the firemen. There used to be ten to twelve men for each truck; now there are only two to three and they rely on Mutual Aid, which brings out volunteers from all six companies.

There are more fire companies than are needed for fighting fires and it is their role as active neighborhood social clubs with a hall and bar that makes them such a significant feature in town life. They held block parties (up until the early 1990s these "picnics" were annual for each company), canvass door to door, and have bingo three nights a week to raise funds to buy equipment; they host parades, contests, dinners, dances, parties and clambakes; and they organize sports teams and sponsor scout troops for children, and softball, pool and darts for adults; hold concerts in the Fireman's Park in the middle of town; and now two of them hold *soupie* contests, the new popular event in the town. Retired firefighters spend a lot of time socializing in them, like the ethnic clubs their beer is cheaper than in the bars. This wide range of activities helps to sustain social life and community ties. In 1991, there were 150 active fire company members and more than 2,000 social members.

The significance of the fire companies as a local institution is apparent in various other ways also: Shamokin has a monument to firefighters and a small museum on the history of fire-fighting;[34] the fire companies are always part of town parades; and Memorial Day events recognize not only servicemen but also firemen and on this day all the firemen in the city make their rounds to the different fire stations to celebrate and pay their respects to one another.[35] In 2002, the funeral procession of a volunteer fireman killed in a fire at Trevorton, the first fireman ever killed in the line of duty, was unparalleled in the history of Shamokin: it stretched for about five miles.[36] Such a turnout was a unifying event and signified the contribution of the fire companies and firemen to town life.

Economic, Demographic and Political Change

In assessing Shamokin/Coal Township today, following the collapse of the coal and garment industries of the town and the loss of over two-thirds of the population, it is clear that the economy is reviving into a different form: people see the area's potential as a good home base but not any longer as an industrial and manufacturing or shopping and entertainment center. Ethnicity is becoming politically irrelevant, and the class structure of the town has changed.

The Economy

Few career opportunities exist today to keep the young in the area and most of them leave. But the loyalty and attachment of some of the young and middle aged is sufficient to keep a number of them wishing to stay and raise their families, so that some commute to better jobs in the cities while others work in the medical and prison service jobs offered by the large institutions that have appeared in the area, and a good number of former residents return to retire. The town is thus becoming a bedroom community for the nearby, and not so nearby, towns and cities, and a retirement community. More recently it has also become a haven for welfare migrants from the big cities seeking cheaper housing, so that it is confronting a new welfare migration that brings an increasing need for social services when there is already a problematic decline in the tax base because of economic and demographic change.

There are several prisons in north central Pennsylvania which provide some local career opportunities and a number of people commute to work in them. In 1993, a state prison was built within three miles of Shamokin/Coal Township. In 2004, it had 1,850 inmates and more than five hundred staff. Working there brings good salaries, retirement pay and benefits. One staff member from Shamokin, in charge of the breakfast and lunch kitchens, said that for someone with only a high school education, it was a great place to work.[37] He likes the job; it is so varied in its responsibilities.

Medical facilities, the other source of service occupations are provided by the managed care of the huge Geisinger Health Systems, headquartered in Sunbury, which has numerous branches in the towns of the region. Shamokin has a hospital and so does Ashland. Some school leavers take advantage of many small scholarships offered for further education to study medical technology and qualify for these employment opportunities in the area.

In the coal areas, some strip mining still continues. But strip mining and the re-mining of the culm banks employ very few people; it is all done by huge machines. The land must now be filled in after it is mined, and planted with grass; it is very unstable and is thus unsuitable for industrial sites. Small family coal businesses have operated what little remains of the mining industry.[38]

A tax relief program exists for new businesses in Pennsylvania, the Keystone Opportunity Zones (KOZ), which gives freedom from taxes for fourteen years from the day the land is declared a KOZ. It is usually raw land with no buildings on it since KOZ tax relief is intended as an incentive to get land developed. Pennsylvania taxes are relatively high, so these zones help make the state more competitive for attracting new businesses. Some manufacturing and small industry has come to restore something of the economy since the decline of the coal and garment industries, and some of these have failed, but there are recent signs of some new developments for the region as a whole.

Several new businesses have come into the area attracted by the tax advantage, by the available work force, and by a quite adequate local road system connecting to the big highways. These include two big Distribution Centers with huge warehouses. There are also a number of small manufacturing companies in the area. The Coal Region as a whole can expect an economic boost from a proposed cargo-only airport near Hazleton, currently underway, that would provide a cost-effective alternative to congested and expensive airports in New York, Newark and Philadelphia, offer easy access to freight lines and interstate highways, and create 4,533 high technical jobs and, indirectly, 161,000 others (*News Item*, February 1, 2007). This development has the potential to re-connect the region to the international economy. It is being built on former coal land; a $17 billion impact from it is forecast for the region.

Ethnic Niches

Since the later years of the twentieth century, small stores in the coal towns have found it hard to stay in business because of competition from the chain stores and malls in the towns and cities of the wider region, to which people will drive out on a weekend. But once in the way of driving to these malls and stores elsewhere, it turns out that people will also drive to the ethnic food stores in different towns of the region to buy their favorite foods and smoked meats. These stores have found an economic niche by supplying the ethnic foods still in demand in the area and by residents who have moved away but still crave the foods of home.

In Tamaqua there is a bakery with the last coal-fired ovens in Pennsylvania where all they make is old-time, crusty Italian bread. In Frackville they make the Eastern European huge rye bread loaf, which they sell in quarters; the Weis supermarket in Shamokin/Coal Township, obtains a quantity of this bread to sell in its store on one day a week. In Shenandoah, Kowalonek's, a Polish butcher, makes *kielbasa* meatloaf, and other renowned specialty meats. Nanticoke also has a *kielbasa* store. Such stores do a large business at festive seasons: you have to wait in line for hours in Kowalonek's at Easter and other festivals because it is so crowded with customers coming in from out of town. There are similar stores in other Coal Region towns.

In Shamokin/Coal Township the long-surviving family business of Anthracite Provisions is such a store. The Mahers were the family who owned this business originally. They were a very well-to-do Irish family in Shamokin, in the late 1800s and through the early 1900s. Some of them still live in town or in the area. Three generations back, Thomas Maher started a wholesale liquor business, selling whisky, soda, wine, and cigars. He married into the prominent and wealthy Graeber family (see chapter 4) with whom he became partner in several mining enterprises. Vincent Maher, returning from service in World War II, was encouraged by his family to buy a wholesale food business with their help: the Anthracite Provisions Company. This store supplies meat to grocery stores and restaurants locally and in nearby towns, and is a retail butcher store that sells also the ethnic foods that were formerly cooked at home but are now commoditized and sold commercially. Vince built the business up from nothing into a flourishing concern, continued after his death by his daughter and his son-in-law, Earl Sheriff.

They make the old-fashioned *faggots*,[39] Welsh in origin, which made good hand-held food for miners' lunches. They make them all year round. These date back to the Mollie Maguires, but today are only found in this local area, Tamaqua does not have them. They also make *soupies* all year round, about 4,000 of them. During Christmas most people buy them in jars for gifts. Former residents come to buy them, and they ship them to Hawaii, Texas, and other states. "Some hear of it on the internet or have had family here at one time. They don't know what it is but they want to try it, and you ship it out," Earl says.

He noted how besides *faggots* and *soupies* they also make *kielbasa* loaf, peppered bacon (another local specialty), ham loaf, country sausage (which is also sold as a hot sandwich with tomato, pepper and onion sauce in the store), as well as all the regular butcher meats. The store is in a back street. "On Friday, Saturday, even Monday, it is jam-packed and people can't get in, I mean it's like there is a football game going on here. . . . They come from all over, Mt. Carmel, Kulpmont, sometimes Harrisburg, Reading. People know me very well." He still has some ten or fifteen good restaurants that buy from him, some smaller sub-shops, and some nicer stores, bigger but not too big. His business is mostly in Hometown, Hazleton, Tamaqua, Coaldale, Summit Hill, Nescahoney, Sunbury, Danville, Bloomsburg, Berwick. The Elks clambake used to have 1,500 people from New York and New Jersey coming to it. They would supply the food and the trucks to get the beer, going round the beer distributors, first to Furman & Schmidt, the long-time family owned local brewery, for around fifty barrels, then to all the others, so that everybody got a piece of the pie. Busloads of returning residents would come even from the cities. "It was a great thing. But I'd have to work 'em." Additionally, when the churches make pizzas for their block parties, they buy the shells and sauce from Anthracite Provisions.

The ethnic and mining heritage and strong sense of place bring people back wanting to buy all this food that they associate with home. Altogether, this seems quite an impressive market for this business. But in 2004, Earl was worried that these organizations were all dwindling. He feared that it is only the old folks who want these ethnic specialties, and those of their children who know what they are, and that with the present trend for fast food restaurants and general disinterest in cooking and family meals, in the next generation the demand for these foods would very much decrease. However, the amount of money still being raised by the sale of them, as documented in chapter 7, would seem to indicate that that day is quite far off. Contrary to Earl's view, a number of people are quite confident that there are enough people waiting in the wings to take over organizing these activities from the older folk when they can no longer carry on doing them.

There are other small businesses that also cater to the diminished ethnicity of today. Aid to the European homelands provides a need for shipping services that will facilitate the sending of goods and money. One company that comes to the Coal Region is a Polish company that has a branch in Gdansk in Poland and another in Philadelphia. A pick-up truck will take twenty-eight to thirty packages from Coal Township to a travel agent in Philadelphia that includes them in a direct container shipment to Gdansk and charges $1 per pound. They are packed in fifty-five- to sixty-pound boxes and donors try to make up ten boxes. The company delivers the packages directly to people's homes in Europe, avoiding the theft that is widespread with other ways of sending.[40]

A Lithuanians runs another such small business based in Boston. He comes to Frackville and other towns in different areas with a truck, and picks up packages for Lithuania, primarily medicines, clothing and money. When he has a box car load, he sends them. He has people over there who work with him and they distribute the packages direct to peoples' homes. He was born there and speaks Lithuanian fluently, which is necessary for making all the arrangements for his business started before 1991. He goes over to Lithuania about three times a year, staying for two months each time. He worked for an airline before he retired and gets reduced fares for trips for life as a benefit.[41] Many people send things there through him. According to him, many Lithuanian immigrants are moving back to Lithuania to retire, especially those who immigrated after World War II. He ships their furniture back for them.[42]

These are small, not large-scale, enterprises, but they show there is enough significance to ethnicity today to provide a market sufficient to create economic niches of which these small businesses can take advantage. Others include Ukrainian crafts, Lithuanian straw art, and the Polish crafts sold at their club. Thus, although the strong ethnic groups that formerly made up the town and structured people's lives have faded away with economic change and population decline, ethnicity remains as an identity option which still has cultural and economic content.

Further changes in the town around the millennium reflect new shifts in power and inequality.

Shifts in Power Relations

There have been indications of a beginning in the breaking down of the barriers of gender and ethnicity in politics. One was the entry into politics of a woman, Eleanor Kuhns, whose life as a union organizer was described in chapter 6. She started her political career in November 1984 as a Democratic National Delegate for Walter Mondale, getting the highest number of votes of all twenty-six candidates in the seven counties of the 11th Congressional District. She was the first woman elected to the Coal Township Board of Commissioners and later the first woman to be elected its President. In 1993, she was selected to fill a vacancy on the Northumberland County Board of Commissioners, and in 1995 she was the first woman in its 140-year history to be elected as Chair. Her achievements in political and community involvement and their significance were recognized in March 1993, when she was presented with the "Outstanding Woman Award" at the annual Columbia-Montour Counties Women's Conference at Bloomsburg University.[43]

In November 2003, the election of Frank Sawicki as a Northumberland County Commissioner indicated a change in the ethnic bias in politics. His election as a commissioner was perceived as a triumph because he achieved it without changing his Eastern European name. People gathered for a group discussion at the time, commented on the election of a county commissioner with a Polish name of Polish-Italian parentage: "In years gone by, you could not run for office if you had an ethnic name. If you did not have a Protestant name, you would never get a vote north of the Cameron Bridge;" formerly if you had an ethnic name like Sawicki you'd have to change your name to be elected in Northumberland County. . . . The whole county is not Coal Region and the northern district looks down on us, the southern district."[44]

Changes have taken place in the relationship of the town to the bigger towns and cities to which its people have moved or to which they commute. The city folk are perceived to consider themselves as a class above Coal Region people, an attitude made explicit in the way the former may refer to the latter as "Fish Wrappers" (Catholics who eat fish on Fridays). It is to these larger towns that people moved as they acquired the skills and education for the better jobs that made them socially mobile and which, for the most part, cannot be found in the Coal Region. This mobility has class connotations both for those who leave and for those who stay,[45] and is a consequence of a shift in power relations as the town economy has declined and is no longer a source of wealth and power.

A staff writer for the local newspaper makes it clear that social mobility corresponds to geographic mobility as he talks about people in Elysburg, a town to the north of Shamokin, within the boundaries of the seven anthracite coal counties but not in an actual mining area, and about Coal Region people who have moved to the bigger towns and cities.

Elysburg, he says, is on the edge of the Shamokin, Kulpmont, Mt. Carmel region, but, although they technically are, people there do not like to be considered Coal Region. It is because they were a farming, and more or less rural, region. But it is still considered the Coal Region. A lot of people there work at Geisinger in the hospital, or at the Merck Chemical Co. which is at Riverside near Danville. Some have fine homes and they are more affluent than the people here, and there is some sort of stigma there. So they don't like to be considered Coal Region. It is the same thing for the people that moved out and live in Harrisburg. If you look at the names of the people that came from there, they all came from Mt. Carmel or Shamokin/Coal Township or Trevorton. They went to high school here. Sometimes they feel they are better than the people who live in the Coal Region. They come back in the summer and come to the local block parties. The majority of them come back at some time or another. But there are some people who just refuse to return, they have nothing, their family doesn't live here for some reason anymore, "they think it is below them to come back to an area that they grew up in. But for the most part we have a lot of people who make some kind of contact, whether it is coming back just for some kind of food, or to see relatives, or to go to some church." He has friends who have good jobs, a couple of them work at the Pentagon, they come in and they all go out for pizza and beer. They are good friends, he says, and do not consider themselves above you, they love it and love going back to the spots they went to when they were teenagers. But there are some others who do not mingle, who just think, "I'm an affluent attorney in Harrisburg or Pittsburgh," or wherever. They want to move on.

These comments reference the upward mobility represented in the names of those from the Eastern European ethnic groups of the Coal Region, who came from the laboring class of their parents in the mines and are now in professional employment in Harrisburg and do not want to preserve their ties with the Coal Region. They have moved up. Others, however, want to maintain their ties with the Region and love to come back.[46] These are the people who form a wider community of belonging and identity, and whose continuing involvement in the town makes a positive contribution to its struggle to recover from economic decline and population loss and rebuild its sense of community. The rural urban class division is not so rigid here.

Chapter 4 showed the local perception of the identity of the people of the region as Coal Crackers, who would fiercely unite in situations in which they confronted outsiders. Some say that to be a Coal Cracker, you must be descended from a miner, others just that you live, or have lived, there. In the process of being socially mobile, Coal Region people will shed this identity in the outside world and deliberately stop using the characteristic dialect of the region known as "Coalspeak." This is identified by an accent but also by vocabulary and colloquialisms. For example, a "Proosey" is a Protestant; "half a double" is half a duplex; "Chendo" is Shenandoah; "Ho-Butt" means "Hey, buddy," and so on. A Lithuanian gave an example:

> If you say someone is "thick as a felt boot," it means a stupid person, greenhorn (immigrant), or country type. It refers to a felt boot from Russia. The miners wore rubber boots and to keep their feet warm, they would stuff felt in them, so there was a thickness to them. So if they wanted to say that you were a little thick, or dense in not getting something, they would say, "He's thick as a felt boot." I would be enraged by that comment, it would mean I am not intelligent, I just don't get it. And that still carries on in the Coal Region, everybody knows what it means, and if you called someone that he'd get up and punch you in the mouth. Elsewhere in Pennsylvania they would not know what I was talking about and they would not be offended. It is Coalspeak.[47]
>
> He also said: "I try not to use coal speech, and pressure my children, and my brother is the same. He is an international manager and he knows the derogatory connotations of being called a Coal Cracker—although there are a lot of good things, like loyal, hardworking, honest, that are positive aspects of the coal cracker label, there's a lot of negative connotations also, just as there are negative connotations between the [ethnic] groups within the Coal Region."

Components of a sense of place vary according to social position. Besides comments on the bleak landscape of mountains of coal waste, in recollections of the past descendants of miners often voiced a harsh component of their sense of place in their frequent mention of the sound of the breaker whistle blown outside its regular marking of daily working hours, and the dread this aroused of a mine accident. This sound signified the violence done to the miners and their families by the callousness of the company's reluctance to spend what was needed to make the mines safer places. Often mentioned also was how mine company personnel just callously dumped a dead or injured miner, either someone of the speaker's family or someone they knew, on the porch or in the kitchen of his house after accidental death or injury in the mine. No compensation was paid to the family.

Since the late 1980s, a new underclass has emerged in the town as a consequence of demographic change: a flow of migrants, poor and on welfare, have arrived in Shamokin/Coal Township, replacing some of the population loss. These new arrivals, initially a trickle from the cities in the late 1980s, became a steady stream by 2003, according to Police Chief Richard Nicholls. He could not put a number on it but thought that it was substantial for a city the size of Shamokin/Coal Township. This is not an immigration of recovery substance abuse addicts, like that experienced by Williamsport in the 1980s (Milofsky et al. 1993), but is made up of poor inner city residents, on welfare and fleeing from the big east coast cities. They are Caucasian, Hispanic and African American and are attracted by the cheap housing that is available in Shamokin/Coal Township as a consequence of the population exodus.

The new migrants bring the ways of the inner city into the town: a more confrontational culture and a lifestyle based on overcrowded apartments. Drug trading has been here for a long time, but it got worse in the 1990s, as drug gangs reached down from New York City to Shamokin/Coal Township, where it is much easier to obtain hand gun permits than it is in New York.[48]

These new arrivals are not integrating into the town community because they are constantly on the move in search of other welfare possibilities. This combined with low skills makes their job prospects poor. Additionally, they are despised by the locals for accepting welfare. In a 2006 interview, a union organizer emphasized that the Slavs would not ask for or take welfare. "The AFL/CIO has millions of benefits available but people aren't taking them, because hard work does not phase these people at all and they don't want to owe anything to anyone."[49] The newcomers are looked down upon, as were the Irish in the early years of the mines, fleeing from the famine (when signs for job postings would say "No Irish need apply"), and as later were the Slavs. But nevertheless both gradually moved up the social hierarchy over time. If the regional economy recovers, perhaps this new population will find the opportunities to integrate more into the town. At present, it means that the town is confronting a new welfare migration that brings an increasing need for social services when there is already a problematic decline in the tax base.

Communities evolve and change over time in a continuing process, contingent on economic and political factors; any stopping point in studying them has to be arbitrary. This study has had to end without a detailed investigation of this new population and how it impacts the town.

To conclude, in the aftermath of economic and population decline, the townspeople are attempting to reconstruct the sense of community of the past. In this process, they draw upon the anthracite heritage and the ethnic foods and modified ethnic traditions of the past that still remain, and on their high level of community pride and strong sense of place. This brings the continuing involvement of the many former residents who form a wider community of identity and belonging in the big towns and cities. They continue to contribute to the life of the town and to its economy, as they return for events: for life cycle celebrations, town and church festivals, football matches, high school and family reunions, and for buying the ethnic foods of their childhood, and they may finally retire and live in the town. The sense of pride and community heritage manifest in the festival described at the beginning of this chapter and the strong sense of place of the people are thus assets for the town in its efforts to recover from economic downturn and population loss. Shamokin/Coal Township is not unique: small towns and cities throughout the country have been brought to similar straits by the decline of the manufacturing base in America contingent on the globalization of capital. But the basis of the town's mining and ethnic heritage in reconstructing a sense of community and the boost the town gets from the loyalty and involvement of its wider community of former residents in towns and cities are more valuable assets than exist for many small towns likewise afflicted by this economic change.

Notes

1. They used to be held regularly on Memorial Day, Independence Day, Columbus Day, Halloween and Armistice Day (Marlok 1976, 5).
2. Mt. Carmel football coach February 25, 2003.
3. Joe Chowka February 26, 2004.
4. As well as high school sports, there was also the Polish Dramatic Club organized in 1928 at St. Stanislaus Kostka Church. The purpose was to put on theatrical programs but it developed strong baseball and basketball teams (Greater Shamokin Centennial Committee Souvenir Committee 1874–1974).
5. Chuck Yoder, by permission, April 8, 2003.
6. Chuck Yoder, by permission.
7. Paul Lima, unpublished paper, Bucknell University, 1999.
8. Jazz Diminick, April 21, 2003.

9. Paul Lima, unpublished paper.

10. Ronald Frankenberg notes these features for the football team in his study of a Welsh village (Frankenberg 1957).

11. Shamokin has turned out eight or nine state wrestling champions. There is a big board listing their names on the way into the town from the east.

12. In the past it was baseball. The Covaleski brothers of Shamokin were famous baseball players. Three of the five made it to the major leagues, and Stanley was inducted into the Hall of Fame in 1969. A memorial to him in polished coal stands downtown in Shamokin. Harry played with the Philadelphia Phillies in 1908; John with the St. Louis Browns; Stanley with the Cleveland Indians, the Washington Senators, and, finally, with the New York Yankees.

13. Dave Shade, November 10, 2003.

14. Mark Gilger, February 12, 2003.

15. Gerald Breslin, April 29, 2003.

16. Casey McCracken, March 2, 2004.

17. Bob Chesnay.

18. Mary Lenig, March 27, 2002.

19. Dave Kinder, January 15, 2005, with permission.

20. Walter Neary, February 1, 2007.

21. Bob Chesnay, February 25, 2003.

22. Casey McCracken, Mt. Carmel, 2004.

23. Vince Chesnay, February 25, 2003

24. Harry Derk, April 9, 2003.

25. Mark Gilger, February 12, 2003.

26. Bob Chesnay, February 25, 2003.

27. Mel Farrow, February 24, 2004.

28. From Garth Hall's detailed documentation of town life: "Shamokin, My Home Town," available in the local libraries.

29. Joe Chowka, one of those who returned to Shamokin to retire, took me on a tour of the restaurants that are special features of the town for its inhabitants, 2004.

30. The Maurer family was advertising its restaurant and ice cream mart in the *1939 Jubilee Booklet*. They sold it to the present owner, who has expanded the production of ice cream from 350 gallons a week to that much in one day, and 500 gallons of bittersweet in a week.

31. Paul Palmitessa, May 6, 2004; *News Item*, March 17–18, 2001.

32. Carl Milofsky, in his study of institutionalizing community in a Pennsylvania town on the Susquehanna, calls the volunteer fire companies "institutions of localism" because of the role they play in the lifestyle of active neighbor networks in the town (Milofsky 2008, 42).

33. The Friendship Fire Company at Rock and Chestnut Streets, the Liberty at Sunbury and Liberty Streets, the Rescue at Lincoln and Liberty Streets, the Independence at Market and Arch Streets and the West End at 5th and Pine Streets (see figure 4.1).

34. The museum was created and is maintained by John Smith. It has a meticulously organized collection, much of it computerized, of the past history of the companies and of how they were organized, including photographs, newspaper accounts

and videos; the Fire Chief's logs from 1874 to the present day; and a collection of equipment, uniforms, trophies and tools of fire-fighting and memorabilia.

35. Sources on the fire companies: interviews with John Smith, fire historian, April 15, 2003; and Mel Farrow, February 24, 2004, and research projects by two of my students, Shelley Simonds and Maulik Trivedi, in 1991 at Bucknell University, Lewisburg, PA.

36. Mark Gilger, February 4, 2003.

37. Ron Burns, February 4, 2004.

38. There are extensive articles on these family owned mines in the *News Item*, Sunday March 21, Monday March 22, Tuesday March 23, November 26, 2004. These independent deep mines were producing about 200 thousand tons a year as coal mining expanded somewhat in 1990, due to cogeneration plants producing steam, electricity and aluminum from culm, and to its use in industrial and residential heating. But by November 2004, only twelve family anthracite mines remained in Pennsylvania, down from sixty in 1995 and 140 in 1985. The number of these mines in Northumberland County has dwindled to three.

39. "We take the pork hearts and the pork livers and a little bit of breadcrumbs and egg, and we put a bit of fresh sausage in ours, and you mix that into a ball like a meatball and wrap them in pork netting, then you bake them in the oven and freeze them in broth." Earl Sheriff, February 24, 2004.

40. Len Oszko, February 8, 2002.

41. Research on unrecorded transnational trade between the Democratic Republic of Congo, Europe, and other countries of the world, has showed that employers using the perk of airlines' free tickets for their personnel, as a means to facilitate trade, is practiced in other parts of the world today (MacGaffey and Bazenguissa-Ganga 2000).

42. Eleanor Vaicaitis, Frackville, June 18, 2004.

43. Dick Morgan, "The Achievers Series," *News Item*, 2006.

44. Len Oszko, February 28, 2002.

45. A similar identification of geographic mobility corresponding to social mobility has been described in the Suffolk village of Elmdon in England by Marylyn Strathern (1982).

46. It would be interesting to seek out people who do not return and compare them in terms of economic success with those who retire in the town, but that is beyond this study.

47. Dave Kinder, by permission. A glossary of *Coalspeak* can be found on the Web, www.coalregion.com.

48. Police Chief Nicholls, March 3, 2003. More recently, there were reports in the newspaper of vans of undocumented migrants also coming into the area and being set up in sweat-shop working conditions and housing.

49. Marty Burger, formerly Organizer of the International Ladies Garment Workers union in the town 1978–1981. Interview in Philadelphia January 21, 2006.

CHAPTER NINE

Conclusion

In the early years of the coal era, ethnicity structured people's lives in the town. It was expressed in the language they spoke, where they lived, the churches they belonged to, whom they married, the associations they joined, the foods they ate every day, and the traditional arts, crafts, music and festive events that enriched their lives. These were the symbols of ethnicity and their practice marked the ethnic groups of the town. During the period of the late nineteenth and early twentieth centuries, ethnicity, religion, and class converged, and the structured inequality of ethnic groups in the town was marked in class, ethnic and religious neighborhoods, but gradually with the rise of the labor movement in the 1880s and 1890s, working class interests overrode ethnic interests as labor organized strikes against the big national corporations of the coal and railroad companies and the significance of ethnicity diminished.

After reaching its peak during World War I, the coal industry declined with the competition from alternative fuels, the increasing power of organized labor, and the Great Depression of the 1930s. The setting up of the factories of the New York garment industry in the Coal Region as it searched for cheaper labor in the 1920s brought prosperity to the town after the Depression, but the effects of World War II and the opportunities it provided thereafter through the G.I. Bill brought social mobility and the attraction of better jobs in bigger towns and cities for many people in the town. After the war, the cumulative effect of the competition of the new fuels and the disruption in filling demand because of the bitter struggle between the unions and the big companies in long strikes brought the coal industry into severe decline and many more of the townspeople left in search of work. Finally, in the 1970s and 1980s, the garment industry moved overseas in search again of cheaper labor, causing another exodus of the population. With the loss of over two-thirds of its people and the severe decline of the economy, the significance of ethnicity and of religion in town life waned.

Ethnicity, however, has not gone away. After these changes, it no longer structures people's lives, but it remains as an identity for many and as a valued part of their heritage. A feature of this study is the comparison of the component ethnic groups of the town over time. This has showed that they were differently located in the town hierarchy and that their relative position altered over time with changes in historical circumstances. Ethnicity is shown to be a process and the transformations of ethnic culture and identity as contingent on shifts in power relations and economic and demographic change.

The ethnic and mining heritage of the town, the popularity for everyone of ethnic foods of no matter what group, the participation in the modified ethnic events that still take place, are now all recognized features of the Coal Region as a whole and perceived to contrast with surrounding areas. This solidarity, however, is experienced as a class solidarity in opposition to those outside the Region. It is expressed in the identity of Coal Crackers which unites people against the derogatory perceptions of them by city dwellers and by some of the people who moved away to job opportunities and the social mobility of professional employment. The townspeople perceive the new underclass of today that has come with an influx of poor Caucasian, African American, and Hispanic migrants from the big east coast cities, more as a welfare class than in ethnic terms.

The practices of ethnicity are thus no longer identified with ethnic groups because they no longer define them: everybody eats everybody else's ethnic foods, enjoys musical performances—be they Welsh hymns or Polish polkas—competes in *soupie* competitions, or admires church festival decorations. But power relations have shifted again as the town and the Region have lost their economic importance with the decline of the coal and garment industries, and as the town becomes a bedroom community for the nearby large towns and cities, a retirement town, and a haven for the poor of the big east coast cities.

The dominant locus of political and economic power is now in these larger cities and at the state and national level. Among those who move away, however, there are many who return, keep up their ties in the town, visit regularly and sometimes retire there. The networks of connections between past and present residents of the town have meant that the town community extends beyond the Coal Region into a wider community of belonging and identity. The people of this wider community contribute to the town's economy and life by returning to participate in town events and festivals, to eat in the restaurants and buy the ethnic foods which together with family ties make the town home to them. Some of them assert this bond by belonging to the Coal Cracker Club with its organized meetings for dinners at regular intervals. These staunch supporters of the town are drawn back by a strong sense of place and community, by family ties, and by the ties of churches and associations.

A distinctive element in the town today is the strong sense of place of so many of its residents, both past and present. It is rooted in its prosperous past when droves of shoppers came to buy the fine clothes of the garment industry, in its ethnic heritage, in town and church festivals (for which ethnic foods are produced in vast quantities), in recollections of the militant heritage of the unions' struggle against the coal and rail companies, and in the great banks of coal waste of the countryside. What remains for those still resident in the town and for those who come back to visit and retire, is this sense of identity and place, and they draw on it as they strive to restore the sense of community of the past and to recover the economy into a different form. The strength of this sense of community in the town is articulated in the comment on the Saturday afternoon football game: "Everybody was there and if you weren't, they wanted to know why" (see chapter 8).

This fits with what Marion Kempny terms localism, "a feeling of being rooted in a place, of experiencing a sense of continuity over time as part of a bonded entity" (2002, 72). Chapter 8 describes some institutions of this localism: the fire companies, certain restaurants, and the Coal Cracker Club. Vered Amit's idea of a community, which has shifted away from an actualized social form to be an idea or quality of sociality, a collective identity rather than interaction (ibid., 3), is applicable here to the wider community of Shamokin/Coal Township's dispersed population of former town residents that are still so important for its life.

The commoditization of ethnic foods, arts and crafts, music and dance has accompanied the decline of ethnicity: massive quantities of ethnic foods are produced for fundraisers; arts and crafts are bought for display in glass fronted cabinets; and, with a few exceptions, music and dance happen as paid public performances. This constitutes the economic content of the ethnicity of today. It is very different from the days when ethnic culture was celebrated in the great ethnic days of each group, when Ukrainian sword dancers rolled back the rugs in their homes to dance when they gathered together, and ethnic foods constituted the daily diet of families.

The details in this study of the economy of favors of the mining era, what it consisted of, how it worked, and its significance in the life of the town, contribute to the discussion of James C. Scott's (1985) idea that such everyday resistance constituted the "weapons of the weak" in a form of political action among subordinated groups, and of Michel de Certeau (1984), who sees that every day practices are sometimes ways of operating to give the weak victories over the strong, and may consist of clever tricks and maneuvers. These ideas recognize that there are numerous instances throughout the world in which the hegemony of the state and other powerful organizations are challenged by various kinds of everyday small-scale resistance rather than through violent uprising and organized rebellion. Scott (1990) has argued in addition, that because social scientists focus on official public transcripts of culture, everyday forms of resistance have been underestimated because transcripts in the public eye reflect only the compliance of both the weak and the powerful while everyday forms of resistance to the powerful are hidden.

In a critique of Scott, Deborah Reed-Danahay suggests that the term resistance implies impact and conflict, while the cunning and manipulation often involved in the everyday practices that Scott talks about, have a fluidity that make "resistance" perhaps too rigid a term. From the perspective of the Lavallois villagers of the Auvergne in Central France, where she worked, engaging in such everyday resistance is part of a more general notion of skillfully "making out" or "making do" in difficult situations (Reed-Danahay 1993, 223). Rhoda Halperin's description, in her book *The Kentucky Way*, includes similar coping strategies (1990). The economy of favors of the Coal Region seems to come into the same category as these two examples: people made do and survived oppressive conditions through "helping each other out." But Coal Region mining families differ from these other examples because their highly developed system of reciprocal exchange of favors was not only a way of making out in the harsh circumstances of everyday life: the use of networks developed in this system also helped mineworkers to rapidly mobilize and organize their overt and confrontational resistance to the big coal companies and the state through strikes and then through marches and demonstrations of massive numbers of people to eventually achieve the legalization of independent mining operations. The miners thus utilized these everyday practices of helping each other out as a basis for political action also. In this way, these practices were part of the resistance to the power structure, which had some impact on it.

The account given here of the part played by the economy of favors in helping the miners to hold out and be successful in their struggle against corporate capitalism through the effectiveness of their networks of communication and mutual support, also contributes to studies of the labor history of this period.

To conclude, I share Lorand Matory's view that historians who document the interactive character of multiethnic, trans-geographical regions offer a major challenge to the ethnographer (Matory, 2005). My historical ethnography of a town, set in the wider European home background of its immigrants and in the context of national and international affairs, is an attempt to confront this challenge. The course of this history has generated the strong sense of place that marks its people and has given rise to a wider community of former residents in the towns and cities who contribute in some measure to sustaining the town today, and also help to rejuvenate the sense of community of the past.

In moving into such a broad research field, I found particularly valuable what Michael Herzfeld calls "anthropology's resolute insistence on the significance of the particular" (1997, 11). Peoples' own words and particular histories are given to show the effects on their lives of events and changing power relations in the local, national or global arena. This usage is endorsed in Paul Willis' insistence that "social reproduction and contradiction must be shown not as abstract entities, but as embedded dynamically within the real lives of real people" (Willis 1981, 201).

The documentation that one might supply in such an ethnography could be encyclopedic but would be of unreadable dimensions and scope for a book. Therefore the material I have drawn upon to fill the canvas of so wide a view has to be far from complete; my intention has been to show to a limited and practical degree how wider national and global power relations have impinged upon the town, and how they have affected the lives of its inhabitants over the last approximately one hundred and fifty years.

My study seeks to follow Matory's historical ethnography in drawing upon a new kind of ethnographic field site with a cultural field that spans continents as well as centuries. As technology increasingly facilitates the interconnectedness of the peoples of the world, developing approaches and techniques for the study of such sites becomes a pressing need for anthropologists. The historical perspective of longitudinal studies are as illuminating for understanding the present features of communities today, as are the understanding and knowledge of the unofficial economic and political interconnections that are made over sometimes immense distances of geographical space that I have described in my previous publications. Use of the communication technologies that increase these connections are expanding so rapidly and so creatively over such wide areas of the world that their consequences are of extraordinary interest and importance. They constitute the ways by which economics and politics really operate worldwide today. The implications of this are significant not just for anthropology but also for economics, political science and international relations. The insights and methods of anthropology are potentially highly useful for such studies. Despite the difficulties in adapting them to fields of such wide scope and historical depth, more such studies need to be attempted.

Bibliography

The American Association of University Women. 1985. *Women of the Looms: Women's Work in the Textile and Weaving Mills of Shamokin Coal Region 1900–1937.* Shamokin Oral History Project. Organized by Catholic Social Services, Shamokin and the International Ladies Garment Workers Union, Shamokin, with a grant from the Pennsylvania Historical and Museum Commission, Harrisburg, PA. Typescripts of interviews. Unpublished.

Akenson, Donald H. 1992. "The Historiography of the Irish in the United States of America." In *The Irish World Wide: History, Heritage, Identity. The Irish in the New Communities*, edited by Patrick O'Sullivan, vol. 2, 99–127. Leicester: Leicester University Press.

Alisauskas, Arunas. 1980. "Lithuanians." In *Harvard Encyclopedia of American Ethnic Groups*, edited by Stephan Thernstrom, 665–76. Cambridge MA: Harvard University Press.

Amit, Vered, ed. 2002. *Realizing Community: Concepts, Social Relationships and Sentiments.* New York: Routledge.

Anderson, Benedict. 1991. *Imagined Communities: Reflections on the Origin and Spread of Nationalism.* London: Verso.

Appadurai, Arjun. 1988. "Introduction: Place and Voice in Anthropological Theory." *Cultural Anthropology* 3(1):16–20.

Arensberg, Conrad, and Solon T. Kimball. 1940/1968. *Family and Community in Ireland.* 2nd ed. Cambridge, MA: Harvard University Press.

Aurand, Harold W. 1971. *Coal Cracker Culture: Work and Values in Pennsylvania Anthracite, 1835–1935.* Selinsgrove, PA: Susquehanna University Press. London: Associated University Presses.

Banks, Marcus. 1996. *Ethnicity: Anthropological Constructions.* New York: Routledge.

Barendse, Michael A. 1981. *Social Expectations and Perception: The Case of the Slavic Anthracite Workers*. University Park: Pennsylvania State University Press.

Bartoletti, Susan Campbell. 1996. *Growing Up in Coal Country*. Boston: Houghton Mifflin Co.

Bazelon, Bruce. 1986. *The Jews in Pennsylvania*. Peoples of Pennsylvania Series 2. Harrisburg, PA: Pennsylvania Historical and Museum Commission, Commonwealth of Pennsylvania.

Bell, Herbert C., and J. J. John. 1891. *History of Northumberland County, Pennsylvania*, edited by Herbert C. Bell. Chicago: Brown, Runk and Co.

Berthoff, Roland. 1980. "Welsh." In *Harvard Encyclopedia of Ethnic Groups*, edited by Stephan Thernstrom, 1011–17. Cambridge MA: Harvard University Press.

Blatz, Perry K. 1994. *Democratic Miners: Work and Labor Relations in the Anthracite Coal Industry, 1875–1925*. SUNY Series in American Labor History. Albany, NY: State University of New York Press.

Blessing, Patrick J. 1980. "Irish." In *Harvard Encyclopedia of American Ethnic Groups*, edited by Stephan Thernstrom, 524–45. Cambridge MA: Harvard University Press.

Blu, Karen I. 1996. "'Where Do You Stay At?' Home Place and Community among the Lumbee." In *Senses of Place*, edited by Steven Feld and Keith H. Basso, 197–227. Santa Fe, NM: School of American Research Press.

Boback, John. 1994. "History of the Eagle Silk Mill. Unpublished manuscript.

Bodnar, John. 1979. "Immigration and Modernization: The Case of Slavic Peasants in Industrial America." In *American Working Class Culture: Explorations in American Labor and Social History*, edited by Milton Cantor, 333–60. Westport, CT: Greenwood Press.

———. 1982. *Workers' World: Kinship, Community, and Protest in an Industrial Society, 1900–1940*. Baltimore: Johns Hopkins University Press.

———. 1983. *Anthracite People: Families, Unions, and Work, 1900–1940*. Harrisburg, PA: Pennsylvania Historical and Museum Commission.

———. 1984. "The Family Economy and Labor Protest in Industrial America: Hard Coal Miners in the 1930s." In *Hard Coal, Hard Times: Ethnicity and Labor in the Anthracite Region*, edited by David L. Salay, 78–93. Scranton, PA: Anthracite Museum Press.

Broehl, Wayne G., Jr. 1964. *The Molly Maguires*. Cambridge, MA: Harvard University Press.

Brown, Keith, and Dimitrios Theodossoupoulos. 2004. "Others' Others: Talking About Stereotypes and Constructions of Otherness in Southeastern Europe." *History and Anthropology* 15(1): 3–14.

Budreckis, Algirdas M., ed. 1976. *The Lithuanians in America 1651–1975: A Chronology and Fact Book*. Ethnic Chronology Series 21. Dobbs Ferry, NY: Oceana Publications Inc.

Burrows, Francis G. 1930. "Early Newspapers of Northumberland County." *Proceedings of Northumberland County Historical Society* (1930): 54–81.

Campisi, Paul J. 1948. "Ethnic Family Patterns: The Italian Family in the United States." *American Journal of Sociology* 53(6): 443–49.

Canavan, Bernard. 1994. "Story-Tellers and Writers: Irish Identity in the Immigrant Labourers' Autobiographies 1870–1970." In *The Irish World Wide: History, Heritage, Identity. The Creative Migrant*, edited by Patrick O'Sullivan, vol. 3, 154–69. Leicester: Leicester University Press.

Carter, John M. 1936. "The Himmel Church." *Proceedings of Northumberland County Historical Society* 8 (1936): 67–97.

Centennial Committee. 1964. *Greater Shamokin Centennial 1864–1964*. Shamokin: Centennial Committee.

Chandler, Alfred D. 1972. "Anthracite Coal and the Beginnings of the Industrial Revolution in the United States." *Business History Review* 46 (2): 141–81.

Chapman, Malcolm. 1992. *The Celts: The Construction of a Myth*. New York: St. Martin's Press.

Chernoski, John J. 2004. "Little Lithuania, USA": Schuylkill County, PA. *Lithuanian Heritage* (May/June): 14–23.

Chrypinski, Anna, ed. 1977. *Polish Customs*. Detroit, MI. Friends of Polish Art.

Cnaan, Ram A., and Carl Milofsky, eds. 2007. *Handbook of Community Movements and Local Organizations*. New York: Springer.

Cohen, Abner. 1969. *Custom and Politics in Urban Africa: A Study of Hausa Migrants in Yoruba Towns*. London: Routledge and Kegan Paul.

———. 1981. *The Politics of Elite Culture: Explorations in the Dramaturgy of Power in Modern African Society*. Berkeley: University of California Press.

Cohen, Robin, ed. 1995. *The Cambridge Survey of World Migration*. Cambridge: Cambridge University Press.

Comaroff, John L., and Jean Comaroff. 1992. *Ethnography and the Historical Imagination*. Boulder, CO: Westview Press.

Conway, Alan, ed. 1961. *The Welsh in America: Letters from the Immigrants*. Minneapolis: University of Minnesota Press.

Conzen, Kathleen Neils. 1980. "Germans." In *Harvard Encyclopedia of American Ethnic Groups*, edited by Stephan Thernstrom, 405–25. Cambridge MA: Harvard University Press.

———. 1985. "German-Americans and the Invention of Ethnicity." In *America and the Germans: An Assessment of a Three-Hundred-Year History*, edited by Frank Trommler and Joseph McVeigh, vol. 1, 131–47. Philadelphia: University of Pennsylvania Press.

———. 1989. "Ethnicity as Festive Culture: Nineteenth-Century German America on Parade." In *The Invention of Ethnicity*, edited by Werner Sollors, 44–76. New York: Oxford University Press.

Corbin, John. 1979. "Social Class and Patron-Clientage in Andalusia: Some Problems of Comparing Ethnographies." *Anthropological Quarterly* 52(2): 99–114.

Cullinane, John. 1994. "Irish Dance World-Wide: Irish Migrants and the Shaping of Irish Traditional Dance." In *The Irish World Wide: History, Heritage, Identity. The Creative Migrant*, edited by Patrick O'Sullivan, vol. 3, 192–220. Leicester: Leicester University Press.

David, Jono. 2000. "The Jews of Riga." *Jewish Magazine* 34 (July). http://www.jewishmag.co.il/34mag/riga/riga.htm.

Davies, Edward J., II. 1985. *The Anthracite Aristocracy: Leadership and Social Change in the Hard Coal Regions of Northeastern Pennsylvania, 1800–1930*. DeKalb, IL: Northern Illinois University Press.

De Certeau, Michel. 1984. *The Practice of Everyday Life*. Berkeley: University of California Press.

Dowling, P. J. 1935. *The Hedge Schools of Ireland*. New York and London: Longman's Green.

Dragan, Anthony. 1964. *Ukrainian National Association: Its Past and Present (1896–1964)* Jersey City, NJ: Svoboda Press.

Dublin, Thomas. 1998. *When the Mines Closed: Stories of Struggles in Hard Times*. Ithaca, NY: Cornell University Press.

Duffy, Anne. 1986. "Reformulating Power for Women." *Canadian Review of Sociology and Anthropology*. 23(1): 22–46.

Fedunkiw, Marianne P. 1995. "Ukrainian Americans." In *Gale Encyclopedia of Multicultural America*, edited by Judy Galens, Anna Sheets, Robyn U. Young, 1374–91. New York: Gale Research, Inc.

Feld, Steven, and Keith H. Basso, eds. 1996. *Senses of Place*. Santa Fe, NM: School of American Research Press.

Frankenberg, Ronald. 1957. *Village on the Border: A Social Study of Religion, Politics and Football in a North Wales Community*. London: Cohan & West.

Freese, Barbara. 2003. *Coal: A Human History*. Cambridge MA: Perseus Publishing.

Frisch, Michael.1990. *A Shared Authority: Essays on the Craft and Meaning of Oral and Public History*. New York: State University of New York Press.

Galens, Judy, Anna Sheets, and Robyn U. Young, eds. 1995. *Gale Encyclopedia of Multicultural America*. New York: Gale Research, Inc.

Gans, Herbert J. 1962. *The Urban Villagers: Group and Class in the Life of Italian-Americans*. New York: Free Press of Glencoe.

Genealogical and Biographical Annals of Northumberland County. 1911. Chicago: J. Floyd and Co.

Glazer, Nathan, and Daniel P. Moynihan. 1963. *Beyond the Melting Pot: The Negroes, Puerto Ricans, Jews, Italians and Irish of New York City*. Cambridge MA: MIT Press and Harvard University Press.

Golab, Caroline. 1977. *Immigrant Destinations*. Philadelphia: Temple University Press.

Gouldner, Alvin W. 1960. "The Norm of Reciprocity: A Preliminary Statement." *American Sociological Review* 25(2): 161–78.

Graeber, Kathleen Neuman. 1981. *A History of the Greber/Graeber/Graber Family, 1680–1980*. Unpublished paper.

Granquist, Mark A. 1995. "Lithuanian Americans." In *Gale Encyclopedia of Multicultural America*, edited by Judy Galens, Anna Sheets, Robyn U. Young, vol. 2, 881–94. New York: Gale Research, Inc.

Graves, Thomas E. 1973. "Keeping Ukraine Alive Through Death: Ukrainian American Gravestones as Cultural Markers." In *Ethnicity and the American Cemetery*, edited by Richard E. Meyer, 36–79. Bowling Green, OH: Bowling Green State University Popular Press.

Greater Shamokin Centennial Committee. 1964. *Greater Shamokin Centennial: 1864–1964*. Shamokin, PA.

Greene, Victor R. 1968. *The Slavic Community on Strike: Immigrant Labor in Pennsylvania Anthracite*. Notre Dame, IN: University of Notre Dame Press.

———. 1980. "Poles." In *Harvard Encyclopedia of American Ethnic Groups*, edited by Stephan Thernstrom, vol. 2, 787–803. Cambridge, MA: Harvard University Press.

Grifo, Richard D., and Anthony F. Noto. 1990. "Italian Presence in Pennsylvania." *Pennsylvania History Studies* 19. University Park, PA: The Pennsylvania Historical Association.

Gudelunas, William A. 1984. "The Ethno-Religious Factor Reaches Fruition: the Politics of Hard Coal, 1945–1972." In *Hard Coal, Hard Times: Ethnicity and Labor in the Anthracite Region*, edited by David L. Salay, 169–88. Scranton, PA: Anthracite Museum Press.

———. 1986. "The Lithuanians of Pennsylvania's Lower Anthracite Region: A Study in the Persistence of Ethnic Identification." *Lituanus Lithuanian Quarterly Journal* 32(3): 1–5.

Gupta, Akhil, and James Ferguson, eds. 1992. "Beyond 'Culture': Space, Identity, and the Politics of Difference." *Cultural Anthropology* 7(1): 6–23.

———. 1997/2001. *Culture, Power, Place: Explorations in Critical Anthropology*. Durham, NC: Duke University Press.

Gutman, Herbert G. 1987. *Power and Culture: Essays on the American Working Class*, edited by Ira Berlin. New York: Pantheon Books.

Halperin, Rhoda H. 1990. *The Livelihood of Kin: Making Ends Meet "The Kentucky Way."* Austin, TX: University of Texas Press.

Hanney, Joseph M. 1985. "Schuylkill County: Built on Coal." *Pennsylvania Heritage* 11 (Winter): 10–17.

Heimlich, Evan. 1995. "Welsh Americans." In *Gale Encyclopedia of Multicultural America*, edited by Judy Galens, Anna Sheets, Robyn U. Young, vol. 2, 1408–19. New York: Gale Research, Inc.

Herzfeld, Michael. 1997. *Cultural Intimacy: Social Poetics in the Nation State*. New York: Routledge.

Hobsbawm, Eric, and Terence Ranger, eds. 1983. *The Invention of Tradition*. Cambridge: Cambridge University Press.

Howard, Walter T. 2001. "The National Miners Union: Communists and Miners in the Pennsylvania Anthracite, 1928–1931." *Pennsylvania Magazine of History and Biography* 125(1/2): 91–124.

Huffines, Marion L. 1985. "Language-Maintenance Efforts Among German Immigrants and Their Descendants in the United States." In *America and the Germans: An Assessment of a Three-Hundred-Year History*, edited by Frank Trommler and Joseph McVeigh, vol. 1, 241–50. Philadelphia: University of Pennsylvania Press.

Humphrey, Theodore C., and Lin T. Humphrey, eds. 1988. "We Gather Together:" In *Food and Festival in American Life*. Ann Arbor, MI: UMI Research Press.

Hunter, Albert. 2007. "Creating a Frame for Understanding Local Organizations." In *Handbook of Community Movements and Local Organizations*, edited by Ram A. Cnaan and Carl Milofsky, 20–33. New York: Springer.

Hyden, Goran. 1980. *Beyond Ujamaa in Tanzania: Underdevelopment and an Uncaptured Peasantry*. London: Heinemann.

Isajiw, Wsevolod W. 1979. "Organizational Difference and Persistence of the Ethnic Community: Ukrainians in the United States." In *The Ukrainian Immigrant Experience in the United States: A Symposium*, edited by Paul R. Magocsi, 79–95. Cambridge, MA: Harvard Ukrainian Research Institute.

Jacobs, Neil G. 2005. Yiddish: *A Linguistic Introduction*. Cambridge: Cambridge University Press.

Jacobson, Matthew Frye. 1995. *Special Sorrows: The Diasporic Imagination of Irish, Polish and Jewish Immigrants to the United States*. Cambridge, MA: Harvard University Press.

Jaeger, Katherine. 2001. *The Molly Maguires of Northumberland County, Pennsylvania*. Unpublished paper.

Jones, Hugh A. 1978. "The Importance of Welsh Immigration into the Anthracite Region of Northumberland County." *Proceedings of the Northumberland County Historical Society* 27 (1978): 138–47.

Jones, Syd. 1995. "Polish Americans." In *Gale Encyclopedia of Multicultural America*, edited by Judy Galens, Anna Sheets, Robyn U. Young, vol. 2, 1083–99. New York: Gale Research, Inc.

Jones, William D. 1993. *Wales in America: Scranton and the Welsh, 1860–1920*. Scranton, PA: University of Wales Press and Scranton University Press.

Kantz, Robert W., and Roger B. Saylor. 1956. *Mt. Carmel, PA: An Industrial Survey of the Area*. Bureau of Business Research, College of Business Administration, University Park: Pennsylvania State University.

Kellas, James. G. 1991. *The Politics of Nationalism and Ethnicity*. New York: St. Martin's Press.

Kempny, Marian. 2002. "Cultural Islands in the Globalizing World: Community-Cum-Locality of the Cieszyn Silesian Lutherans" In *Realizing Community: Concept, Social Relationships and Sentiments*, edited by Vered Amit, 60–83. London, New York: Routledge.

Kenny, Kevin. 1998. *Making Sense of the Molly Maguires*. Oxford: Oxford University Press.

Klein, Philip S., and Ari Hoogenboom. 1989. *A History of Pennsylvania*. 2nd. ed. University Park: Pennsylvania State University Press.

Kopytoff, Igor. 1986. "The Cultural Biography of Things: Commoditization as Process." In *The Social Life of Things: Commodities in Cultural Perspective*, edited by Arjun Appadurai, 64–91. Cambridge: Cambridge University Press.

Kozura, Michael. 1996. "We Stood Our Ground: Anthracite Miners and the Expropriation of Corporate Property, 1930–1941." In *"We Are All Leaders!": The Alternative Unionism of the Early 1930s*, edited by Staughton Lynd, 199–237. Urbana: University of Illinois Press.

Kuropas, Myron B. 1972. *Ukrainians in America*. Minneapolis, MN: Lerner Publications Co.

Kuznets, Simon. 1975. "Immigration of Russian Jews to the United States: Background and Structure." *Perspectives in American History* 9: 35–126.

Ledeneva, Alena V. 1998. *Russia's Economy of Favours: Blat, Networking and Informal Exchange*. Cambridge: Cambridge University Press.

Leeds, Anthony. 1965/1974. "Brazilian Careers and Social Structures: a Case History and Model." In *Contemporary Cultures and Societies of Latin America*, edited by Dwight B. Heath, 2nd ed. 285–307. New York: Random House.

Le Roy Ladurie, Emmanuel. c1975. *Montaillou—Village Occiten de 1294 à1324*. Paris: Gallimard.

Linden-Ward, Blanche. 1989. "Strange but Genteel Pleasure Grounds: Tourist and Leisure Uses of Nineteenth Century Rural Cemeteries." In *Cemeteries and Gravemarkers: Voices of American Culture*, edited by Richard E. Meyer, 239–328. Ann Arbor, MI: UMI Research Press.

Litt, Edgar. 1970. *Beyond Pluralism: Ethnic Politics in America*. Glenview, IL: Scott Foresman and Co.

Lomnitz, Larissa. 1971. "Reciprocity of Favors in the Urban Middle Class of Chile." In *Studies in Economic Anthropology*, edited by George Dalton, 93–106. Anthropological Studies 7. Washington, DC: American Anthropological Association.

Luciuk, Lubomyr L. 1995. "A Continuing Presence: North America's Ukrainians." In *The Cambridge Survey of World Migration*, edited by Robin Cohen, 109–13. Cambridge: Cambridge University Press.

MacCormack, Geoffrey. 1976. "Reciprocity." *Man* 11: 89–103.

MacGaffey, Janet. 1991. *The Real Economy of Zaire: The Contribution of Smuggling and Other Unofficial Activities to National Wealth*. With Vwakyanakazi Mukohya, Rukaranagira wa Nkera, Brooke Grundfest Schoepf, Makwala ma Mavambu ye Beda, Walu Engundu. London and Philadelphia: James Currey and University of Pennsylvania Press.

———. 2005. "New Forms of Remuneration for Labour in Congo-Kinshasa's Economy of Favours." In *Workers in the Informal Sector: Studies in Labor History 1800–2000*, edited by Sabyasachi Bhattacharya and Jan Lucassen, Delhi: MacMillan India Ltd.

MacGaffey, Janet, and Rémy Bazenguissa-Ganga. 2000. *Congo-Paris: Transnational Traders on the Margins of the Law*. Oxford and Bloomington, IN: James Currey and Indiana University Press.

Magda, Matthew S. 1986. *The Welsh in Pennsylvania*. Peoples of Pennsylvania Series 1. Harrisburg, PA: Pennsylvania Historical and Museum Commission.

Magocsi, Paul R., ed. 1979. "Problems in the History of the Ukrainian Immigration to the United States." In *The Ukrainian Immigrant Experience in the United States: A Symposium*, 1–15. Cambridge, MA: Harvard Ukrainian Research Institute.

———. 1980. "Ukrainians." In *Harvard Encyclopedia of American Ethnic Groups*, edited by Stephan Thernstrom, 997–1009. Cambridge MA: Harvard University Press.

———. 1995. "Carpatho-Rusyn Americans." In *Gale Encyclopedia of Multicultural America*, edited by Judy Galens, Anna Sheets, Robyn U. Young, vol. 1, 252–61. New York: Gale Research, Inc.

Marlok, Edgar. 1976. "My Shamokin: A Collection of Stories from the News-Dispatch, 1954–1968." In *Bicentennial Year Presentation*. Shamokin, PA: News Publication and Printing Company.

Marsh, Ben. 1987. "Continuity and Decline in the Anthracite Towns of Pennsylvania." Annals of the Association of American Geographers. 77 (3): 337–52.

Martz, Sterling P. 1965. "Jacob's or Reed's Church." *Proceedings of Northumberland County Historical Society* (1965): 59–61.

Matory, J. Lorand. 2005. *Black Atlantic Religion: Tradition, Transnationalism and Matriarchy in the Afro-Brazilian Candomblé*. Princeton, NJ: Princeton University Press.

McCafferty, Hugh J. 1929. *Locust Gap, Northumberland County, Pennsylvania: A History*. Mt. Carmel, PA: H. J. McCafferty.

McCaffrey, Lawrence J. 1976. *The Irish Diaspora in America*. Washington, DC: Catholic University of America Press.

Michrina, Barry P. 1993. *Pennsylvania Mining Families: The Search for Dignity in the Coalfield*. Lexington, KY: University Press of Kentucky.

Miller, Donald L., and Richard E. Sharpless. 1985. *The Kingdom of Coal: Work, Enterprise, and Ethnic Communities in the Mine Fields*. Philadelphia: University of Pennsylvania Press.

Miller, Kerby A. 1985. *Emigrants and Exiles: Ireland and the Irish Exodus to North America*. New York: Oxford University Press.

———. 1990. "Class, Culture, and Immigrant Group Identity in the United States: The Case of Irish-American Ethnicity." In *Immigration Reconsidered: History, Sociology, and Politics*, edited by Virginia Yans-McLaughlin, 96–129. New York and Oxford: Oxford University Press.

Milofsky, Carl. 2008. *Smallville: Institutionalizing Community in Twenty-First-Century America*. Lebanon NH: Tufts University Press.

Milofsky, Carl, Anthony Butto, Michael Gross, and Jim Baumohl. 1993. "Small Town in Mass Society: Substance Abuse Treatment and Urban-Rural Migration." *Contemporary Drug Problems* 20 (Fall): 433–71.

Milspaw, Yvonne J. 1980. "Segregated in Life, Segregated in Death: Landscape of an Ethnic Cemetery." *Pennsylvania Folk Life* 30(1): 36–40.

Moore, Sally Falk. 1981. *Social Facts and Fabrications. "Customary" Law on Kilimanjaro, 1880–1980*. Cambridge: Cambridge University Press.

———. 1987. "Explaining the Present: Theoretical Dilemmas in Processual Ethnography." *American Ethnologist* 14(4): 727–36.

Morawska, Ewa. 1995. "Eastern Europeans on the Move." In *The Cambridge Survey of World Migration*, edited by Robin Cohen, 97–102. Cambridge: Cambridge University Press.

Morgan, Prys. 1983. "From a Death to a View: The Hunt for the Welsh Past in the Romantic Period." In *The Invention of Tradition*, edited by Eric Hobsbawm and Terence Ranger, 43–100. Cambridge: Cambridge University Press.

Morris, Charles R. 1997. *American Catholic: The Saints and Sinners who Built America's Most Powerful Church*. New York: Times Books, Random House.

Muller, Edward K., ed. 1989. A *Concise Historical Atlas of Pennsylvania*. Philadelphia: Temple University Press.
Nash, June. 1979. *We Eat the Mines and the Mines Eat Us: Dependency and Exploitation in Bolivian Tin Mines*. New York: Columbia University Press.
Nelli, Humbert S. 1964. "The Italian Padrone System in the US." *Labor History* 5(Spring): 153–67.
———. 1980. "Italians." In *Harvard Encyclopedia of American Ethnic Groups*, edited by Stephan Thernstrom, 545–60. Cambridge MA: Harvard University Press.
Nugent, Walter. 1990. "Pennsylvania German in Public Life." *Pennsylvania Folklife* 39(1): 117–25.
———. 1995. "Migration from the German and Austro-Hungarian Empires to North America." In *The Cambridge Survey of World Migration*, edited by Robin Cohen, 103–8. Cambridge: Cambridge University Press.
O'Dea, John. 1923. *History of the Ancient Order of Hibernians and Ladies' Auxiliary*. 3 vols. Philadelphia: Keystone Printing Co.
Olwig, Karen Fog. 2002. "The Ethnographic Field Revisited: Towards a Study of Common and Not So Common Fields of Belonging." In *Realizing Community: Concepts, Social Relationships and Sentiments*, edited by Vered Amit, 124–45. London and New York: Routledge.
———. 2003. "Global Places and Place-Identities: Lessons from Caribbean Research." In *Globalisation: Studies in Anthropology*, edited by Thomas Hylland Eriksen, 58–77. London and Sterling, VA: Pluto Press.
Poliniak, Louis. 1970. *When Coal Was King: Mining Pennsylvania's Anthracite*. Lebanon, PA: Applied Arts Publishers.
Poore, Carol. 1985. "Whose Celebration?: The Centennial of 1876 and German-American Socialist Culture." In *America and the Germans: An Assessment of a Three-Hundred-Year History*, edited by Frank Trommler and Joseph McVeigh, vol. 1, 176–88. Philadelphia: University of Pennsylvania Press.
Portelli, Alessandro. 1998. "Oral History as Genre." In *Narrative and Genre*, edited by Mary Chamberlin and Paul Thompson, 23–45. New York: Routledge.
Pozetta, George E. 1995. "Italians." In *Gale Encyclopedia of Multicultural America*, edited by Judy Galens, Anna Sheets, Robyn U. Young, vol. 2, 765–82. New York: Gale Research Inc.
Procko, Bohdan, P. 1973. "Pennsylvania: Focal Point of Ukrainian Immigration." In *The Ethnic Experience in Pennsylvania*, edited by John E. Bodnar, 216–32. Lewisburg, PA: Bucknell University Press.
———. 1979. "The Rise of Ukrainian Ethnic Consciousness in America During the 1890s." In *The Ukrainian Experience in the United States: A Symposium*, edited by Paul R. Magocsi, 51–63, Cambridge, MA: Harvard Ukrainian Research Institute.
Ranger, Terence. 1993. "The Invention of Tradition Revisited: The Case of Colonial Africa." In *Legitimacy and the State in Twentieth-Century Africa*, edited by Terence Ranger and Ofumeli Vaughan, 62–111. London: MacMillan Press.

Rauche, Anthony T. 1988. "Festa Italiano in Hartford, Conneticut: The Pastries, the Pizza, and the People Who 'Parla Italiano.'" In *"We Gather Together:" Food and Festival in American Life*, edited by Theodore C. Humphrey and Lin T. Humphrey, 205–17. Ann Arbor, MI: UMI Research Press.

Reed-Danahay, Deborah. 1993. "Talking About Resistance: Ethnography and Theory in Rural France." *Anthropological Quarterly* 66(4): 221–29.

Rippley, La Vern J. 1995. "German Americans." In *Gale Encyclopedia of Multicultural America*, edited by Judy Galens, Anna Sheets, Robyn U. Young, vol. 1, 565–75. New York: Gale Research, Inc.

Roberts, Bryan R. 1973. *Organizing Strangers: Poor Families in Guatemala City*. Austin, TX: University of Texas Press.

Roberts, Peter. 1904/1970. *Anthracite Coal Communities: A Study of the Demography, the Social, Educational and Moral Life of the Anthracite Regions*. New York: Arms Press and New York Times.

Rodechko, James P. 1973. "Irish American Society in the Pennsylvania Anthracite Region, 1870–1880." In *The Ethnic Experience in Pennsylvania*, edited by John E. Bodnar, 19–32. Lewisburg, PA: Bucknell University Press.

Romanucci-Ross, Lola, and George A. De Vos, eds. 1995. *Ethnic Identity: Creation, Conflict and Accommodation*. London and Walnut Creek, CA: AltaMira Press.

Roseberry, William. 1983. *Coffee and Capitalism in the Venezuelan Andes*. Austin, TX: University of Texas Press.

———. 1988. "Domestic Modes, Domesticated Models." *Journal of the Historical Society* 1(4): 423–30.

———. 1989/1991. *Anthropologies and Histories: Essays in Culture, History and Political Economy*. New Brunswick, NJ: Rutgers University Press.

Rottenberg, Dan. 2003. *In the Kingdom of Coal: An American Family and the Rock that Changed the World*. New York: Routledge.

Royce, Anya Peterson. 1982. *Identity: Strategies of Diversity*. Bloomington: Indiana University Press.

Schneider, David M. 1968. *American Kinship: A Cultural Account*. Chicago: Chicago University Press.

Scott, James C. 1985. *Weapons of the Weak: Everyday Forms of Peasant Resistance*. New Haven, CT: Yale University Press.

———. 1990. *Domination and the Arts of Resistance: Hidden Transcripts*. New Haven, CT: Yale University Press.

Shankovskj, Lev. 1982. "Ukraine and the Ukrainians." In *Ukraine and the Ukrainians: A Collection of Selected Articles*, edited by I. Dmytriw and J. Wasyluk, 43–68. London: Association of Ukrainians in Great Britain.

Shawda, Geraldine E., and Ruth G. Meyer, eds. n.d. *The Witnesses: The History of the German Reformed Churches in Central Pennsylvania, Forerunner of the United Church of Christ Churches of Northern Association of the Penn Central Conference, Beginning 1790*.

Shomper, Harold. 1967. "Kimber Cleaver." *Northumberland Historical Society Proceedings* 25 (1967): 71–89.

———. 1987. "Coal and Coal Township." *Coal Township 150th Year Anniversary 1837–1987*. 41–97.

Smith, Anthony D. 1991. "The Nation: Invented, Imagined, Reconstructed." *Millennium: Journal of International Studies* 20(3): 353–68.

Smith, Graeme. 1994. "My Love is in America: Migration and Irish Music." In *The Irish World Wide: History, Heritage, Identity. The Creative Migrant*, edited by Patrick O'Sullivan, vol. 3, 221–36. Leicester: Leicester University Press.

Smith, M. G. 1982. "Ethnicity and Ethnic Groups in America: The View from Harvard." *Ethnic and Racial Studies*, 5(1): 1–22.

Sollors, Werner, ed. 1989. *The Invention of Ethnicity*. Oxford: Oxford University Press.

Sowell, Thomas. 1996. *Migrations and Cultures: A World View*. New York: Basic Books.

Spencer, Jonathan. 1989. "Anthropology as a Kind of Writing." *Man* 24(1): 145–64.

Sperry, James R. 1973. "Rebellion within the Ranks: Pennsylvania Anthracite, John L. Lewis, and the Coal Strikes of 1943." *Pennsylvania History* 40: 293–312.

Sterba, Christopher M. 1996. "Family, Work, and Nation: Hazleton, Pennsylvania, and the 1934 General Strike in Textiles." *Pennsylvania Magazine of History and Biography* 120(1/2): 3–35.

Stewart, Kathleen. 1996. "An Occupied Place." In *Senses of Place*, edited by Steven Feld and Keith H. Basso, 137–65. Santa Fe, NM: School of American Research Press.

Stewart, Pamela J., and Andrew Strathern, eds. 2003. "Introduction." In *Landscape, Memory and History*, 1–15. London: Pluto Press.

Stocking, George W., ed. 1983. *Observers Observed: Essays on Ethnographic Fieldwork*. Madison: University of Wisconsin Press.

Stoller, Paul. 1997. "Globalizing Method: The Problems of Doing Ethnography in Transnational Spaces." *Anthropology and Humanism* 22(1): 81–94.

———. 2002. *Money Has No Smell: The Africanization of New York City*. Chicago: Chicago University Press.

Strathern, Marilyn. 1982. "The Village as an Idea: Constructs of Village-ness in Elmdon, Essex." In *Belonging: Identity and Social Organisation in British Rural Cultures*, edited by Anthony P. Cohen, 247–77. Manchester: Manchester University Press.

———. 1984. "The Social Meanings of Localism." In *Locality and Rurality: Economy and Society in Rural Regions*, edited by Tony Bradley and Philip Lowe, 181–97. Norwich: Geo Books.

———. 1988. "Place and Voice in Anthropological Theory. Commentary: Concrete Topographies." *Cultural Anthropology* 3(1): 88–96.

Thernstrom, Stephan, ed. 1980. *Harvard Encyclopedia of American Ethnic Groups*. Cambridge MA: Harvard University Press.

Tonkin, Elizabeth, Maryon McDonald, and Malcolm Chapman, eds. 1989. *History and Ethnicity*. London: Routledge.

Toscano, Mark. 2000. "The Effect of the Great Depression on Shamokin, Pennsylvania." Honors Paper in History. Collegeville, PA: Ursinus College.

Ukrainian Weekly (compiled by editors). 1983/1988. "The Great Famine in Ukraine: the Unknown Holocaust." 2nd ed. Jersey City, NJ: National Ukrainian Association.

Van Reenan, Antanas J. 1990. *Lithuanian Diaspora: Konigsberg to Chicago*. New York: University Press of America.

Vardys, Vytas Stanley, and Judith B. Sedaitis. 1997. *Lithuania, the Rebel Nation*. Boulder, CO: Westview Press.

Vecoli, Rudolph J. 1995. "The Italian Diaspora, 1876–1976." In *The Cambridge Survey of World Migration*, edited by Robin Cohen, 114–22. Cambridge: Cambridge University Press.

Vincent, Joan. 1986. "System and Process, 1974–1985." *Annual Review of Anthropology* 15(1): 99–119.

Wallace, Anthony F. C. 1981. *St. Clair: A Nineteenth-Century Coal Town's Experience with a Disaster-Prone Industry*. New York: Alfred Knopf.

Wasserman, Stanley, and Katherine Faust. 1994. *Social Network Analysis: Methods and Applications*. Cambridge: Cambridge University Press.

Waters, Mary C. 1990. *Ethnic Options: Choosing Identities in America*. Berkeley and Los Angeles: California University Press.

Wiest, William Harvey. 1978. "Early German and Hessian Settlement in Lower Northumberland County." *Proceedings of Northumberland County Historical Association* 27 (1978): 130–37.

Willis, Paul E. 1981. *Learning to Labour: How Working Class Kids Get Working Class Jobs*. New York: Columbia University Press.

Wimmer, Andreas. 2002. *Nationalist Exclusion and Ethnic Conflict: Shadows of Modernity*. Cambridge. Cambridge University Press.

Wolf, Eric R. 1982. *Europe and the People Without History*. Berkeley, CA: University of California Press.

Wolfgang, Thomas. n.d. Northumberland County and the Shamokin Region, 1615–2000. Unpublished manuscript.

Wolkovich-Valkavicius, William. 1988. *Lithuanian Fraternalism: Seventiy-Five Years of the US Knights of Lithuania*. Brooklyn, NY: Knights of Lithuania.

Yoder, Don. 1961a. "Sauerkraut in Pennsylvania Folk Culture." *Pennsylvania Folk Life* 122 (Summer): 56–69.

———. 1961b. "Schnitz in the Pennsylvania Folk Culture." *Pennsylvania Folk Life* 122 (Fall): 44–53.

Znaniecki, William I., and Florian Znaniecki, 1984. *The Polish Peasant in Europe and America: A Classic Work in Immigration History*. Edited and abridged by Eli Zaretsky. Chicago: University of Illinois Press.

~

Index

About the Author

Janet MacGaffey is professor emeritus of anthropology at Bucknell University. Previously an Africanist, she focused her research on unrecorded trade across the borders of the Republic of Congo in Central Africa and on its huge scale. She has published and lectured widely in the United States and other countries on the extent of such unrecorded trade in Africa and all over the world and on its economic and political significance.

While teaching at Bucknell in Lewisburg, Pennsylvania, she became fascinated by the nearby anthracite coal towns in the northeastern area of the state because of their significance in the industrial revolution, their part in the rise of organized labor, and the rich variety of ethnic culture in their history. In following her new interest in the anthracite towns, she discovered that miners' families survived in the nineteenth and twentieth centuries by means of unrecorded nonmonetary exchange of goods and services between members of family, church, and neighborhood. After retirement, she undertook the intensive historical and ethnographic investigation over time focusing on one of the towns, Shamokin/Coal Township, which is the subject of this book.

www.ingramcontent.com/pod-product-compliance
Lightning Source LLC
Chambersburg PA
CBHW071200300425
25951CB00025B/52